Power is an illusion.

Illusion. Mirrors and blue smoke, beautiful blue smoke rolling over the surface of highly polished mirrors, first a thin veil of blue smoke, then a thick cloud that suddenly dissolves into wisps of blue smoke, the mirrors catching it all, bouncing it back and forth. If somebody tells you how to look, there can be seen in the smoke great, magnificent shapes, castles and kingdoms, and maybe they can be yours. All this becomes particularly dynamic when the person telling you where to look knows how to adjust the mirrors, tilt one forward, walk to the other side, and turn one on its base a few degrees to the right, suddenly causing the refractions to be different everywhere. And then going to the blue smoke, lessening it, intensifying it, and all the time keeping those watching transfixed, hoping, believing himself. Believing perhaps more than anybody else in the room. And at the same time knowing that what he is believing in is mirrors and blue smoke.

—JIMMY BRESLIN
How the Good Guys Finally Won

The Rise of Political Consultants

THE RISE OF
POLITICAL
CONSULTANTS

*New Ways of Winning
Elections*

L A R R Y   J .   S A B A T O

Basic Books, Inc., Publishers
NEW YORK

Library of Congress Cataloging in Publication Data

Sabato, Larry J.
  The rise of political consultants.

  Includes bibliographical references and index.
    1.   Political consultants—United States.   2.   Campaign
management—United States.   3.   Electioneering—United
States.   I.   Title.
JK2281.S2   324.7′0973   81–66104
ISBN 0–465–07040–X (cloth)   AACR2
ISBN 0–465–07041–8 (paper)

TO

Weldon Cooper
Clifton McCleskey
H. G. Nicholas

In grateful appreciation
for favors great and small

Contents

I

Political Consultants and Their Wares

II

Democracy and the New Campaign Technology

Contents

List of Tables and Figures

Acknowledgments

The election, proclaimed H. G. Wells, is "democracy's ceremonial, its feast, its great function." Most studies of "democracy's ceremonial" quite naturally center on candidates and voters, who are presumed to be the central characters in any election. Yet my own work as a campaign staff member in several dozen campaigns has convinced me that other actors, particularly political consultants, are sometimes as important as voters and candidates in determining the conduct and outcome of elections.

This belief, coupled with the realization that the current literature on campaigns had not given enough attention to the phenomenon of politicians' use of consultants and the growth of new campaign technology, led me to undertake the writing of this book. After an impoverished beginning, this project eventually enjoyed the embarrassment of rich support, and for that happy turn of events I have many agents to thank: the National Endowment for the Humanities (whose award of a Category B Fellowship enabled me to spend a year in full-time research and writing); the American Philosophical Society (for a generous grant from the Hays Fund); the LBJ Foundation (for a Moody grant-in-aid, financing a productive research trip to the LBJ Presidential Library); and The Brookings Institution and New College, Oxford (for the welcome provisions of quiet places to work and write for extended periods of time). My own University of Virginia was enormously helpful and supportive, and I am grateful to the Institute of Government, the White Burkett Miller Center for Public Affairs, the University Research Policy Council, the Dean of the Faculty of Arts and Sciences' Office, the Small Grants Committee, and, of course, the Department of Government and Foreign Affairs. Several of my university colleagues—Edwin Floyd, Clifton McCleskey, Kenneth Thompson, and Vincent Shea—were kind enough to secure one or more of these grants for my research.

The resources that came my way sustained four dozen extensive personal interviews with political consultants, as well as with journalists and academics familiar with their work. (See appendix B for a complete list of personal interviews.) All personal sessions, some lasting as long as seven hours, were tape-recorded and transcribed, except when the interviewee requested otherwise. Several dozen other telephone interviews and briefer, unrecorded sessions with consultants were conducted as well (often at trade conferences). The personal interviews and many of the less formal encounters were unquestionably the most revealing and fascinating part of my research, providing access to hundreds of political television and radio advertisements, polls, and direct-mail letters, and to the personal thoughts and reminiscences of some of the United States' most seasoned electoral activists. The relative dearth of published materials on consultants made interviewing absolutely necessary.

Few candidates appear in the list of interviewees, nor were many consulted informally. That was not my original intention, but preliminary conversations with a former president, several governors, and half a dozen U.S. senators, representatives, and state legislators were so unproductive that plans for formal interviews with officeholders were scrapped. At first I was astounded at how little candidates knew about either the men and women they had hired at great cost or the tools of the consultant's trade, but in retrospect this is less surprising. The new campaign technology is more complex than ever before, and an understanding of it requires specialized training and experience that most candidates simply have not had. In a demanding campaign a candidate's time and personal resources are too divided to afford him a chance to learn the techniques in much detail. So most candidates know they want consultants and vaguely know consultants are "necessary" without quite understanding what consultants do. Candidates often "take it on faith" (as one told me), exalting their consultants' wisdom in victory and decrying their collective stupidity in defeat, a situation that is both predictable and essentially unenlightening for someone with my research goals. (The sometimes strange—and strained—relationship between the candidate and the political consultant is a major topic of chapter 1.)

The interviews I did conduct were a considerable imposition on many of the consultants and their staffs, and I am grateful for the time and materials they so generously gave me again and again. (Their good humor will prove sustaining, I trust, when they encounter disagreeable passages in this book.) The tapes and transcripts of the interviews have been preserved. Quotations from them have occasionally been altered slightly to correct grammar and syntax, but in no case

Acknowledgments

was the substance of any statement changed. Unless noted otherwise, all quotations in the text have been taken from the personal interviews.

Several consultants and some of my academic colleagues and associates were kind enough to review all or a portion of the manuscript. I deeply appreciate the many helpful corrections and alterations suggested by Weldon Cooper, Walter DeVries, Charles Guggenheim, Jim Loyd, Clifton McCleskey, Thomas Mann, H. G. Nicholas, Robert Odell, Austin Ranney, A. James Reichley, Barry Sussman, and Lance Tarrance. A special note of appreciation is due Phyllis Brotman, past President of the American Association of Political Consultants, for her support and assistance. I was also very fortunate in having the editorial and production assistance ably provided by Martin Kessler, Linda Carbone, and Janet Byrne of Basic Books.

For essential research help, I would like to acknowledge and thank the staffs of the Republican National Committee, the Democratic National Committee, the LBJ Library, Rhodes House Library, Alderman Library at the University of Virginia, and Plus Publications. Secretarial support was provided by the Department of Government and Foreign Affairs and the Institute of Government at the University of Virginia, and due particular thanks are Susan Antonik, Maggie Applewhite, Lynda Cook, Taylor Harbison, Barbara Jones, Edna Mitchell, Robert Mowbray, Cora Pitts, Martha Rucker, Bunny Stinnett, and Sharon Wolford.

Rarely has an instructor been blessed with as many able and enthusiastic student assistants as I have had on this project. Deserving very special mention for service far above the call of duty are Wade Atkinson, Ray Granger, Linda McClain, Carmen Matarazza, Jeffrey Nuechterlein, Jim Reagen, Tom Shadyac, Susan Sullivan, David Whitescarver, and Ellen Zisook. Also making a contribution were Jesse Beasley, Hal Carlson, Henry Carretta, John Fishetti, Suzette Haynie, Brad Jones, Stephanie Kennan, Andrew Kingston, Wendy Knepper, Jeffrey Kramer, William Lascara, Haber McCarthy, Patricia Maggio, Charles Metz, Cassandra Newby, Richard Norman, Joshua Rales, Susan Shearer, Andrew Spaulding, Adele Stockham, Steven Strnisha, Ron Suskind, and David Troller.

Last, but hardly least, comes acknowledgment of the scholars who have contributed so much to my own academic development and that of this project. In the bibliographical essay at the conclusion of this book, I acknowledge the debt I owe to other researchers in the field, particularly Stanley Kelley, Dan Nimmo, and Robert Agranoff, whose works on politicians' use of consultants have been trailblazers.

Acknowledgments

Here also, though, I must mention three scholars who have given me much and asked little in return. My association with Professors Weldon Cooper and Clifton McCleskey of the University of Virginia and Professor H. G. Nicholas of New College, Oxford, has been intellectually rewarding and personally cherished. I owe them more than I can ever repay, and this volume is warmly dedicated to them. I only hope that the remaining errors in the pages to follow, for which I accept the customary responsibility, are few enough to do them justice.

LARRY J. SABATO
Charlottesville, Virginia
July 1981

I

Political Consultants
and Their Wares

"I'm sure our firm can handle your campaign, Senator, but first we
have to answer the question 'Who are you?'"

Chapter 1

The Consultant Corps

I AM A POLITICAL CONSULTANT. My business is helping elect candidates to high office. I don't see anything particularly sinister about that, but some people do.

—JOSEPH NAPOLITAN[1]

Television and polling have bred a new profession of electronic manipulators. Assembled in election-management firms, the media specialists, working indifferently for one party or the other, reduce campaigns to displays not of content but of technique.

—ARTHUR SCHLESINGER, JR.[2]

Controversy is raging about the role and influence of the political consultant in American elections, and properly so. There is no more significant change in the conduct of campaigns than the consultant's recent rise to prominence, if not preeminence, during the election season. Political consultants, answerable only to their client-candidates and independent of the political parties, have inflicted severe damage upon the party system and masterminded the modern triumph of personality cults over party politics in the United States. All the while they have gradually but steadily accumulated almost unchecked and unrivaled power and influence in a system that is partly their handiwork.

For a group of political elites so prominent and powerful, consultants have been remarkably little investigated and understood. Indeed, the argument about their role and influence in the electoral system has operated essentially in a vacuum—a vacuum this book attempts to fill. Until now far more misinformation than fact has surfaced in the debate about politicians' use of political consultants, and there are many reasons for this. The consultants themselves make the task of separating fact from fiction and image from reality as difficult as possible. They enhance their own images and increase the fees they can command by keeping their campaign techniques as mysterious and bewildering as possible. Most consultants have been intimately involved with politics for decades, and they know better than most elected officials that, in politics, style is closely intertwined with substance. Fame and fortune—not to mention electoral success—come to those who can adjust the mirrors in just the right way and produce sufficient quantities of blue smoke in the public arena.

In using the blue smoke and mirrors of politics to cloud the view of their profession, consultants have found a valuable ally, the working press. Not only do many journalists fail to understand what it is consultants do and how they do it; those same print and television journalists are responsible in good measure for the glow of expertise and omniscience that surrounds the consultant's every pronouncement. Consultants have become prime and semipermanent sources of information and insight for political reporters, and the election professionals are rewarded with an uncritical press and frequent, beatific headlines.

No one reads these headlines more closely than the prospective candidates, and as a consequence virtually no nominee for public office at any level thinks he can survive without a consultant or two. Remarkably, though, if reporters are ignorant of the consultant trade and technology, candidates are far more so. President Gerald Ford, for instance, would admit almost total ignorance of his 1976 direct-mail operation and even decry "junk mail" after leaving the Oval Office, despite the fact that direct mail had been one of the most successful aspects of his campaign for the Republican presidential nomination. Many other candidates have hired media and polling consultants at great cost without even a superficial comprehension of their techniques or their real worth—taking on faith what they had read and heard about these election wizards, believing all the while that consultants were essential for victory without knowing whether or why the common wisdom was true. Understandably, candidates lack the specialized training in election technology that their consultants possess and have little time to learn in a demanding, pressure-cooker campaign. This leaves the consultant a seemingly indispensable commodity, someone with immense leverage not merely during the election but also after the campaign is over. Few are the politicians who never seek office again, and their relationships with consultants are as permanent as their campaigns. Pollster Patrick Caddell's and media man Gerald

Rafshoon's extraordinary alliance with President Carter is by no means exceptional any more.

If a thorough examination of the consultants' profession is in order, so too is an exhaustive study of their much-acclaimed techniques. A glance at any election-year newspaper or political trade journal tells why. In the praise being heaped upon the media masters and soothsayers and direct-mail artists, all sorts of wondrous things are being attributed to them. Upon actually meeting these political wizards, after preparatory reading of hundreds of articles by awe-struck commentators, one inevitably is reminded of Dorothy's disappointment when she unmasked the Wizard of Oz. For, despite their clever public posturings, consultants have no potions or crystal balls, and most of them will admit it forthrightly, at least in private. "If I knew the successful formula," conceded one long-time professional, "I would patent it."

It is reassuring (perhaps deceptively so) to hear one of the most widely experienced generalist consultants, Stuart Spencer, proclaim that "There are good politicians and there are bad politicians, and all the computers and all the research in the world are not going to make the campaign situation any better when bad politicians are involved." Spencer may well be right that consultants cannot turn a sow's ear into a silk purse (although at least a couple of exceptions come to mind). But this book will certainly provide some evidence that a less radical transformation at the consultant's hand is possible, that a black sheep can become a white one upon application of a little dye and a corroded silver dollar can be transformed into a shiny one with a chemical and a bit of polish. Consultants and the new campaign technology have not changed the essence of politics. Politics is still persuasion, still a firm, friendly handshake. But the media of persuasion are no longer the same, and the handshake may be a projection or even an illusion.

Whatever the degree of their electoral influence, consultants—most of them—have talent and enormous experience. One hastens to add that a few well-publicized consultants do not live up even vaguely to their advance billing. As one top professional observed: "The only thing that keeps some of them alive is luck and being in the right place at the right time. They don't really affect anything in a dramatic way because they don't have the political instinct to do it." By and large, however, consultants are hard-working professionals: very bright and capable, politically shrewd and calculating, and impressively articulate. They travel tens of thousands of miles every year, work on campaigns in a dozen or more states simultaneously, and eat, breathe, and live politics. They are no less political junkies than the candidates they serve. For the most part, they are even less concerned with issues, the parties, and the substance of politics than their clients. They are businessmen, not ideologues.

While admired for their abilities and acumen, consultants also suffer an unsavory reputation in some quarters, and certainly among the general public, whose distrust of seamy, "smoke-filled–room" political operatives is traditional and enduring. At best consultants are seen as encouraging the natural instincts of plastic politicians. ("Gripp, Grinn, Waffle, & Faykit" is the sign cartoonist Jeff MacNelly hangs outside his fictional consulting firm.) At worst, consultants are denounced as "hustlers and con men," as Joe Napolitan put it.[3] Consultants bristle at the slightest mention of any unfavorable press, blaming the criticism on the politicians they work for. As media consultant Michael Kaye expressed it:

People don't like politicians. So no matter how skillfully a political consultant like me does his work, I am a bad guy. I am a packager. I am a manipulator. Now, is it because of what I do, or is it the product that I sell?

Yet widespread doubt about the work of consultants has a basis more thoughtful than Kaye's analysis suggests. That basis is a deep concern for the health and well-being of the democratic process. What consultants seem to forget is that their work cannot be evaluated solely within the context of their profession. "Is this artful media?" or "Is this an effective piece of direct mail?" or "Did this action by a political consultant help to elect candidate X?" are legitimate questions and necessary ones for any judgment of a particular consultant's worth. But the ultimate standard by which the *profession* of political consulting is judged cannot merely be success in electing or defeating candidates. There are much more vital considerations of ethics and democracy to ponder, because electoral politics is the foundation of any democratic society, and important actors in the political sphere must necessarily be the subject of special scrutiny.

This book attempts to provide that scrutiny and to offer an informed discussion of the consequences of the consultant's trade and his new campaign technology. While an observer can reasonably conclude from subsequent chapters that most politicians have been fairly well served by their election professionals, it simply does not follow that the public and the political system have been equal beneficiaries. As the influence of consultants has grown, some very disquieting questions have begun to loom large. Influence peddling, all kinds of financial misconduct, shameful acts of deception and trickery, and improprieties with former clients who are in public office are only a few of the compromising and unethical practices found in far too many consultants' portfolios. At the root of some of the worst offenses is a profit motive unrestrained by ties to party, ideology, or ideals. Sadly, the truth is much as political columnist Jack Germond suggests: "Philosophy and party don't motivate most of the political consultants. Money does, partially, and there is a lot of money to be made if you're any good."

As distressing as they are, the ethical concerns fade by comparison to the democratic effects wrought by consultants. Political professionals and their techniques have helped homogenize American politics, added significantly to campaign costs, lengthened campaigns, and narrowed the focus of elections. Consultants have emphasized personality and gimmickry over issues, often exploiting emotional and negative themes rather than encouraging rational discussion. They have sought candidates who fit their technologies more than the requirements of office and have given an extra boost to candidates who are more skilled at electioneering than governing. They have encouraged candidates' own worst instincts to blow with the prevailing winds of public opinion. Consultants have even consciously increased nonvoting on occasion and meddled in the politics of other countries.

These activities have not occurred in a vacuum. The rules of the political game have been altered dramatically, with consultants clearly benefiting from the changes. The decline of the political parties and the establishment of a radically different system of campaign finance are foremost among the developments that consultants have turned to their advantage. For example, as a direct consequence of the diminution of party strength, a diminution to which consultants have themselves contributed and, in some cases, cheered, consultants have replaced party leaders in key campaign roles.

Yet the power flow from party leaders to political consultants does not have to continue, nor must unethical practices remain unchecked. Consultants and their apologists quite naturally can see no system better than the current one, and they will always have a ready excuse for distasteful doings in their profession. But those who lament the recent technological changes in electioneering have only to look to one of the major parties to see the path of renewal that these same new campaign technologies have made possible. A revitalized national and state Republican party organization, fueled by the marvels consultants had previously harnessed for themselves and monopolized, has provided the model that can tame consultant abuses and develop a healthier, party-based electoral system in the future. This auspicious development and its considerable potential for good will be the object of special examination later.

I have attempted to keep the organization of this book as simple as the subject is elusive. This chapter examines the consultants as a group apart from their techniques and distills a set of general principles of political consulting from a collection of very different individuals. In chapters 2 to 4 the consultants' new campaign technology and their attitudes about it are dissected in considerable detail for the three main consulting specialties or subfields (political polling, paid media, and direct mail). In chapter 5 the odd love-hate relationship between political consultants and the political parties is reviewed, as are the effects of the recent campaign finance laws and the growth of political action committees on both the consultants and the parties. In chapter 6 the broader questions of ethics and democracy raised by this study are discussed. This concluding chapter analyzes the ills apparent in the new age of political consultants and prescribes remedies for some of the most severe ailments.

Images and Roles of Political Consultants

The term "political consultant" is bandied about so loosely that any discourse on the subject must begin by attempting to define it. A *political consultant* is a campaign professional who is engaged primarily in the provision of advice and services (such as polling, media creation and production, and direct-mail fund raising) to candidates, their campaigns, and other political committees. Broadly the title can adorn almost any paid staffer on even the most minor of campaigns. Here, however, we shall concentrate on the relatively small and elite corps of interstate political consultants who usually work on many campaigns simultaneously and have served hundreds of campaigns in their careers. They are the sellers, and often the creators, of advanced campaign technology and technique.*

* Appendix A lists the major American political consulting firms and contains information about their location, party and ideological leanings, and services. Many of the individuals and firms are repeatedly cited throughout the book, and almost all of the individuals were interviewed for this study, as appendix B notes.

The Consultant Corps

There are basically two kinds of consultants. A *generalist* consultant advises a candidate on most or all phases of his campaign and coordinates most or all aspects of the technology employed by the campaign. A *specialist* consultant concentrates on one or two aspects of the campaign and peddles expertise in one or two technological specialties. While almost all of the early consultants were generalists, most consultants today are specialists (who nevertheless often advertise themselves as generalists).

Whether generalist or specialist, the consultant's primary role is the same: to provide services to campaigns. A consultant is hired to conduct a series of public opinion surveys or create a precinct organization or orchestrate a direct-mail fund-raising effort. The secondary roles played by consultants, however, are sometimes more intriguing and just as substantive as the provision of technological services. There is, for example, the "expert" role, a position accorded the consultant by the campaign staff and the candidate because of his wide experience and masterful reputation. (In many campaigns the consultant probably has more influence, and his every word is weighed more carefully than his actual experience or his degree of involvement with the campaign can justify.) Even though he may only visit the campaign once a month or talk with campaign officials weekly, the political professional frequently becomes the grand strategist, designing and supervising the "game plan," orchestrating the press, and selecting the candidate's issues.

Because of the respect he is given as "the expert," the consultant more often than not also seems to assume the role of the candidate's confidant. As media consultant Douglas Bailey has suggested, "Most candidates are hiring outside consultants because within the campaign and within their circle of friends, they don't have anyone whom they feel has the experience or the savvy to satisfy their need for reassurance that they're doing it right or that they can win."

Another media professional, Robert Goodman (who produced advertisements for George Bush's 1980 Republican presidential bid), emphasizes the psychological aspects of the consultant's tour of duty:

George Bush said to me after four hours with him one day at his house, "Are you a psychiatrist or a filmmaker?" We're really into psychiatry. . . . It is incumbent upon the media guy to really look at the candidate and try to lead him past those personality landmines that will destroy him if he doesn't loosen up and do his thing.

These roles are hardly the only ones in the consultant's repertoire. He often finds himself a trusted postelection adviser when his clients win public office. Most significantly, and regrettably, he and his technological wares are "party pinch hitters," substituting for the weakened parties in a variety of ways.

A Brief History of Political Consulting

There have always been political consultants in one form or another in American politics, but the campaign professionals of earlier eras were strategists without benefit of the campaign technologies so standard today. Usually, too, consultants were tied to one or a few candidates, or perhaps to a state or local party organization. Before consulting became a full-time profession, lawyers were often assigned campaign management chores since they had a flexible work schedule as well as the personal finances and community contacts to do the job properly.[4] The old-time press agent, usually a newspaperman familiar with the locale,[5] was also a crucial and influential figure in campaign organization. But in most cases these lawyers and press agents were only functionaries when compared to party leaders and organization bosses who wielded far greater authority in political matters.

On a separate track, one supported by the business community, the profession of public relations was developing. As Stanley Kelley, Jr. has stated, "Business was, and is still, the public relation man's most important patron."[6] Businessmen saw image making as a way to counter a rising tide of business criticism. The federal government followed in close pursuit of public relations professionals, expanding their role considerably during the New Deal. State and local governments, charities, religions, and colleges in succession all saw the "P.R. promise."

Dan Nimmo has called political consultants the "direct descendants" of the public relations professionals,[7] and the growth of both groups is clearly related to some similar phenomena, especially the revolution in mass media communications. Yet political consulting has causes all its own. The decline of the political parties has created opportunities for consultants and the tools of their trade. New means of financing campaigns, telling the candidate's story, and getting the candidate's voters to the polls became necessary as the parties' power waned.

The Consultant Corps

The new campaign techniques and the development of air travel, television, and the computer combined to give consultants the substitutes candidates desired. The fact that these techniques quickly became too complex for laymen to grasp easily—consultants themselves were forced to specialize to keep up with changes—and the acknowledged American need for, and trust in, experts, made professionals that much more attractive. Even if false, the belief that consultants' tricks could somehow bring order out of the chaos of a campaign was enormously reassuring to a candidate. And rising campaign costs (and expenditure and contribution limitations) have placed a premium on the wise use of every campaign dollar. All of these alterations of the political map seemed powerful arguments for hiring political consultants, who gradually became an unquestioned essential for serious campaigns. Everyone now needs them if only because everyone else has them.

The consulting movement coalesced first in California.[8] The state's traditionally anemic party system was weakened further in the twentieth century by the addition of new social welfare programs, a broadened civil service system, and a sprawling suburban shift from the central cities matched by the influx of hundreds of thousands of migrants from the East, Midwest, and South. The sheer growth in the size of the electorate made organizing difficult (and redistricting an even more wrenching and enveloping process). Finally, California was in the forefront of the popular initiative and referendum movement, and had an exceptionally long ballot and a multiplicity of elections.

It was during an initiative campaign, in fact, that modern political consultants first had a major effect.[9] In 1933 the California legislature passed a bill authorizing a flood control and irrigation development in northern California (called the Central Valley Project), which the Pacific Gas and Electric Company (PG&E) believed to be a threat to private power. The utility promptly launched a ballot initiative to reverse the decision. The project's proponents hastily enlisted Clem Whitaker, a Sacramento newsman and press agent, and Leone Smith Baxter, a public relations specialist, to mastermind a campaign to defeat PG&E's initiative. On a limited budget of $39,000, and using radio and newspaper appeals, Whitaker and Baxter managed to save the Central Valley Project.

Not only did PG&E hold no grudge, it actually put Whitaker and Baxter on annual retainer! The two consultants incorporated themselves (as Campaigns, Inc., and later as Whitaker and Baxter Campaigns) and eventually married as well.[10] There were two decades of smooth sailing for the firm, operating out of San Francisco, and the lack of extensive competition[11] enabled it to post a 90 percent success rate in seventy-five major campaigns. Eventually, rival California consultants (such as Republicans Stuart Spencer and Bill Roberts and Democrats Don Bradley, Joseph Cerrell, and Sanford Weiner) came to the fore and reduced Whitaker and Baxter's edge and win-loss record.[12]

By the early 1950s it had become obvious that political professionals were playing an increasingly important part in electoral politics, so much so that Neil Staebler, then chairman of Michigan's Democratic party, alarmed a congressional committee with his prediction that ". . . elections will increasingly become contests not between candidates but between great advertising firms."[13]

While Staebler's vision seems a bit exaggerated even today, he was surely right in suggesting a role for consultants far beyond their relatively limited involvement in some statewide and national races in 1952. Political scientist Alexander Heard's survey of state party committees in 1956–1957 showed remarkable growth in a short time. Democratic state party committees in fifteen states and GOP committees in eighteen states employed public relations firms at some point during those years, and in many cases a high proportion of the committees' funds was spent for retainers.[14] Of the 130 public relations firms he contacted, 60 percent had had some kind of political account between 1952 and 1957, and forty firms in fifteen states reported that they could assume complete responsibility for a campaign.

Two decades later political consultants had become a campaign standard across the United States, and not just for major national and statewide contests. State races for lesser offices and U.S. House seats, and elections for local posts and even judicial offices, frequently had the services of one or more consultants. For example, a 1972–1973 survey indicated that 168 of 208 candidates running for state office had hired at least one political professional: sixty-one of sixty-seven U.S. Senate candidates, thirty-eight of forty-two gubernatorial candidates, thirty of thirty-seven attorney general contenders, and even nineteen of thirty-one and twenty of thirty-two aspirants for secretary of state and state treasurer.[15] Most politicians seeking major office attract a small committee of consultants. A *National Journal* review of sixty-seven opposed campaigns for U.S. Senate in 1970 revealed that sixty-two had an advertising firm, twenty-four had a pollster, and twenty secured help from some sort of campaign management firm.[16] Just five candidates made do with no consultants.

Consultants, moreover, rarely miss an opportunity to expand their domain. The judicial field in California is a classic illustration. In Orange

County a judge seeking another term was defeated in 1940, and none ever lost again until 1978 when four county judges were beaten simultaneously. Sitting judges became understandably nervous and sought professional assistance. Joseph Cerrell and Associates, which had never done a judicial campaign until 1978, suddenly had nine at once. The agency's candidates, all incumbents up for reelection, made a clean sweep (at $7,500 apiece). Flushed with success, Cerrell sponsored a conference on Judicial Campaigning in 1979, designed for judges of the superior and municipal courts. For a $100 registration fee a judge would be treated to sessions on topics such as "Campaigning with Dignity: Maintaining the Judicial Image."

The number of consultants has skyrocketed along with the demand for their services. As late as 1960 there were relatively few full-time professionals in the field; twenty years later there are hundreds—thousands if local advertising agency executives specializing in politics are counted. In addition, they handle a great deal besides candidates' campaigns. Referenda, initiatives, bond issues, and political action committees (PACs) sustain many firms. Some consultants enjoy overseas work in foreign campaigns or specialize in primary and convention nomination battles as well as general elections. Today the average modern professional manages more campaigns in a year than his predecessors did in a lifetime.

Consultant Services: The New Campaign Technology

Generalist consultants offer an especially wide range of service packages to prospective clients. They will do as much, or as little, as the campaign organization desires. Generalist Joseph Cerrell occasionally has done little more than let his firm's name (and, by implication, its successful reputation) be used in a campaign's directory or roster. "Selling your name," as Cerrell calls it, is done almost as an endorsement—in exchange for payment, of course. Cerrell and his associates will also sell their time on a per diem or other basis, for which "we don't do a thing except be a critic." But the firm is also an "A to Z shop" where "we'll sit in the back room and make all of the radio spots right here" and attend to the details of a multitude of other campaign chores. (Some of the major American generalist consultants are sketched in appendix C.)

Specialist consultants usually provide more restrictive services. But those who have been in the business for a long time seem inevitably to diversify their offerings, both because they become more familiar with other technological specialties the longer they are associated with campaigns and because there is a good deal of additional money in it and candidates often request other services. (Having been "sold" on a consultant's product in one area, candidates are often eager to thrust even more responsibility on to a "trusted expert.") Thus it is quite common to find established media consultants such as Douglas Bailey and John Deardourff being hired to write a "soup to nuts" campaign plan or to give per diem strategy advice. Whether the candidate actually benefits from this sort of arrangement is another question. Some consultants, such as Bailey and Deardourff, clearly have the background to be a bit expansive, but many others learn one specialty well and then offer a series of "add-on" services that are cheap imitations of the work done by competent professionals.

A consultant is undeniably at his best when concentrating on his specialty, and the new campaign technology has become advanced enough in several areas to be well worth having. Yet some political participants emphatically deny that this is so. "Campaign technology hasn't changed since the three-by-five card,"[17] claims the executive director of a liberal political action committee. While it is true that the new campaign technology (like all technologies) builds upon older, established principles of political communication and organization, Matt Reese, a generalist consultant, has the weight of evidence behind his assertion that "the whole political world has changed. . . . It's unbelievable what is available to Ted Kennedy in 1980 as opposed to what was available to his brother in 1960."*

Most political technicians trace the advances in political polling, direct mail, demographic precinct targeting, and most media innovations to the private sector, whose marketing needs financed volumes of research and much trial-and-error experimentation. The development of computers for government and business purposes also had major impact on the political sphere.

Not only did consultants borrow heavily from business technology, but they also found each other's work a tempting cookie jar from which to snatch a sweet or two. As a consequence, no new item of campaign technology stays dazzling very long. All consultants in the

---

* Ironically, it was Ted Kennedy's opponent in 1980, Jimmy Carter, who marshalled all the up-to-date techniques in support of his candidacy, while Kennedy's operatives ran a campaign whose technology was, except for direct mail, vastly inferior.

field grab hold of it, and it becomes standard. One campaign professional saw the process as a kind of political détente: "Everything neutralizes out. It's just like the U.S. versus Russia: They get a new missile, then we get it, and on and on." Standard though the techniques may be generally, a good number of technology-deficient campaigns (lacking the necessary financing or with an overconfident incumbent) serve as convincing case studies of the difference technology can make. U.S. Senator Clifford Case's defeat for renomination in New Jersey's 1978 Republican primary is a classic example.[18] Case's opponent was Jeffrey Bell, a young and unknown right-wing activist who targeted Case's liberal record with devastatingly effective direct-mail pieces produced by Eberle and Associates, conservative direct-mail consultants. Bell's extensive use of telephone banks with excellent Republican voter lists was in pointed contrast to the absence of any on Case's behalf. The senator had also used a quickly produced, $3,000 poll whose methodology was questionable.

Still, the importance of campaign technology to electoral success can easily be overstated (and usually is). Elections, and the choices voters make among candidates, are too complex and involve too many variables to be determined by a single element. In most elections the new campaign techniques, and the consultants themselves, probably do not make the difference between winning and losing, although they make some difference and in at least a few cases can convincingly be given credit or blame for the margin of victory or defeat. This alone would serve to make consultants modestly influential in the conduct of the campaign. But due in good measure to journalists' "hype" and consultants' own superb sense of self-promotion, the *perception* is that consultants and technology make the difference in a greater percentage of elections than they likely do. This perception among the press and political people simply means that consultants and the new campaign techniques are even more important than their actual electoral effect would justify—more important, certainly, than they deserve to be.

This is not to say that consultants and their technologies are worthless. In general, the new techniques are more effective than many "old-fashioned" methods. Moreover, consultants and the new techniques can and do influence virtually every significant part of a campaign, and the campaign certainly makes some difference in the outcome of an election. While it is still true that most voters make their choices in good part on the basis of party loyalty and many if not most have their minds almost made up before the campaign even begins, it is also true that in just about every election as much as a third or even more of the electorate is honestly uncommitted or switchable, and that number may be growing as the strength of party identification declines. Voter turnout is also variable. Even if persuasive action is fruitless, a campaign's success depends heavily on its ability to stimulate those favorable to it to vote and, alas, to encourage those unfavorable to it to stay at home, mainly through negative advertising directed almost solely at the opponent's weaknesses.

Technology provides the means to both these ends: New organizational techniques (to be discussed in chapter 3) have been developed to stimulate turnout, and a disturbing proportion of the innovative modern media is negative. Also, for all practical purposes campaigning is now continuous, and voters can be influenced by television, direct mail, and other campaign aids long before the outset of the official campaign season. There is some evidence that at state as well as national levels, campaign technology is being employed increasingly early.

Still another situation in which campaign technology is especially influential is during primary elections, where party identification (absent a preprimary party endorsement) can play no role at all. Many political consultants love to work in primaries, where they believe relatively low turnouts and the lack of party ties give the new campaign technology its broadest potential use. Finally, it should be noted that campaigns have other functions besides winning, which a European would acknowledge sooner than an American. Party building for future elections (or candidate building within the personality-centered American system) is a perfectly legitimate and useful campaign goal.[19]

Inevitably, anyone who attempts to assess the effectiveness of modern campaign techniques is humbled by the scarcity of empirical evidence to support any hard and fast conclusions. There have been few solid election-day and postelection surveys, for example, and, compared to the extensive privately supported research in product advertising, little thorough testing of the impact of political media advertisements during campaigns. The impact of any consultant or any technology, then, can usually only be guessed at. No one has the foggiest notion of what percentage of the vote a consultant or a piece of new campaign technology can or does add to a candidate in any given set of circumstances. Campaign observers rarely even have a precise idea of what event or series of events produced the election result. Campaigning remains a complex, unpredictable, and very unscientific process, and one may expect and be grateful that it always will be.

Consultants' understanding of the new campaign technology is often just as inexact. Most political consultants, even some of the best, "don't know why they are doing what they're doing. They just mechanically learn some new technique, but they don't really understand it," says media professional Tony Schwartz. Matt Reese admits that after 187 campaigns at every level, "I know more what not to do than what to do."[20] Even with other professionals in their own specialty, consultants rarely seem to agree on anything. They disagree violently about the most basic of campaign questions (such as the allocation of the budget between media and organization). They delight in deriding the "rules" of the political game—the origin of the rules is never disclosed—and relish telling an interviewer of their most recent successful rulebendings. Yet they create much of the currently accepted political wisdom and generalize about campaigning and electioneering with abandon "because they like to believe they have the answer, and everyone expects them to have some handle on the truth." But, continues Charles Guggenheim, a respected Democratic media professional, "none of us has *the answer,* and every race is so different that the generalizations are either obvious or not useful."

If we can be grateful that campaigning cannot be completely quantified, we can also give thanks that the profession of consulting is still far more of an art than a science. As Bob Goodman sees himself and his fellows:

We are still artists, trying to develop a dramatic way of capturing the attention and then inspiring resolve. The new technology is in its infant stage for those who practice the media arts. What we learn is what doesn't work, by trial and error. My value to a candidate right now is that after ten years of doing media, I won't try an idea that I had five years ago and I found bombed. We're becoming a little more error free. But we really don't know a great deal. If we knew more we would be dangerous.

Winning and Losing in the Election Game

Let no one doubt it: Consultants care very much about winning the campaigns they take on. They need victories for their business to survive, above all. In addition, there is a not insubstantial investment of ego and emotion in their clients' fates. William Butcher of Butcher-Forde Consulting agency minces no words about his goal: "When it comes to political consulting, the name of the game is winning on election day. We do everything we are legally and morally able to do to win."[21] (Later chapters will suggest that some consultants' moral standards are extraordinarily flexible and tolerant.)

There is nothing consultants enjoy more than citing their win-loss records, and as they count them the records are phenomenally and uniformly successful, rarely falling below 60 to 70 percent triumphant. The numbers are almost always partial or exaggerated citations, winked at by others in the business who understand the polite fictions necessary for self-promotion. Genial Matt Reese, commenting on a well-known consultant's record, was more honest than most: "He hasn't had as much success as he claims—that's off the record. None of us has. I've always mentioned the names of the ones that I've won and forgotten to mention the ones that I haven't won."

Reese's "trinity of necessity" for political consultants explains why the win-loss records are so consistently overblown: "There are three things in this business that are important. Winning, or the reputation of winning—you need a pretty good record; working for people whose names are known; and winning when you're not supposed to."[22] Consultants do more than cheat on their records to support their reputations. They mix and match the clients they take to insure a healthy percentage of victories. Most professionals enjoy a challenge or two, and need to be on board at least occasionally when a long shot manages to confound the experts. (Sometimes consultants are partly responsible for these come-from-behind surprises.) But it is the rare consultant who loads up on long shots in any single year. The largest number of a consultant's clients are almost always incumbents or reasonable bets for open seats.

Consultants' need to insure a winning record is yet another advantage incumbents have over their challengers. It is always easier for an incumbent, including one in electoral trouble, to secure top-flight consulting services since even incumbents who appear to be in danger usually wind up in the winner's column on election day. Challengers are not nearly as good bets for consultants, and frequently they are refused assistance for that reason. A major consultant who requested anonymity on the matter confessed that "There were two long-shot races last year that I just didn't want to take because I didn't want the losses on my record." Ironically, most incumbents would probably win easily without professional services. Reese, who did some work for Democratic House Speaker Thomas P. O'Neill and U.S. Senator Edward M. Kennedy (D-Mass.) in 1976, humbly notes that "They would have won had I never been born." Challengers have their best opportunity to snare national consultants in the "off-off" years of the election cycle (the year immediately before and the one immediately after the presidential election year) because there is relatively little political work available then. Only a few states (Kentucky, Louisiana, Mississippi, New Jersey, and Virginia) and localities (such as New York City) have major elections scheduled then, but candidates in those areas are often spoiled by the attention lavished upon them by the band of national political professionals—people whose services they probably could not hope to secure in a busier year.

While all consultants try to end up with a winning balance, they go about it in widely different ways. Some, such as Democratic media professional Robert Squier, who has only a couple of full-time assistants, take on just a few campaigns each year. Having signed on nineteen campaigns one year and found the load to be far too heavy, he has settled into a pattern of about five major statewide campaigns per year, supplemented by a number of smaller, less intense local or congressional races. The large polling firm of Decision Making Information, by contrast, has four senior political project directors, each of whom takes on five or six statewide campaigns and a dozen or more congressional races, for a total of twenty to twenty-four statewide and fifty to seventy-five congressional campaigns each election year. Not just the size of the firm but also the demands of a consultant's technological specialty and the financial rewards from it seem to determine his caseload. On a rough average pollsters sign on the greatest number of clients, followed closely by direct-mail agencies, with media professionals taking a dozen or fewer candidates per election calendar. Much of the work, as in any profession, is repeat business when the customer is satisfied, and the proportion of steady clientele can range quite high—close to three-quarters in at least one case,[23] but usually about a third.

One of the most dramatic changes in the history of political consulting has been the complete transformation of the political professional from private, behind-the-scenes adviser to the most public of election actors (except for the candidate himself). Consultants have become media stars. They are signals to the press and, through them, to the activists and general public, about the rising and falling fortunes of politicians. Douglas Bailey, a national Republican media consultant, explained (and deprecated) the importance that the candidates themselves attach to "name" consultants:

We have been through the ego trip over the past six or eight months of talking with no less than twelve either actual or potential Republican candidates for

president who had wanted us to sign on. Three of them have said to us something that we have heard frequently on the state level and I just think is
absurd, a sign of the weakness of their candidacy. They sort of make the
assumption: If I've got you guys in my corner, that gives me credibility from
the outside, and I have made the decision that with you, I will run, and without
you, I will not run. I don't like to be put in that situation. That's very flattering
and so forth, but that's kind of a dumb conclusion for a candidate to reach.

It may well be a sign of weakness, but it is not an unreasonable
conclusion for a candidate to make, so climactic is the nod from a
top-flight consultant considered to be in some circles.

The consultants successfully recruited by a candidate have become
status symbols. A candidate is not merely hiring consultants. Through
the consultant he is purchasing acceptance from other politicians, insurance that his campaign will be taken seriously, and favorable mention
by journalists. He is also buying association with a consultant's past
clientele, particularly the winners. He is securing access to the web
of relationships that a consultant and his firm have developed. Finally,
he is acquiring the public services of a surrogate, for political consultants hold press conferences to discuss their work (and the candidate's
chances), build supporters' morale, attract headlines, enhance fund
raising, and send a signal to groups such as the national party committees and PACs that their support services would not be wasted on
this client. It is little wonder that a candidate often schedules some
of his grandest press gatherings to announce the identities of his consultants and to ballyhoo his good fortune.

Political activists and working journalists alike, recognizing the
importance and influence of the choice of consultants, naturally ask
whether each candidate is keeping up with the Joneses. The press
has taken to designating "front runners" among consultants as well
as candidates, and a new political wizard is crowned each election
year.[24] In 1974 it was John Martilla of the Boston firm of Martilla,
Payne, Kiley, and Thorne, mainly because of his masterminding of
Democrat Richard F. Vander Veen's takeover of the Michigan U.S.
House seat formerly held by Gerald R. Ford (who had just taken office
as Vice-President). In 1976 Douglas Bailey and his partner, John Deardourff, were given much of the credit for President Ford's home-stretch
surge after trailing Carter badly in the early polls. In 1977 New York
media man David Garth grabbed the publicity spotlight with two triumphs for underdogs Ed Koch (in the New York City mayoralty contest) and Brendan Byrne (the incumbent New Jersey governor who

won reelection against long odds). In 1978 Deardourff had another happy year in gubernatorial elections, and Democratic advertiser Michael Kaye got his first dose of national exposure in a New Jersey Democratic primary for U.S. Senate when his man, Bill Bradley, trounced state treasurer Richard Leone, the candidate represented by David Garth. In 1979 Robert Squier hit the jackpot in a dry off-year when he produced the advertisements for John Y. Brown's victorious media blitz campaign for the Kentucky governorship. Squier also managed the effort of William Winter, the surprise winner of Mississippi's protracted 1979 statehouse battle. In 1980 Robert Goodman was on the air almost as much as his candidate George Bush when Bush was riding high in the polls after the Iowa caucuses. On the Democratic side Gerald Rafshoon received a more favorable appraisal from his previously harsh critics for Carter's much-improved 1980 advertising effort, compared to his near-disastrous 1976 general election offering for Carter.*

Some consultants get glowing reputations from campaigns in which they were not deeply involved or were more lucky than skillful. Stuart Spencer, whose firm reaped a publicity bonanza after its management of Ronald Reagan's winning California gubernatorial quest in 1966, remembers the race quite differently than the instant histories of the time: "I never saw an easier campaign in my life: Everything fell into place. We got a great reputation out of it but it wasn't that hard." Spencer correctly believes that simple luck still plays as great a role in politics as all the technologies put together, and at least a few prominent members of the consulting clan surely owe their gratitude more to *fortuna* than their own ability.

In the consulting business, one can lose by winning and win by losing. A winning streak can produce overconfidence and a false sense of security. Several consultants recalled instances similar to Michael Kaye's chastening experience of a string of wins crowned by the mighty loss of Democratic U.S. Senator Dick Clark's 1978 bid for reelection in Iowa:

Maybe before Dick Clark's campaign I was feeling a little bit invincible. I had never lost and . . . I was starting to feel a little godlike. . . . But the Clark campaign woke me up because I did basically the same things in that campaign that I had done in every other campaign, and we lost.

* Ironically, Carter won when Rafshoon was "bad" and lost when he was "good"— a reminder that media consultants are usually assigned too much credit for victories and too much blame for defeats.

Conversely, a campaign that achieves victory in a closer race than the polls and pundits predicted is adjudged a loss for the "winning" consultant. Gerald Rafshoon's candidate may have gotten to the White House, but Bailey and Deardourff were perceived to have won the 1976 presidential contest. Hubert Humphrey lost the 1968 presidential election, but Joseph Napolitan and the Democratic nominee's managers won the blue ribbons from the panel of judges in politics and the press.[25]

All of this is not to underprice the costs of losing, whatever the circumstances. Hell hath no fury like a candidate scorned, and as newspaper columnist Jack Germond surmised from his long experience observing campaigns, "When the candidate's campaign goes sour, he has to put the rap on someone and the consultant is very handy." It is not uncommon for a losing candidate, dissatisfied (in retrospect) with his consultant, to refuse to pay remaining debts or to challenge the consultant's accounting (a wise idea that should be standard practice when dealing with some firms). Most damaging to the consultant, though, is the scuttlebutt that makes the political rounds about "how I supposedly screwed up," as one consultant put it. "When I win I'm a genius, a hero, and when I lose I'm a jerk." Professionals often are branded with a loss even when they have had little to do with the actual conduct of the campaign, or when the candidate and staff ignored their advice. However unfair these circumstances may be, the glories of the profession seem to exceed the sorrows by a wide margin.

In fact, an observer is struck by the agility of most consultants in evading blame even in highly publicized losing battles. How is it that we always see the triumphs of consulting magic emblazoned across the sky (and the tops of most newspapers), while the defeats are kept as quiet as an Anglo-Saxon family's secrets? It is not that the cases of failed campaign wizardry are few or minor. Just in 1978 there were dozens of noteworthy examples.[26] Maryland Attorney General Francis Burch's bid for the Democratic gubernatorial nomination cost one-third of a million dollars, and Burch did all the "right" things and secured some of the best and the brightest the consulting profession has to offer (including Bob Squier to do his media and William R. Hamilton to conduct his surveys). Yet Burch consistently fell in the polls, his financial support dried up, and he was forced to withdraw in July before the September primary, which was won by Harry R. Hughes, who had strong endorsements from the *Sunpapers* but almost no advanced campaign technology and consultant assistance. Next door in Washington, D.C., home port for so many large and renowned consulting firms, three candidates were locked in a contest for mayor in a simultaneous September party primary. The incumbent, Walter Washington, had Matt Reese on his campaign roster. Sterling Tucker, the city council chairman and early favorite, had Bailey and Deardourff leading his effort. Supposedly trailing the field was Councilman Marion S. Barry, who had no prominent consultants working on his behalf.[27] With the help of editorial backing from *The Washington Post,* Barry defeated his opponents and all of their professional troops.

Consultants are not salesmen for nothing, of course, and they are as resourceful at packaging themselves as they are their candidates. But the working political press must be credited with the lion's share of myth creation. As chapter 6 will highlight, consultants have become prime sources for journalists, too valuable to treat badly, fellow members of the traveling band of the semipermanent political elite. Journalists are in good part responsible for helping the public and even some of the powerful forget, as Matt Reese suggested, "in the final analysis, it is not we who win campaigns and not we who lose them."[28]

With all of the emphasis on winning, and a life-style built around the power, glory, and rewards of politics, it is not surprising to discover that many political consultants have had a stray thought or two of running for office themselves. One conservative consultant, direct mail's Richard Viguerie, actually toyed publicly with a 1976 vice-presidential bid on the American Independent party ticket, George Wallace's 1968 presidential election vehicle. (Viguerie gave up the idea when the zany former governor of Georgia, Lester Maddox, became the A.I.P.'s presidential nominee.) What prevents them from taking the plunge is not fear of defeat. Their substantial egos and considerable faith in their own electoral devices lead most to believe their elections would be, in the words of one, "a piece of cake." Rather, it is a dislike of the thought of actually having to *serve* in office, as well as a belief that merely holding a single office would mean a considerable reduction in the influence to which they have become accustomed. "I think I could probably elect myself and I don't think it would be terribly difficult," remarked Bob Squier. "But it wouldn't be as much fun as being a consultant, and I would lose my leverage. I would just be one vote someplace." Stuart Spencer would relish *running* for office— every other year for the U.S. House is "not often enough" for his tastes—"but I'd hate like hell to serve. I'd be bored to death."[29]

Party Loyalty, Personal Ideology, and the Selection of Candidate-Clients

There are several methods by which candidates are matched up with political consultants. The first is consultant solicitation. When the principals in Butcher-Forde Consulting, for instance, heard that there was no professional management team supporting Howard Jarvis's 1978 Proposition 13 tax-cutting drive in California, they arranged a meeting with Jarvis, presented a plan of action, and hustled the extremely lucrative account.[30] While solicitation is a common and necessary practice for lesser-known consultants, occasionally the national firms also seek the account of a campaign that has either great financial potential or a capacity to enhance their winning image and reputation. The D.M.I. polling firm systematically compiles a "druthers list" of the most desirable campaigns and contacts them in an attempt to sign them up (approaching political consultants working for the campaigns instead of the candidates on occasion).

Rarely in past times did consultants actually recruit an individual to make a race, but the practice is becoming disturbingly common due to the expansion of ideological political action committees. A professional manager like Roy Day was once the exception in his role as Richard Nixon's original sponsor.[31] Day, though, was also chairman of the Republican Central Committee of Los Angeles when he formed the Committee of One Hundred in 1946 to find an opponent for the Democratic incumbent U.S. congressman, Gerald Voorhis. Day placed advertisements on the front pages of twenty-six newspapers, and Nixon was one of the respondents. The future president was chosen to make his first race, launching his long political career. Today, however, consultants active in recruiting candidates have weak or nonexistent party credentials and sometimes are agents of party-rivaling political action committees, such as the Committee for the Survival of a Free Congress or the National Committee for an Effective Congress.[32]

Most major consultants do not bother to recruit because ideologically they are not very choosy and they have far more business that walks in the door unsolicited than they can possibly handle. In the vast proportion of client-consultant matchings, the original contact is made by the future client, and the odds are great that prominent consultants will not be interested or able to take them. Richard Viguerie claims to turn away 98 percent of all the people who come to him.[33] David Garth reports that, while he took only five campaigns in 1978, he was approached by statewide candidates in thirty-nine states, and in twelve of those states (or twenty-eight—he cited different figures in two separately published interviews) he was offered both sides of the race.[34]

It is little wonder that a few consultants are so swamped with requests. Candidates and their staffs usually know little about the national professionals or their campaign technologies and are likely to seize upon one of the periodic glowing press accounts of one or another consultant's miracles, after which the candidate or campaign manager issues the order to secure consultant "X" at any cost. A bit of campaign shopping could do wonders for a campaign budget, but there is astoundingly little of that. When it occurs, it is worth noting. U.S. Senator Birch Bayh's well-organized 1974 reelection effort, for example, arranged interviews with eight political pollsters. The two finalists, Peter Hart and Patrick Caddell, were not well known at the time. (After final interviews of one and a half hours each, Caddell was chosen over Hart.) Demand for consultant services has so increased since 1974 that it is doubtful that any such carefully staged selection is possible today. Most potential clients would simply not be worth the preliminary investment of so much of a consultant's time.[35] Regrettably, the consultant crunch at the first level is forcing candidates to solicit help from much less experienced and sometimes less scrupulous second- and third-level professionals. Many of the unethical practices in the consulting business find their origin there.

One other method of matching candidates and consultants should be mentioned. Candidates are frequently referred to a particular consulting firm by a third party. Sometimes a firm's previous candidate-clients who were satisfied by the services rendered will pass along the experience while offering advice to new candidates. A consultant who is too busy to sign the candidate on will sometimes suggest the names of friendly associates or some young, struggling firm with which he is acquainted. Many PACs have semipermanent relationships with certain consultants and will suggest a linking of arms to a candidate being supported with PAC money. Finally, the candidate's state or national political party committee may work on a regular basis with consultants, and a recommendation may be forthcoming from party officials. In some midwestern states, particularly in the Republican camp, a few consultants have done all of a party's major candidates for a number of years and are hired almost by habit.

For the most part, one problem candidates do not have to worry about is locating ideologically compatible consultants. While the professionals are not without political belief, they rarely let it overrule their business sense. For most consultants ideology is a surprisingly minor criterion in the selection of clients. Party affiliation plays a larger role for some, but usually because serving candidates of both parties is impractical and hurts business. (A significant minority of the professionals, however, are actively hostile to the parties—even to the very notion of a political system.) Political reporter David Broder connected the consultants' party links and lack of pronounced ideology to the credibility and professionalism required for success in their business: "I think the nonideological style they adopt is not dissimilar to that of political reporters, mainly that they try to really separate their own feelings and emotions so that they don't get in the way of making a professional judgment."

But the full explanation has a major financial component, as political consultant Sanford L. Weiner, addressing his peers, frankly surmised:

We would all like to think we have only worked for candidates we believed in, and who represented our own individual political thinking. . . . Unfortunately, as with any profession, economics enter the picture. We have all, from time to time, represented clients whom we didn't particularly love, but who could help us pay the overhead.[36]

The businessman's profit motive is admittedly powerful, and when combined with most political professionals' disinterest in issues and the stuff of government, a remarkable tolerance results. Robert Goodman can say without blush, "I call myself a Jacob Javits Republican, but I can stretch to the conservative ends without a problem." His standard of judgment for potential clients is heroic, not ideological: "We see politics as theater, living theater, and it is classic theater. There is a hero and there is a villain. Now we won't knowingly take on a villain. We like to feel that our candidate has the potential of being the hero." Fellow Republican consultant John Deardourff has a less charitable assessment of the "heroic standard": "Bob Goodman doesn't care who he works for. He'll build a big, noisy campaign, with a forty-seven-piece band, around anyone."[37]

As its literature notes, Deardourff's firm makes its services "available to candidates we wish to see in public office." His partner, Doug Bailey, identified two areas (civil rights and women's issues) where "unless we generally shared the candidate's philosophy, we would feel so uncomfortable it would be a nonproductive and unpleasant relationship." Yet he admits to working for candidates who have opposed the Equal Rights Amendment and racial balancing of school systems through busing. In 1978 the Bailey-Deardourff firm also handled at least three candidates with solid antiabortion records.[38] Chuck Winner of California's Winner-Wagner organization proclaims insistently and forthrightly his undying resistance to his state's often-used initiative and referendum process: "I oppose the idea of law by mob rule. I oppose the idea of doing away with representative democracy. I oppose the idea of losing basic protections for the minority." But almost all of his lucrative political work is referendum- and initiative-related. (Someone has to do it, of course.)

Generalist consultant Hank Parkinson (who claims to have worked for both the Democratic and Republican national committees) explains his lack of issue orientation by calling himself "a technician, not an ideologue. . . . I have turned down extremists on both ends of the spectrum, but mostly because they simply can't win." Some professionals are addicted to sports analogies to communicate their love of the game and disinterest in the philosophy behind the plays. Others report that their ideological attachments are fading over time as their exposure to politics lengthens, and that ideological rigidity is part of the problem in the political system they observe. Says Patrick Caddell:

I'm basically a liberal, but also basically convinced that most of those answers aren't working either. Rigid ideological structures are helping to screw up what's going on in terms of our ability to solve our real problems. I've said to people who say, "How do you work for McGovern and work for Carter?" it's very simple. In both cases, I happen to think that they were the best people running for President at the time.

These comments would be an anathema to a small but growing band of political consultants who are more rigid in their ideological prerequisites for candidate-clients. Conservative Richard Viguerie has never been accused of ignoring his direct-mail firm's business interests, yet he carefully considers the ideology of all his prospective clients and organizational subordinates. The right-wing political action committees, which Viguerie often helps to coordinate, sometimes have prospective candidates fill out written ideological examinations. Paul Weyrich, executive director of the Committee for the Survival of a Free Congress, gives a seventy-part questionnaire on issues and ideology to each candidate who approaches the group for assistance, and the answers are crucial to chances for funding.

Perhaps because the contemporary United States is in a conservative-dominated political era and a period of retrenchment for liberals, most tests of ideological purity are administered on the right. But in a recent time more attuned to left-wing philosophy, the 1960s, the same degree of selectiveness by liberal political professionals existed. Only days before President Johnson withdrew from the 1968 presidential race, one of his campaign assistants was forced to tell Johnson that his staff had had great difficulty finding a New York advertising agency willing to take him on "because they are all [Vietnam] 'doves.'"[39]

Ideology is also at least one of a number of considerations for some consultants not at the liberal or conservative extremes of the spectrum. The direct-mail firm of Craver, Mathews, Smith and Co. has been known to reject issue groups because they were philosophically in conflict with the partners' views. David Garth has his staff carefully research the records of his petitioners (because he has learned not to trust their own accounting of their voting histories), and he pays careful attention to views on a number of social issues. Generalist Walter DeVries eventually switched from the Republican to the Democratic party to accommodate his progressivism, although business needs entered into the decision. As he wryly noted, "If you work only for progressive Republicans, your market is getting pretty small."[40] Regional media consultant Marvin Chernoff insists on working for "the most progressive or liberal candidate in the race," yet this carefully worded criterion often allows signing on a moderate or conservative.

Even consultants who put ideology on the back burner (or off the stove entirely) have some rock-bottom standards and very general prohibitive criteria. Joseph Cerrell will not work for anybody that he would "have trouble voting for." Pollster William Hamilton, a moderate-liberal Democrat who has worked for conservatives, had the opportunity to take one of George Wallace's presidential campaigns but refused it. Bob Goodman also rejected Wallace and did not respond to preliminary soundings from a U.S. Senate candidate from Virginia (who was eventually successful in his electoral bid) because he was "a guy who would have taken the rent from poor little Nellie and thrown her on the streets." He continued: "We will not handle people we don't like as human beings. We will not handle people we think are dangerous at either extreme. We could not handle a John Bircher, a racist."

It is a delicious commentary on the American system that some of the least ideological professionals take their chosen political party dead seriously, and anyone who cares about the party system can be grateful that they do. A few are fierce partisans, having had their political baptism as party functionaries and occasionally having had years of direct party employment. One of these, Robert Odell, is inclined to take on just about any Republican in his direct-mail firm because, "Democrats do little or nothing that I respect and Republicans do nearly everything I respect." Striking a rare pose for a private consultant, Odell declares, "The most important goal for me is to make the Republican party effective." Matt Reese holds the Democratic party in similar esteem, observing only half in jest that he is "a partisan without apology. I don't even *like* Republicans, except for Abraham Lincoln." And few professionals have shown as long and abiding a concern for a political party as Stuart Spencer and his partner, Bill Roberts, who both began their political careers as volunteers for the Republican party in California. Their consulting shop actually developed around the GOP and was encouraged by the party. Spencer explained that he and Roberts "wanted to be an extension of the party, a management tool that the party could use" and that they viewed each of their early consulting outings as "an opportunity for the Republican party." With the party's interests in mind, Spencer and Roberts gave Ronald Reagan an extended grilling when he approached them about his impending 1966 gubernatorial campaign in California. After a number of questions about his depth and experience, and whether he could win for the party or might instead become another Goldwater disaster, reportedly Reagan became exasperated and demanded: "Now, goddammit, I want to get some answers from you guys. Are you going to work for me or not?"[41] The Spencer-Roberts agency finally did agree to handle him.

The greatest number of consultants, though, are simply not committed in any real sense to a political party. Michael Kaye, for instance, proclaims himself to be an Independent and the parties to be "bullshit." Revealingly, however, he still sensed that it was a mistake to work both sides of the street, comparing it to his practice while a product advertiser:

People in political office, most of them are paranoid anyway. And I think it would make someone uncomfortable to think that I was working for a Republican at the same time I was working for a Democrat. That is why I work only for Democrats. I don't work for just Democrats because I think they are the only good pure people on this planet. It is the same reason that in the [product] advertising business I didn't work for two clients in the same business.

Yet for all of the danger supposedly involved in crossing party lines, consultants seem to yield frequently to the temptation. Democrat Peter Hart conducted Republican U.S. Senate nominee John Heinz's surveys in Pennsylvania in 1976 (and claimed he was told he could not take polls for Jimmy Carter as a consequence). David Garth has been "all over the lot," as one of his detractors termed his tendency to take moderate-to-liberal Democrats and Republicans indiscriminantly, and it was a surprise to no one in the profession when GOP Congressman John Anderson tapped Garth to help with his 1980 Independent presidential bid. Another Democratic-leaning liberal firm, Craver, Mathews, Smith, and Co., took on Anderson's direct-mail program. The now-defunct firm of Baus and Ross in California secured the accounts of Richard Nixon, Barry Goldwater, and Edmund G. "Pat" Brown, Sr., within a few years of one another. The survey firm of D.M.I. not only once worked for both Democrats and Republicans, they actually polled both sides of the same congressional election district in 1966. Vincent Breglio, the D.M.I. vice president, took one side, and President Richard Wirthlin took the other. They ran the research independent of one another and provided consulting services to each side without crossing communications. Apparently the candidates were rather trusting souls who reportedly agreed to this outrageous arrangement (although it was quite a useful one for the firm's "win ratio"). D.M.I. converted permanently to Republicanism in 1967 when Michigan Governor George Romney asked the firm to join his presidential effort on the condition that they work only for the GOP. Convinced that the move was good for business, Wirthlin and Breglio made the switch over the objections of the Democratic members of the firm, who nevertheless stayed.[42]

It is one thing to be apathetic about the party system and quite another to be hostile to it. The nonideological nature of American parties is the object of venomous rebuke by right-wing consultants such as Richard Viguerie and PAC leaders such as Paul Weyrich. Viguerie has flirted with a personal Independent candidacy and publicly expressed his hopes for a new conservative party to replace the GOP. Urging cross-party consulting for conservative candidates, Viguerie insisted that "conservatives must learn to disregard meaningless party labels."[43] Weyrich's Committee for the Survival of a Free Congress practices Viguerie's preaching and has involved itself in party congressional primaries on both sides of the aisle, assisting the 1978 victories of the presidents of both the freshman Democratic and freshman Republican U.S. House classes. A "militant supporter" of Independent

U.S. Senator Harry Byrd of Virginia, Weyrich believes that conservatives' "political victory will not come by the Republicans winning control but rather by a coalition of conservatives of both political parties getting together." The conservative Republican takeover of the U.S. Senate in 1980 may have given Weyrich second thoughts, but it hardly instilled in him any greater loyalty to the GOP. Barely had the votes been counted than Weyrich and other New Right leaders warned President-elect Ronald Reagan to hew closely to conservative ideology. Vice-President-elect George Bush, suspected of moderate tendencies, was threatened in much stronger terms.

With the exception of the ideological PACs, party affiliation and ideology are by no means the only, or even the dominant, criteria for consultants in selecting their clients. The personal mesh between consultant and client seems to be of paramount importance, followed by the need for a balanced and economically rewarding program for the firm. There is a sort of ritualized mating dance when consultants and prospective clients meet, a mutual sizing-up and testing of one another that can sometimes be quite intense for all parties. Most consultants in preparing to meet with a candidate learn as much as possible about the individual ahead of time and request a full day of the candidate's time for the interview. They grill the candidate, peppering him with questions, many of them personal (in an attempt to ferret out scandal in advance). David Garth's interrogation is unusually issue-oriented: "How should the state or city be run? How should the money be distributed? What do you think about welfare?" Walter DeVries is particularly interested in the response to one query: " 'What makes you think you ought to be governor or United States senator?' And a lot of guys don't have very good answers. And if they haven't articulated in their own mind why they want to be governor, you can't do it for them." Matt Reese's mind is more directly on the prospects of winning when he confronts the candidate: "I ask how many people they've got and how much money. I know how to run a campaign with lots of people and little money. I know how to run a campaign with lots of money and few people. I love it when I've got lots of money and lots of people. I don't know what to do when I don't have any money and any people." In his interview sessions, Pat Caddell tries above all to test character to find the "real patriots in the sense of really caring about the country. If I were to apply one single criterion, it would be whether the individual really gives a good damn about what happens to the United States. Large numbers of politicians, frankly, could care less as long as they stay in office."

The personal interviews are enormously useful, and normally essential, for both the candidate and the professional. Sometimes serious potential problems are exposed and explored so that all parties can anticipate the campaign ahead. Frequently a consultant encounters a reluctant candidate and after a rewarding session actively encourages his candidacy. On the other hand, as one consultant reported, "Many times what you find out is that that person really shouldn't be running for office. Either they have problems or when you really get down to it they are running because somebody else wants them to run . . . or because they see a lot of glamour in it."

The interviews are not always revealing, of course, and many consultants (at least the ones who have sufficient clientele to afford the luxury of leisurely choice) often require a number of interviews over several weeks or months before an agreement is concluded. But even with multiple meetings, decisions on taking clients are always gambles. Media consultant Tony Schwartz asks rhetorically, "How well can you really know a guy? You get to know your wife better after you get married and your secretary better after you've hired her." Still, most professionals believe they can sense whether the client understands and appreciates what they do and whether the personal relationship in the campaign is likely to be a pleasant, satisfying, and effective one.

While the personal evaluation and relationship is the most crucial nonpartisan element in the selection process, at least half a dozen other factors are taken into consideration. The revenue-producing potential of a campaign is almost always at the top of the list. A major race that will contribute substantially to a firm's economic objectives is a good bet to be selected, and campaigns are scrutinized to determine the likelihood they will meet their projected budgets. Consultants also consider the stress that a campaign will add to their personal schedules. Most have a fairly fixed limit on the number of campaigns they will take in any year, and they often try to cluster them geographically, which saves traveling wear and tear. No consultant forgets about the overall batting average, either; a reputation that has been so lovingly nurtured must be protected with a sufficient quota of expected victories and upset wins. And a spirit of cooperation and an appreciation of the consultant's role must be manifested not only by the candidate but also by the spouse and the key internal campaign staff aides.

Some consultants are reluctant to take on campaigns at certain levels (usually local or presidential, although some firms refuse gubernatorial clients). At least until John Anderson came along, David Garth refused to consider presidential clients, saying, "I don't really have any great desire to elect a president. . . . The kind of physical and emotional expenditure it takes doesn't make sense for the company."[44] Garth also claims to use a form of collegial decision making absent in most firms, wherein his staffers and associates participate fully in the client selection process rather than accept his dictation of choices.

The direct-mail firms have a number of specialized criteria peculiar to their technology. Viguerie's organization insists that candidates prove they can raise significant funds on their own, partially because of the huge initial costs involved in a direct-mail program. And some firms, such as Craver, Mathews, Smith, and Co., refuse a significant percentage of the candidates and organizations that approach them because direct mail is not an appropriate device in many cases and will not turn a profit for the company or the clients.

Each consultant applies these criteria quite differently, giving more emphasis to some than others, and consequently he can judge particular candidates differently than his peers. The case of Bill Bradley's 1978 bid for the Democratic U.S. Senate nomination in New Jersey will serve to illustrate. Bradley's personal charm and flattering appeal to Michael Kaye's professional pride won the consultant over:

Bill saw my work for the first time. Apparently, as he tells me, he instantly realized I was the guy without a doubt. . . . I liked the fact that he genuinely wanted me. I told him I would give him a decision after the weekend, because I was still wondering if I really wanted to fly back and forth to New Jersey all the time. I said, "Bill, don't bother me until next Monday." The next morning, he calls me. He said, "Mike, I know I've broken the rules, but I just have to tell you how much I want you to do this campaign. Maybe I didn't get that point across the other night, but I want you to know that we loved meeting you." That was very nice. Anyway, I did it and it was a marvelous year.

Kaye had not been Bradley's first choice, however; David Garth was. But Bradley's wooing of Garth had been much less successful, and Garth not only declined Bradley but signed on for Richard Leone, one of his opponents. Said Garth:

I didn't like Bradley. I interviewed him. It was awful. I asked him five or six questions. I asked him questions about energy, housing, the kind of things I think as a candidate for the U.S. Senate from the state of New Jersey he ought to know. He didn't know anything. I didn't ask him any questions like "Do you want to win?" or "Will you change your clothes?" I don't like that. Dick Leone was a personal friend of ours. We had worked with him in several campaigns. He probably would have been the best qualified guy in that race.

He was also an Italian and I felt there was a shortage, quite frankly, of Italians in office, that we need more because it's a group that really feels unrepresented, the same as the blacks do.[45]

Garth's comments make obvious the fact that political consultants have become preselectors in the nominating process, encouraging and dissuading candidacies often with the mere announcements of their choices of clients in a race. In this respect and in others—slate balancing, for example, as in Garth's determination that more Italians should be in office—modern political consultants have substituted for the party bosses of old and make decisions today that should more properly be the prerogative of party leaders. Peter Hart sounds like a more grammatical version of Tammany Hall's George Washington Plunkitt when he relates this anecdote:

I worked with [one candidate] in 1978 and came to the conclusion that he's a very, very bad human being and that I made a mistake. The person decided he'd seek office in 1980 and the guy made an appointment with me. I said, "I'm sorry to tell you, but I think you've got a character flaw. I'm sorry if nobody else has ever told you. I don't believe in you. I can't work to see that you get elected."

It is not that most political consultants look upon their preselector role cavalierly; some see it for what it is, a sobering responsiblity. Sanford Weiner reminded his fellow consultants in a session of the American Association of Political Consultants that, in Watergate's wake, they had "a duty and a responsibility to screen would-be candidates more carefully than ever."[46] But is it better for society to lodge this obligation with the political parties or with private individuals in the profit-making profession of consulting?

Relationships with Clients and Campaigns

The formal relationship between a consultant and his candidate is defined by the contractual arrangement to which both parties agree. Because of the candidate's relative unfamiliarity with technology and consulting, and the professional's much wider background and experience in the field, a consulting firm's standard contract is normally accepted with minimal alteration. (Many a candidate, perhaps like an author desperate to be published, is so grateful to have been among the chosen ones that he fears to tamper with the instrument of finality.) Some clauses vary little from consultant to consultant and specialty to specialty. Twenty years ago verbal contracts were the norm, but along with the codification of virtually everything in the United States, written contracts are now required by almost all professionals. The agreements can be as short as one page or as long as a dozen or so. The duration of the contract (usually in force until about a week after the election) is specified, and the obligations incumbent upon the consultant are enumerated, some in precise terms and others quite generally. The exact total of fees and per diem and the schedule of payments is described, often in elaborate detail. Clients are always required to pay the full fixed costs of services as well as the necessary personal expenses of the consultant and his staff, and sometimes several thousand dollars of expense money must be paid in advance, with interest penalties noted for overdue payments of fees and expenses. The client usually must permit the consultant to subcontract, normally with the client's agreement, and occasionally the candidate guarantees that he will lease computer facilities for the consultant's use or that he will provide a professional random-sample survey to a media or organizational consultant. Last, "opt-out" clauses are included that can be exercised by either client or consultant to terminate the contract. Direct-mail agreements are automatically cancelable after the testing phase in most cases. When a contract in any technological specialty is abrogated, the consultant or candidate gives thirty to sixty days' notice of intent to withdraw. If the candidate ends the relationship without the concurrence of the consultant, payment of a "termination bonus" may be required.

Rarely has a candidate had enough experience with consultants to realize that "overbooking" of clients is an all-too-common practice, with the result that an overextended consultant short-changes each campaign. When George Bush signed Bob Goodman for his 1980 presidential effort, the contract specified that Goodman could accept involvement in only seven other statewide or congressional campaigns while Bush was still in the race.[47] Consultants can be just as jealous of their client's attentions. Some direct-mail firms contractually stipulate that a client can deal only with their outfits for a specified number of years.

The contract cannot determine the shape of the informal relationship between consultant and candidate, however, and as in any marriage the informal bond can override the narrow legal prescriptions. According to Bob Goodman, the consultant becomes "very intimate with the candidate, involved with his ego and feelings."[48] Like many of his peers, Goodman becomes animated and expansive when discussing the emotional ties he establishes with his clients:

I am interested in that candidate. . . . It is very psychological. . . . Election night is the worst night of the year for us unless all [my candidates] win. They become family. We socialize together and we love each other.

Goodman's candidates, or the winners among them, return his affection. U.S. Senator Alan Simpson (R-Wyoming) was enthusiastic: "By George, what he did for me was stunning." His Wyoming GOP colleague, Malcolm Wallop, acknowledged Goodman's emotional commitment to his campaign, commenting, "With his zeal and my volunteers, we brought it off." Calling Goodman's media spots for him "great stuff," U.S. Senator Rudy Boschwitz (R-Minn.) admitted that he went along with Goodman's judgments despite his own misgivings: "I'm still in shock over the seventy-eight piece orchestra he hired. It cost me nine thousand dollars, and when I was running my lumber business, I turned down music for commercials that would have cost me two hundred."[49]

Boschwitz's deference to his consultant is hardly out of the ordinary. After all, if a campaign is going to pay a small fortune for a consultant's advice, the candidate is probably going to listen to him most of the time. Moreover, the candidate probably does not understand much about the new campaign technology and is impressed at the very sight of a computer printout. The consultant's winning reputation, wide experience, and technological expertise naturally encourages deference. "We're the big experts from the outside; we are prophets from another country," says Charles Guggenheim, whose "biggest problem is that they defer to me too much. I want to get their reactions [to my media ads] but they hold back. If I said, 'You've got to play that,' I'd be scared they'd do it unquestioningly."

A professional's influence does not merely extend to technical matters. Consultants are having an increasingly greater voice in the setting of basic strategy and the selection of (and relative emphasis on) campaign issues. As political scientist Stanley Kelley has observed, the development and evolution of the consultant's role from a purely technical one to one that influences policy and choice of campaign issues is to be expected.[50] In private business, public relations chiefs are also policy makers, a natural extension of their skills. Propagandists are necessarily strategists, and strategy in politics involves choice and interpretation of issues as a matter of course. Political scientist Xandra Kayden's rule of influence in decision making for the campaigns she studied was that "decisions are made by whoever happens to be in the room at the time."[51] Access to the candidate, his campaign manager, and other key officials is one of the consultant's strengths. He can intervene at any time he desires, sometimes merely by inference, through his reports, polls, campaign plans, and so on. Kayden also stresses the uncertainty of campaigning (causing reliance on tradition *and* innovation), the limited organizational life of the structure, and the win/lose payoff that allows for no partial satisfaction.[52] All of these campaign characteristics tend to increase the influence of the outside professional. The consultant knows best both the devices that have worked in the past and the newest innovations. The limited organizational life discourages the orderliness of hierarchical decision making, making more valuable the services of someone experienced enough to function in spite of a campaign's chaos. An all-or-nothing payoff must necessarily humble those with lesser experience, and with stakes so high, great faith is placed in the wisdom of an expert.

It is not hard to find intimate illustrations of a consultant's issue influence. Dan Nimmo tells the tale of Ronald Reagan's 1966 governorship election in California, when Reagan's poorly versed posture forced Spencer-Roberts to hire a team of academicians at the Behavior Science Corporation (BASICO) to research all major state problems and summarize them with suggested solutions on a set of index cards.[53] Reagan, in what was to become his standard technique, studied the file thoroughly, memorized his lines, and passed the try-outs with flying colors. The same Stuart Spencer offered two instances of his 1976 issue advising to President Ford, one where the President accepted and another where he rejected Spencer's proposed course of action:

When I'm working with a client I try to get him to do things that I think are politically wise. I went to President Ford in 1976 when [Secretary of State Henry] Kissinger had trips scheduled to Africa just before the Georgia and Alabama primaries. I went to the President and I said, "Mr. President, you can't let him go to Africa before these two primaries. There are too many racial overtones in the South." But he looked me in the eye and said, "You're probably right, Stu, but I'm doing the right thing for the country." Well, I don't argue with that. I made my point, and he said no. . . . I did get him to change sides on the common situs picketing bill. [The bill, strongly favored by labor, was vetoed by Ford after he had promised to support it.] I don't even care about common situs picketing, but a lot of people on the right in the Republican party did, and it became a cause célèbre.

Like Spencer most consultants offer morally and ideologically neutral advice; their sole goal is to elect the candidate, and, not surprisingly, they want their clients to do anything that is politically advantageous, everything that will maximize their chances for victory.

By no means are all candidates susceptible to a consultant's urgings. At least on occasion Joe Napolitan claims he "can't even get them to change the color of their socks."[54] "Some candidates just won't listen, they won't do what they are told," says Vincent Breglio with a sigh. He reports that "the extent to which a candidate is manageable" is one of the variables D.M.I. considers in selecting its clients. Breglio continues:

Contrasting with the mavericks, other candidates are . . . almost too manageable. You have to put some backbone into a candidate who is otherwise pretty wishy-washy. But some place in the middle is the ideal guy who has his own stands and positions but is willing to be influenced to some degree by what our surveys are showing. . . .

Then, too, there is a countervailing force, the internal campaign staffers, who sometimes attempt to weaken and discredit an outside professional because they believe he is giving bad advice, or for reasons of envy or usually misplaced fear that the consultant will interfere with their postelection job aspirations. Resentment can also stem from salary differentials, since the consultant is paid handsomely for a relatively minor investment of time, while most staffers are poorly paid or not paid at all. (Staff salaries—but not the consultant's—are the first to go in a fiscal crunch.) Normally the consultant's expertise and potential contribution to the candidate's victory—the key to any volunteer's hopes of future glory—are sufficiently respected to override jealousies. But staffers have been known to play games and perhaps twist the consultant's work or his conclusions in his absence. On the other hand, the day-to-day frictions between candidates and personal staff are great, and usually the outside professional is on better terms with the candidate, being considered far more indispensable. Machiavellian plotting is a staple of campaigns, but it can be a high-risk venture for any staffer with postelection designs.

David Garth strikes a Hamlet-like pose in describing his reactions to the election defeat of one of his clients: "I bleed as much for him as for myself."[55] Most consultants bleed, all right, but many times not voluntarily. The sunniest of campaign relationships can turn remarkably acrimonious overnight (specifically, the night of the election). Not only is the consultant almost automatically blamed, at least in part, for the loss, but the candidate sometimes refuses to pay remaining

contractual debts, and not always because the coffers are empty. Walter
DeVries was forced to sue campaign committees of his former clients
five times in seven years to collect his due. Robert Squier had to sue
a Maryland U.S. House candidate for his full fee of $10,000, which as
a special favor had been greatly reduced from the usual amount. Despite facing the chairman of the state Democratic party in the Maryland
courts (whom the ex-client had secured as his lawyer), Squier was
awarded the entire fee.

Nor does a campaign victory insure that a good relationship persists. There was strong resentment against Doyle, Dane, and Bernbach
advertising agency in the Johnson White House for the "royal financial
clipping" supposedly administered LBJ's 1964 campaign.[56] Successful
clients, when they are dissatisfied or "ungrateful" (as some consultants
put it), also slight their former consultants in meat-and-potatoes fashion
by refusing to recommend them to other candidates.

In fairness, it should be noted that consultants do their share of
blame shifting after an election defeat. Characteristically, the client
was difficult to work with, had an incompetent staff, and repeatedly
refused their advice. When Acting Governor Blair Lee of Maryland
lost a large lead and failed in his 1978 bid for a term of his own, for
instance, his consultant, Joe Napolitan, claimed afterward that Lee
was "a candidate who assumed there was no way he could lose, and
had his son running the campaign." Only rarely will a consultant admit
he might have had a role, however partial, in a loss. The press as
well is reluctant to pin blame on consultants, not really understanding
what it is they do or being indebted to them for the "inside" information they provided during the campaign.

In a small percentage of the consultant's caseload, the campaign
is over before the election is, because either the consultant or candidate
exercises the "opt-out" clause in the contract. Virtually every major
consultant has had at least one major contract dissolution in the past
few years: Gerald Rafshoon with 1977 New York City mayoral candidate
Mario Cuomo; Robert Teeter with 1978 GOP gubernatorial candidate
Perry Duryea of New York; David Garth with Pennsylvania's Republican candidate for governor in 1978, Richard Thornburgh; Richard Viguerie with 1980 GOP presidential candidate Philip Crane (after which
Viguerie sued Crane for several hundred thousand dollars in back fees
and, in a great flourish of publicity, joined John Connally's presidential
effort); and on and on. Doug Bailey suggests some of the reasons why
a break becomes necessary:

We've opted out in a couple of situations where the politics were bleak, the political conditions had changed, plus the personal relationship just wasn't working. Once we have committed ourselves to somebody and the personal relationship stays good, we're with that person. We're going to be there through thick or thin. Sometimes you know pretty quickly that it is going to be a long haul, but you do it anyway. You've given your word. But where the personal relations are bad and the political conditions are bad too, then it's just very unpleasant for everybody and you might as well do what you can to get out either by exercising the clause that's there or by sitting down and saying this isn't going to work.

No consultant takes an "opt-out" decision lightly, because it can drastically affect his reputation, and the effect on the candidate is usually taken into consideration as well. Breaking of the contract is so unpalatable to some consultants that they will try to do anything short of it. Bill Hamilton, for instance, related that on several occasions "We just stopped talking to the candidates." There is little a consultant can do when the candidate decides to end the arrangement, of course. Ronald Reagan dumped C. T. Clyne Company advertising agency after his 1980 Iowa caucus loss and hired a Philadelphia ad man to produce harder-hitting spots.[57] Advertising, in fact, had little to do with Reagan's defeat in a situation depending heavily on organizational preparation, but the agency was a convenient scapegoat for the campaign's woes.

The Postelection Relationship

Most of the older generation of current political consultants would agree with one of the early leaders in the field, Clem Whitaker, who believed that campaign professionals should "strive to be good craftsmen, . . . never . . . bosses" and should "never [seek] political patronage and power" from candidates they had helped elect.[58] Stuart Spencer, considering himself the technician and not the ideologue, has a firm proscription against contacting former clients about political issues. He has never gotten a service contract through a public official who was formerly his client, and he considers it unethical to take contracts from special interests in order to lobby the people he has helped elect. Joseph Napolitan concurs: "My interest and my area of expertise is in the electoral process—getting people elected. There are thousands of people in this country more qualified than I am to run the government. . . ."

Most of Spencer's and Napolitan's newer colleagues clearly disagree with their viewpoint. While a consultant's influence undoubtedly is at its peak during the campaign itself, it hardly vanishes after the election. The same tools and experience that make the political professional so necessary to the operation of the modern campaign can be quite useful to a public official as he attempts to influence his constituency and refine his image. Indeed, holding public office depends on winning reelection, and many politicians in office campaign almost continuously do retain their posts. The consultant's magic and expert advice are welcomed by many clients after the election, and consultants are well aware of that fact. Some professionals consider it a legitimate part of their role[59] and consider themselves fully qualified to offer policy analysis, certainly as qualified as some of the candidates they have assisted. (Spencer said many of his colleagues "think they are so much smarter than the people they're electing.") The pollsters, in particular, are called upon frequently in their role of vox populi. Robert Teeter has given both political and policy advice on many occasions to former clients, has a few times initiated the contacts himself, and, like almost all younger consultants, indicates that if he personally felt strongly enough about a public issue—a Vietnamlike conflict was suggested—he would not hesitate to use his influence to affect public policy.

Breglio of D.M.I. stresses that he, like Teeter, mixes in his interpretive views because the client wants it: "They expect you to give a personal opinion, more than simply numbers." Consultants such as Doug Bailey and John Deardourff go a bit beyond expectations, since they contact their elected clients to "lobby" for their views "all the time." Whether officials take their advice is another matter. A good politician seeks counsel from a number of sources, and a political professional's offering is just one piece of intelligence, albeit usually a major one. Everything depends on the personal relationship that developed between consultant and client during the campaign. If it was close and has been continuing, a consultant can have a major impact on the votes and decisions of his ex-client. If, however, the consultant has relatively little access to the candidate and works mainly with the staff through the election, his postelection power will be minimal. Direct-mail consultants (with the possible exception of Richard Viguerie) are included in this category. Candidates rarely understand the technique's importance; it lacks the glamour of media and polling. A direct-mail firm works mainly with the staff, not the candidate, and as Bob Odell commented, "Win, lose, or draw, we're not perceived to be the ones who made the difference."

A few issue-oriented consultants informally monitor their success-ful clients' performance in office to see whether campaign promises are being fulfilled. David Garth exclaims unhesitatingly that if one of his former candidates ever reversed himself on a major issue, "I would probably call the guy up and take him apart. And what I could very well do is run a campaign against him." Douglas Bailey cited the case of Pennsylvania's Republican U.S. Senator Richard Schweiker, a former Bailey/Deardourff moderate-liberal client who, after Ronald Reagan selected him as his 1976 vice-presidential running-mate, began voting strongly conservative:

There is a guy who turned around completely. . . . It's a matter of being elected one day, seeing another opportunity and turning around. I don't like that. . . . In all probability it is hard for me to imagine that we would ever work for Dick Schweiker again. We would undoubtedly, under circumstances like that, express that view to him and to his people. Taking to denouncing him publicly, I don't think that we would hesitate [to do that] if we felt it was appropriate. . . . If I had felt that in some way the denunciation of Dick Schweiker would have clearly helped safeguard Gerald Ford's nomination at the 1976 GOP convention, I would have done it.[60]

All in all, though, consultants appear more concerned with substan-tive postelection favors and contracts than with issues or voting records. This finding is wholly in concert with the earlier depiction of consul-tants as businessmen rather than ideologues, or, in a few cases, business-men first and ideologues second. Over the years there has been a number of victor's plums that consultants have found particularly tasty. Most highly prized are state contracts and personal retainers. It is common for the governor's old political consultants to be awarded contracts with state agencies (state travel bureaus seem to be particu-larly popular). Another way to channel victory money is through the political party. Like Pat Caddell, who had a lucrative survey arrange-ment with the Democratic National Committee during the Carter ad-ministration, other consultants are put on retainer for years to advise the state parties. Sometimes the consultants receive annual retainers directly from public officials' office or election accounts, heightening their postelection influence as well as providing additional remunera-tion. This even occurs internationally. The president of Venezuela, for whom Joseph Napolitan served as campaign consultant, retained Napolitan's company to help plan the president's trips to the United States and other tasks. Occasionally consultants change hats entirely, as did Gerald Rafshoon (for more than a year of the Carter administration) or California's Don Bradley (during Democratic Governor Pat Brown's term), and take full-time jobs in the offices of their successful candidates.[61] Consultants are also likely to use their influence to secure jobs for their subordinates, as David Garth and many others have done. Another form of largesse is the lobbying contract, which a powerful U.S. senator or governor may secure for his former consultant. Special interests crave influence, and they hire consultants such as Joseph Cerrell to give them access to his ex-clients. Cerrell delivers the goods in various ways: by asking friends in office "to perform in pony shows [conventions and the like] for a commercial client," by advising on "how to approach public officials," and by contacting those officials directly to endorse a group's requests.

The consultants are also fond of less tangible perquisites available through association with the powerful. They all relish their closeness to the great and may-be great, and it is a rare consultant who does not have a "wall of intimidation" in his office—space crammed with pictures of the consultant with leaders of the U.S. and other countries, with gushing inscriptions attesting to his magic and genius. Some Washington-based consultants frequently socialize with their former clients, even introduce them to the city's political and social elite when they first move into town. And the consultant on retainer to high government officials has special joys, as Pat Caddell related:

You have cars to go places when you need to on official business, and support staff and communications. You can get things videotaped. You can get things moved quickly. You can reach people around the world—fast. The greatest thrill in the world I ever had was picking up the phone on Air Force One and calling the ground and having a conversation. There's nothing like saying, "Hi," and they say, "Where are you?" and I say, "I'm on Air Force One. We're just flying over—"[62]

Relationships Among Political Consultants

The band of national political professionals like to appear to be a jovial, if hard-charging, fraternity. They generally try to refrain from criticizing each other in public media. Many of them are genuine friends (irrespective of party affiliation or ideology), if only because, as William Sweeney, Executive Director of the Democratic Congressional Campaign Committee, suggests: "Professionals of the opposing camps . . .

all go into the same town with the same mission. There's only one hotel and there's only one bar. And at the end of the day there is no one else to talk to except your friend from the other campaign." Consultants with similar ideologies and the same party ties (such as Bob Teeter and Douglas Bailey) work together repeatedly and know each other very well. They often steer business to one another (when they are full up or when a media adviser is asked to recommend a pollster, for instance), and the monopolization of the campaign goodies by such a practice is usually at the expense of lesser-known consultants or academics who can sometimes do the same work at less cost to the candidate. But the top-rung professionals nearly always prefer "dependable" and "known" quantities—in other words, each other. Matt Reese remarked:

I will often say, "Hey, why don't we talk with [Peter] Hart or [Pat] Caddell, or [Bill] Hamilton?" The candidate has always got some professor—forgive me, Professor—someplace who could really do a poll cheaply. And he may be brilliant but I don't have the necessary qualifications to judge, nor does [the candidate]. And so I want to go to somebody I know is dependable.

Many outside observers, and some consultants as well, believe this "all in the family" practice is detrimental to campaigns for reasons in addition to cost. In the interest of personal friendship and a continuing good working relationship, for example, consultants are too likely to submerge their differences with one another's work as the campaign progresses. This effect is perhaps exaggerated when a generalist professional is hired to assemble and coordinate a team of specialty consultants.

Despite the public image, professional jealousy and pettiness is widespread within the consulting corps. In ventures as competitive as campaigns, personal conflict and recrimination among the principal figures is inevitable and even, to a degree, understandable. Yet it is somewhat amusing to discover the extent of the rivalries. In one brief interview, for example, David Garth made the following statements about his esteemed colleagues:

I wake up a lot of mornings thanking God there is a Gerry Rafshoon. Very few people could have destroyed Mario Cuomo [1977 New York City mayoralty candidate] the way Rafshoon did. . . . I think Rafshoon is full of it.

The biggest weakness [in the Cuomo campaign] was [Patrick] Caddell. . . . He can't interpret. . . . Pat has gotten carried away with himself and I think he's on a trip, a very dangerous trip.

I don't think John Deardourff knows politics well.

I don't believe that Bob Squier understands politics.

There's a guy named David Sawyer who has made a total career out of literally copying our commercials. . . .

Garth also came in for his fair share of criticism, as did virtually every major professional during the interviews of their fellow consultants for this book. Robert Goodman, for example, while respecting "what Garth charges," termed the New Yorker "not very creative": "Last year he gave the same blue-plate special to every candidate he ran. He had some little [television advertisements] with a trailer at the bottom. And everyone said, 'Oh, isn't that fantastic!' For $25,000 a month you *ought* to have a good line."

The criticism may flow freely, but consultants offer the highest form of praise, imitation, to one another with every passing year. The professionals' tendency to borrow from one other—"steal" is a less polite term—insures the spread of new campaign technology and is a form of electoral cross-pollination. "My penchant for larceny is one of my greatest advantages," quipped Matt Reese. "My skill is having the taste to know what's good enough to steal."

The theft and other consultant interrelationships were institutionalized with the formation of the American Association of Political Consultants (AAPC) in 1969. The prime mover was Joseph Napolitan, and the original membership was about two dozen, all "close friends," according to Napolitan. It was clear from the start that the organization would not be an activist one, that its mission was more along the lines of a trade association, giving consultants a forum for exchanging ideas and viewpoints. The AAPC has grown significantly in membership to several times its original size,[63] but its functions have never been broadened. It remains generally inactive, sponsoring an annual conference and occasional seminars and meetings. Matt Reese, a former AAPC president, admitted that it was "not a strong organization" and that he had had "a difficult time keeping it together." Many major consultants have refused to join, some of them labeling it a "personal vehicle" and a "front" for several of its presidents, particularly Napolitan. As Douglas Bailey critiqued the AAPC:

Essentially it was set up as a plaything by its original founders, and it is a waste of time. It may be very enjoyable and it may be a perfectly good excuse to make good trips and so forth. But it has no particular attraction for us, and the thought that consultants are somehow going to get together and share their secrets with one another is ludicrous; it is not going to happen.

Bailey's latter contention is hotly disputed by AAPC participants such as Roy Pfautch who, likening the organization to a consultants' Rotary Club, claims that "Anyone who doesn't join is just missing a good chance to cross-fertilize." While some of the AAPC's critics are mavericks whose self-evaluation is so glowing that they could scarcely conceive of learning anything from the lesser mortals in their business, it is also true that the AAPC is a disappointment, that it is far less than it could be. At the least the organization should be setting clear ethical standards for its profession, ones that (as chapter 6 will indicate) are sorely needed.

The Consultant Firms

Tracing the rise and fall of consultant firms is a dizzying task. Many consultants are themselves like meteors, streaking brightly across the sky for a few election seasons, then disappearing from sight. As the consultants rise to prominence or sink into obscurity, richly deserved or not, so go their firms. The rapid reorganizations and name changes come about for any number of reasons. It is not uncommon for a firm to break up because of personal or political conflicts among its partners. A "very amicable" disassociation was made by Chuck Winner and Joseph Cerrell shortly after the end of the 1968 campaign because of "incompatibility of philosophies." Cerrell had leaned to President Johnson that year, while Winner favored either of Johnson's Democratic challengers, Senators Eugene McCarthy or Robert F. Kennedy. The once-premiere liberal consulting firm of Martilla, Payne, Kiley, and Thorne, based in Boston, fell prey to hard times in 1976 and 1978, losing a collection of well-publicized battles and breaking up shortly thereafter to pursue separate political interests.[64] Ill health forced Bill Roberts to withdraw from Spencer-Roberts Agency in 1974. Though Stuart Spencer bought his partner's share of the company, he kept the original name, a widely recognized star in the political firmament.

There is no shortage of applicants for the senior or junior positions frequently available in the firms. Consulting organizations are now seen by the politically interested and ambitious as ports of entry into the political world. Surveying the resumes on his desk, one consultant noted that he gets "four or five applicants a week, every week of the year, [including] the pick of the *cum laude* crop from the Ivy

League."[65] Many are willing to work without pay for the opportunity
to apprentice and learn the ropes. Those accepted into the firms are
acknowledged to be quite good, and their work is often the equal of
anything the firm's partners can produce. "The truth of the matter
is that if I fell out that window, this organization would have the same
record that it would have with me alive," admitted David Garth. The
national political professionals are many times just the public faces
for organizations of considerable campaign talent. It is accepted as
an inevitability that some of a firm's employees will eventually break
off and start rival agencies, though a few organizations try to tie down
their key personnel with formal contracts and confidentiality pledges.
Many of the currently successful consulting firms began as spin-offs:
V. Lance Tarrance and Associates from D.M.I., Woodward and Mc-
Dowell media agency from Spencer-Roberts, and Stephen Winchell
and Associates direct-mail group from Richard A. Viguerie Company,
just to name a few.

Not only has there been a significant increase in the number of
national consultants and firms over the past quarter century, but also
the size of each surviving firm has shot upward. Outside of Viguerie's
rapidly expanding direct-mail outfit, which has about 300 employees,
most of the largest consulting firms are polling organizations, with
40 to 80 full-time workers and many more part-time interviewers and
telephone bank operators. D.M.I. is typical, with offices in Santa Ana,
California; Washington, D.C.; and a new branch in Toronto, Canada.
There are 49 full-time employees and between 100 and 300 part-time
interviewers and data collectors, the exact number depending on the
workload. The media agencies travel more lightly, the normal employment range being between 10 and 25. (All consulting firms expand
and contract with the workload, which means that they are almost
always larger in election years than off-years.) Some of the best-known
generalists and media consultants (including Tony Schwartz, Joseph
Napolitan, Walter DeVries, Michael Kaye, and Roy Pfautch), though,
have shops consisting just of themselves and perhaps one assistant.
The firms are kept slim despite heavy workloads through the use of
subcontracting and informal association. For example, Matt Reese and
Associates normally has 6 or 7 full-time employees, but 25 to 30 other
individuals are associated with the group because of frequent subcontracting. Some are associated almost exclusively with Reese, rarely
taking on assignments from other sources. Yet Reese has no obligation
to pay them if business is slack, and the associates operate out of their
own homes.

Almost all consulting firms have patterns of subcontracting, but they differ widely in the specific pieces of work they delegate to outside individuals. Bailey and Deardourff subcontract nothing in the consulting and planning areas, but in the advertising field, creation and production usually devolves upon a group of freelance people (editors, writers, camera crews, art directors, etc.) who do work exclusively for them. Winner-Wagner and Associates subcontracts pieces of each service: the sampling and computer work for surveys (doing the analysis in-house); the production of all radio and television advertisements (with the conceptualization, writing, and direction coming from within the firm); and the mechanics of direct mailing (with the letters written by Winner-Wagner's employees). Stuart Spencer prefers to subcontract because it is "difficult to keep talented people with you rather than having them start their own firm"; he has "access to more talent" by subcontracting; and his clients are better served by outstanding regional consultants who know their turf.

Subcontracting can easily mean that a client who signs with a "name" consultant, expecting a great deal of his personal attention, is actually (if unknowingly) purchasing the services of possibly second-rate satellite associates. There are real truth-in-advertising problems here, and candidates should always be alert—though they hardly ever are—to the subcontracting policies of the firm and the percentage of time the firm's leading professionals intend to devote to them.

The allocation of work within each consulting firm varies as much as the subcontracting practices. Bailey/Deardourff, for instance, is almost two separate organizations, "somewhat interchangeable but not totally," and the staff is divided up between the two principal partners. Bailey has taken all of the firm's Illinois campaigns, and Deardourff has concentrated on Ohio. In fact, President Ford's 1976 campaign is the only one on which Bailey and Deardourff have worked jointly, and their collusion was at the specific request of Ford's pollster, Robert Teeter. The Bailey/Deardourff operation illustrates yet another change in focus for consulting groups. It could once be written of the Whitaker and Baxter agency that "the ideal of the firm is the interchangeability of its members, each having both a broad experience in all phases of the work and a specific knowledge of the details of current projects."[66] But campaigns and their technologies have become far too complex for this sort of generalist approach. Specialization of technique, of region, and of personal interest and expertise has necessarily become the rule. This specialization has led to diversification in a number of firms. D.M.I. now has an associated organization, Decima Research, that does governmental survey research projects. Though under the D.M.I. umbrella, with the same president and vice-president, Decima is kept separate publicly because D.M.I. itself has become strongly associated with right-wing Republicans such as Barry Goldwater and Ronald Reagan. "These guys must be to the right of Attila the Hun," Vincent Breglio imagined government officials to be saying, and the subsidiary's new name removed the stigma. Richard Viguerie's empire includes a number of corporate entities that supply lists, produce mass mailings, and handle public relations. Spencer-Roberts agency founded Datamatics, Inc., to compile demographic and computer analyses of electoral data. Whitaker and Baxter organized the California Feature Service to distribute weekly political newssheets to the state's newspapers.[67] And these are but a few of many examples.

The Costs of Advice and Technology

Talk is cheap, except when lawyers or political consultants are doing the talking. No one has ever accused consultants of undercharging, and, like most businessmen, they charge what the market will bear. Robert Goodman well expressed the arbitrary nature of the political mercenary's financial decisions: "I'm a big round-number guy. I look at a candidate or a project or a campaign and I say, 'What do I want to make out of this thing?' I try to be fair to the client and consider the campaign's degree of affluence, the candidacy, my particular feelings for it, how big the state is." The cost of the technology itself figures heavily, of course. Some of the new techniques become cost effective over time, as more campaigns use them and mass production of some items lowers the price of each unit. There is considerable evidence, cited in chapter 5, that campaign technology's inflation index has far outstripped the Consumer Price Index, but, wholly aside from inflation, the constant refinements in old techniques and the swift development of innovative gadgets have kept campaign costs soaring. The consultant, despite his protests, has done his part to assist the cost spiral. The ever-frank Matt Reese could have been describing much of any consultant's business when he said, "My secret of success is that I find things that work politically, and put names on them, and sell them." One of his colleagues gleefully described his plans for some 1980 Census Bureau data available to the general public for

$80 per computer tape: "We will take this data and put it in printout form, really make it attractive, put a nice cover on it, and sell it at one hell of a profit."

Many professionals angrily counter the assertion that they are making "one hell of a profit" on the American electoral system. The nationally recognized consultants claim, with some justification, that the mere signing on of an agency with a winning reputation can attract contributions and help in all fund-raising efforts. Experienced political action committees (PACs) are particularly interested in the identity of a campaign's aides, considered a "sure" indication of the fate awaiting a candidacy. David Garth confidently states that a campaign fortunate enough to enlist his support will "end up getting at least enough money to make up for the fees."[68] Consultants also insist that they actually save a campaign's money by getting "more bang for every buck. If I can't save my fee there's something wrong with me," says Reese. Joe Napolitan offers some evidence that he has held down the cost of campaigning by knowing where money can be most effectively spent: "I saved Jay Rockefeller [Democratic Governor of West Virginia] a quarter of a million dollars in one afternoon in 1976. He was about to embark on a big, ridiculous direct-mail program that didn't make any sense, and I stopped him." (Both Napolitan and Reese can be forgiven for forgetting that direct mail and many of the other new campaign technologies would not be nearly as widespread, and certainly not as expensive, without their promotion of them.) Finally, in answer to the accusations of greed, campaign professionals always cite the far more lucrative careers they could be pursuing among a private clientele. "I could pick up ten times more commercial business," remarks Michael Kaye. "It's more financially rewarding by a long shot—but not as fulfilling."

Like it or not, the reality is that good consultants cost a bundle, and it is to a campaign's advantage to sign the best available professionals. The most expensive election is a lost election, so to a candidate bent on winning—and what serious candidate is not?—money can be no object to acquiring what he needs to win. Stuart Spencer has "seen consultants and management people who have worked for me go into business for themselves and charge fees I think are outrageous—but they get them!" Local agencies may be cheaper and easier to secure, and "they may have the reputation of doing a wonderful job for the local Pontiac dealer, but they just don't understand politics—and it's usually a disaster," concludes PAC director Paul Weyrich.[69]

The actual charging patterns and practices of consulting firms are

like mazes—and, at times, amazing. In general, there are three main
categories of charges: (1) consulting (or "creative") fees; (2) incurred
costs and personal expenses; and (3) commissions. The consulting fee
is simply what it takes to secure the services of the firm or consultant,
usually a flat fee (ranging from $10,000 to $75,000) paid in monthly
installments or in thirds (one-third at the contract signing, one-third
midway during the campaign, and one-third right before—not after—
election day). The incurred costs and personal expenses are merely
reimbursements to the consultant for actual outlays made for television
production, survey interviewing, or whatever. The richest source of
revenue is commissions, or "markups"; the consulting fee is just icing,
albeit thick, on the cake by comparison. The commission is a set percentage of money from sales (normally 15 percent) allotted to the consultant. That is, a commodity is purchased for a campaign through
the consulting firm, and the candidate is billed for it at its cost *plus*
15 percent as a commission. Virtually anything can be, and is, commissionable: production work for media advertisements, printing, computer work, even mass-mailing postage fees.

There are no two consultants with precisely the same practices.[70]
Stuart Spencer mainly subsists on fees, charging $1,000 per diem, or
on a contract basis from $20,000 to $50,000 for a statewide campaign's
election year consulting, and up to $100,000 for complete management
of the effort. Bob Goodman charges a fee of $50,000 to $100,000 (which
includes both primary and general elections), as well as a 15 percent
commission on production and placement of his media advertisements.
Joe Napolitan assesses a separate fee of $25,000 to $30,000 for a seriously
contested primary election in addition to a similar charge for the general election. Joseph Cerrell's fees range from $1,000 to $10,000 a month
(hefty, perhaps, but rather pale next to his charge of $100 per *hour*
for his private commercial clients.) David Garth, in addition to media
commissions, has charged $10,000 a month and more for a creative
fee, but he is adamant that his clients get their money's worth: "I
have never had a client who ever said, 'You didn't work hard enough
for us. We never got what we paid for.'" Marvin Chernoff sets no
creative fee, relying entirely on his 33 percent advertising production
commission and 17.65 percent placement commission. Matt Reese lev-
ies a flat fee of about $50,000 for a major statewide campaign and
bills the client separately for the per diem services of his firm's associates (at $250 a day for a senior associate's time, $150 a day for a writer's
work, etc.). Aside from their media commissions, Bailey and Deardourff
use a per diem rate of $750 for their consulting advice. Robert Squier

has an unusual creative fee structure. He charges a client the same $50,000 fee whether he is hired two years or two months prior to the election, obviously encouraging candidates to come to him early: "I can't tell you how frustrating it is to sit here and have a candidate tell me he announced last Saturday and now he wants to talk about his campaign."

In general, the less subcontracting there is, the shorter and lighter is the client's final bill since there is usually less of a markup, or none at all, when the work is done in-house. Buying a "full-service" consultant can also reduce costs by securing all the necessary pieces in a package that has only one creative fee. There are unbilled "costs" with this method, though. A client does not have the competitive creative talents of a group of specialists at his disposal, and a firm offering a complete set of services is rarely expert in all, or even most, of them.

Consultant fees, expenses, and commissions are estimated to comprise about 20 percent of the average campaign budget,[71] and with million dollar–plus budgets very common today, it is clear that consultants do very well. Referenda and initiative campaigns are even more rewarding than candidate campaigns, and media commissions are the primary explanation. Candidates are certainly not stingy when it comes to television and radio advertising. In a not untypical race for governor of Louisiana in 1979, Charles Guggenheim's unsuccessful client spent about $400,000 to air his commercials; at the standard 15 percent commission, Guggenheim received $60,000. This considerable sum appears meager when compared to the Woodward & McDowell agency's profit from their 1978 California campaign to defeat Proposition 5, a ballot measure to regulate and limit smoking in public places. With fees and commissions in excess of $400,000, one can see why Richard Woodward would jest with more than a little hope and anticipation, "We ought to try to get this on the ballot in every state."[72] The initiative was so profitable in part because ballot measures tend to have an extraordinarily high proportion of the budget devoted to commissionable media advertising. (Fully 68 percent of the anti-Proposition 5 campaign budget was spent on media-related activities.)[73]

Initiatives are so remunerative that Winner-Wagner and Associates, another California firm specializing in ballot initiatives, agrees in most cases to apply one-third or more of all commissions against their established creative fee of $100,000. For example, if the ballot campaign spends $1 million on commissionable items, Winner-Wagner would receive 15 percent, or $150,000. One-third of this amount, or

$50,000, would then be subtracted from the creative fee, reducing it by half. Winner-Wagner would garner $200,000 in all ($150,000 in commissions and $50,000 as a creative fee). This practice benefits both consultant and client. The creative fee becomes a smaller part of the client's budget, and most of the money earned by the client's agency does not actually come from the campaign budget but from the television and radio stations in the form of commissions.[74] The consultant also finds this arrangement advantageous because the campaign is encouraged to raise and spend more (which means more commissions) because the more it expends, the more of the consultant's creative fee is, in effect, returned to the campaign's coffers through substitution of commission fees.

It should be added that consulting firms, as any business, also lose money on occasion. Clients sometimes balk at paying their bills or dispute the accounting of their debts, and court suits to force payment are often more trouble than they are worth to political professionals. In rare circumstances a consultant actually becomes a major contributor to a campaign by waiving or reducing his set fee. Sometimes this is done of necessity, when a campaign's fund-raising well goes dry. Other times the consultant may volunteer his time or reduce his fees to help a cause or a candidacy he favors. Many consultants view this as their profession's *pro bono publico* work. Those consultants who get emotionally wrapped up in a client's campaign are less likely to turn a deaf ear to pleas for assistance when money becomes scarce. Joseph Cerrell's close involvement in a 1974 California Democratic primary campaign for state controller, for instance, reportedly led him to turn over his commissions to the campaign treasury at a critical juncture, leaving him at campaign's end with $30,000 in unpaid bills, which were eventually written off. There are also political reasons for reducing fees or signing on a less than lucrative campaign. Chuck Winner indicated that his agency took a financially unrewarding 1976 California ballot initiative (Proposition 2), a bond issue for beaches, parks, and recreation, in order to rebuild bridges with environmentalists upset at the firm for handling the pro-nuclear side of another initiative.

The Nonpolitical Side of Political Consultants

Politics is a jealous mistress, but somehow consultants have been able to devote themselves to other pursuits during a fair portion of the working day. David Rosenbloom's national survey of 360 campaign management firms in 1972 indicated that 58 percent had less than half of their business in the political sphere.[75] Most major political consulting organizations (as opposed to more localized advertising agencies) devote considerably more of their time and energy to campaigns than Rosenbloom's figures suggest, and their business is consequently substantially more political. Nevertheless there is a definite trend in many national firms to reduce the political proportion of their work.

There is wide variation in attitude among professionals toward nonpolitical work. Stuart Spencer and Joseph Napolitan keep their businesses almost totally political. Says Spencer, "I am a political animal. I love politics; that's my life-style. I am totally bored to death in dealing with corporate types." Napolitan emphatically agrees: "What I really like about campaigns is that they are finite: you know at the end whether you won or lost; you can do corporate public relations for ten years and not know if you helped one bit. It can get pretty boring."

Yet a growing number of professionals restrict campaigns to a lesser, if still dominant, position on their agendas. Some have purposefully reduced the number of political accounts. Patrick Caddell's Cambridge Survey Research has switched from entirely political to 85 percent nonpolitical, by Caddell's estimate. Most observers might be excused for thinking campaigns provide quite a handsome margin of profit, but Caddell says his company's new nonpolitical posture is due to "the very low dollar margin of politics. The amount of effort that you have to put in is immense, far beyond what you're being compensated for generally, because a campaign is life and death and you feel compelled to do it. And it's a very erratic business." Caddell also takes less political work because of his growing cynicism and disgust for many of his past politician-clients:

Frankly, politicians are probably the greediest individuals I have ever seen. Never have a group of people asked for more and given less in return, and been less appreciative. And when they lose they always blame other people, when they win nobody else had any impact usually. Politicians as a breed are not very . . . charitable. They're not really very nice people, basically. They may be good politicians, but I'm not sure how many of them you would want to have in your home.

Robert Smith of Craver, Mathews, Smith direct-mail firm, whose business now takes only a quarter of its work from campaigns, commented that "The nonpolitical side is certainly more profitable, it's longer term, it makes more sense, and it's less frenetic. There is more time for sensible financial and administrative procedures." Joseph Cerrell, who has decreased his political work by two-thirds, believes it is "difficult to do justice" to nonpolitical clients during election periods, and many large advertising agencies are refusing to take any more political clients at all, their experience with campaigns having been traumatic—the ruination of the carefully conceived bookkeeping procedures and internal systems so characteristic of those organizations.[76] And a few professionals, such as Charles Guggenheim, simply appear to have become bored by politics. Once overwhelmingly political, Guggenheim's operation now takes only an occasional campaign (about 15 percent of his accounts) because "Fundamentally, political campaigns don't interest me. It's like running on a treadmill . . . not particularly challenging in a creative sense."

Most consulting firms seem stabilized with between one-third and two-thirds of their accounts being political. Even some of these firms, though, are starting to deemphasize campaigns to the benefit of political action committees, lobby groups, special interests, and state political party committees, all of which provide a permanency and orderly planning capacity that campaigns, by their very nature, lack. (It was the electoral connection, ironically, that first brought the firms in contact with most of these subsidiary groups.) Roy Pfautch is an example of a former campaign consultant who phased out of elections entirely to concentrate on PACs and corporate public affairs. While his motive for doing so—entanglement with the Watergate scandal made him unwelcome in his old political haunts—is somewhat unrepresentative, he sounds a common note when he reveals that "quite a few of my corporate clients [but not PACs] were not particularly happy with simultaneous candidate involvement." While businessmen might welcome contacts with the powerful, they fear recriminations from victorious opponents and resent the unavailability of their consultants during the height of the campaign season. Pfautch is certainly correct in contending that there are fewer conflicts of interest when a consultant makes a clear choice between campaigns and public/private interest groups, but most of his colleagues clearly prefer to have a bit of both worlds. And that suits the PACs and lobbies quite well.

One other in-between arena for the consultant is the referendum or initiative campaign. It is clearly political, yet has some of the advantages of noncandidate work (in addition to being exceptionally lucrative). More than a few consultants refuse ballot initiatives without a second look, evaluating them much as Douglas Bailey did after a couple of disappointing issue campaigns:

Frankly, a personal candidate race is a far more exciting thing normally than an issues race. I think it is less likely that you can enjoy yourself than you can in the guts of a real personal candidate campaign. Somebody may have filled your ears with stories about the difficulty of dealing with candidates and candidates' wives. I can tell stories about how difficult it is to get associations and organizations of people to take decisive action. I would much rather work with a candidate who can say yes or no than with a board of fifty people who must say yes or no.

A few consultants who have seized upon ballot measures for much of their livelihood naturally disagree with Bailey's assessment. The political consultant is almost certainly given greater leverage in most referendum or initiative efforts. First of all, there is no party involvement or partisan identification to contend with either in the workings of the campaign or the electorate. Second, most groups sponsoring (and opposing) ballot measures are well funded and have a mass membership. Moreover, these groups often have little electoral experience and desperately need expert campaign guidance.

Winner-Wagner and Associates is one of several California firms that handle ballot questions. Forty percent of its work is in this area, with the balance controlled by nonpolitical "issues communication" for major corporations and agencies such as Rockwell International and Westinghouse. The two areas are related; after Winner-Wagner helped to defeat an antinuclear initiative, for instance, it established continuing consulting accounts with a number of utility companies. It has developed a national reputation among nuclear energy proponents and has helped defeat antinuclear measures in several states. Chuck Winner hotly disputes the contention that ballot campaigns are less interesting than the candidate variety, terming his previous initiative efforts "intense and intriguing." He also finds them more profitable, less worrisome to his Republican-leaning corporate clients than the Democratic liberals he once managed, and less contentious than a candidate and his family and staff. Winner is not alone. The San Francisco-based Woodward & McDowell agency had great success in defeating a recent antismoking ballot proposition in California and became the first choice of the well-heeled tobacco industry to fight similar initiatives all over the country. Butcher-Forde agency is handling tax and spending limitation referenda across the nation after its guidance of Howard Jarvis's Proposition 13 in California, and Solem and Associates of San Francisco specializes in rent-control measures. Other consultants have begun to see the advantages of ballot campaigns and seek similar work. Lance Tarrance reports that his firm is "getting more and more into this area," and has polled for supporters of a death-penalty proposition in California and opponents of smoking bans in half a dozen other states.

The original political consulting firm, Whitaker and Baxter, has come over to the ballot measure side, now no longer taking candidates at all and specializing in initiatives and corporate public relations. A whole new campaign industry is also springing up around the process of qualifying initiatives for the ballot. Several agencies center part of their business around collecting the hundreds of thousands of signatures required to place any question before the voters. Direct mail is often used to accomplish the task, on a charge-per-signature basis. Finally, issue campaigns are even being waged absent actual elections by consultants, primarily through the medium of television advertising. The American Conservative Union, for example, produced a program opposing the ratification of the SALT II Treaty using a Miami agency, with a filmed fund-raising appeal complete with toll-free numbers (similar to the technique candidates are now using and the "electronic churches" have employed for years[77]). The liberal side is not inactive in this field, and Marvin Chernoff has created some Equal Rights Amendment television spots for the National League of Women Voters.

International Campaigning: The Ugly American?

The involvement of American consultants in other countries' elections has been somewhat obscured. The Americans and particularly their clients abroad are usually deathly afraid of the "ugly American" label.* So subdued and evasive are many of the normally ebullient U.S. professionals when on foreign soil that a *New York Times* report on their international activities declared that only Costa Rica, Puerto Rico, and Venezuela "are known to have used American experts in recent

* The "Ugly American" was actually the hero of Eugene Burdick and William J. Lederer's novel of the same name (New York: Norton, 1958), but colloquially the label has come to embody the vices of American representatives abroad. See William Safire, *Safire's Political Dictionary* (New York: Random House, 1978), p. 751.

campaigns."[78] In fact, at least thirty other countries have been invaded by the Yanks at election time in recent years. In addition to the nations listed by the *Times,* Australia, Belgium, Canada, several Caribbean islands, Colombia, France, Guam, Israel, Italy, Japan, Mexico, the Philippines, Spain, Sweden, the United Kingdom, Venezuela, and a dozen other Latin and South American countries have seen American consultants advising one or more major contenders in at least one national election.[79] Every subgroup of consultants has been called upon. David Garth produced media advertisements for about 170 of Venezuela's Social Christian Party's municipal candidates in June 1979.[80] Robert Squier also has done media work in Venezuela, and for President Ferdinand Marcos of the Philippines and Premier Adolfo Suarez of Spain. Robert Teeter has polled for the Conservative party of Canada for the past four consecutive general elections. As mentioned earlier, D.M.I. now has a Canadian office, which handles a growing number of political and governmental contracts, and the firm has also surveyed for clients in Mexico, Japan, and Great Britain.[81] Robert Odell has organized direct-mail programs in Canada.

The godfather of all American international campaigning, though, is undoubtedly Joseph Napolitan. He was perhaps the first consultant to recognize that the advanced political technologies developed in the United States could be transferred to other nations.[82] Napolitan made his foreign premiere in 1969, when he aided the Philippines' Marcos in his triumphant quest to become the first president of his country ever to be reelected. (At the time, no one suspected it would be a permanent reelection.) From that initial success, Napolitan branched out to Europe, Latin America, Asia, and the Caribbean, although at times he refuses to specify the countries or elections "because of the fear of what the opposition might do if it were known that an American was serving as a consultant to the other side."[83] (This caution might well be merited, yet an observer must note that in those few elections abroad in which the participation of Americans has been prominent in the local press, no great upheavals or internal protests have occurred.) In 1978 alone Napolitan made thirty-three separate international trips to fulfill contracts made with President Giscard's party in France (for legislative elections) and for contests in Guam (the governorship), Israel (the mayoralty of Tel Aviv), and Venezuela (the presidency). He has established a branch office in London and is taking proportionately more campaigns abroad than domestic ones because of the additional challenge and his slackening interest in U.S. elections, which "all seem alike" after so many years of consulting.

The Consultant Corps

In no foreign country's elections have American consultants been more publicly prominent than in Venezuela.[84] For several successive presidential and legislative elections, Americans have swarmed over the candidates and parties in South America's liveliest democracy. The 1978 presidential election, for instance, was fought primarily on television under the complete direction of a set of well-known U.S. professionals. (Seven out of ten urban households have televisions, and the nation is 75 percent urban.) David Garth was the consultant to the eventual surprise winner, centrist Luis Herrera Campins of the Social Christian party. Garth subcontracted nine surveys for Herrera and, relying on his Spanish-speaking staff members, designed television spots around the slogan "Enough Already!" focusing on bureaucratic inefficiency, inflation, street crime, poverty, and the broken promises of the current government. (This list should be proof enough that the issues are the same everywhere.) Joseph Napolitan and F. Clifton White (one of Barry Goldwater's 1964 key strategists) managed the campaign of the other major contender, Luis Piñerua Ordaz, the nominee of the ruling left-liberal Acción Democrática party. Napolitan knew Venezuela well, having helped to run the 1973 campaign of the current president, Carlos Andrés Pérez, and, portraying Piñerua almost as an incumbent, Napolitan centered Piñerua's effort around florid, musical commercials with the closing slogan "Capacity and firmness to govern. Correct." White and Napolitan also tried to paint Herrera with Communist colors, featuring an advertisement comparing him to a watermelon—green on the outside (Herrera's party's color) and red on the inside. Piñerua's campaign received subterranean assistance from President Pérez, who hired Robert Squier to dress up his own image (and, indirectly, that of the candidate he was supporting) with media advertisements before the election. As if all of these American consultants were not sufficient, a third candidate in the race, Diego Arria of the "Common Cause" party, brought John Deardourff and Patrick Caddell on board his organization. With Caddell's surveys as guides, Deardourff created a series of spots around a theme of "The People Come First."

And thus a showcase of Latin American democracy became a showcase for American political consultants, who showed that the pursuit of electoral profit recognizes no territorial boundaries. In fact, crossing the borders seems to have been ideologically liberating for many of the professionals. Democrat Caddell worked with Republican Deardourff while the staunchly Republican Goldwaterite, Clifton White, teamed with moderate Democrat Napolitan to back the leftist nominee being opposed by the very liberal Garth's centrist candidate. Could it have been the $8 million apiece spent by Herrera and Piñerua and the $100 million estimated to have been expended by all parties on the election that served as such an irresistible lure to foreign adventure?

At least until recently, Great Britain has been at the other extreme from Venezuela, with both major parties there having traditionally been resistant to the campaign technology used elsewhere. Napolitan reported that he scheduled an international meeting of consultants in London shortly after the Labour party had been soundly defeated in a 1970 upset victory by the Conservatives. But most British pols, especially those on the Labour side, "virtually boycotted the meetings and the British press generally gave us a roasting."[85] Napolitan also complained that the British seemed to regard all private polling as "unethical" in politics.[86] Yet public relations men have been at least tolerated in general election campaigns for some time,[87] and the Tories especially have been willing to experiment. In 1969 the Conservative party, with a £2 million budget, contracted with Davidson, Pearce, Berry and Tuck advertising agency to help them prepare for the upcoming national election.[88] A survey research program was subcontracted to the MARPLAN group as well.[89] In 1975 an American consultant, Charles Guggenheim, was hired to produce television advertisements in the Common Market referendum election—an indication, perhaps, that media politics was beginning to find acceptance in the U.K.

In every one of the British general elections of the 1970s, advertising agencies played a part in one or both parties' efforts, but none came close to matching the Conservative party's 1979 technological spree.[90] The Tories hired a London advertising firm, Saatchi & Saatchi Garland—Compton Ltd., which had its international corporate home (Compton Advertising) in the United States, and they had the financing to wage a major battle, £1.5 million to Labour's guerrilla war chest of £300,000.[91] A clever series of poster, movie, and television advertisements was prepared, an audience pretested,[92] and extensive survey research was conducted, all aimed at securing the support of the "swing" voters (those without strong party allegiances who would determine the election's outcome). A BBC/Gallup election-day poll provided some evidence that the Conservatives succeeded in doing precisely that in their sweeping 1979 victory. While about the same number of voters identified with the Tories (41 percent) as with Labour (42 percent), 46 percent of the electorate voted Conservative and 38 percent Labour. Of the defectors from Labour, 26 percent cited the

Tory political advertisements as a reason for switching sides; none of the fewer defectors from the Conservative party named Labour broadcasts as influencing their decisions. The explanation for the disparity was not difficult to find. While the Tory party had been modernizing itself and its election machinery, the Labourites had been latter-day know-nothings, using little polling data, no thorough advance planning, no pretesting of what primitive media advertising there was.[93] The Labour party leader and incumbent prime minister, James Callaghan, piously derided the Tory program, declaring: "I don't intend to end this campaign packaged like cornflakes. I shall continue to be myself."[94] The Conservative party leader, Margaret Thatcher, apparently preferred to be prime minister.

With even aloof and skeptical British politicians coming around, it is obvious that consultants are becoming accepted tools of the election trade all around the world; the new campaign technology is one of the most highly prized exports of the United States. The involvement of U.S. professionals in foreign campaigns will almost certainly increase in the near future, and the development of a cadre of native consultants versed in the American techniques can be anticipated. Most U.S. consultants sign on local advisers and technicians when they take up temporary residence, and these apprenticeships will provide sufficient training to produce independent spin-offs eventually—not unlike the process that occurs naturally within American firms already.

There is also an International Association of Political Consultants (IAPC), begun like the AAPC by the redoubtable Joseph Napolitan in November 1968.[95] (Michel Bongrand, a French consultant, was Napolitan's founding partner.) The IAPC has a membership of about fifty, half of them Americans and half Europeans. As one would suspect, the association is dominated by Americans but also has Spanish, Portuguese, French, and Dutch representatives on its board of directors. An annual three-day conference, in which contemporary elections across the globe are reviewed and previewed, is held in such lovely vacation spots as London, Paris, Florence, Brussels, Amsterdam, Madrid, and Majorca, and each conference usually draws a total of about forty-five to seventy participants from more than a dozen countries. The IAPC, like the AAPC, is a commendable and potentially worthy venture, but it suffers from a limited scope of function, activity, and control—all weaknesses in common with its American counterpart.

It is also far from rare to discover in attendance at AAPC meetings in the United States foreign election agents such as Gordon Ashworth, the campaign director for the Liberal party of Canada. (Ashworth and his associates helped to engineer a remarkable comeback for Pierre Trudeau in the 1980 national election with superb television advertisements in the best American tradition.) Although a few non-American professionals have done political consulting work in other nations,[96] none has apparently ever done so within the United States. However, American consultants have, on occasion, brought back with them techniques forged in different political cultures. In Europe, for example, there has long been a greater emphasis on print and display media than in the U.S., and American consultants report learning how to use print media and billboards more effectively from their experience in such countries as Britain, France, and Belgium. While American billboards have usually, and uncreatively, been used solely to establish a candidate's name identification, European parties often employ the "situational billboard," which is the equivalent of a frozen frame of film focusing on a key issue, with the "frames" changing frequently and often appearing in sequence. More recently an American party has imitated a European counterpart extensively. The National Republican Congressional Committee was so impressed with the 1979 triumph of the GOP's British soulmate, the Conservative party, that it designed a $9.5 million television advertising effort airing in 1980 based on the humorous but hard-hitting Tory spots.[97]

Conclusion

The performance of American consultants on foreign soil reconfirms strong suspicions that business interests and profit usually take precedence over the professionals' ideological concerns and that issues are for them the means to the greatest end of all, winning. Whether generalist or specialist, the consultant's wide experience and acknowledged talent give him access to the corridors of campaign power. He is the provider of technological services, the modern magic of successful electoral efforts. As the respected and sought-after expert, he is the grand strategist, the candidate's confidante, the contemporary substitute for the party professional of days past who encourages, discourages, and arbitrates candidacies.

To a consultant there can be no substitute for triumph, and there are no final victories, either. Through exaggerated performance records and careful choosing and matching of a clientele each election year (to the great benefit of incumbents), a professional tries to insure that the winning aura is maintained, the arrangement garnished with lavish media attention from time to time. (Woe is the burden of losers, with debts unpaid, reputations shattered, and magic dissipated—at least until the next election.) With glowing press notices and good references from PACs, party committees, and former clients, a major national consultant generally waits for his business to come to him unsolicited, with far more petitioners refused than taken. Those who are signed are chosen not by ideology, in most cases, but because of a combination of personal and financial factors: the prospects of victory, a campaign's financial promise, personality chemistry, the degree of stress likely to be imposed on the professional, and so forth. Party affiliation is normally a consideration as well, but only for the sake of the firm's credibility and financial solvency.

Assuming that candidate and consultant survive the election without a broken contract or love lost between them, a fulfilling postelection relationship can begin. The more issue-oriented professional monitors his ex-client's performance and influences his votes and decisions, while the consultant with one eye on his bank account and the other on social status enjoys the spoils of victory: lucrative state and party contracts, the perquisites of proximity to the powerful, arrangements with special-interest lobbies impressed with the consultant's friends, and retainers from the officeholders themselves who feel in need of a new kind of image making.

With his peers it is more difficult for a professional's life to be idyllic. The fiercely competitive nature of the business leads many a professional to less than kind assessments of his colleagues. The carping and criticism do not prevent cooperation in the workplace, however, and clients are referred from one to the other and techniques "borrowed" with abandon. Permissive larceny occurs on a grand scale at meetings of the American Association of Political Consultants, which, similar to its international equivalent, the IAPC, is a worthy but vastly underused venture.

The professionals are far more concerned with their individual firms, now prime entry points for young political activists, some of whom eventually break off to form their own consulting groups. Each firm has different norms and patterns, but most encourage specialization within the ranks and subcontract a great deal (sometimes to the detriment of the client). The proportion of campaign work done in most is gradually shrinking, being replaced by more lucrative and orderly corporate and lobby contracts. Not that campaigning chores are financially displeasing; the compensation is handsome, a generous reward for the enhancement of fund raising, the efficient targeting of resources, and the other advantages that professionals confer with their imprimatur.

Political consultants are not measured merely by the size of their firms and by the list of their clients. The wares of their trade, the new technologies that are transforming electoral politics in the United States, are an essential part of any comprehensive analysis of the extent of the political professionals' influence and power. The next three chapters will examine in turn the key weapons in the consultant's arsenal: polls, media advertisements, and direct mail.

NOTES

1. Joseph Napolitan, *The Election Game and How to Win It* (New York: Doubleday, 1972), p. 1.

2. *The Wall Street Journal*, May 14, 1979.

3. Napolitan, *The Election Game and How to Win It*, p. 11.

4. W. E. Barnes in *The San Francisco Examiner*, July 25, 1979.

5. Stanley Kelley, Jr., *Professional Public Relations and Political Power* (Baltimore: Johns Hopkins, 1956), pp. 26–30; see also pp. 9–25, 31–38.

6. Ibid., p. 13.

7. Dan Nimmo, *The Political Persuaders: The Techniques of Modern Election Campaigns* (Englewood Cliffs, N.J.: Prentice-Hall, 1970), p. 35.

8. Ibid., pp. 35–37.

9. Barnes in *The San Francisco Examiner*.

10. See Kelley, *Professional Public Relations and Political Power*, pp. 39–66, for a history of the Whitaker and Baxter firm.

11. Baus and Ross of Los Angeles, a rival consulting firm started by one of Whitaker-Baxter's former employees, provided what competition existed. Both firms primarily handled Republicans.

12. Nimmo, *The Political Persuaders*, p. 36, n. 2. Whitaker and Baxter has now effectively withdrawn from candidate campaigns.

13. Hearings before the Special Committee to Investigate Campaign Expenditures, 1952, House of Representatives, 82nd Congress, 2nd session, p. 76: as quoted in Kelley, *Professional Public Relations and Political Power*, p. 2.

14. Alexander Heard, *The Costs of Democracy* (Chapel Hill: University of North Carolina, 1960), pp. 415–477. Heard notes that his totals were probably understated because of the limitations of his survey.

15. Robert Agranoff, (ed.) *The New Style in Election Campaigns* (2nd ed.) (Boston: Holbrook Press, 1976), p. 8. See also David Rosenbloom, *The Election Men: Professional Campaign Managers and American Democracy* (New York: Quadrangle, 1973). Rosenbloom indicates a 650 percent growth rate in consulting firms overall between 1952 and 1970, an 842 percent increase in consultant involvement in U.S. House of Representatives contests, and a 300 percent increase in their employment for local elections.

16. See *National Journal*, September 26, 1970, pp. 2084–2085.

17. Personal interview with Russell Hemenway, executive director of the National Committee for an Effective Congress.

18. *Campaign Insights*, vol. 9, no. 13 (July 1, 1978): 14.

19. See Nimmo, *The Political Persuaders*, pp. 3–5.

20. Remarks delivered at the annual meeting of the American Association of Political Consultants, Washington, D.C., November 16, 1979.

21. Quoted by W. E. Barnes in the *San Francisco Examiner*, July 24, 1979.

22. See *National Journal*, November 4, 1978, p. 1776.

23. See *Campaigning Reports*, vol. 2, no. 3 (February 7, 1980): 7.

24. See *Congressional Quarterly Weekly*, July 22, 1978, p. 1860.

25. See Napolitan, *The Election Game and How to Win It*, pp. 20–63, 283–292, for a fascinating review of the 1968 Humphrey campaign from the consultant's perspective.

26. See the excellent series in the *Washington Star*, September 7, 8, 9, 1979.

27. Barry did have an accomplished but basically nonpolitical pollster, Herschel Shosteck, conduct a number of well-done surveys for him, and he also used a local advertising agency.

28. See *National Journal*, November 4, 1978, p. 1777.

29. *National Journal*, November 4, 1978, pp. 1772–1773.

30. Nora B. Jacob, "Butcher and Forde, Wizards of the Computer Letter," *The California Journal* 10 (May 1979): 162.

31. See Nimmo, *The Political Persuaders*, pp. 42–43.

32. These developments will be discussed in full in chapter 5.

33. See *National Journal*, January 21, 1978, p. 91.

34. This is yet another example of the bravado and exaggeration that is so much a part of consultants' character. Garth used the figure "twelve" in a *Washington Post Magazine* interview appearing July 29, 1979, while the figure "twenty-eight" was cited in a *Washington Star* article on September 7, 1978. Despite the unreliability of consultant self-reporting, there are some well-documented cases, about which the candidates concur, of one consultant being offered all major contenders in a contest. See *Congressional Quarterly Weekly*, July 22, 1978, pp. 1859–1860, which gives a valid example involving Garth (the 1978 New Jersey Democratic U.S. Senate primary).

35. See the *Washington Star*, April 7, 1978.

36. Sanford L. Weiner, "The Role of the Political Consultant," in Robert Agranoff (ed.), *The New Style in Election Campaigns*, p. 69.

37. *The Wall Street Journal*, September 24, 1979.

38. *The Washington Post*, November 9, 1979.

39. Memorandum to President Lyndon B. Johnson from James Rowe (who was serving as a 1968 Johnson campaign adviser outside of the formal structure), March 15, 1968, in the *Papers of Lyndon Baines Johnson*, Files of Marvin Watson, Box 30 (1375B and 1375C). Rowe had been an assistant to FDR and was a law partner of Tommy "the Cork" Corcoran.

40. DeVries basically broke ties with Republicans in 1970, but he did work for Republican Mississippi gubernatorial nominee Gil Carmichael in 1975.

41. Nimmo, *The Political Persuaders*, pp. 43–45.

42. D.M.I. has, however, taken about ten Democratic candidates in nominally nonpartisan local races since 1967.

43. *Conservative Digest*, February 1976.

44. *E.P.O.*, vol. 1, no. 1 (January/February 1979): 58.

45. Personal interview with the author. Bradley won the nomination and the general election.

46. Weiner, in Agranoff, ed., *The New Style in Election Campaigns*, pp. 68–69.

47. *The Wall Street Journal*, September 24, 1979.

48. *National Journal*, November 4, 1978, p. 1772.

49. All senatorial quotations are taken from *The Wall Street Journal*, September 24, 1979.

50. Kelley, *Professional Public Relations and Political Power*, pp. 210–213.

51. Xandra Kayden, *Campaign Organization* (Lexington, Mass.: D.C. Heath, 1978), p. 11.

52. Ibid., pp. 62–63.

53. Nimmo, *The Political Persuaders*, pp. 47–48.

54. Elinor C. Hartshorn, "The World of Joseph Napolitan," *Practical Politics*, vol. 1, no. 6 (September/October 1978): 16.

55. *E.P.O.*, vol. 1, no. 1 (January/February 1979): 55.

56. Memorandum to President Johnson from James Rowe, March 15, 1968, in the *Papers of Lyndon Baines Johnson*, Files of Marvin Watson, Box 30 (1375B and 1375C).

57. Yet another media director, Peter Dailey of Los Angeles, was hired by the Reagan forces to conduct the television campaign in the general election.

58. Kelley, *Professional Public Relations and Political Power*, p. 60, n. 28.

59. See Weiner in Agranoff, ed., *The New Style in Election Campaigns*, pp. 69–70.

60. Schweiker did not seek reelection in 1980 and was appointed secretary of Health and Human Services in Ronald Reagan's cabinet.

61. Bradley's salary was actually paid by the state Democratic party, at Brown's behest. See *The San Francisco Examiner*, July 23, 1979.

62. Quoted in *Playboy* magazine, "Interview with Patrick Caddell," February 1980, p. 84.

63. However, most pollsters do not belong to the AAPC, preferring several trade associations of their own.

64. *Campaigning Reports*, vol. 1, no. 8 (September 20, 1979): 12. Martilla and Associates replaced the parent firm and remains in Boston.

65. *The Washington Post*, November 4, 1978.

66. Kelley, *Professional Public Relations and Political Power*, p. 40.

67. Nimmo, *The Political Persuaders*, p. 37.

68. *E.P.O.*, vol. 1, no. 1 (January/February 1979): 56.

69. *National Journal*, November 4, 1978, p. 1775.

70. All charging information cited here was extracted from the author's personal interviews with the consultants.

71. Estimate of Hank Parkinson, editor of *Campaigning Reports*, borne out by several other consultants and campaign managers in personal interviews.

72. Gail Robinson, "How to Package a Politician," *Environmental Action*, vol. 10, nos. 16 and 17 (January 1979): 9.

73. *The San Francisco Examiner*, July 23, 1979. The exact breakdown presented was: 68 percent media; 9 percent political consultants' fees (except pollsters); 4 percent pollsters' fees; 1 percent accounting; 17 percent miscellaneous, including staff salaries, travel, photocopying, and office supplies.

74. The client cannot save some of the commissions by making advertising placement personally. The advertising rates charged by stations include the standard commission, and if placement is not made by an intermediary who can collect the commission, the stations keep it.

75. Rosenbloom, *The Election Men*, p. 50. The exact figures were: 200 firms under half political, 100 firms completely political, 60 firms less than completely but greater than half political. Note that this total includes local advertising agencies with political accounts; thus both the total number of management firms and the percentage of firms under half political are somewhat exaggerated.

76. *Campaigning Reports*, vol. 1, no. 4 (July 12, 1979): 4–5.

77. *Los Angeles Times*, August 8, 1979.

78. *The New York Times*, August 2, 1979.

79. This compilation was made primarily using information obtained during personal interviews, with bibliographical materials serving as supplementary sources. The listing is almost certainly incomplete, and thus even this analysis probably understates the extent of the American campaign activity abroad.

80. *Campaigning Reports*, vol. 1, no. 4 (July 12, 1979): 1.

81. The private pollsters have competition from the public survey organizations. George Gallup now has twenty-six international affiliates scattered all over the world, and Louis Harris has been expanding in the foreign sphere as well. The polling firms, public and private, are not given government contracts only in democracies. Some authoritarian regimes apparently have an insatiable thirst for polls because, one conjectures, surveys are used to gauge popular feelings as a substitute for the free elections that are never held.

82. See Napolitan, *The Election Game and How to Win It*, pp. 244–257.

83. Ibid.

84. See *The New York Times*, August 2, 1978; *Time* magazine, December 18, 1978; *The Washington Post*, December 5, 1978.

85. Napolitan, *The Election Game and How to Win It*, pp. 254–255.

86. Ibid., p. 132.

87. Accounts of the roles played by public relations men in two British elections are contained in D. E. Butler and Richard Rose, *The British General Election of 1959* (London: Macmillan, 1960), and D. E. Butler and Anthony King, *The British General Election of 1964* (New York: St. Martin's, 1965).

88. Nimmo, *The Political Persuaders*, p. 194, n. 63.

89. Ibid.

90. See David Lipsey, "What Swings the Elections?" *New Society*, vol. 52, no. 916 (April 24, 1980): 165–166.

91. These are the estimated amounts spent by the parties in the eighteen months prior to the election.

92. Some of these advertisements will be highlighted in chapter 3.

93. Labour did have some volunteer help from an ad agency, and the private polls of Market and Opinion Research's Robert Worcester, but the depth and quality of these provisions pale by comparison to the Tory arsenal.

94. *Time* magazine, April 23, 1979, p. 40.

95. The IAPC was actually founded two months before the AAPC. Recently a European Association of Political Consultants was also started, but it has a much smaller membership than the AAPC.

96. Joseph Napolitan, for example, cited a French pollster who had surveyed in several African countries with French colonial backgrounds, and another French consultant who had worked in preindependence Rhodesia (now Zimbabwe). Napolitan, *The Election Game and How to Win It*, p. 257.

97. The chairman of Republicans Abroad, James Killough, had worked for Compton Advertising, whose U.K. subsidiary designed the Tory ads.

Chapter 2

The Pols and the Polls

John White, former chairman of the Democratic National Committee, is not exactly enamored of polls. "Good politicians," he says, "already know what people are worried about. If you've got a candidate who doesn't know, get yourself another candidate."[1] Perhaps good politicians can rely on instinct, but virtually none are left who trust instinct alone. The political pollster and his surveys are omnipresent, measuring moods, sounding out opinions, interpreting trends, reassuring the pols, and revealing the shape of political things to come. Protestations to the contrary notwithstanding, candidates, officeholders, other political consultants, and the general public are fascinated, even mesmerized, by the steady stream of survey statistics that cascade down every conceivable outlet—business, labor, education, political parties and campaigns, and the news media. From the three national television networks alone in 1976 came fifty-seven separate major surveys on the presidential campaign.[2] By the end of the 1980 campaign, CBS and NBC together had exceeded the 1976 grand total, issuing about sixty-five polls between them.

In this chapter the polls and the pollsters will be scrutinized critically, with a look at polling's roots and the pollster's roles and practices. The polling instruments and the potential sources of error in the surveying process will be emphasized in particular. It should be clear at the conclusion of this examination that polls are far less "scientific" and reliable than is commonly believed and that pollsters are not always the vox populi the press acclaims.

The Development of Political Polling

It was a newspaper, the *Harrisburg Pennsylvanian,* that in 1824 published the first political poll in the United States. The electorate of Wilmington, Delaware, was surveyed on presidential preferences, with Andrew Jackson winning the straw ballot two to one over the eventual Electoral College winner, John Quincy Adams.[3] Similar newspaper straw polls became the fashion by the 1880s, with the *Boston Globe,* the *New York Herald Tribune,* the *St. Louis Republic,* and the *Los Angeles Times* all joining in the fun. The practice continued to be prominent until the most famous straw poll in history brought the process into disrepute. In 1936 a widely read weekly magazine, *Literary Digest,* mailed a sample presidential ballot to ten million Americans (together with a subscription solicitation) and, from the returns, arrived at the startling conclusion that President Franklin D. Roosevelt was about to be upended by GOP challenger Alf Landon. In the end, however, FDR had won a historic landslide, and straw polling and the magazine itself became the victims, never recovering from the enormous public embarrassment. The poll's essential error was inherent in its process. The *Digest* had mailed only to Americans who owned telephones or automobiles, and the Republican, upper-class bias of the sampling universe was never taken into account.

Polling as an enterprise was far from finished by the *Digest* debacle, though. Mrs. Alex Miller was the first candidate to benefit from campaign polling, as her son-in-law, George H. Gallup, assisted her successful 1932 Republican bid to become the first female secretary of state in Iowa.[4] Gallup's doctoral thesis on sampling techniques led to the founding of a polling industry in 1935, as he and two other early pollsters, Archibald Crossley and Elmo Roper, began taking surveys independently. The next disaster to befall the polling profession, the presidential election of 1948, when Gallup and others predicted a Dewey victory over President Truman, caused much hand wringing among the professionals and perhaps engendered among the public a lingering and altogether healthy skepticism about polls. Yet the polling industry survived and prospered greatly. In the next presidential contest Dwight Eisenhower's advertising agencies consulted Gallup in designing themes for the Republicans' 1952 television spots.[5] However, extensive use of polling in a presidential campaign did not occur until 1960, when Louis Harris analyzed public opinion in the most important primary states for John F. Kennedy. (Harris's polling enabled the Kennedy managers to target the West Virginia primary for an "upset." Though superficially appearing to be hostile territory, the state that gave JFK a key boost to the Democratic nomination in fact showed a healthy Kennedy lead over Senator Hubert H. Humphrey.)

In whirlwind fashion political pollsters began to crop up in campaign headquarters across the nation. By 1962 two-thirds of all U.S. Senate candidates used surveys, and four years later 85 percent of all winning Senate contenders, virtually all gubernatorial candidates, and about half of the victorious U.S. representatives had commissioned polls.[6] For a few of the pollsters the campaign trail led to the White House. As long ago as 1939 Franklin Roosevelt had recognized the utility of an in-house pollster, and Hadley Cantril, a Princeton psychologist, was hired to help interpret prewar public opinion. John Kennedy had also had sufficient exposure to polling's delights during his presidential quest to remain interested once in office. But it was Lyndon Johnson who almost institutionalized the polling function in the Executive Office. Hadley Cantril's son, Albert H. "Tad" Cantril, was put on LBJ's staff to interpret the published polls and analyze public opinion for the president, and pollster Oliver Quayle had a close association with the administration too. When riding high on the popularity charts Johnson was known to have kept the latest newspaper clips on his person, always at the ready to impress visiting diplomats and disrespectful journalists. Even when his popularity declined rapidly after the midpoint of his elected term, Johnson retained an obsession with polls, and his in-box was literally cluttered with poll readings and staff memoranda about polls in every state.[7]

Jimmy Carter's interest in, and respect for, survey research perhaps surpassed even Johnson's. By means of a generous contract with the Democratic National Committee and with an office a block away from the White House, Patrick H. Caddell had the closest relationship with an incumbent president of any pollster in history. From his position as Carter's 1976 campaign pollster—he had done the same for George McGovern in 1972—Caddell became a member of the President's inner circle, and he influenced major decisions during the Carter administration. Caddell's prognosis that a "crisis of confidence" existed in the nation (not to mention in President Carter) helped to precipitate Carter's Camp David reassessment in the summer of 1979, for instance. So influential had Caddell become by the time of Carter's reelection bid that Steven Smith, brother-in-law of Senator Edward Kennedy and manager of Kennedy's ill-fated presidential effort, toyed with the idea of making the Caddell-Carter relationship a major issue in 1980.[8]

The Pols and the Polls

The number of polling organizations at all levels has expanded to fill the modern demand, with many survey outfits evolving from purely market research groups designed to serve business alone, to firms that take political clients as well. There are now estimated to be more than 200 polling firms throughout the country, nearly 150 operating primarily at the state and local level, and approximately 50 to 75 operating regionally or countrywide with a national reputation.[9] The widely recognized public opinion polls are taken by divisions in a number of well-established national commercial firms: Gallup; Harris; Yankelovich, Skelly & White; John F. Kraft, Inc.; Sindlinger; Opinion Research Corporation; Roper; and Cambridge Research Reports. Dozens of other smaller commercial and public relations companies also poll nationally.[10] There are a few outstanding state polling outfits, such as Field Research Institute of San Francisco. Its founder, Mervin D. Field, is director of the renowned California Poll, a public, media-sponsored survey begun in 1947. Some state newspapers and an occasional university sponsor regular surveys, such as the Des Moines *Register* and *Tribune's* Iowa Poll, the *Minneapolis Tribune's* Minnesota Poll, and the New Jersey Poll of Rutgers University's Eagleton Institute.[11] Two independent academic survey units are located at American universities: the Survey Research Center at the University of Michigan and the National Opinion Research Center (NORC) at the University of Chicago. And the three commercial networks have joined forces with major newspapers, news services, or commercial pollsters to produce their own opinion samplings.[12] *The Washington Post*, which initially polled in conjunction with the Associated Press, now regularly conducts surveys under the direction of its in-house polling reporter, Barry Sussman. Other newspapers hire academicians as advisers.

At least one national network, NBC, has tried a revolutionary and potentially dangerous "polling" device, the Qube System. Essentially an "instant straw poll," Qube is the first viewer-response system fitted to the television set.[13] Used on an experimental basis in the summer of 1979 after President Carter's crucial "crisis of confidence" speech, the immediate reactions to the talk of 29,000 viewers in Columbus, Ohio were given national attention. While the network gave warnings that the nonrandom sample was the equivalent of a "man on the street" interview, the definition was probably lost on most viewers, especially when the commentator also referred to Qube as an "electronic poll." Albert H. Cantril, president of the National Council on Public Polls, chastised NBC severely, correctly noting that the "poll" results cited on the air were not an accurate measure of opinion even in Columbus, much less the nation. But with the system scheduled for expansion to Houston, Cincinnati, and undoubtedly other areas, the age of plebiscitary democracy—with instant "polls" on the nightly news programs—may lie in wait up ahead.[14]

While there are hundreds of polling organizations, only a minority take political campaigns, and a tiny number monopolize almost all major political contests. (Most of them are sketched in appendix C, and a few others are briefly listed in appendix A.) Three Republican firms (V. Lance Tarrance and Associates; Market Opinion Research, Inc.; and Richard Wirthin's Decision Making Information) and three Democratic ones (Patrick Caddell's Cambridge Survey Research; William R. Hamilton and Staff, Inc.; and Peter D. Hart Research Associates, Inc.) dominate the "private political pollsters," as they are normally termed. While, as Peter Hart suggests, "anyone can hang out a shingle and say he's a pollster,"[15] the principals of these polling organizations tend to dominate both public and private election forums. Mervin Field calls the group "a very small cult" compared to the several dozen media consultants who handle national campaigns and maintain a relatively high public profile.[16]

The individuals heading the firms are from widely varying backgrounds, educations, and experiences, although most have been involved in politics in some way from a young age. Their primary collective interest is unquestionably politics, but most of their firms have now diversified to include private and nonpolitical accounts. D.M.I., for example, has a field data collection subsidiary that will sell partial services (such as a randomly drawn sample) to any concern.[17] Market Opinion Research has three other divisions besides the political one, performing more than two-thirds of the firm's tasks: a social research division for government, university, and foundation work; a consumer division for market research; and a media division for television, radio, and newspaper subscriber surveys. Only a half dozen of the seventy-five to eighty full-time employees do political work exclusively; most of the personnel are shared by all divisions. Like most of his fellow polling consultants, though, M.O.R.'s president, Robert Teeter, is primarily interested in politics, and he personally runs the political division of the company. In addition to campaigns, the political divisions of most polling firms are similar to other political consulting firms in taking lobby groups and political action committee (PAC) accounts. Peter Hart has handled the dairy cooperatives; AMPAC (the American Medical Association's political action arm) has hired D.M.I.;

and William R. Hamilton & Staff has been used by the American Federation of State, County, and Municipal Employees.[18]

In 1972 four of the private pollsters (Caddell, Hart, Teeter, and Wirthlin) founded the National Association of Political Pollsters, primarily as a response to the new federal election laws and the regulations concerning polling promulgated by the Federal Election Commission.[19] "We decided it would be useful to speak with one voice," explained Teeter, but though the articles of association open membership to all in the field of private polling, Tarrance and Hamilton, among others, are still excluded, and there is no plan to expand the group's membership.[20] This suggests a polling "cartel," and there is no doubt that recognized pollsters wish to keep the number of equally renowned competitors as small as possible. Yet the competition is stiffening even without new pollsters rising to prominence. In-house polling is becoming much more common in campaigns, especially in the reelection efforts of incumbent congressmen and governors who have often used staff funds to hire or train someone to take regular surveys of the constituency. Such polls are certainly cheaper and more convenient, but they are often poorly conceived and executed by individuals without extensive training. Moreover, the temptation is always present for a loyal or fearful staffer to tinker with unfavorable poll results or present them in a light more to the boss's liking. Some supportive party and PAC groups, such as the Democratic Study Group in the U.S. House of Representatives or the National Committee for an Effective Congress, donate an inexpensive in-house poll to a candidate as their allotted contribution to the campaign. As polling costs continue to rise, this will undoubtedly become more commonplace, to the chagrin of the private pollsters.

In more ways than one, however, candidates with purely in-house polling do not get the whole loaf. For the modern national pollster is far more than an objective data collector or a mere engineer or statistician. He is an analytic interpreter, a grand strategist, and to some, a Delphic oracle. All of the prominent national private pollsters are impressively skillful and extraordinarily well versed in the ways and means of politics. Peter Hart compares himself and his colleagues to highly trained X-ray technicians: "We look for the bones and where the breaks are, and we learn to get the best angle, to get the best profile and the best shot." Once the shot is taken, the interpretive judgments are made, and it is then that the experienced pollster makes a quantum leap from social scientist to strategist and tactician. For example, Pat Caddell's list of his 1976 duties for the Carter presidential campaign is extensive, with several tasks having only a tenuous link to survey research: "In the 1976 Carter campaign I basically had input into the schedule for all the people in the campaign, the media buys, the kind of media messages, the organizational efforts, the dollar priorities. In the primaries I helped to make decisions about which states we went into, which states we did not." Caddell's involvement in virtually all major campaign decisions is not unusual for pollsters. When Ronald Reagan fired his 1980 campaign manager, John Sears, for instance, it was D.M.I. president and campaign pollster Richard Wirthlin whom Reagan tapped to become one of his primary political advisers and strategists.[21]

The serious problem for the pollster in such circumstances becomes that of separating his personal views and opinions from his reporting and interpretation of what the survey data actually show. Most polling consultants will frankly admit that the line between the roles of data interpreter and political strategist is very thin, and that it is crossed frequently without any warning to a client. But if consulting advice mingles so freely with the actual survey research findings, it is because the client wants and expects it. Political writer Alan Baron has called polls "the new holy writ of American politics," and the pollster's advice has come to replace the candidate's intuition and gut instincts.[22] The candidate-client cannot really be blamed for his heavy reliance on his pollster; he is merely responding appropriately to the pollster's own carefully cultivated public image. Through the active pens and cameras of the press, pollsters have become seen as society's doctors, diagnosing our ailments and prescribing cures. They are called upon in public forums to divine who we are and why we are. They are the vox populi, but the voice seems to come from Mount Olympus. The title pollster gives its bearer the right to philosophize grandly, to pontificate in tones normally reserved for a nation's governing elite. Let us take one of Peter Hart's public surmises: "America is still facing hard times. Our people are frustrated and they are willing to go much further than their leaders appear willing to take them. Our people are thirsting for strong leadership, but they are doubtful that they will find any."[23] There can be little doubt that a pollster's philosophizing often falls on fertile ears. In May 1976, before Jimmy Carter was even elected President, pollster Caddell was telling an interviewer:

Today there is a crisis of public confidence, not merely in specific officeholders, but in the functioning of government itself; not merely in bad policies, but in the entire process of policy making. It is a crisis of confidence in the political process and the future of the nation.

This public attitude may be unique for America, at least in our lifetime. At other times people have been worried but they have seen ways out of their problems, even if that meant hard work and sacrifice. They had basic trust in the institutions of the country and in their capacity to respond. But today we are reaping the harvest of more than a decade of national psychological trauma.[24]

President Carter's speechwriters obviously were not overtaxed when it came to preparing a draft of the chief executive's "crisis of confidence" speech after the Camp David domestic summit.

Kinds and Costs of Surveys

Five different kinds of surveys are commonly used today, each with its own special requirements and done for specific purposes.[25] In a major campaign all five types will be employed one or more times. First in the series is the *benchmark poll,* also called a "baseline" survey, which is conducted early in the precampaign period (often a year or more ahead of the election date). The goal is to assess the nation's or state's mood and the public's general perception of the strengths and weaknesses of the candidate and his potential opponents. A statewide or national benchmark poll usually is conducted personally by interviewers visiting the homes of respondents, and the interview is quite lengthy—forty-five substantive questions or more, possibly exceeding twenty pages. The sample size can be unusually large (1,500 to 2,000 respondents, sometimes as many as 4,000). Lately, because of rising costs, many benchmark polls have been conducted over the telephone, and some congressional district benchmarks have sampled as few as 400 people. In any case, the benchmark is a planning, not a predictive, document. Projected "horse races" between candidates are useless at an early stage. As British Prime Minister Harold Wilson once remarked, "A week is an eternity in politics," and a poll that attempts to predict an election result months in advance is a colossal waste of money.

The second phase of polling is a refinement and extension of the first. Once a complete analysis of the benchmark poll has been completed and areas of additional study proposed, one or more *follow-up surveys* are conducted to probe more deeply into topics of concern. Sometimes actions have been taken in response to the benchmark poll to polish the image of the candidate or to strike a new theme, and the follow-up sample can gauge the effectiveness of the efforts. Specific segments of the population may be oversampled to give a clearer indication, within a narrower margin of error, of their views. The sample size in these polls is much smaller than in a benchmark, usually between 500 and 600 individuals. The interviews are sometimes conducted in the home, but more frequently are done over the telephone. Telephone interviewing, combined with the smaller sample size and a much shorter length, makes follow-up surveys (also called "vulnerability polls") far less costly than the larger-scale benchmark ones. Two or more are sometimes conducted, half a year or so prior to the election. Closer to the election, "brushfire" surveys, short polls with small samples focusing on issues that arise during the campaign, are usually taken.

Panel surveys constitute a third major kind of political polling. They involve the reinterviewing of up to half the respondents of a previous follow-up or benchmark poll after the passage of several months to measure opinion shifts. Sample size (about 250 or 300 people) sometimes presents difficulties here, since the results of a respondent group that small has a wide margin of error. Individuals previously interviewed are also not as representative of the population as they once were, because a poll interview has been found to have a measurable impact on the political awareness and participation levels of respondents.[26] Interviewed individuals are much more likely to vote, their alienation is reduced, and their feelings of involvement in the political process increase. As a consequence, it is necessary to set up panels of new respondents who are administered the very same questions as the repeat panel. Panel surveys are conducted by telephone and are usually quite brief, the information sought being well defined. It takes two weeks or less, from start to finish, to complete a panel survey, as compared to a month for a benchmark poll.

The most critical kind of election polling comes last, in the *"tracking" phase*. As the election campaign actually begins, shifts in sentiment among likely voters are "tracked" by calling 50 to 100 or more individuals each night, with half a dozen very specific questions asked (usually about the latest issues, changing perceptions of the candidate, the effect of the media advertisements, etc.). Not enough interviews are conducted each evening to comprise a worthwhile sample, of course, but a system of "moving averages" is instituted.[27] If 100 individuals are interviewed each night, then the last five consecutive nights' interviews constitute the total sample, and with each new evening's additional 100, the oldest nightly accumulation is dropped. The trend line produced in this way can be exceptionally useful to the candidate and his managers as they attempt to make crucial decisions in the pressure-cooker days at a campaign's conclusion.

A fifth category of tool used by pollsters is actually not a random sample poll at all. Called a *"focus group,"* it is a small collection of individuals (a dozen or less) selected nonrandomly to reflect age, sex, race, economic, or life-style characteristics, brought together under the leadership of a trained discussion leader to talk generally about the campaign and the candidates.[28] The discussants are observed from behind a two-way mirror, and extensive notes are made of their comments and the surfacing connections among issues, images, and advertisements. A focus group is somewhat equivalent to asking a series of very open-ended questions on a poll, a process time and money rarely permits. "Focus groups are impossible to quantify," notes Patrick Caddell, "but their advantage is that you get insights that go beyond your numbers. You get a linear thinking process that explores all sorts of unexpected dimensions to the campaign."[29]

The onset of polling in an election campaign, like the campaign itself, has been moved steadily forward on the calendar. In past years the benchmark survey for a campaign was usually scheduled in the spring of the election year, but now it is often done in the prior autumn or even summer or spring of the previous year. The contract with a polling firm is negotiated well in advance of the starting date, of course, and agreement must be reached on the content of the questionnaire and the kind of surveys to be conducted. Pollsters retain sole control over the sample selection and statistical design, however, since their reputation is at stake. Generally an outline of the sequence of polls that the firm projects to do over the entire campaign is approved by the client, but pollsters proceed on a project-by-project basis with the client's renewed approval for each new poll. Since the campaign time is lengthened, more polling is probably being done (adding to campaign costs) simply to keep the assessment of a campaign's progress timely. While tracking surveys were once done only rarely, they are now almost certain to become standard campaign tools unless rising costs make them prohibitive.

The increasing costs of polling also envelop a raging debate among pollsters about the best method of interviewing. All agree that surveys by mail are unreliable, with a low rate of response and an unrepresentative sample returned that even a good system of weighting cannot fully correct. But there is a serious division between those favoring interviews by telephone and those who insist that the most accurate polls are administered in person. Most polling consultants formerly agreed with Charles Roll and Albert Cantril when they insisted that "the attractions of telephone polls are far outweighed by significant drawbacks," making personal interviews "much preferable."[30] Telephone polls incorporate a severe sampling bias, since the polling universe is defined as those citizens rich enough to afford telephone service. About 10 percent of white U.S. households and 15 percent of nonwhite households do not have telephones, and the phoneless concentration is in poorer, more rural areas and also among the highly mobile young. The telephone cannot produce a rapport between interviewer and respondent comparable to that achieved in person, and the respondents cannot peruse exhibits listing a wide range of answers to a question or a pictoral scale, thus forcing reduced complexity in questioning. The interviewer also cannot accurately determine race and income over the telephone, respondents' answers on the latter subject in particular being notoriously at variance with the truth, and telephone interviewees were long thought to be more inclined to refuse to answer questions on controversial subjects.

Yet the tide of opinion in the polling ranks has begun to turn, and almost all political pollsters now use the telephone consistently. On the one hand some rationalization supporting increased use of telephone polling is necessary to justify the rapid decline in personal interviewing. In-home polling is just too expensive anymore for even monied campaigns. ("Only the federal government can come up with the bucks for in-person interviewing," reports Vincent Breglio.) Telephone polls are substantially cheaper, can be done far more quickly (in several days, if necessary), and the dispersion of the randomly selected sample is greater (that is, the individuals selected are likely to come from a larger number of diverse areas than in personal interviewing, which "clusters" interviewers at relatively few geographic points).[31] With the refusal rate for doorstep interviews now exceeding 20 percent in many cases, the in-person advantage has almost disappeared. Telephone polling may actually better the response rate with inner-city dwellers, who are hard to reach in person or actively avoided by nervous and fearful interviewers. D.M.I.'s research has indicated that, once in the door or on the phone, there is less than a 1 percent difference in the refusal rate for most questions. No accommodation can be made for voters without telephones, but many pollsters contend that those individuals are the least likely to vote anyway, so that the polled sample may be more representative of probable voters.[32] Nor can much be done about the reduced sophistication of questioning, or the reduction in the number of questions that can be asked in one sitting over the telephone. In-person interviews usually include sixty to seventy questions, with up to an hour spent answering them; but it is difficult to keep people on the telephone for more than twenty minutes, permitting only thirty or forty simple questions to be posed. Pollsters gloss over this irremedial difficulty by suggesting that in-person interviews often produce "information overkill . . . too much information for a campaign to handle." Contends Vincent Breglio, "A telephone interview gives a campaign about the right amount of data." He seeks follow-up surveys or focus groups with key subsets of the population as an acceptable substitute for an extensive doorstep poll.

The switch to a telephoning standard is one of the changes being wrought in the political polling industry as a result of skyrocketing prices. Polling costs more than doubled from 1972 to 1978, far outstripping the average inflation rate.[33] Not just the method of interview, but also the size of the sample and the length of the questionnaire (and thus the duration of the interview) affect cost. A forty-five-minute in-home benchmark survey, at $20 to $35 per interview, can easily run to six figures, though a campaign version is usually scaled down to $50,000 or less. A twenty-minute follow-up telephone survey with 600 interviews at $15 to $23 apiece costs between $15,000 and $20,000. The longer the poll and the larger the sample, the greater the cost. Reducing the length of the questionnaire means losing data, and reducing the sample size means increasing the margin of error, so a clear trade-off exists between expense and reliability. As the number of interviews is increased, though, the cost of each interview declines because of economy of scale. Yet there is little to be gained, at least as far as the margin of error is concerned, by expanding sample size by increments, because a drastic ballooning of the sample (and total price) is necessary to achieve any major reduction in the error margin.[34]

Estimates vary substantially from firm to firm, and comparative shopping by candidates is always recommended. No two pollsters appear to charge the same rates, although exact comparisons are difficult to make with so many variables involved. For example, statewide telephone polls in Rhode Island are cheaper than elsewhere because no long-distance dialing is involved; Alaska or Wyoming is quite the opposite, being sparsely populated with a great deal of cross-zonal telephoning essential. Generally about half the price of any poll is a product of field service (i.e., interviewing) charges, and the other half is due to data processing, analysis, and consultant fees. The sum of all polling charges usually amounts to between 5 and 8 percent of the total campaign budget. In a million-dollar statewide campaign, then, anywhere from $50,000 to $80,000 would be allocated to the pollster.[35] In close races, where constant tracking is required, the total far exceeds this average. By and large pollsters require a proportion of the money in advance. Half of the total cost of every survey usually must be in hand before fieldwork commences, and the last half is due prior to final presentation of the data and findings. This schedule perhaps exacerbates the cash-flow problem that plagues most campaigns, but it is understandable given the polling firm's own cash needs.

As substantial as the costs appear for political polls, they pale in comparison to the charges levied by the same consultants for commercial projects.[36] Louis Harris, for example, received a $120,000 payment for a research survey conducted for the "Virginia Slims" cigarette makers on women and the feminist movement—a poll that would have cost a political client just several thousand dollars.[37] When one considers that an estimated $4 billion is spent on polling by political, commercial, and scholarly groups each year,[38] it is easier to agree with Peter Hart's assertion that "We're a terribly small part of a campaign's budget. If you're doing it [political polling] for the bucks, then you're in the wrong business." Caddell echoes Hart: "It's much better [financially] to go out and measure most people's attitudes about cereal and milk rather than politics. You do [politics] because it's interesting and fascinating. There's a trade-off there."

Campaign participants have a rather different view. Engaged in political enterprises with limited resources and enormous demand, they see the polling portion of the budget as substantial, and growing. As mentioned, several arrangements to reduce survey costs have been organized in recent years. The House Democratic Study Group (DSG), consisting of most U.S. House Democrats and funded with portions of their office allowances, has established a privately financed campaign warchest that helps candidates conduct local polls for between a fifth and a third of the price asked by the polling professionals. A telephone poll, for example, costs only $1,500 for the first survey and $1,000 for each subsequent poll. The DSG has taken more than 170 surveys since 1974 and is now the most common supplier of polls to House Democrats.[39] "Package deals" have also become a standard cost-cutting measure for candidates. Using the state party committee as the contracting agent, all of a party's major statewide candidates pool their resources and hire a pollster to survey jointly for them.[40] (Obviously not as much individual attention and questionnaire space can be given to each candidate in this arrangement.) The political pollsters have sensed the desire for lower-cost service, and some will make available a polling instrument and sample, and train a candidate's volunteers to administer it. The results of such endeavors have been decidedly mixed. Cambridge Survey Research was heavily criticized for its lackadaisical training of candidate volunteers in the 1978 elections. In one poll conducted by Caddell's "trainees" in New Hampshire shortly before the election, Democratic U.S. Senator Thomas McIntyre was shown to be far ahead of his right-wing Republican challenger, Gordon Humphrey. When Humphrey unseated McIntyre and the Democrat's distraught campaign officials pointed to Caddell's poll, Caddell smugly replied that the poll had been conducted by volunteers, not professionals.[41]

Polls and Political Power

Richard Wirthlin describes polling as "the science of ABC—almost being certain."[42] It is somewhat comforting to know that even with the most advanced computers and after decades of experience, human judgment is still at the heart of polling analysis—one more suggestion that political consulting is less science than art. "What we really do is a bit arbitrary, though it's much more scientific than putting your finger up to the wind," surmises Patrick Caddell. Yet, by the scientist's criterion, polling could never qualify as an experimental discipline because any given poll's results cannot be truly tested and replicated. Every poll is unique, a snapshot of a moment in time. Conditions in our world change from minute to minute; a television news bulletin between polls an hour apart could alter survey results by 20 to 30 percent. Unless a clear flaw in the methodology is exposed, no one can actually ever prove that a poll was right or wrong. Even election results cannot pronounce a judgment with certainty: last-minute shifts and the split of the undecideds can easily explain a variance.[43]

Polls can suggest the direction of a trend, if there is one, but otherwise their forecasting powers are vastly exaggerated. Public opinion is fluid on most matters, including headline items such as impending elections, which, though it pains a political scientist to admit it, are not on the top of every citizen's list of major concerns. The ephemeral nature of poll findings is suggested by the Harris Poll's figures on President Nixon's invasion of Cambodia in 1970.[44] On the eve of the illegal

Pitfalls of polls

incursion, only 7 percent of the American public favored sending U.S. forces into Cambodia and 59 percent were opposed. But after the troops were in, 50 percent said Nixon was right to invade, with only 43 percent demurring. Polls can be deceptive as well. There are several layers or levels of opinion. Someone who says he is a "conservative" in answer to a direct question on ideology may in fact be quite "liberal" when it comes to dispensing certain kinds of federal aid.[45] The intensity of a respondent's opinion is often more vital politically than the direction of the opinion (as single-issue groups have shown), but no special weight is assigned a deeply felt response when the answers are tabulated.[46] There is also plenty of room for error in polls, as will be discussed later. Polling is subjective and the results turn, in part, on the question's wording and the interpreter's judgment. Merely asking the question generally produces an opinion, whether the respondent had ever considered the subject before or not; polls often manufacture public opinion in this way.

When all of polling's pitfalls are considered, it becomes apparent that opinion surveys can never substitute for good sense and thoughtful study. Nor for conscience, it must be hoped. After all, today's profile in courage may be well within tomorrow's opinion mainstream. The pollsters themselves caution candidates against a strict reading of the results to the exclusion of other factors. Robert Teeter notes:

There's an incorrect public perception that polls are infallible and that they can measure everything to a precise degree. Polls should provide some guidance on what candidates ought to talk about or how they should frame their presentations—but I don't think polls should ever override good judgment or replace people's brains.[47]

Candidates for office are often more inclined to follow poll results than even the pollsters like. "I've seen candidates who were far too flexible for my tastes in being willing to realign their positions," reports Teeter. When Republican John W. Warner was entering the race for U.S. Senator from Virginia in 1978 (which he eventually won), he was asked about his position on the proposed constitutional amendment giving the District of Columbia full congressional representation. Warner reportedly turned to his pollster, Arthur Finkelstein, and asked, "Art, where do we stand?"[48] But polls do not usually change a candidate's views, or even create an opinion where none had existed. More common is a change in emphasis on one issue as opposed to others. When Democratic U.S. Representative Henry Helstoski of New Jersey called for an end to the bombing of North Vietnam in 1966, polls taken by

problem: conform to voters rather than convince them.

his consultant, Joseph Napolitan, indicated that 70 percent of his constituents opposed his viewpoint. So without repudiating his stand, Helstoski simply stopped talking about this issue and went on to others.[49]

Perhaps if candidates understood the art of polling better, they would be less likely to rely on survey results for inappropriate purposes. They would probably also get more use out of the polls they pay dearly for, by seeking more advantageous information. "Candidates are often more concerned with asking questions that are interesting, not questions that are of strategic use," laments Peter Hart.[50] Most politicians read polls as carefully as the election returns, but there are exceptions. Three 1980 presidential contenders were privately hostile and sometimes openly contemptuous of campaigning by poll. U.S. Senator Edward Kennedy, California Governor Jerry Brown, and former Texas Governor John Connally all preferred to rely on their own instincts and those of their staffs. It may be just a coincidence that their campaigns floundered, while the three candidates who polled most extensively (Carter, Reagan, and Bush) met with greater success.

Polls seem to be misused as much as they are used, and the influence they wield often leads to regrettable consequences.[51] One of the worst decisions a politician can make on the basis of polls is the determination of whether to run or not. The early trial-heat match-ups are usually nothing more than name-identification contests or pairings based on expectations and assumptions that can be deflated or dispelled during a campaign. Elections are decided in good part by the events of the campaign, sometimes the very last event. A "horse-race" poll months (or years) before an election is utterly useless as a predictive device, though for the candidate with the chimerical lead it often works wonders as a press magnet or fund-raising tool. ("When the polls go good for me, the cash register really rings," candidate Nixon was quoted as saying during the 1968 campaign.)

The reality, however, is that many a candidate has let the trial heats decide his fate. Michigan Governor George Romney withdrew from the 1968 GOP presidential contest because of Market Opinion Research polls showing him trailing in New Hampshire. (The mayor of Rockledge, Florida, was so angry that a poll and not an actual election had forced his favorite candidate out of the race that he proposed an ordinance forbidding national pollsters from interviewing his town's residents.[52]) In 1980 U.S. Senator Lowell Weicker of Connecticut followed the Romney pattern and dropped out of the GOP presidential scramble, attributing his decision to a poll showing him running third in his home state.[53]

On the other hand, some potential candidates have ignored admittedly depressing early poll figures, thrown their hats into the ring, and walked off with the grand prize or at least a consolation gift. Jimmy Carter's less than 3 percent support rating in the Gallup poll of October 1975 and George Bush's virtually nonexistent poll rating throughout most of 1979 did not deter them from making very respectable showings in their presidential bids. On the other hand, early poll leaders are not infrequently unemployed on election day. Michael Dukakis, former governor of Massachusetts who lost his renomination bid in a 1978 Democratic primary, became a Harvard instructor after he left office and wryly commented on his educational goals: "For one thing, I'll try to keep my students from believing polls too readily. The early polls had me so far ahead in the primary that it was impossible to get voters to take the race seriously. So now I'm a teacher."[54]

Another regrettable misuse of survey data can be pinned squarely on American journalists. Referred to by political veterans as "the numbers game," this misreading of the deceptive early trial-heat polls can set up wholly unrealistic expectations that a candidate must meet. Failing to reach the artificial straw-man percentage set for him can result in a plurality or clear majority victory being converted by press interpretation into a measured defeat. Recent American history is replete with shameful illustrations. In 1972 an early *Boston Globe* poll of New Hampshire primary voters gave nearby Maine Senator Edmund Muskie an overwhelming 65 to 18 percent edge over his little-known competitor, Senator George McGovern.[55] When Muskie secured a decisive plurality (46 to 37 percent) from New Hampshire's discriminating and fickle electorate, reporters promptly declared McGovern the "winner," having earlier christened the 65 percent figure as the standard by which Muskie would be judged.

Later in the same presidential year the tables were turned on McGovern. The California primary was set to determine whether Hubert Humphrey continued his acid challenge to the McGovern bandwagon's steady roll toward the Democratic nomination. Three polls in series had a critical effect on the nomination contest, and possibly on McGovern's chances in the general election as well. The first survey, conducted by ABC and released a week before the election, showed a McGovern lead of 22 percent.[56] Two other polls, one by ABC and the other by Mervin Field, were made public four days prior to the election, and indicated a McGovern lead of 17 and 20 percent, respectively. When McGovern defeated Humphrey by 6 percent, the press viewed it as a setback for the front-runner because he did not live up to the expectations created by the surveys. Humphrey (and Muskie, too) got the encouragement needed to continue the nomination fight, creating a deeper rift among the Democrats and helping Nixon to paint McGovern into an extremist corner from which he could not extricate himself. Yet at least one of the pollsters involved, Mervin Field, was concerned after the California contest that this survey might have "interfered with the electoral process" by making McGovernites complacent and Humphrey supporters firmer in their resolve to vote.[57]

While the "complacency theory" is mere conjecture, there is a frequently demonstrated problem with preprimary polls that could have a direct bearing on the disparity between the polls' predictions and the voting results in California. The determination of who among the respondents is likely to vote—as opposed to those who *claim* intention of voting—in relatively low turnout party primaries is the most crucial decision a pollster can make, since it affects the universe from which the results are tabulated. It is an extremely difficult determination as well, and the screening process is often a matter of educated guesswork, still rather primitive (and certainly so in 1972). Yet the methodological complexities were never mentioned, and few thought to question the instruments of judgment. Instead, the failures of the polls and their interpreters became the failures of a candidate. Lamentably the "numbers game" appears to have intensified in the subsequent presidential contests of 1976 and 1980, and seems to be on its way to becoming a fixture in the presidential selection process. And with the growth of the caucus method of delegate selection, which is characterized generally by an even smaller absolute voter turnout that is heavily dependent on the variable get-out-the-vote organizational efforts of candidates, the difficulty in conducting polls representative of the participating electorate can only increase.

Public polls, combined with the leaking (usually very selectively) of private surveys, are thought by some to create a "bandwagon effect" for the front-runner. Patrick Caddell insisted in 1972 that the reason McGovern registered so low in the polls was because voters were ashamed or afraid to identify themselves with an unpopular candidate ("unpopular" as determined by highly publicized previous surveys). Caddell noted this reticence particularly in doorstep interviewing when a respondent's identity and location were most clearly established. The Goldwater managers had postulated the existence of the same phenomenon, but the 1964 and 1972 election returns have not added much supporting evidence.[58] Academic survey researchers and the pollsters themselves disagree on whether favorable polls can have great positive effect on a campaign, little or no effect, or even a reverse bandwagon influence stimulating movement toward an underdog.[59] It is true perhaps that Americans, more than most people, love winners, but there is usually enough contradictory polling information bandied about to give some hope to everyone.

Bandwagons would seem to be more in the province of party officials, activists, and patronage appointees who have the most to gain or lose from the election result. Indeed, campaign polls are often leaked (many times with a deceptive arrangement of polling results) merely to influence party leaders and contributors who are on the fence. Fund raising by poll has proven to be a successful means of filling campaign coffers not only with large contributions but also with small gifts solicited with a direct-mail package highlighting favorable poll results (as discussed in chapter 4). The suspicion that poll findings have been manipulated for the purpose often leads to charges of deceit. A vicious verbal battle erupted between two pollsters, Patrick Caddell and Lance Tarrance, over just such an incident in the 1978 U.S. Senate contest in Texas between incumbent Republican John Tower and Democratic challenger Robert Krueger. Tarrance charged Caddell with permitting his poll to be used in a "less than professional" manner to help Krueger's fund raising, intimating that Caddell had made the contest look closer than it was. Caddell angrily denied the suggestion.[60]

With all of the ways polls can be misjudged and misused, some may be tempted to think that campaigns would be better off without them. Yet nothing could be further from the truth. The alternatives to good polling are far more fallible and less satisfying. Crowd size and warmth, newspaper editorials and letters, mail to an officeholder or candidate, and intuition unquestionably have a much greater margin for error than any properly conducted random-sample survey of reasonable size. And none of these other devices can be nearly as informative as a comprehensive poll. A good private poll literally can help a candidate change the election results, even if it cannot precisely predict them. A poll aids a candidate in determining his most likely majority coalition and suggests ways of appealing to them. This essential task is accomplished in a number of ways.[61] The concerns of the electorate are measured, and all sides of each major issue are examined from the voters' perspectives, helping the candidate position himself and choose which issues to emphasize. The analysis is done for all large subgroups of the population, permitting targeting and refinement of appeals where the odds for gain are greatest. A poll can serve as a signal of potential or growing difficulty, indicating to the candidate how his strengths and weaknesses (and those of his opponent) are perceived and weighted. Most important for the science of campaigning, a poll is the determinant of resource allocation, suggesting the media time-buying strategies, the optimal scheduling of the candidate's time, and the best allotment of volunteer resources. These tasks are done by first using the poll data to identify the subgroups of the electorate or regions of the constituency to be targeted, then buying television and radio time at the hours when targeted groups are concentrated in the viewing or listening audience, and scheduling the candidate and volunteers for areas or tasks designed to shore up support.

To accomplish these varied goals, most campaign polls ask a list of questions on standardized topics (although the wording of the questions differs considerably from pollster to pollster). After a brief, authoritative introduction designed to induce participation,[62] an interviewer, with the permission of the respondent, proceeds immediately to determine whether the respondent is registered and whether he or she is likely to vote in the forthcoming election. If not registered and without a clear indication of intent to register and vote, or if the voter suggests that he will not cast a ballot in the upcoming contest, the interview is terminated and is not counted toward the sample total. A good poll does not stop at this basic registration screening. Participation in recent elections (for primaries or general elections, depending on the purpose of the survey) is also used as a guide. Many people, wishing to be thought good citizens, lie and report that they voted when they did not, so the question should include good excuses for nonvoting.[63] If the respondent has not previously cast a ballot for the office at stake in the forthcoming election, assuming he was of age and registered, then the interview can also be ended at that point.

The respondents who pass the initial screens are closely examined on their party identification. Independents are prodded in a number of ways to disclose their weak party leaning (if any). One major political pollster poses the following question:

Let us suppose that there were two candidates running for a lesser statewide office and you had not heard of either candidate. If you got into the voting booth and realized that one of these two candidates would be elected, would you vote for the Democrat, the Republican, or would you just not vote in that election?

Respondents are asked to disclose their choices in past elections, as a means of checking party identification and classifying by ideology (and the surprising thing is that most people reveal their votes without much hesitation). There are all sorts of ingenious ways to determine a candidate's philosophical disposition. In several cases pollsters have constructed a question on the presupposition that the Republican and Democratic parties "no longer existed." The respondent, having been told the question was in good fun, is asked which of a fictitious list of parties he would favor (Labor, Progressive, Conservative, Free Enterprise, "Taxpayers," "Consumers," etc.) if all he had to judge the parties on were their names.

Normally, a lengthy series of issues questions follows, many of them open-ended if the interview is in-person, allowing for extended remarks by the respondents. Identification of the most serious problems at national, state, and local levels is requested, and respondents are often forced to weigh one against the other to determine priorities. Interviewees are called upon to identify major public figures and to rate them in various ways, primarily on job performance and personality.[64] Peter Hart uses a "thermometer" approach to evoke feelings about his candidates. The respondent is asked to place a series of individuals on a 10-point scale; those who warm the heart are put near 10, and those who chill the spine situated near 1. The inevitable, if often useless, horse-race match-ups are included to satisfy the candidate and his fundraisers. Finally, the poll is concluded with invaluable sections on the respondent's pattern of television viewing, radio listening, and newspaper reading, as well as his or her vital personal characteristics (age, education, religion, ethnic group, race [if by telephone], income, etc.). These concluding questions permit the most revealing cross-tabulations to be run, so that a campaign can say (almost) that if middle-aged lower income white Catholic men of Lithuanian descent who watch *Laverne and Shirley* can only be won over, victory is assured.

"There are only X number of ways to ask a question," says Peter Hart. "Most of the difference comes from what you do with the answers." Hart and his fellow political pollsters are attempting to analyze polling data in ways far more precise and complex than that done just a few years ago. Most of the efforts center around "multidimensional scaling" (MDS).[65] Unlike simple cross-tabulation, which correlates only two factors simultaneously, MDS utilizes computer regression techniques to analyze multiple dimensions of a interviewee's responses. Most voters' electoral decisions are based on a multitude of issues, prejudices, emotions, and judgments, and simplistic interpretation cannot adequately project this intricate web. MDS presents each factor in relation to all others and roughly establishes the relative importance of each item comprising the voting decision, including personal ideology and party affiliation, issue beliefs, reactions to candidates, and so forth. Peter Hart uses MDS to scale respondents' issue and ideological beliefs. He first asks an "open-ended" question[66] to elicit the respondent's views on "the most important problems facing the country today." A follow-up open-ended question requests solutions to those problems. After a series of intervening and mentally distracting queries, a closed list of as many as two dozen issues is handed to the interviewee, and he or she is asked, in a carefully designed sequence of questions, to gauge the success or failure of incumbent officeholders' attempts to deal with each issue; to evaluate the progress being made in each area; to identify the issue or issues that would be most likely to determine his or her electoral choices; to judge both the candidates and the parties' abilities to improve conditions; and to agree or disagree with a wide range of different formulated "solutions" to each major problem. The idea of MDS analysis is that, having plumbed a voter's mind at several conscious and subconscious levels in a variety of ways, the resulting "map" of all the answers will piece together a coherent picture of political motivation. When further correlated with personal and demographic responses given in the poll, the data can suggest which ways, and on what themes, the campaign should move forward.

An additional example perhaps can serve to clarify this remarkably complex and advanced technique. Robert Teeter found MDS had great utility in the 1976 Ford presidential campaign. He grouped his respondents' replies onto two main axes: One, a "vertical dimension," represented "traditional American social values" (arrived at through a series of questions on topics such as amnesty, abortion, national defense, etc.); the other, a "horizontal dimension," signified party preference and ideology (also the product of a series of queries). Among other surprises, the MDS analysis showed that President Ford was perceived as liberal or untraditional on social values, while Carter was positioned almost perfectly to appeal to a broader electoral base. Ford's media advisers designed a series of television advertisements portraying Ford as a "solid guy with a typical American family," and later MDS interpretation using subsequent poll data indicated that the effort was successful, as Ford's perception became more appealing to the electorate and better positioned.

A number of other advanced survey techniques are being used in political polling. D.M.I.'s polling strategy sometimes calls for a telephone survey to identify the population subgroups a candidate must attract to win, then another telephone survey targeted specifically to those subgroups with the questions having been formulated after focus-group interviews with representatives of the selected subgroups. D.M.I. also employs a fascinating open-ended device called the "ECHO technique" in many of its in-home interviews. Having found closed questions, even ones with dozens of alternative answers, to be overly inhibiting and stifling sometimes, D.M.I. survey researchers adopted a sequence of open-ended questions with repeated themes. A respondent is asked: "What's a good thing that ought to happen in the country today?" Then, a follow-up: "Who or what could cause that to happen?" Next, a repeat version of the first query: "What's another good thing that should happen in the country today?" The sequence continues until all levels of an individual's life (from national government to personal family) are covered, after which the questions are asked again in the negative ("What's something that ought *not* to happen in the country today?") Vincent Breglio considers the ECHO technique an expensive but superior substitute for focus groups, since a representative random sample is used in ECHO, permitting firmer conclusions to be drawn than for the unrepresentative sample of a focus session. He also advocates ECHO because of its revealing results: "You get a whole group of verbatim responses that begin to flesh out what people really mean when they say they're concerned about inflation or education or whatever."

William Hamilton has begun to adopt a fascinating new tool, a geodemographic targeting system, in conjunction with his polling. Using "clustering" census data refined in marketing research and specially programmed voter registration lists, Hamilton is able to pinpoint groups of swing voters. As Hamilton describes the advantages:

Never before has anyone had a situation where a pollster can tell a campaign, "Look, we have problems with people who live in new towns, who are white and upper middle class," and then tell the candidate that 40 of these people live in this county, 60 here, and 120 in the northwest part of the state. And here are their names, addresses, and phone numbers.

A full discussion of this advanced form of polling research—which also has revolutionary application to the field of campaign organization—follows in chapter 3.

The difficulty in briefly explaining and illustrating new polling techniques is reassuring, because political survey research has long been accused of oversimplification in form and interpretation. While 70 percent or more of the citizenry might enthusiastically answer in the affirmative a question about whether they would like their taxes lowered, most of the same respondents would strenuously object to a reduction in governmental services. Analysis that cannot combine these two contending sentiments is not particularly worthwhile or useful to a campaign. When the analysis is sophisticated and the pollster politically shrewd, survey research *can* benefit a candidate enormously, and even make the difference between experiencing the proverbial thrill of victory and the agony of defeat.[67] Unquestionably, Patrick Caddell's 1976 polling for Jimmy Carter was a major assist in the series of well-positioned breakthroughs that propelled an obscure former governor to a presidential nomination. In the Florida primary, for instance, Carter's defeat of George Wallace brought him a massive dose of favorable national publicity. It was Caddell's polling that helped to secure a decisive victory, shifting the campaign's media focus to the Tampa–St. Petersburg and Miami "Gold Coast" urban areas, which had been earlier ignored by Carter even though his vote harvest was shown to be potentially great. (Carter did, in the end, carry both areas by larger than expected margins.) Caddell also helped to design Carter's "something for everyone" appeal that held the diverse Democratic coalition together. Voters preferred drastically reduced federal spending and bureaucracy in Caddell's polls, while they endorsed strenuously governmental intervention in the health-care field. The electorate felt no need for greater consistency and did not demand it of Carter, either, who made both a balanced budget and a moderate national health-care insurance program prominent planks in his campaign platform. Caddell was a match for one of the GOP's best pollsters in the general election as well. President Ford's consultant, Robert Teeter, had discovered the fundamentalist Carter's weakness among Catholics during the primary season, and on the basis of that finding, urged Ford to concentrate on Louisiana (with a 37 percent Catholic population) as a potential breakthrough in Carter's solid phalanx of southern support. But Caddell had detected Catholics' reluctance to back Carter at about the same time as Teeter, and he made certain Carter gave inordinate attention to the Bayou state. The Democrat's forays were well received and, in a mild reversal of expectations, Carter carried the state against Ford.[68]

Ronald Reagan has also been especially well served by his survey researchers. His chief pollster, Richard Wirthlin of D.M.I., supervised a comprehensive polling program for the 1976 campaign that included a 2,100-person random-sample benchmark survey of extraordinary length (almost 100 questions, generating 212 elements of information per respondent in September 1975) and extensive, repetitive telephone polls and near-continual tracking surveys. But Wirthlin, who is credited by Reagan (and others) with rescuing his floundering candidacy after his narrow New Hampshire primary loss to President Ford in February 1976, proves that a pollster's real value goes far beyond the survey data that is produced. Because polls indicated that foreign policy issues had little appeal to most voters,[69] Reagan had concentrated on other matters during the early phase of his campaign. Yet Wirthlin himself sensed that Reagan's challenge to an incumbent president had lacked definition and that the greater gap between Reagan and Ford lay in the foreign policy sphere. Trusting his instincts as a veteran consultant more than the cold facts of his polling data, he urged Reagan to "confront the President with our own issue."[70] Using U.S.–U.S.S.R. détente and the Panama Canal treaties as the focal points—the latter an issue so low in public recognition that it had not even shown up in Wirthlin's open-ended polls—Reagan pumped life into his campaign, and in quick succession won the North Carolina, Texas, Indiana, and Nebraska primaries. Wirthlin's strategy was unwittingly assisted by Ford's Robert Teeter who, in a rare but major error in judgment, recommended against any more tracking polls in North Carolina when his surveys several weeks before the state's primary showed Ford with a comfortable lead. Reagan again benefited from Wirthlin's expertise early in 1980 when D.M.I.'s almost daily tracking was a major assist in Reagan's skillful outmaneuvering of GOP opponent George Bush in the New Hampshire primary.[71] Incredibly, Bush had done his last New Hampshire poll in December. In the general election Wirthlin employed advanced MDS techniques to guide the Reagan campaign. Wirthlin's polls were generally more accurate, and certainly more analytical, than any of the public surveys.

Misses and Mistakes: Sources of Error in Polls

In spite of glowing accounts of pollsters' exploits such as the ones just related, some campaigns remain cautious. U.S. Senator Birch Bayh's sophisticated 1974 reelection organization, for example, had its own in-house pollster, who checked and did further analysis of the outside polling consultant's surveys as well as additional telephone surveys of her own.[72] The Bayh campaign's care and caution were fully justified, for the history of political polling is littered with the remains of campaigns that were misled by wayward pollsters brandishing defective polls. Just a week after the 1978 midterm elections, a front-page headline in *The Washington Post* advertised a string of embarrassing survey failures: "The Biggest Losers: Public Opinion Polls Widely Refuted by Election Results."[73] The lead paragraph summed up the scathing commentaries being aired across the country:

In Colorado "there must have been a colossal breakdown"; in South Dakota there was "a colossal screwup"; in Iowa the results were simply "wrong." In state after state this year, public opinion polls—the ball and bat of American politics—miscued, sometimes with disastrous consequences for candidates.[74]

Virtually the same biting evaluations of the polls were headlined again in November 1980 after surveys failed to predict the Reagan presidential landslide and the GOP takeover of the U.S. Senate.

Part of the criticism was a classic overreaction, based on ignorance about the substance and purpose of polling and the understandable if reckless postelection search for scapegoats. Yet a critical view of polling is warranted—and desperately needed. Polling is oversold as a "scientific" profession and as a campaign tonic. Its weaknesses are at least as apparent as its strengths, and there is a frightfully large number of entry points for error in the polling process. Many polls are just plain wrong—poorly done or poorly interpreted. Several sources of potential error stand out, including prior prejudices and question bias; the construction, analysis, and interpretation of the polling instrument and results, including the sampling and respondent screening processes; and a host of problems with interviewers and respondents.

PREJUDICE AND QUESTION BIAS

Mervin Field has bluntly posed the "crisis of conscience" question for political pollsters: "Do they provide objective reports, or are they deliberately or inadvertently influenced by the positions of their political clients?"[75] As he suggests, the prejudice may be subconscious and unintentional, but pollsters are not exempt from the quite natural human desire to avoid being the messengers of bad news. Pollsters also sometimes feel pressure to demonstrate change and reveal unsuspected facts of public opinion. (It is a rare client who will gladly pay thousands of dollars to verify everything he knew all along.) It is surprisingly easy to skew the results in any direction. Phrasing and ordering of the questions are critical, and one can poll quite "scientifically" to reach a predestined conclusion.

Political writer Alan Baron has drawn a superb illustration in examining pollsters' work for the opposing sides of recent labor-law reform legislation.[76] Both the Chamber of Commerce and the American Retail Federation fought the legislation, designed to reduce obstacles to union organizing, and hired Opinion Research Corporation (ORC) and Patrick Caddell's Cambridge Survey Research respectively. Union leaders were infuriated that Caddell took business's side since he had a lucrative, standing contract with the Democratic National Committee, partially funded by labor. The liberal Caddell saw no conflict of interest between the two financially rewarding packages, however. The AFL-CIO countered by securing the polling services of Public Interest Opinion Research. To no one's astonishment, all of the pollsters found substantial survey evidence that the public supported their clients. The polls were not fabricated—although this has been known to happen in and out of politics.[77] Rather, the various findings were a function of how the question was posed. ORC's interviewers asked whether "federal legislation should be passed that makes it easier than it now is for unions to organize nonunion employees." The triad of potential answers—favoring the easing of strictures, desiring to make it even harder for unions to organize, or advocating no change at all—would be expected to encourage the "middle way," no-change alternative. Pollsters have long noted that respondents, given three choices of amount or degree, will likely select the moderate alternative.[78] Americans' inherent tendency toward compromise and support for the status quo in the absence of compelling need for change was also heightened in this case by a lack of information about the whole problem. The question had no elaborate prefacing that could have given rudimentary background.

As expected, 22 percent of the respondents favored the proposed legislation, 25 percent wanted a tougher union organizing posture, and 40 percent said the status quo seemed perfectly acceptable. The survey on labor's behalf demonstrated just as convincingly that public opinion was squarely in their corner. Between 67 and 73 percent of the public favored "a law making it easier for workers in a company to vote on whether or not they wish to join a labor union."[79] The issue for the respondent now turned on the great American qualities of individualism and a citizen's freedom of choice.

These poll results, contradictory on their face, demonstrate the schizophrenic nature of public opinion. As every individual knows from listening to debate, there are usually popular and valid points to be made on both sides of the same issue, and one can find oneself agreeing with principles that lead unavoidably to antithetical conclusions. Careful wording of a question can tap the desired response, as the labor law example showed. In that case one suspects that the bias was intentional, but the chastening discovery for pollsters was how frequently bias of some type affects the responses of truly "nonpartisan" surveys. (Since no word is really neutral, and every word communicates or symbolizes something, bias in some direction is absolutely unavoidable.) In 1953 two Korean War opinion surveys taken within a month by the same polling firm showed a 37 percent variation in the public's evaluation of the war.[80] Only 27 percent responded favorably to this question: "As things stand now, do you feel the war in Korea has been worth fighting, or not?" But in answer to a subsequent question, which some observers believe tested patriotism more than anything else, 64 percent of the respondents agreed that "the United States was right" to have sent in troops.[81] Long after the Korean War had ended—shortly after U.S. withdrawal from the Vietnam War, in fact—Louis Harris asked a pair of questions about Korea again. Only 14 percent favored U.S. military involvement "if North Korea attacked South Korea."[82] But a 43 percent plurality favored military action when the question included prefatory background information:

The U.S. has 36,000 troops and airmen in South Korea. If North Korea invaded South Korea, we have a firm commitment to defend South Korea with our own military forces. If South Korea were invaded by Communist North Korea, would you favor or oppose the U.S. using troops, air power and naval power to defend South Korea?[83]

Part of the explanation for the wide variance is obviously the pollster's decision to "educate" the ignorant respondent on the issue. In doing so, though, the pollster is "on dangerous ground," as Mervin Field flatly declared.[84] In seeking to tap a latent disposition, a survey researcher may be *creating* an opinion where none existed before. On many a prominent public issue, a shocking proportion of the public has no view at all; many people, in fact, may be only dimly aware of its existence. Pollsters had been puzzled by the wide divergence in public surveys on the U.S.–U.S.S.R.'s Strategic Arms Limitation Treaties (SALT II) until a *New York Times*/CBS News poll found that 77 percent of the respondents could not identify the two nations involved.[85] There are other difficulties with question wording as well. Some questions are vague and baffling, making respondents feel that no answer really fits. Cultural biases may also be present. Psychologist Kenneth B. Clark and Percy Sutton, the Manhattan Borough president, formed a new black-oriented survey research firm (Data Black Public Opinion Polls) in 1979 because of alleged culturally biased wording in the prominent national polls and the relatively low number of blacks in most polling samples.[86]

CONSTRUCTION, ANALYSIS, AND INTERPRETATION

It would be grossly misleading to suggest that polling firms are Chinese take-outs, where what you want is what you get. But the polling instrument and how it is designed are major determinants of a poll's results. Every serious pollster—and the best-known political pollsters in both parties are certainly in this category—takes the greatest care in the construction of his survey. Pollsters estimate that, depending on the purposes for which they are conducted, between one-third and three-quarters of the questions in their political surveys are standard and used repeatedly. The exact wordings have been devised and tested over time so that there can be a high degree of confidence in their relative objectivity. Identical questions on a series of polls are also useful for comparative purposes (in assessing regional or national trends, for example). Standardization is overdone by some pollsters, of course, and the consultant's convenience can unfortunately substitute for personalized attention. On occasion the prefabricated, "cut-and-paste" polls leave telltale traces. One prominent national political pollster distributed a draft questionnaire to a Virginia client that repeatedly asked respondents about conditions in New Jersey. In fairness, most pollsters do make a conscientious effort to research each campaign before drawing up the questionnaire, often journeying to the state or national campaign headquarters to consult at length with the strategists and in-house analysts.

Professional pollsters permit no consultation about the selection of the sample; that task is strictly their own. Even with an expert in charge, however, there is still plenty of room for error. The only acceptable, reliable method of sampling is the "random" or probability one. In this method each person in the population universe has, theoretically, an equal chance to be selected for the survey, and no element of nonrandom human choice is involved in the selection of respondents. Using census tracts, atlases, and computers, a polling firm first randomly selects a set of sampling points for its in-home interviewees (towns, cities, and so on, where specific respondents will be chosen); finally, the actual homes and even sometimes the individuals within each home are randomly designated.[87] Every major survey research organization now uses random sampling, although this was not always the case.

Another form of sampling, the "quota," was assigned part of the blame for the 1948 Truman-Dewey fiasco,[88] and was widely employed prior to that time. In a quota sample the choice of the respondents is left up to the interviewer, who is merely assigned quotas of each major population subgroup to interview based on each group's proportion of the population. Quota surveys are nonrandom since the element of human choice is involved, and therefore the theory of probability does not apply.[89]

Clustering interviews within sampling points does not affect randomness; rather it makes the selection of respondents a two-step random process. But the technique does require that a reasonable number of interview sites be selected and that their geographic locations be diverse. If too many interviews are conducted at a single spot, there is too little heterogeneity to assure a representative sample, and this is where many modern political surveys fall short.[90] The number of interviews conducted at each geographic sampling point ranges from as few as four to as many as a dozen or more. The Gallup Organization used to assign ten interviews to each of 150 sampling points (producing its total sample size of 1,500), but in the interest of increasing dispersion, just five interviews are now assigned to more than 300 sampling points. Obviously, the costs are greater, but the results are much sounder. It is not uncommon for some political polling firms to maximize their profit margins by clustering fifteen or more interviews at a single place, putting the representative reliability of their surveys at great risk.

Whatever the number of sampling points and the total size of the sample, an automatic probability margin of error exists. The larger the sample, the lower is the margin of error. A sample size of about 1,000 carries with it a 3 percent margin of error—that is, the percentages in the survey's responses are representative of the population within 3 percentage points in either direction. A 5 percent margin of error is found with a 400-person survey.[91]

These statements are made at a "95 percent confidence level." Therefore, in 95 out of 100 surveys of the same population with a comparable sample size, any error in the polls will be within the indicated margin; in the other 5 surveys, the margin of error would probably be above or below the suggested range. Since hundreds of political polls are conducted each election year, statistical probability discloses that at least a few will likely be off the mark even if conducted flawlessly, with potentially disastrous consequences for the unlucky candidates who have purchased them.

The possibility of disaster is increased by the growing use of "weighting techniques" to "perfect" incomplete samples. In short, pollsters sometimes find it necessary to give extra weight to the answers of respondents belonging to subgroups still underrepresented when all the interviewing is done. These subgroups are by no means purely demographic ones. Gallup increases the weight of respondents who indicate they had been away from home during several previous evenings, assuming they are much like the people the interviewer could not find in their residences. This guesswork gives more room for error, but its use often cannot be avoided because of the mushrooming proportion of "refuse-to-reply" and "not-at-home" respondents. While once gauged at between 10 and 22 percent of the sample, those who are unavailable or refuse to be polled now total between 40 and 55 percent for in-home interviews and between 25 and 35 percent for telephone samples.[92] About 20 percent of all actual respondents are also "reluctant interviewees," who evade, object, or refuse to answer one or more questions on the poll, so some data is less randomly representative than the overall margin of error would indicate. However justified, weighting is a risky business, as the *Minneapolis Tribune* recently discovered. A market research firm based in Phoenix, Arizona, that had contracted to do the newspaper's Minnesota poll severed ties with the paper after the 1978 midterm elections, charging that the *Tribune's* editors had wrongfully adjusted survey results prior to publication. The original survey findings had correctly predicted a GOP sweep of the major statewide posts, but the newspaper (perhaps getting cold feet about the mildly surprising forecast) weighted the data to reflect what it believed would be a more representative cross-section of the state's electorate, with the effect of inflating the projected Democratic vote. Election day, though, showed the original poll had probably done a better job of surveying *likely* voters, and the newspaper had egg on its front page.

Flagrant violations of polling procedure occur frequently in yet another area, subgroup analysis. A 400-person poll's summary results, which are drawn from the responses of the entire interviewed sample, may have a 5 percent margin of error, but the subgroup breakdowns by smaller state or national regions or racial and ethnic classifications have much greater margins of error (easily 10 percent or more). A 10 percent error margin means that if the poll showed 50 percent of the black respondents favoring a candidate, the real figure could actually lie anywhere between 40 percent and 60 percent—an enormous margin. Subgroup analysis in small-sample polls is greatly suspect, then, but analyses of the data breakdowns are often made by pollsters as though the margin of error was minimal. A "trend" is established when a candidate gains 4 percentage points among black respondents from one poll to another, even though the 10 percent error margin clearly forecloses any such conclusion. As polling costs increase, the pressure on campaigns to have smaller samples increases, but it does not seem to be accepted that a smaller sample must necessarily entail the price of more detailed analysis.

Loss of precise analysis is an excruciating price to pay, for interpretation is the finest art of the pollster, and also the area where a lack of data can seriously impede a poll's campaign utility. Interpretation can only follow the purposeful and insightful construction of a tightly drawn polling instrument.[93] Only rarely do polls adequately explore the complex mental set of voter attitudes about campaigns, and consequently the findings are superficial. Peter Hart ruefully gave as one example his 1978 polling in Minnesota for U.S. Senate candidate Donald Fraser. Three months before the Democratic primary, Fraser led his opponent, Robert Short, 67 to 16 percent in a trial heat. Hart was uneasy about the figures, suspecting they did not tell the full story, so he devised a "horse-race" question that dropped the two candidates' names and merely described them using their backgrounds and issue positions. Under these conditions, Fraser had a marginal 49 to 42 percent edge, presaging Short's eventual come-from-behind victory.[94] Screening questions to determine likely voters are also notoriously unreliable and are becoming more so, as voter turnout declines and the Independent bloc in the electorate continues to grow and delays the voting decision until just before the election, or election day itself. Although they are just elaborate forms of guesswork, pollsters have devised complex formulas for screening respondents. Lance Tarrance, for example, classifies respondents on a four-point "propensity-to-vote" scale based on a number of screening questions in the poll and a predictive barometer that uses personal data (such as educational level, age, length of residence, and type of housing).[95] Pollsters are finding it increasingly difficult to deal with the undecided. Should their electoral choices be inferred from the clues they give in answer to other questions, or should they be assigned to candidates on a strict proportional basis? One solution that can be applied to in-home interviewing is the use of the secret ballot. Gallup reduced the percentage of undecideds from 15 percent to 4 percent with the use of this simple device.[96]

Methodological difficulties notwithstanding, no richer source of polling error exists than the pollster's own frailties. Unless a pollster is extremely careful, he can selectively interpret, seeing what he and his candidate want to see. Not only do pollsters often become too close to their candidates to remain sufficiently objective, but they develop a stake in their own analyses, which can have detrimental consequences for their clients. "If a pollster has done an early survey and made recommendations on how the campaign should go, then as a counselor he's committed to that course of action," Mervin Field explained. "Every poll he takes thereafter is a test of those recommendations. If the policies aren't working, the human thing to do is to say the evidence is not clear-cut." [97] Moreover, pollsters sometimes use the data to inject their personal opinions, or they assume their own views are shared by the general public. "Their surveys may be more a reflection of the pollsters' assumptions than of the electorate's mood," surmised Albert Cantril. [98] Patrick Caddell's determination that the nation was experiencing a "crisis of confidence" is a case in point. Caddell rather testily rejects criticism that he interpolated rather than interpreted in reaching his famous conclusion:

I think, frankly, people are often more critical of the messenger than the message, because everybody's data support my conclusion. Nobody can contend anything other than that people's confidence in our institutions or their optimism about the country has declined. . . . As I said, most of it is data-generated. A lot of people who criticize it try to pretend that there's no data that exists—the Peter Pan principle that if you keep wishing, if we all chant "I believe, I believe," then Tinkerbell will live. There is a lot of that among political commentators. . . .

Yet political scientist Warren E. Miller, among others, using extensive survey research data, vigorously contests Caddell's contentions and refutes his suggestion that "everybody's data support" them. [99] Some polling experts apparently are quite convinced that Tinkerbell lives.

PROBLEMS WITH INTERVIEWERS AND RESPONDENTS

Even with a perfectly selected sample and a thoughtfully constructed questionnaire, a poll can easily fail. Few observers outside the polling field are aware of the crucial role played in survey research by the interviewers. The interviewers' degree of skill and training is absolutely critical to the quality of a poll's data. The interviewer must be able quickly to establish a rapport (even on the telephone) with a wide range of respondents, who must feel comfortable during the interview if full and revealing replies are to be forthcoming. The interviewer, while appearing at ease, must be on guard at all times to avoid biased phrasing or remarks that might unintentionally sway a respondent. He must be able to stick to the script exactly and to probe delicately, and he must be patient and persistent in the field, not only during interviews, but also in the frustrating task of catching his chosen respondents at home.

Finding good interviewers, training them properly, and assuring appropriate supervision of their activities are constant headaches for every polling firm, and because the measurement of interviewers' preparedness is qualitative rather than quantitative, some firms cut corners in this area without fear of detection. Especially questionable are many of the "partial package" arrangements where a firm provides the questionnaire and sample and the campaign provides the volunteers to conduct the poll. The volunteers are ostensibly trained by the firm, but the instruction is usually rudimentary and the supervision during the interviews wholly inadequate. The unfortunately widespread belief among campaign officials that anyone can conduct a poll, and the willingness of some of the large political polling firms to participate in schemes of this sort, has produced a number of inferior surveys. These cut-rate polls save money, of course, but they are usually cheap in worth as well as cost. Most reputable polling firms have a full-time field director just to do the hiring and training for the high-turnover interviewer posts.[100] Interviewers tend to be students, people between jobs, and middle-aged housewives (who are much preferred because of their tendency to keep the job for longer periods). Strict supervision is required to insure quality control, and quite commonly plug-in supervision monitors are used in telephone polling.

It is much more difficult to ascertain the validity of in-home interviewing, and cheating by interviewers is a problem of unknown proportions. While some pollsters claim that less than 3 percent of all professional interviewers falsify questionnaires (i.e., never actually conduct real interviews and fill out the forms themselves), other observers claim that at least a fifth of all interviewers make up some of their returns.[101] There are ways of checking up, of course. Business-reply postal cards can be sent to interviewees to verify that an interview occurred and that certain questions were asked, and sometimes, when there are suspicions, respondents can be telephoned directly and quizzed. But most pollsters do not bother to check regularly, lacking the time, the resources, and even the interest to do so.

Fiddling interviewers may be apprehended, but virtually nothing can be done about fibbing respondents. Many people try to please, or at least not offend, polltakers, telling them what they believe they want to hear.[102] Spanish-speaking interviewers in Puerto Rican, Cuban, or Mexican-American neighborhoods might improve frankness, but this is no cure for selective memory. The Survey Research Center at the University of Michigan discovered evidence either of massive ballot fraud or of an amnesia epidemic in 1964 when fully 64 percent of adult voters distinctly remembered having cast their 1960 ballots for John F. Kennedy, who won one of the closest presidential elections in U.S. history.[103] In preelection polls, voters can also lie about their choices,[104] but this dishonesty can be unintentional since, at the time of the questioning, individuals sometimes have not thought through their choices. Patrick Caddell found this occurrence to be widespread in primaries, where decisions are of a less serious, more preliminary nature. Because of it he instituted a two-step method to force a respondent to consider many of the factors that will determine his choice in the end. After a person is asked to reveal the name of the candidate he is tentatively supporting, the interviewer immediately follows up with a short series of probes and open-ended questions about his decisions, gently coaxing the respondent to evaluate his choice. Finally the interviewer again asks the respondent to name his candidate, and a startling shift sometimes occurs in the results of the trial heat.[105]

Peter Hart also found that people are unwilling to admit forthrightly their prejudices, even to themselves, so the bias must be plumbed obliquely. When Congresswoman Ella Grasso sought the governorship of Connecticut in 1974, voters denied they had much of a worry about electing a woman when pointedly asked about it, but 39 percent confided their belief that a male chief executive would be better when Hart couched the question in terms that made sexism seem more acceptable.[106] (Grasso overcame the prejudices and won overwhelmingly.) People do not readily admit their ignorance, either. A recent survey experiment, asking respondents for their views on the Public Affairs Act of 1975, found fully a third of the interviewees had very definite opinions on the subject. This was especially intriguing because the legislation is nonexistent.[107]

Survey research has made great strides since the primitive and highly inaccurate straw polls of a half century ago, and virtually all politicians, from president to city councillor, have been convinced of polls' campaign utility. As the number of private and public polling firms has skyrocketed, the political pollster has gradually outgrown the role of mere technician, emerging from the cocoon a full-fledged strategist who influences campaign activity in a wide variety of areas.

The Pols and the Polls

Beyond the campaign, pollsters have assumed the mantel of vox populi, becoming in some eyes oracles and philosopher-kings.

An elaborate technology has grown up around polling, and there are many weapons in the polling consultant's arsenal of blue smoke and mirrors. Specialized, calendar-oriented forms of surveys (such as the benchmark, follow-up telephone, panel, and tracking polls) have been developed, and the price of each kind has risen significantly. Increased costs in turn have led to widespread abandonment of political in-home surveying and a concomitant surge in telephone polling (with an accompanying sacrifice in data quality). Cheap-rate "package deals" that cut corners in questionable ways have also become more common.

The political power of pollsters and their polls is considerable. They affect the choice of issues in a campaign (and thus eventual governmental policy), especially when their candidate-clients are "flexible." Unquestionably, they help elect candidates, providing reams of enormously useful information on issues, perceptions, and so forth. The quality of the data is constantly improving, thanks to statistical innovations such as multidimensional scaling. Some of the new devices, such as the Qube system, also have rather frightening implications for a polling-addicted society.

Yet for all their impressive qualities and offerings, on closer inspection both pollsters and polls appear surprisingly frail. Polls, after all, are like computers in at least one crucial respect: However awe-inspiring are their powers, they can only do what they are programmed to do. The mistakes of the designer, the interviewer, and the analyst become the poll's failures and, ultimately, the campaign's failures, when combined with the misuse of polling data by the candidate. Like all other new campaign technologies, survey research is more art than science, and the art has notable flaws. At base, public opinion is too fluid for polls to be more than a brief second's snapshot of an object moving in time; viewed in this manner, polls can properly be seen as more historical than predictive. Neither can they quite pierce the interwoven layers of opinions, some brightly colored and others pale, that are held by a public sometimes believing quite contradictory principles simultaneously. Even error-free polls are frequently misconstrued by candidates (in a desperate search for mystical guidance in their "to run or not to run" decisions) and by the press, who recklessly play the absurd numbers game of false expectations with great abandon.

Error-free polls are as rare as perfect specimens in any craft, though. Pollster and client prejudice not uncommonly shape a poll's results even before the data is collected. Moreover, wholly objective surveys are many times just as biased, however unintentionally. The wording of questions is unavoidably prejudiced, sometimes culturally, always attitudinally. The simple inclusion of a particular question can create, unsuspectingly, a false result by manufacturing an opinion where none actually existed. The construction, analysis, and interpretation of polls is similarly fraught with opportunities for error. The selection of the sample is of fundamental importance, and many factors (such as lack of dispersion) can have harmful side effects. By themselves, the statistical probabilities associated with random sampling guarantee a small degree of error, and the possibilities are multiplied by faulty subgroup analysis, the risky practice of weighting, and the baffling process of screening likely voters. Pollsters can misinterpret surveys quite easily by reading their own views and opinions into the data. Interviewers as well have plenty of chances to skew polling results, and thorough training, proper supervision, and checks to avoid cheating are called for (but not always done adequately). Individuals who are imposed upon to submit to interviews occasionally take subconscious revenge by lying, or selectively remembering, or obscuring their real attitudes (even to themselves), practices that are normally beyond correction but that nevertheless produce faulty polls.

With all this room for error, the average political poll is almost certain to be flawed in at least a couple of respects, and the sooner this is accepted and understood by candidates, press, and public, the healthier and more realistic will be the perceptions of the polling consultant's role in the election campaign and beyond.

NOTES

1. Speech given at the annual meeting of the American Association of Political Consultants, Washington, D.C., November 30, 1978.

2. See Woodrow Wilson International Center for Scholars, "TV News and the 1976 Election: A Dialogue," *The Wilson Quarterly*, vol. 1, no. 3 (Spring 1977), p. 87n. By the editor's tabulation, CBS and *The New York Times* jointly conducted twenty polls; NBC aired thirty polls; ABC commissioned seven Louis Harris surveys and assigned a maximum of fifteen correspondents to the task.

3. See Charles W. Roll, Jr., and Albert H. Cantril, *Polls: Their Use and Misuse in Politics* (New York: Basic Books, 1972), pp. 7–11. See also: Richard Jensen, "Democracy

The Pols and the Polls

by the Numbers," *Public Opinion*, vol. 3, no. 1A (February/March 1980): 53–59; Dan Nimmo, *The Political Persuaders: The Techniques of Modern Election Campaigns* (Englewood Cliffs, N.J.: Prentice-Hall, 1970), pp. 85–86; and David Gergen and William Schambra, "Pollsters and Polling," *The Wilson Quarterly*, vol. 3, no. 3 (Spring 1979): 61–72.

4. The first *paid*, privately conducted poll for a political candidate was taken in 1946 by Elmo Roper for Jacob K. Javits. Later Republican U.S. senator from New York, Javits was seeking his first political office, the U.S. representative's seat from New York's twenty-first congressional district. See Jacob Javits, "How I Used a Poll in Campaigning for Congress," *Public Opinion Quarterly*, vol. 11 (Summer 1947): 222–226.

5. Stanley Kelley, Jr., *Professional Public Relations and Political Power* (Baltimore: Johns Hopkins, 1956), p. 189.

6. Nimmo, *The Political Persuaders*, p. 85. Almost all of these polls were privately contracted to professionals.

7. An examination of the files of Johnson's major White House political aides at the LBJ Library uncovered literally dozens of presidential memoranda about polls all through Johnson's term of office. Apparently Oliver Quayle would have served as the President's permanent campaign pollster had LBJ decided to seek reelection in 1968. See "Memorandum from Marvin Watson to the President," December 5, 1967, Office Files of LBJ aide Marvin Watson: Arthur Krim, Box 26 (1375A), LBJ Library.

8. Alan Baron, "The Slippery Art of Polls," *Politics Today*, vol. 6, no. 5 (January/February 1980): 51.

9. See Robert Agranoff, ed. *The New Style in Election Campaigns* (2nd ed.) (Boston: Holbrook Press, 1976), p. 146; and Jensen, "Democracy by the Numbers," p. 53.

10. See Kelley, *Professional Public Relations and Political Power*, p. 53, n. 22.

11. About three dozen newspapers conduct polls at regular intervals, and the number doing so is almost certainly increasing. See Nimmo, *The Political Persuaders*, pp. 209–210.

12. CBS and *The New York Times* work together; NBC polls in conjunction with the Associated Press; and ABC has contracted surveys and commentary from Louis Harris. More recently, ABC has joined forces with *The Washington Post*.

13. The Qube system was installed in 29,000 homes in Columbus, Ohio, by Warner Cable Company. Each subscriber pays an additional $3.45 monthly for the use of ten extra free channels and access to ten more special pay-per-view ones. The polling component operates through a miniature computer terminal in each home connected to the television set, which has buttons respondents can push to answer questions superimposed on the screen.

14. See *The Washington Post*, July 7, 1979, and August 24, 1979. The ABC network also tried a different sort of instant participation poll after the Carter-Reagan presidential debate in October 1980. Viewers called special telephone lines to "vote" for the candidate they believed had "won" the debate. ABC's gimmick was widely and properly criticized, and the results (about two to one for Reagan) were skewed by a number of methodological problems, including (a) timing—the East Coast was retiring, while Reagan's western strongholds were in prime time; (b) the 50-cent charge to participate; (c) the self-selection involved (as opposed to random sampling); and (d) the discrimination of the telephone setup, which apparently recorded "votes" from rural regions more readily than those from congested urban areas. While ABC commentators occasionally mentioned on air that their poll was "unscientific," an untrained public could hardly be expected to make the distinction, particularly when the results were presented on an official-looking, psuedo-election night tally board. Judging by the banner headlines accorded the ABC "poll" results on the day after the debate, it is apparent that many journalists also failed to recognize the bogus nature of the ABC gimmick.

15. Baron, "The Slippery Art of Polls," p. 21. In fact, Gallup majored in journalism and Elmo Roper began as a jewelry salesman.

16. As quoted in *National Journal*, December 15, 1979, p. 2093.

17. The sample is sold without D.M.I.'s name attached to it, however, so that the organization is not directly associated with an undertaking over which it has no control (but which could potentially affect its reputation).

18. *National Journal*, April 10, 1976, p. 475.

19. Most of the "name" private pollsters do not belong to the American Association

of Political Consultants, the more general trade association that has long been dominated by generalist and media professionals. Pollsters seem to prefer the company of their peers, and there are several other organizations designed exclusively for the polling profession, including the National Council on Public Polls, the American Association of Public Opinion Research, and the American Institute of Public Opinion.

20. *National Journal*, December 15, 1979, p. 2093; and "Articles of Association—National Association of Political Pollsters" (1972), Article III, Section 1: Qualifications (for Membership).

21. *The Washington Post*, February 28, 1980.

22. Baron, "The Slippery Art of Polls," p. 21.

23. *National Journal*, May 1, 1976, p. 574.

24. Ibid., p. 575.

25. The primary sources for much of this discussion are the author's personal interviews with pollsters. See also *National Journal*, December 15, 1979, p. 2094.

26. See *Campaign Insights*, vol. 8, no. 2 (January 15, 1972): 9.

27. See *Campaigning Reports*, vol. 2, no. 3 (February 7, 1980): 3.

28. Focus groups will be discussed more fully in the next chapter. Their use by media consultants (to test completed advisements) is actually more widespread and common than their utilization by pollsters.

29. *National Journal*, December 15, 1979, p. 2094.

30. Roll and Cantril, *Polls*, pp. 96–102. See also Gergen and Schramba, "Pollsters and Polling," p. 67.

31. Dispersion is an important element in sample selection. See Roll and Cantril, *Polls*.

32. There is another sampling problem with telephone interviews: how to account for the significant proportion of unlisted telephone numbers. Random-digit dialing, giving every number an equal chance of being selected, is one less-than-perfect solution. Other pollsters prefer a well-controlled and stratified regular telephone sample (using telephone books to select the respondents), claiming that random-digit dialing is not stratified sufficiently, calls commercial listings as well as personal listings indiscriminately (adding to interviewer fatigue), and generally leaves too much control up to the interviewer. (The more discretion an interviewer has, the greater the chances of error.)

33. Campaign Study Group, Institute of Politics, JFK School of Government, Harvard University, "An Analysis of the Impact of the Federal Election Campaign Act, 1972–78" (Cambridge, Mass.: May 1979): 175.

34. Richard Wirthlin suggested this example to the *National Journal* (December 15, 1979, p. 2094):

A sample of 384 persons would provide a 95 percent chance that the margin of error would not exceed 5 percent. A sample that size cost $35 per interview, for a total of $13,440. To reduce the margin of error to 4 percent, the sample would have to be increased to 600, at a cost of $33 per interview and $19,800 in all; for 3 percent, a sample of 1,065 at $31 each and a total of $33,015; for 2 percent, 2,390 persons at $27 each and a total of $64,530; and for 1 percent, 9,423 persons at $25 each and $235,575 in all.

35. This estimate was given by several pollsters, and the *National Journal* calculated similarly (May 1, 1976, p. 578). See also Nimmo, *The Political Persuaders*, p. 87. This percentage has grown slightly from Roll and Cantril's 3 to 5 percent estimate for campaigns in the 1960s (*Polls*, pp. 3–4).

36. Gergen and Schambra, "Pollsters and Polling," pp. 64–65; see also *National Journal*, May 1, 1976, pp. 576–577.

37. This instance and the practice of sliding scales and parallel charges for commercial clients are mentioned in the *National Journal*, ibid.

38. Estimated figure is for the year 1978 in Gergen and Schambra, "Pollsters and Polling," pp. 64–65.

39. *National Journal*, January, 1980, p. 20.

40. *National Journal*, May 1, 1976, p. 578. In 1976 package deals were contracted with Hart in Rhode Island and Maryland, with Market Opinion Research in Ohio and Pennsylvania, and with D.M.I. in numerous areas.

41. Several interviewees indicated that this case was not an isolated one. A partial

services agreement is a risky investment, because interviewer training and performance are absolutely essential to a well-done poll.

42. *National Journal,* December 15, 1979, p. 2092.

43. The closest polling comes to scientific precision is probably the final Gallup preelection-day poll, when the number of interviewees is doubled to 3,000 from the usual 1,500 (a result of the Truman-Dewey debacle of 1948). As Alan Baron suggests,

> The question in that final survey is clear-cut. There is no ambiguity in its phrasing, no uncertainty in the meanings of the responses. The voters have focused their attention on the subject; the vast majority have made up their minds. The pollster is, in effect, asking a question of fact (what will you do?) as much as one of opinion (what do you believe?).

See Alan Baron, "The Slippery Art of Polls," pp. 21–22. Even the final Gallup Poll was less than impressive in 1980, however, when a Reagan victory was forecast as probable but narrow.

Retrospective postelection polls also permit more leisurely and considered analysis. Unfortunately, they are rare because of the extra expense and a lack of candidate interest after the election is over. Opinion Research Corporation conducted one for Goldwater in 1964, and since then the National Republican Congressional Committee has shown the greatest interest in postelection polls.

44. Cited in Gergen and Schambra, "Pollsters and Polling," p. 71.

45. See Roll and Cantril, *Polls,* pp. 117–135.

46. Scaling, which measures intensity, should always be used in a campaign poll so that cross-tabulations can show the voter subgroups most usefully targeted.

47. *National Journal,* May 1, 1976, pp. 575–576.

48. Baron, "The Slippery Art of Polls," p. 21.

49. Nimmo, *The Political Persuaders,* p. 93. Helstoski went on to win reelection narrowly in 1966.

50. *National Journal,* December 15, 1979, p. 2094.

51. See Roll and Cantril, *Polls,* pp. 18–37.

52. See *The Wilson Quarterly,* vol. 3, no. 3 (Spring 1979): 85.

53. *The New York Times,* May 17, 1979.

54. *E.P.O.,* vol. 1, no. 1 (January/February 1979): 8.

55. Preprimary polls not only have to contend with voter disinterest, but also with the notoriously thorny problem of determining which voters are likely to cast a ballot in a relatively low turnout contest. Both of these factors *should* humble the purveyors of primary polls but rarely do.

56. This sequence is taken from Timothy Crouse, *The Boys on the Bus* (New York: Ballantine, 1973), pp. 153–56, 366. The ABC poll was actually leaked to rival CBS News, which announced the results first. Polls have become so attractive to news departments that they are worth scooping.

57. The poll might also have had precisely the opposite effect: emboldening McGovern voters and discouraging those backing Humphrey. There is no data to support either conclusion.

58. However, a Roper survey in 1964 found that Goldwater did 4 percent better in a secret ballot than in an open interview format. See Gergen and Schambra, "Pollsters and Polling," p. 70. Interestingly, Ronald Reagan—perceived by some as an ideologically extreme candidate during his four gubernatorial and presidential campaigns—has usually won by larger margins on election days than campaign polls predicted, but this could be due to differential turnout as easily as the diffidence of voters in being identified with a socially unacceptable candidate.

59. See Agranoff, ed., *The New Style in Election Campaigns,* p. 363. Also see Harold A. Mendelsohn and Irving Crespi, *Polls, Television, and the New Politics* (New York: Chandler, 1970). Mendelsohn and Crespi, after a careful examination of polls in presidential elections from 1952 to 1968, dispute the bandwagon effect. There is at least as much circumstantial evidence to justify belief in a reverse bandwagon effect. For example, in the 1978 Illinois U.S. Senate contest, the publication of a *Sun-Times* newspaper poll showing Democratic challenger Alex Smith unexpectedly leading GOP incumbent Charles Percy stunned and mobilized Republican workers. Said Percy's consultant,

Douglas Bailey: "The *Sun-Times* poll saved Percy." See *The Washington Post*, November 15, 1978.

60. *The Houston Post*, November 26, 1978.

61. See Roll and Cantrill, *Polls*, pp. 39–64; also *National Journal*, December 15, 1979, p. 2094.

62. Normally, the introduction will read something like this for a doorstep interview: "Hello, I'm _____ from Public Opinion Company, an international research company with headquarters in Chicago. We are making a study of problems and political figures in [name of state or locality] and would like to have your opinion." Because mobile young voters are often underinterviewed, the interviewer will ask to speak to a registered voter between the ages of eighteen and twenty-four. If there is no such person currently living at the address, any registered voter is fair game, although each interviewer has a strict quota of male and female respondents.

63. One pollster phrases his question like this: "There are many reasons why people are unable to get to the polls on election day, but did you happen to have a chance to vote for [name of office] in [year]?"

64. The National Republican Congressional Committee's research has suggested that such "objective" data can be used to indicate which candidates have the greatest chance of victory. Winning candidates in one NRCC study achieved at least 50 percent name identification by Labor Day and at least 70 percent by election day. Winners also had an overall favorability rating (i.e., respondents felt generally good about them) at least four times as great as the unfavorability rating. See NRCC, "1978 Congressional Post-Election Survey" (Washington, D.C., 1979): 22, 26.

65. See *National Journal*, May 1, 1976, p. 577.

66. An open-ended question elicits a spontaneous and wholly volunteered response, without the interviewer suggesting specific alternative answers. A closed question has a list of responses attached from which the respondent chooses.

67. The 1976 Carter and Reagan illustrations that follow are taken from personal interviews and the *National Journal*, May 1, 1976, p. 579, and December 15, 1979, p. 2092. For additional examples of professional polling's successes, see Joseph Napolitan, *The Election Game and How to Win It* (New York: Doubleday, 1972), pp. 113–136; and *E.P.O.*, vol. 1, no. 1 (January/February, 1979): 65.

68. Immediately before the general election most political prognosticators had bet that Louisiana would end up in Ford's column.

69. When asked to rank issues of importance to them, voters had placed the foreign policy group fifteenth or lower. Absent international crisis, pollsters almost always find domestic issues predominant.

70. *National Journal*, December 15, 1978, p. 2092.

71. *The Washington Post*, February 28, 1980.

72. Xandra Kayden, *Campaign Organization* (Lexington, Mass.: D.C. Health, 1978), p. 113.

73. *The Washington Post*, November 15, 1978.

74. Ibid.

75. *Los Angeles Times*, August 5, 1979.

76. Baron, "The Slippery Art of Polls," pp. 22–23.

77. See *National Journal*, November 4, 1978, p. 1777.

78. See Roll and Cantril, *Polls*, pp. 115–116, n. 7. The authors suggest that an even number of alternatives should be provided whenever possible (e.g., four answers of degree such as "a great deal," "a fair amount," "not very much," "none at all").

79. The law was favored by 73 percent for large companies, and 67 percent wished to see it apply to small business as well.

80. In this example and in all the cases cited in this section, it is theoretically possible for the variation in results to have been due to time lag—that is, one poll was taken later than another, after major events had intervened to change public opinion. However, it appears unlikely that this occurred to any great degree in any of these instances.

81. Gergen and Schambra, "Pollsters and Polling," pp. 69–70.

82. See *Public Opinion*, vol. 3, no. 1A (February/March 1979): 26. The exact wording of the question was: "There has been a lot of discussion about what circumstances

might justify United States military involvement, including the use of United States troops. Do you feel you would favor or oppose U.S. military involvement if North Korea attacked South Korea?"

83. This question was asked in a May 1975 Harris poll, the other in a December 1974 survey.

84. *Los Angeles Times,* August 5, 1979.

85. Gergen and Schramba, "Pollsters and Polling," p. 71. Two almost simultaneous SALT polls cited in Baron ("The Slippery Art of Polls," p. 22) indicated unusual variations in response distribution. A Harris Poll asking, "Do you favor or oppose the U.S. and Russia coming to a new SALT arms control agreement?" found 72 percent in favor and 17 percent opposed. A *Time*/Yankelovich poll queried: "The government is attempting to negotiate a new agreement with Moscow called SALT II, limiting the number of strategic nuclear weapons either country will manufacture. Do you favor our signing this kind of agreement with the Russians or do you think its too risky?" This time only 32 percent favored SALT and 56 percent opposed it. Clearly, the more cautious language of the second question took its toll, but it is also true that most respondents' lack of much of an information base about the subject facilitated the wording's apparent influence. Because of findings like those in the SALT polls, the Yankelovich firm has recently developed a "mushiness index" to test respondents' knowledge and concern about any subject being surveyed. Each respondent is asked a series of questions about whether he talks much with family or friends about the subject, whether he is strongly committed to his position or likely to change his mind, and so forth. From these questions an index is calculated that measures the indefiniteness or "mushiness" of a respondent's opinion, and it is a useful device for determining whether the public's view is formed or fluid, and for separating those with firm, established opinions from those who have yet to make a definite, knowledgeable choice.

86. Even in a sample as large as 1,500, there would probably be only about 140 blacks, an adequate reflection of their percentage in the general population but hopelessly inadequate for drawing conclusions about subgroups within the black populace (such as college-educated blacks).

87. See Nimmo, *The Political Persuaders,* pp. 95–105, and Roll and Cantril, *Polls,* pp. 65–93, for a further discussion of sampling techniques. For reasons of cost, all in-home interviewers cannot be selected at random directly from the population; travel expenses and convenience require selection of relatively few geographical locations. This is technically called "modified random sampling." Sampling problems with telephone polling were discussed in a previous section. See especially note 32 above.

88. The 1948 lesson was apparently lost on the British. Quota samples were used as late as 1970 in the United Kingdom, when pollsters who had almost unanimously predicted a substantial Labour victory had to explain a large Tory electoral triumph.

89. Another form of nonrandom survey, the "purposive" sample, is sometimes required. To get a sample of centenarians, for instance, one would have to restrict the search to nursing homes, and choosiness would be a financial luxury.

90. See especially Roll and Cantril, *Polls,* pp. 77–79.

91. The margin of error is actually slightly greater than these estimates suggest as the percentages get closer to a 50–50 split, but the implications of this statistical quirk in political surveys are negligible. Also, as one can see by comparing these two examples, sample size has to be drastically increased to achieve a relatively small reduction in the margin of error. See note 34 above.

92. See Nimmo, *The Political Persuaders,* pp. 101–102, and Baron, "The Slippery Art of Polls," p. 25. People appear to be more mobile in the evenings, or less accessible, and also more reluctant to answer their doors, perhaps because of rising crime rates.

93. A separate methodological subfield has developed around the construction of the questionnaire, which should have a logical sequence of questions (perhaps placing the most difficult and prying items last), good transitions between sections, "relaxer" questions to put the respondent at ease, adequate interviewer instructions, and so forth.

94. *The Washington Post,* November 15, 1978. Short, a multimillionaire businessman, spent heavily in the race, overcoming Fraser's name-identification advantage and insuring that the voters actually recognized the differences described in Hart's nameless

pairing. Short's victory badly split the Democratic-Farmer-Labor party in Minnesota, and he lost the general election to the Republican Senate candidate, David Durenberger.

95. Tarrance classifies respondents as having a very high, high, medium, or low propensity to vote. He assumes that 90, 70, 50, and 30 percent, respectively, of each category will actually vote. See *Campaigning Reports*, vol. 2, no. 1 (January 10, 1980): 7–8. Also see *Campaigning Reports*, vol. 1, no. 7 (September 6, 1979): 5–8, where Professor Will Adams describes another advanced screening method using registered voter data revealing past participation frequency.

96. Nimmo, *The Political Persuaders*, p. 103.

97. See *National Journal*, December 15, 1979, p. 2095.

98. Ibid.

99. See *Public Opinion*, vol. 2, no. 5 (October/November 1979): 2–15, 27–37, 52–60. Miller and Caddell have back-to-back articles challenging each other's interpretations.

100. Small polling outfits contract out their interviewing to the field services provided by several large public and private polling firms.

101. The lower estimate is given by Roll and Cantril, *Polls*, p. 102; the higher one by Baron, "The Slippery Art of Polls," p. 25.

102. Obviously the respondents have never met the interviewer, but they quite naturally make certain assumptions based on looks, demeanor, accent, and so forth, even if these first impressions are misleading.

103. Gergen and Schrambra, "Pollsters and Polling, p. 70.

104. See note 58 above.

105. See *The Washington Post*, April 24, 1980. Caddell discovered that some of President Carter's wide margin over Senator Edward Kennedy often disappeared in the second step. Apparently, Kennedy's negatives produced a knee-jerk pro-Carter choice among some voters who, after consideration of Carter's job performance and Kennedy's issues, decided to vote against Carter and for Kennedy. The "second-round" results were far more accurate a predictor of the 1980 Democratic presidential primary returns than the first poll question's results.

106. *The Washington Post*, November 13, 1979. Hart began the question by stating that "often people feel some government positions are better held by men and others by women," then asked the respondents which sex was more appropriate for a lengthy list of jobs, including governor.

107. Baron, "The Slippery Art of Polls," p. 25. This is a superb example of how opinions can be created out of nothingness.

Chapter 3

The Media Masters

... Behind each [candidate] is a team of advertising experts whose vision does not extend beyond their cubicles. They are not concerned with who is the best candidate or how their candidate is superior to the others. They pay no attention to their candidate's grasp of the issues. They are concerned with selling the candidate, obtaining maximum exposure so the voters will recognize and trust the name, providing a "youthful" look or a "grandfatherly" look.

—*A New York advertising agency executive*[1]

Media consultants are merely the stage managers and the creative writers of living theater politics.

—*Media consultant* ROBERT GOODMAN

For years political observers have wondered aloud why more and more successful politicians resembled television game-show hosts. Television itself is the answer, of course. No single medium has ever transformed American politics to the extent that television has, and the development of a group of political media experts was an inevitable consequence. Mixing style with substance and imagery with reality, media consultants have developed a wide range of formats, strategies, techniques, and gimmicks both to inform and to deceive a television-addicted electorate. The candidate advertisements they produce are perhaps the most precisely and carefully crafted part of a modern campaign. Nothing has been left to chance; every aspect has been included for some purpose—from the colors to the background scenery to the inflections in the announcer's voice. In the hands of a media master, a political commercial can become a work of art—impressive, effective, enthralling, and, in afterthought, disturbing.

The strongest case *for* any candidate (and *against* his opponent) is crystallized in the advertisement package, and the approach and often the themes are the product of a consultant's political instincts. If the instincts are good, and the capacity to convert instinct into effective communication is present, the media consultant *can* have an influence on the results of an election. What is more important, the consultant is normally *thought* to have had an impact by the candidates he supports. Even though most media experts believe that in 1976 Jimmy Carter was ill-served by his media consultant, Gerald Rafshoon, a letter from an appreciative President-elect was prominently displayed in Rafshoon's office near the Carter White House. Said Carter, "I'll always be grateful that I was able to contribute in a small way to the victory of Rafshoon agency."

Media consulting is the most prominent and popular subfield among political professionals, and this chapter will explore some major facets of political television and the multimillion dollar consulting industry that has grown up and around it.

Media Consulting Comes of Age

By 11:15 [of election night], John Deardourff is on the phone to [Pennsylvania Governor-elect Richard] Thornburgh, "Hey! I don't suppose on some obscure corner of the capitol grounds I could have a statue? . . . Well, I'm proud of YOU. All you've got to do is produce. We've got you this far."[2]

Media consultants are now the ones who often claim election-night credit for victories and offer paternal congratulations to exuberant candidates. It would have been difficult for the ward leaders and political bosses three decades ago to imagine how completely they would be replaced by professionals independent of the party. In 1948 television would hardly have looked like much of a threat to party leaders. Less than 3 percent of the population owned a set, and President Harry Truman taped just a single spot announcement (and that one, merely encouraging citizens to vote, was more of a public service than a political advertisement). Two years later, during the 1950 midterm elections, a few candidates began to see television's potential.

Republican Governor Thomas E. Dewey of New York used television extensively in his reelection bid, and GOP candidate John Butler's spot announcements in Maryland's vicious U.S. Senate campaign assisted his victory over incumbent Democrat Millard Tydings.[3]

The initial landmark year for political television, though, was 1952. Television had become truly national, not just regional, and portions of the political parties' national conventions were broadcast first then. With 45 percent of the nation's households owning televisions,[4] the presidential campaign was forced to take notice. Dwight Eisenhower's advisers were particularly intrigued with the device, seeing it as a way to counter his stumbling press conference performances and to make him appear more knowledgeable.[5] Eisenhower's advertising campaign was a glimpse of the future. Two associates of Ted Bates and Company advertising agency of New York designed the spots, targeted them to play in key swing areas of the country, and arranged a television and radio saturation blitz in the last three weeks of the campaign along with Batten, Barton, Durstine, and Osborn (BBD & O) agency, which actually bought the air time. The three primary themes of the commercials (centering on corruption, high prices, and the Korean War) were chosen after consultation with pollster George Gallup. There was an extraordinarily large number of spots (forty-nine produced for television, twenty-nine for radio); most of them were twenty seconds in length, the rest sixty seconds. They played repeatedly in forty-nine selected counties in twelve nonsouthern states as well as a few targeted southern states. In New York City alone, 130 Eisenhower television ads were broadcast at station breaks just on the day before the election. The GOP's media strategy appeared to have been successful, and the Neilson ratings showed Eisenhower's telecasts consistently drew higher ratings than those of Democratic opponent Adlai Stevenson.[6]

The commercials themselves were simplistic and technically very primitive by comparison with modern fare. Eisenhower had a peculiarly stilted way of speaking while reading cue cards, and his rendition was amateurish if sincere and appealing. If nothing else, the GOP commercials from 1952 reveal that the issues in American politics never seem to change. Eisenhower's slogan "It's Time for a Change" is a perennial production, for example. Most of the commercials produced for the Republicans in 1952 would not have been thematically out of place in 1980—one declared that "Eisenhower knows how to deal with the Russians." The same advertisement was a clever adaptation of

"The March of Time" newsreel series that preceded the main features in American movie theaters of the period, and various newsclips of Eisenhower accompanied the audio:

NARRATOR: The man from Abilene. Out of the heartland of America, out of this small-frame house in Abilene, Kansas, came a man, Dwight D. Eisenhower. Through the crucial hours of historic D-Day, he brought us to the triumph and peace of VE-Day. Now, another crucial hour in our history. The big question. . . .

MAN'S VOICE: General, if war comes, is this country really ready?

EISENHOWER: It is not. The administration has spent many billions of dollars for national defense. Yet today we haven't enough tanks for the fighting men in Korea. It is time for a change.

NARRATOR: The nation, haunted by the stalemate in Korea, looks to Eisenhower. Eisenhower knows how to deal with the Russians. He has met with Europe's leaders, has got them working with us. Elect the number-one man for the number-one job of our time. November fourth, vote for peace, vote for Eisenhower.

Yet this approach ignored the intimate nature of television, which reaches its viewers in the home's cozy quarters as opposed to the blare of a newsreel in an auditorium. Some other Eisenhower commercials used an even less effective format where Eisenhower was filmed mechanically giving his responses to off-camera questions.

By the best estimates this first media blitz cost the Republicans close to $1.5 million. During that campaign the Democrats spent only about $77,000 on television, and the few spots they produced played on New Deal themes and Republican responsibility for the Great Depression: "Sh-h-h-h. Don't mention it to a soul, don't spread it around . . . but the Republican party was in power back in 1932 . . . 13 million people were unemployed . . . bank doors shut in your face. . . ." The Democrats, who had wanted to run an ad blitz but could not raise the money, turned instead to broadsides about the GOP's "soap campaign." George Ball, then a staffer in Stevenson's organization and later a major figure in the Johnson White House, set the tone for all the critical reactions to media politics that would follow when he charged that the Republican ad managers:

conceived not an election campaign in the usual sense, but a super colossal, multimillion-dollar production designed to sell an inadequate ticket to the American people in precisely the way they sell soap, ammoniated toothpaste, hair tonic, or bubble gum. They guarantee their candidates to be 99⁴⁴/₁₀₀ percent pure; whether or not they will float remains to be seen.[7]

Poet Marya Mannes was moved to write "Sales Campaign" in reaction to the Eisenhower advertising effort. It read, in part: "Phillip Morris, Lucky Strike, Alka Seltzer, I like Ike."[8]

For better or worse, the pattern was set for future campaigns, and the media battleground gradually came to be important enough to require full-time commanders who reported directly to the candidate rather than to subordinate aides, as was the case in 1952.[9] Richard Nixon's political career is, to a great extent, a measure of the influence of media politics. His vice-presidential nomination had been saved in 1952 by the judicious use of television.[10] A "secret fund" of $18,000 to help Senator Nixon defray his office expenses was exposed by the *New York Post* during the presidential campaign, and prominent newspapers called for Nixon's withdrawal from the GOP ticket. But BBD & O bought $75,000 of program time on Tuesday, September 23, and carefully rehearsed a speech with Nixon. Nine million television sets were tuned in and the maudlin spectacle of "The Checkers' Speech" (named after a dog that had been given to the Nixons and that Nixon refused to return because his daughters loved it so much) was generally credited with rescuing Nixon from early oblivion. Nixon became television's victim in 1960 when he rather surprisingly refused a BBD & O proposal to organize his first presidential campaign around the latest media techniques.[11] Preferring a more traditional approach, Nixon ended up a perceived loser of his initial and most important television debate with Democratic nominee John F. Kennedy because he was not well rested or well made up and did not look the part of a president. (On radio, by contrast, where visual appearances were irrelevant, Nixon made a far better impression and was thought by listeners to have had the better of Kennedy.) Eight years later, chastened by his 1960 defeat and his subsequent 1962 loss of the California governorship, Nixon used television to stage one of the most remarkable comebacks in U.S. history. Nixon's sensitive, well-planned media campaign was aided by the widespread introduction of color to the television screen. Color, combined with better makeup and more frequent shavings, helped to eliminate the jowly, shadowy look that had so haunted Nixon's previous television image.[12]

At the same time media politics was becoming a major component of almost all major statewide elections. Following the 1964 presidential race, when 10,000 spot announcements were broadcast in the nation's top seventy-five media markets, the 1966 midterm contests became a showcase of television's political splendors. In California Spencer-Roberts agency was masterminding an effective and nationally renowned televison package for a seasoned veteran of the medium, ex-actor and TV host Ronald Reagan, for his gubernatorial quest. Across the continent Jack Tinker and Partners of New York, better known for their work with Alka Seltzer and Braniff Airlines, were designing a series of creative advertisements for Governor Nelson Rockefeller's come-from-behind reelection effort. The commercials, which were given much of the credit for Rockefeller's unexpected triumph, never featured the candidate at all, so unpopular had he personally become. Instead Rockefeller's accomplishments were highlighted in an eye-catching fashion.[13] For example, one of the advertisements (which was aired 208 times in New York City alone) begins with the film of the white lines of a highway hypnotically swishing by, taken by a camera mounted on the front of a car, as the announcer intones:

If you took all the roads Governor Rockefeller has built and all the roads he's widened and straightened and smoothed out, if you took all those roads and layed them end to end, they'd stretch all the way to Hawaii. . . . [The road ends in the sand of a beach.] All the way to Hawaii and all the way back.

The Pervasiveness of Political Television

Performances like that of Jack Tinker in New York earned a permanent place for the media consultant in virtually all serious campaigns. A 1968 survey indicated that more than half of all congressional campaigns used paid broadcasting on television or radio, and by 1972 85 percent of major U.S. Senate contenders and 53 percent of major U.S. House candidates had purchased at least some television time.[14] For the first time a President of the United States (Carter) appointed a political media consultant (Rafshoon) to his full-time staff and inner circle.[15] That same President, hemmed in by foreign crises, would later use advertisements prepared by his agent as a surrogate for personal campaigning during his bid for renomination in 1980.[16]

Just six days after he won the presidency, John F. Kennedy attributed his victory to television: "It was TV more than anything else that turned the tide."[17] Pollster Elmo Roper confirmed Kennedy's hunch. Of the 4 million voters who claimed to have made their 1960 presidential decision based on the debates, 3 million voted for Kennedy in an election he won by only 112,000 votes. Never again would an election see the likes of Earl Long, who won the last pretelevision gubernatorial race in Louisiana. During one election contest Long ridiculed an opponent for wearing "pancake makeup" and "$400 suits." "You know what one of those $400 suits would look like on Uncle Earl?" he would ask his crowds. "Like socks on a rooster."

It is true that occasionally one observes a long-shot candidate such as Harry R. Hughes managing to win a major statewide office without benefit of much television advertising (as Hughes did in Maryland's 1978 gubernatorial contest.)[18] Far more commonly, though, one reads of a U.S. senator such as Adlai E. Stevenson III of Illinois, who shared with his father an inability to adapt his fertile mind and articulate manner to the strictures of political media. With his performance rating and even his name-identification level slipping, Stevenson chose not to run for reelection in 1980.[19] In that same year Edward Kennedy failed to pay heed to his brother John's experience and observations twenty years before, as his lack of a sophisticated media campaign (and absence of much else in advanced campaign technology) was one of half a dozen major factors in the thwarting of his presidential hopes.[20] Five different media advisers were on board the Kennedy campaign at various times, including nationally known Charles Guggenheim, Tony Schwartz, and David Sawyer, but none were ever given either enough authority by jealous staffers or any polling data by a campaign that curiously refrained from hiring a polling consultant until nearly the onset of the primary season.[21]

The United States is far more a video culture than a word culture, and television is the major cause. In 1950 under 10 percent of all households had a television set, but by 1980 almost 99 percent did; more than half of all homes have two or more sets.[22] During the 1977–1978 television year, the set was on in the average household six and one-half hours per day (seven hours during the season itself and five and one-half hours during the summer). The average American now watches over three hours of television per day, an increase of forty-five minutes since 1965.[23] It comes as no surprise, then, that television is the most important source of campaign information for voters, and it has been so since 1952.[24] Almost nine out of ten Americans say they follow television reports about campaigns, and media information (not just advertising but news programs as well) is almost always at the top of a voter's list of causal factors explaining his ballot decision.[25] In fact, about two-thirds of all Americans consider television their primary source of news and about half claim to rely on television whenever there are conflicting reports in the various media.[26]

Despite virtually unanimous agreement that television has a substantial influence on politics, media experts have long disagreed on the electoral effects of paid television advertising. Political scientists Thomas E. Patterson and Robert D. McClure provided a partial answer in their extensive study of the media during the 1972 presidential election.[27] They found that while commercials have no effect on voters' images of presidential candidates, they do have a substantial influence on voters' perceptions of the candidates' issues and platforms. The electorate apparently learns a good deal from paid advertisements, enough so that the researchers could make a rather startling assertion: "Spot commercials educate rather than hoodwink the voters." Moreover, the ads were discovered to be considerably more issue substantive than the nightly network newscasts, which are obsessed with "trial-heat" polls, the horse-race standings, and the visual hoopla of electioneering.[28] On the other hand, advertisements are far more selective in their choice of content. The only issues raised by a candidate in his paid commercials are those he thinks will help him or hurt his opponent.

One suspects that some of McClure and Patterson's findings would not be entirely borne out at electoral levels below the presidential, and especially that paid ads would be more effective at image making for state and local offices.[29] The average voter knows far less about candidates at these levels, and the press covers them far less extensively. Image probably becomes correspondingly more important as a voter's information level declines. It is particularly crucial in party primaries and nonpartisan elections where the party cue is obscured or nonexistent.[30]

Television may well be used most effectively when it subtly reinforces our existing attitudes and prejudices rather than when it attempts to change current ones or create new ones.[31] It is thought that an advertising campaign can only rarely "convert" a staunch supporter of one party to the support of the other party's nominee. But moving a voter one step in either direction is much easier: for example, reinforcing a weak Democrat's predilection to support his party's candidate *or* encouraging a weak Democrat not to vote or to become an Independent. Television commercials are believed to appeal particularly to Independents, both the largely inattentive and uninformed Independent voter and the floating, highly reactive "ticket splitter" who is unusually aware of politics.[32]

Television has also altered the ways in which voters are corraled. The old-style politics called for "retail" campaigning, seeking customers one by one. Media politics is "wholesale" campaigning, and the wholesale politician secures his voters in bunches and by markets. (The irony today, as both Jimmy Carter and George Bush proved in, respectively, the 1976 and 1980 Iowa presidential caucuses, is that one of the best ways to get the attention of the wholesale media is to prove one's success at retailing.) Television gives name identification to challengers, probably increasing the opportunity for an incumbent's upset in a highly publicized race, but it also lets incumbents sharpen, soften, or refine their own images (and they usually have much more money to spend on media than their opponents). Paid television can be used to overcome unfavorable publicity in the uncontrolled media—news programs and the like. Commercials are proven "morale boosters" for a candidate's workers as well, and give volunteers invaluable ammunition to use on the hustings.[33]

Political communicators recognize that television is not purely informational; it is also an entertainment medium, and, regrettably, they sometimes cater to the audience's lowest common denominator (much as the networks' prime-time programmers seem to do). In the rush to be creative, entertaining, and pleasing, many of paid political television's greatest offenses are committed. Candidates often do not even appear, much less speak at length, in their campaign advertisements—especially if their voices are raspy or their features unappealing. Gimmicks and insignificant elements become writ large on the distorting tube. There is no better illustration than that of Canada's 1979–1980 general election campaigns. In May 1979 Tim Raife, the Conservative party's press chief and a former television broadcaster, fashioned a devastating series of advertisements for the Tories centered around contrasting parliamentary excerpts of Tory leader Joe Clark and the Liberal prime minister, Pierre Trudeau. At Raife's suggestion, the Conservative members of Parliament had changed from the traditional adulatory desk thumping to hand clapping as a means of expressing approval of their party leader's statements, while the Liberals retained desk thumping. Part of the Tory appeal, according to election observers, was that hand clapping gave a pleasing sound and normal appearance to the Tory portion of the advertisements, while the Liberals' desk thumping came across as odd, discordant, and jarring.[34] The image-making tables were turned on the Tories just eight months later, after their minority government had collapsed. The media focus was on Prime Minister Clark, who became saddled with the image of a weak and indecisive leader. All sides agreed that the perception had been amplified by Clark's physical appearance (a "multiple chin, shaky hands, awkward manners, and plainness," as a newspaper report read).[35] Before Clark's defeat, the *Ottawa Journal* editorialized that "The Canadian political process is in very bad shape if governments are to be elected on the basis of a man's laugh, or his walk, or a habit of drumming his fingers on a tabletop."[36]

It is at least possible that paid political television will diminish in importance with the growth of noncommercial television, pay cable, home video sets, and the gradual reduction of the three commercial networks' hold on the viewing audience. Even under those conditions, though, network advertisements can be better targeted and perhaps made more effective as affluent voters are siphoned off and less well educated, poorer, older, and more ethnic voters remain in greater concentrations. Whatever the future may hold for commercial television, the present demands that a serious candidate devote a large share of his resources to the hiring of a media consultant and the preparation of an extensive advertising package.

A Media Consultant's Activities

The political media consultant's influence extends considerably beyond the formal contractual stipulations of his role, but even they are far-reaching. A nationally known media consultant typically pledges to furnish a long list of campaign goods, from the development of themes and strategies to the writing, production, and editing of radio and television advertisements; from the targeting and time buying of spots to the design of graphic materials for billboards, brochures, and news releases.

As the importance of paid media to a campaign has grown, so has the roster of a media consultant's activities. The professional is increasingly involved in all major phases of a campaign, especially in the formulation of basic strategy and the monitoring and critiquing of the candidate and staff's performances. In a real sense he often serves as a campaign's confidante and confessor, keeping his client and the campaign's minions on the straight and narrow path outlined in the original campaign plan. Like his fellow polling consultants, the media master's work and reputation earns him overriding respect and produces inhibition and deference among the campaign staff. A startling, near-absolute faith is frequently placed in the media consultant's ability to insure victory, and the professionals quite naturally are pleased with this attitude. As Robert Squier described his successful 1978 Florida gubernatorial-client, Robert Graham: "Graham was the perfect candidate. He trusted me and he trusted the new campaign technology. He was willing to sit down at one point in the campaign and write a check for $250,000 to keep us going."[37]

Given what the media consultant is usually paid, the deference may be understandable. Occasionally, however, a campaign will switch agencies or hire more than one consultant because of dissatisfaction. The 1976 Carter campaign, stalled in the general election with President Ford moving up rapidly in the polls, decided to supplement Rafshoon's advertising package and hire Tony Schwartz, who produced a last-minute series of commercials. In 1972 the McGovern organization abandoned Charles Guggenheim because he did not want to produce negative advertisements, believing them to be ineffective.[38]

Advertising Format and Length

The national media consultants (many of them sketched in appendix C) could probably agree on little more than a few fundamentals of format and strategy in a media campaign. All recognize that political advertisements have a number of distinct purposes. Commercials can be used to establish name identification and draw attention to a candidate, increasing his visibility. The candidate's personal image can be developed, evoking certain feelings about him based on selected personality characteristics. Campaign issues can be developed, tapping sentiments in the electorate and targeting key constituency groups in the voting population. Advertisements can link the candidate directly with his party or other groups, winning support for his cause through association. Not only can political advertisements stimulate participation in a candidate's campaign and attract new adherents for him, but they can also reinforce and motivate his existing supporters. Finally, campaign commercials can be used to attack opponents—these ads are called "negatives"—or to defend the candidate after an opponent's broadside.

While the goals of political advertising are generally acknowledged, there is hardly any consensus about the best ways and means to accomplish them. Few standard techniques or fixed formulas exist on which most consultants can agree. "We're all kind of probing in the dark. We're out there experimenting with what works," admits Robert Squier.[39] The National Republican Congressional Committee, which regularly conducts audience-reaction tests of political commercials, has found that no format or strategy is necessarily superior, and no style tends consistently to secure more favorable reactions. Almost always the evaluation is dependent on how *appropriate* the selected style, format, and strategy is for the candidate in question, and how well the advertising seemed to fit the circumstances of a particular campaign, the personality of a particular candidate, and the electorate's preconceptions and prior prejudices about politics.

Still, media consultants tend to go about their work on a similar schedule. They first formulate an overall plan of attack, in theory drawing upon the accumulated polling data and issues research compiled by the candidate's staff and by the polling and organizational consultants. Pollsters and other consultants often complain that, in fact, the media masters ignore their carefully compiled pool of research. As Matt Reese describes his media brethren: "One of the biggest problems in campaigns is that the media people have become sort of prima donnas and they go off to do the advertisements on their own, but I present [my research] to them hoping it will be a part of what they do."

Assuming the media consultant actually uses the research, he tries to extract the best "visually oriented" parts and designs spots around them. The narrative is usually written only after the filming is done, when the film results can be seen and analyzed, since the video portion of a television commercial is normally more vital than the audio. In designing the video and writing the audio portions, a media consultant is conscious of the need to be either arresting or entertaining (or both) in order to keep the attention of the viewing audience, especially if the spot is a five-minute one or if a thirty-minute documentary is being planned.

After the filming, editing, and production are completed, and the advertisements have won the approval of the candidate and his staff, a schedule of airing is prepared, based on the budget and the strategy believed best for the campaign. Sometimes there is simply a slow buildup in the airing of the commercials, commencing about a month before the election and peaking on election day. Other times a "saturation blitz" is preferred, and as much time as possible is bought a month or more prior to the election. Occasionally the advertising campaign proceeds in "stop-start" phases, with advertisements running in spring or summer or early September to build name identification, then ceasing, followed by a midcampaign "soft-sell" phase, and finally a series of "hard-sell" advertisements including negatives right before election day. Whatever the actual advertising schedule—and these three examples merely suggest the wide variety of combinations—the advertisements are carefully targeted by program and time slot to reach selected segments of the voting population. (This fascinating process will be discussed later in this chapter.)

Political commercials differ widely in format. Some of the first paid political broadcasts were of candidates delivering speeches to rallies, but this arrangement proved ill-timed and dull.[40] As one consultant suggested, "The process of television communication is living room communication. People do not deliver speeches in their living rooms." Another early format was the "talking head," where the candidate spoke directly into the camera. While most modern consultants consider the "talking head" uncreative and boring, some studies indicate that it has a high recall by the audience and is a good method of communicating both information and personality characteristics.[41] Evaluation of other early formats are harsher. The off-camera questions to the candidate (as in the Eisenhower spots) and staged conversations by the candidate with party leaders and supporters, also common in the 1950s, were noticeably stilted and artificial. One format, though, the "man-in-the-street" interview, has survived and become increasingly popular. First used in politics by BBD & O agency for Governor Thomas E. Dewey's 1950 reelection campaign in New York, "man-in-the-street" has been found to be unusually effective. It generates the highest audience recall of all the standard formats[42] and is helpful in communicating with targeted subgroups. If one's polling results indicate that black women over forty years of age are a swing group, for example, then such an individual, saying just the right thing, is included in the commercial, giving the targeted viewer someone with whom to identify. Modern media consultants, while utilizing all the old formats from time to time, have relied more heavily on "creative" alternatives, using gimmicks of all sorts (including humor and animation). Walter DeVries, for instance, is a believer in the "news look" format, enhancing credibility by presenting political advertisements as mini-documentaries or press conferences, with nonpartisan, factual deliveries sometimes depicting the candidate in the role of an inquiring television news reporter.[43]

The dilemma of commercial length has always been a vexing one for media consultants. They must design their advertisements to fit the spots made available by the networks and their affiliates (which come primarily in ten-second, thirty-second, sixty-second, and four-and-one-half- or five-minute varieties).[44] Network-sold spots within network programs are called "participations," while spots sold by local network affiliates at the half-hour station breaks are termed "adjacencies." Both kinds are subject to complicated pricing regulations that must be taken into account when planning an ad campaign. As one illustration, two thirty-second spots cost more than one sixty-second spot, the exact differential depending on the time of day and day of the week. The thirty- and sixty-second spots comprise the lion's share of political advertisements, variously estimated at 75 to 90 percent of the total.[45] The spot format is heavily favored, first because networks are resistant to making available longer blocks of time, and second because audiences "tune out" lengthy political broadcasts. While there is no measurable reduction in audience for a sixty-second spot, an audience for a thirty-minute documentary will likely be more than a third smaller than the normal audience for a program in any given time slot.[46] Even a five-minute political advertisement regularly loses from 5 to 10 percent of the regular viewing audience.

From time to time television stations refuse to air political commercials shorter than four and one-half minutes because of the alleged superficiality of spot ads. The Federal Communications Commission, however, has since ruled that stations may not predetermine the length of a candidate's advertisements, but the fierce controversy about the proper length of political broadcasts rages on. Edward Ney, president of Young and Rubicam agency, holds the minority viewpoint among advertisers who have taken political candidates: "It is possible to spell out accurately the principal or marginal benefits of a chewing gum in thirty seconds. But it is virtually impossible to do necessary justice to the background, character, and programs of a political candidate in the same time."[47] Other consultants contend that this criticism ignores the cumulative effect of a series of spot advertisements. David Garth filmed forty spot ads for New York Governor Hugh Carey's 1978 reelection campaign and suggested: "If you took a tape and hung those forty spots together, it would be a thirty-six-minute presentation of Carey's accomplishments. All together, you get a total picture—far more than people ever knew about [Franklin] Roosevelt when he ran for governor, far more than they ever knew about [former Governor] Herbert Lehman."[48]

Neither is a short spot necessarily more untruthful or dishonest than a longer broadcast; it is just as easy to lie successfully for five or ten minutes as for thirty or sixty seconds. Nor does a shorter commercial have to have less substantive value. As another consultant commented, "I can think of a lot of things you can say in thirty seconds: 'I love you.' 'I hate you.' 'Will you marry me?' 'I declare war.'"[49] Michael Kaye cited one of his most effective campaign advertisements, an ad just ten seconds in length, designed to demonstrate that San Francisco has one of the highest violent crime rates in the United States. The spot featured a gunman with a pistol turning around, aiming, and firing a visible "hole" directly into the television screen. "I mean that thing wakes you up—in ten seconds!" remarks Kaye. Yet he admits that a brief commerical, while enunciating a fact or a candidate's position on a given item, "does not give anybody the full historical background. It doesn't give anybody the analytical process that helped a candidate arrive at his stand." In that major respect, a spot advertisement is inherently imperfect and lacking. It can clearly, even forcefully, spell out where a candidate stands, but there is not sufficient time to explain why the candidate has taken this position, or to relate it coherently to the other items that comprise a candidate's platform, philosophy, and character. No hit-or-miss, catch-as-catch-can series of spot ads, however comprehensive they may be when viewed as a whole, can really substitute for a well-planned, integrated, and explicated lengthy broadcast.

Documentary thirty-minute political films are increasingly rare, not merely because of audience tune-out, but also due to the extraordinary costs of production (which can easily exceed $100,000). Yet a documentary can enthuse campaign volunteers like no other tool, at home as they watch it on television and at rallies and training sessions. It can also provide the basic footage for shorter commercials and serve as the centerpiece of fund-raising efforts. On occasion a thirty-minute documentary has been judged crucial to a candidate's chances. George McGovern, sick in bed with hepatitis and unable to campaign in the last weeks of his 1962 U.S. Senate campaign, used a thirty-minute program instead of spots to overcome a deficit in the polls and win his first Senate term. Films for John Gilligan of Ohio and Mike Gravel of Alaska in 1968 were probably the most important factors in their upset Democratic primary defeats of, respectively, incumbent U.S. Senators Frank Lausche and Ernest Gruening.[50] Robert Kennedy relied heavily on half-hour documentaries in both his 1964 senate race and his 1968 presidential nomination bid. Hubert Humphrey in 1968 and Ronald Reagan in 1976 were notably successful in using thirty-minute films for fund-raising and tide-turning efforts. In order to expand much beyond a candidate's committed voters, though, a television documentary must have proper promotion, enticing voters to watch; have an engaging opening that encourages viewers to stay tuned; and be as entertaining as it is informative, so that it can compete against alternate commercial programs.[51] Walter DeVries used a series of thirty-minute documentaries in the 1978 campaign of Michigan gubernatorial candidate Pat McCullough, each focusing on a major issue targeted by polling research. All were produced in the news documentary format, with McCullough as newsman-commentator-interviewer, quizzing experts, bureaucrats, and people in the street about the subject at hand. Each show opened with an audience "teaser" of some sort to maintain interest, and the half hour was punctuated with its own "commercials," complete with a toll-free number that voters were encouraged to call for more information. However, most television stations in the key Michigan media markets refused to sell thirty-minute blocks to the McCullough campaign, so this extensive and issue-oriented use of the documentary was stymied and no fair test of its effectiveness was made.

Because of the difficulty in securing ample airing time for documentaries, as well as the large expenditure required to finance their production, many media consultants support the compromise solution of the five-minute commercial (if the networks and affiliates can be induced to sell slots of even that brief duration). Though greater length is no guarantee of enhanced effectiveness, some studies have indicated that both recall by the viewing audience and the viewers' evaluation of the candidate are higher with longer spots.[52] Gerald Rafshoon strongly preferred five-minute slots for Jimmy Carter's 1976 advertisements, contending that "The environment in which you present the thirty-second spot, sandwiched between deodorants and toilet tissue, doesn't lend enough credibility [to the candidate ads]."[53] The Carter campaign repeatedly ran four five-minute broadcasts, two of them minibiographies and the other two devoted to issues. Commented Rafshoon, "I was sure [the five-minute commercial] was the only vehicle short of personally introducing Jimmy Carter to 113 million Americans that would reveal the depth of my candidate."[54]

Advertising Content and Strategy

Beyond the decisions about format and length is the more crucial determination of content. The selection of material about image and issue is as varied as the strategies concocted to elect candidates. Each problem facing a candidate and his campaign has its creative advertising solutions. Name identification is the first gap to be bridged for most challengers in a multicandidate primary field. When Massachusetts Democrat Paul Tsongas ran for his party's U.S. Senate nomination in 1978, he broke out of the pack of lesser-knowns and overtook the recognized leader with a clever advertisement centering around a small child's mispronunciation of his name. Challengers facing incumbents also need to become known quickly. The Bishop and Bryant agency helped Indiana Republican H. Joel Deckard defeat incumbent Democratic U.S. Representative David Cornwell in 1978 with an early advertisement mentioning Deckard's name nine times in thirty seconds.[55]

Each candidate has his own weaknesses. A black contender, for example, has blatant and subtle racial stereotypes to contend with, and unless confronted or circumvented, they can combine to defeat him. When David Garth signed on Tom Bradley's campaign for mayor of Los Angeles in 1973, he designed a perceptive ad package that defused a number of potential time bombs. Bradley's commercials had a number of testimonials from white women and many allusions to his police background and his life's Horatio Alger success ("This city gave me a chance . . ."). His appeal to ethnics and blue-collar voters, presumably the most resistant to his candidacy, was strengthened by several "hard hat" and anticrime spots. Finally, there was heavy stress on his previous accomplishments ("If I could do this as a city councilman, just think what a mayor could do"), suggesting that his work, not his race, had earned him a chance to serve. In a city with a black population far short of a majority, Bradley managed to become Los Angeles's first black mayor.

Advertisements can also be used to enforce prejudices. When William Winter ran against front-running Lieutenant Governor Evelyn Gandy in the 1979 Mississippi Democratic gubernatorial primary and run-off, his media adviser, Robert Squier, described his advertisement goal: "What I want to do is attack her with a machine gun." That he almost did, putting Winter out in the midst of a National Guard battlefield maneuver. With the rumble of tanks in the background and military true grit filling the screen, the candidate solemnly intoned, "The governor is commander-in-chief of the National Guard. He's ultimately responsible for how it performs. The Guard is the first line of national defense. . . ." Riding a slogan of "the toughest job in Mississippi," Winter defeated Gandy and went on to win the general election and four years' command of the state's National Guard. "So that's how you fight a woman," the satisfied Squier says with a smile.

Incumbents have their own special needs, particularly ones who have attracted the voters' brickbats by making unpopular decisions or breaking campaign promises. The "apology" strategy is one that has been followed with some success in recent years. U.S. Senator Charles Percy's 1978 reelection effort will illustrate. Behind in the polls and losing momentum, Percy was convinced by his media consultant, Douglas Bailey, that drastic action was needed. So, surrounded by the members of his family who stared fixedly and frozen-faced at him, Percy filmed a thirty-second spot that is startlingly frank:

The polls say many of you want to send me a message. But after Tuesday I may not be in the Senate to receive it. Believe me, I've gotten the message and you're right. Washington has gone overboard and I'm sure I've made my share of mistakes. But in truth, your priorities are mine too. Stop the waste, cut the spending, cut the taxes. I've worked as hard as I know how for you. I'm not ready to quit now and I don't want to be fired. I want to keep working for you and I'm asking for your vote.

Aired on October 29, this spot and a series of similar advertisements are given partial credit for Percy's last-minute comeback, culminating in an election-day victory.[56]

David Garth has made a reputation out of reelecting unpopular incumbents through the use of similar techniques. The reelection campaigns of New York Mayor John Lindsay in 1969, New Jersey Governor Brendan Byrne in 1977, and New York Governor Hugh Carey in 1978 were all eventually victorious despite long odds at the outset, and part of the reason was a decision to admit their mistakes and run on their records, errors included. "John Lindsay had made so many mistakes that if you didn't point them out, you'd have lost credibility *and* the election," Garth commented.

Garth centered Carey's campaign around the "tough decisions" (i.e., the unpopular ones) the governor had made, declaring that he deserved the respect, not the condemnation, of his constituency. To underline the point, Garth filmed the New York legislative sponsor of a death penalty law endorsing Carey and praising him as a man of conscience for vetoing the legislator's own death penalty bill. Brendan Byrne's theme was similar: "On the record, you've got to respect what he's done." Byrne's cardinal sin had been promising to oppose the enactment of an income tax during his first gubernatorial campaign, then proposing and securing that very levy. A new tax never endears an officerholder to his constituents, but Byrne's 180-degree reversal had multiplied his unpopularity to the extent that he was renominated with just 30 percent of the vote, having attracted ten challengers in his own party (all drawn to the battle scenting Byrne's vulnerability). Despite being labeled a near-hopeless underdog for reelection—Garth himself had encouraged Byrne not to seek another term—Byrne was able to fool the oddsmakers with Garth's help by capitalizing not only on his opponent's mistakes but also his own. Labeling the income tax "a tough decision to make," one advertisement explains, "Sometimes you've got to admit you're wrong in order to do what's right; that's what a *governor* has to do." The Byrne advertisement campaign, like all modern packages, had a number of subplots and secondary themes as well. His specific accomplishments as governor were highlighted by man-in-the-street interviews and ads targeted to the elderly, home-owners, and other groups. Byrne's strongest personal asset was his reputation for honesty, a relative rarity in New Jersey politics, and an endorsement spot featuring New Jersey's U.S. Representative Peter Rodino, chairman of the House Judiciary Committee's Watergate hearings, struck just the right chord. There were a group of negative advertisements directed at Byrne's Republican opponent, State Senator Ray Bateman, but these were unusually issue-based, mainly centering on Bateman's state legislative record and his tax proposals.

No American campaign can compare to a British one in the degree to which issues dominate the political discourse, or so it seems to most transatlantic observers. The 1979 British general election campaign saw the introduction by the Conservative party of slickly produced political commercials on television and in the movie theaters (where commercial advertising is standard). An American is struck by the absence of personality or even the mention of personages in the ads. Instead, in a refreshing change, the concentration is on a clever, if obviously biased, discourse on the issues, with the *party* differences starkly and distinctly etched—a reflection of the strong party system that persists in Great Britain. (By contrast, many American politicians, and especially minority Republicans, will not even so much as permit their party affiliations to be alluded to in their advertising.) Two 1979 Tory commercials, designed by Saatchi and Saatchi agency, are scripted in table 3–1. The second one is particularly fascinating, an imaginative minieconomics lesson that communicates the basic Conservative monetary dogma in an appealing and attention-grabbing manner. It is difficult, perhaps impossible, to find an American political spot advertisement that can compare to this one in comprehensive treatment of a major public issue.[57]

Most American ad campaigns do not even try to be either educa-

TABLE 3–1

Selected Advertisements by Saatchi and Saatchi Agency, Conservative Party of Great Britain (1979 General Election)[a]

---

1. Cinema Spot: The Fifty Pence Queue (60 seconds)

YOUNG BOY [with his girlfriend]:	Excuse me, is this queue for the fifty pence stall?
MAN IN THE QUEUE:	No, mate, this is the queue for the unemployed.
YOUNG BOY:	Excuse me, is this the queue for the fifty pence stall?
WOMAN IN THE QUEUE:	Oh no, this is the queue for serious operations.

[Scene shifts to the Emigration Office]

MAN IN THE QUEUE:	Fifty pence stall? No, you have to leave the country to find a proper job.
YOUNG BOY:	Is this the queue for a fifty pence stall?
WOMAN IN THE QUEUE:	No, this is the queue for buying your own council house. It has hardly moved in the last four years.
ANNOUNCER [voiceover]:	Nowadays the country seems to be standing still, waiting for jobs, operations, homes, everything.
YOUNG BOY:	Is this the queue for a fifty pence stall?
BOY IN THE LINE:	Fifty pence! Haven't you ever heard of inflation?
YOUNG BOY:	All we wanted to see was the Marx brothers, but I can see this Labour Government are another bunch of comedians.
[Poster and voiceover]:	Coming shortly: the Conservatives! A great program for all the family.

---

2. Television Spot: Labour Isn't Working (2½ minutes)

ANNOUNCER:	Once more, since Labour came into power in 1974, the working man is paying more tax than ever before. More direct taxes, like income tax, and more indirect taxes. In fact, more tax on almost everything you earn and much of what you buy. No other major industrialized country in the world extracts a higher rate of income tax from its citizens than the present Labour Government. This government collects a staggering £110 million a day in tax. Now what is the effect of all this taxation?
WORKING MAN:	I am a wage earner. The Labour Government take so much out of my pay in taxes, I'll have to ask him for more pay. [Points to second man.]
INDUSTRIALIST:	I am a manufacturer. And if higher taxes means more payout, I'll have to cover the costs by putting up my prices to him. [Points to third man.]
SMALL BUSINESSMAN:	I am a shopkeeper. If he puts his prices up, I have got to pass them on to her. [Points to woman.]
WORKING MAN'S WIFE:	I am a housewife. If he puts his prices up, I'll have to ask my husband for more housekeeping. [Points to working man.]
WORKING MAN:	If she wants more housekeeping, I'll have to ask him for even more pay. [Points to industrialist.]
INDUSTRIALIST:	And if he does that, I could go bust.
WORKING MAN:	And I'll need another job.

ANNOUNCER:	Today if all the people who didn't have a job went to Westminister to sign on, how far do you think the queue would stretch? It would be a very long way. As far as Birmingham? No, further than that. To Blackburn, perhaps? No, further! To Newcastle? No, further *still!* It would stretch over 300 miles to Glasgow.
	People say that the Labour party is the working man's party but that is nonsense. Their policies of high taxation actually discourage people from working, sometimes stop them altogether, so they end up on the dole.
WORKING MAN:	I am a wage earner. The Conservatives take less out of our pay in taxes, so I could give more housekeeping to my wife. [Points to wife.]
WORKING MAN'S WIFE:	I am a housewife. If he gives me more housekeeping, I can afford to buy more of his goods. [Points to small businessman.]
SMALL BUSINESSMAN:	I am a shopkeeper. If she buys more of my goods, I can buy more from him. [Points to industrialist.]
INDUSTRIALIST:	I am a manufacturer. If he buys more goods, I can afford to pay more and employ more people.
WORKING MAN:	And I have still got a job.

---

* Note to American readers: It was Winston Churchill who once observed that America and Britain are separated by a common language. The following "translations" will be helpful:

Council house: A government-built home available for purchase.

Fifty pence stall: Seats in a movie theater costing half a British pound.

Housekeeping: Money for groceries, home care, etc.

Queue: Waiting line.

Sign on: Go on the welfare roll.

tive or broadly scoped, treating issues as sidelights or playthings for image gimmickry. A case in point is the 1978 Florida governor's contest. For turning an image into a public office, few can match Robert Squier's feat in that election, when a little-known state senator, Bob Graham, used a "working for Governor" theme as a springboard to the executive mansion. Squier had long had the idea of an unknown, liberal candidate using a "work days" gimmick—that is, working a series of mainly blue-collar jobs, one job each day—so as to overcome the liberal stigma with a dose of the Protestant ethic. Squier had Graham work the first 9 of 100 jobs without publicity—bits of each day being filmed, of course—but as Graham punched out on his lunch hour of the tenth job (working in a Tallahassee mobile home factory), he proceeded up to the state capitol, held a press conference, and announced for governor. He refused to answer questions until the next day, explaining that he had to get back to work, which he did, accompanied by a horde of reporters for the remaining 90 of his work days.

The series of commercials Squier created using "work days" footage is masterful. Clips of Graham's day of schoolteaching are accompanied by his discussing his plans for education, his credibility enhanced because he has "been in the teacher's shoes." The "work days" theme became the launching pad for a major campaign proposal to bring 50,000 new jobs to Florida. Mainly, though, it was imagery. "Even the inflection of the announcer, as he says *'working* for Governor,' helps the campaign by contrasting Graham with all those other jerks who are sitting around on their rumps," notes Squier.

In his advertisements, Graham confessed that "work days" were making him a better person, equipping him to restore people's faith in government. Indeed, Squier claims that "work days" literally changed Graham's personality. "He was a very shy, quiet, understated guy when we started, but he opened up as we went along." To prevent the gimmick from appearing too gimmicky, Squier got Graham (who is related to *Washington Post* publisher Katherine Graham) to publish a book on his "work days" experiences. Squier removed all regular commercials from the air for three days in the middle of the campaign in order to run a spot with Graham promoting his book. "The idea behind it was that 'work days' was a serious project, so serious that Graham wrote a book about it," says Squier, adding tongue-in-cheek, "And everybody knows books are serious."

The only break in the "work days" theme came with the production of the seemingly unavoidable negative advertisements. Graham's "Adding Machine" negative was aired in retaliation to a similar spot broadcast by Democratic primary opponent Robert Shevin, whose target was Graham's hefty campaign spending. But whereas Shevin's ad had just *one* adding machine on a desk clicking out all of Graham's expenditures, Graham's anti-Shevin ad pictured *five* machines tallying Shevin's office expenses while serving as the state's attorney general. With this escalation Shevin desisted, the negatives were withdrawn, and both sides reverted to their original advertising campaigns. Graham, who had been expected to finish no better than fourth in the first Democratic primary, ran second, forcing a run-off with Shevin. Graham won both the run-off and the November general election, and secured a full-time job as Florida's governor.[58]

Variations on the "work days" format have been adopted by other candidates before and after Graham, and its success in his case insures that imitations will abound. Advertising themes frequently come in cycles, in approaches that respond to the times. After Watergate, for instance, more candidates began to use the "talking head" format, eschewing slickly produced spots for rough-edged, home-style ones. The content almost invariably led the viewer to regard the candidate as genuine, sincere, humane, and look-you-square-in-the-eyes honest.

Advertisements also frequently use similar approaches and themes because political consultants are inherently cautious, preferring to rely on tried and true techniques. Especially in a close election, a consultant does not want to be tagged with the responsibility for defeat (and commentators always search for out-of-the-ordinary elements in a losing campaign). Media professionals naturally prefer to play it safe. In the 1976 presidential election, both sides rejected potential media gambles. Gerald Rafshoon seriously considered doing a negative spot of President Ford pardoning Richard Nixon but decided, "If we had hit with the pardon stuff, it's possible Carter would have won by a landslide. Or it could have backfired and he would have lost."[59] Douglas Bailey's controversial spot for President Ford was actually produced but never aired. Its highlight had Ford in an open motorcade in Dallas, with the voiceover, "When a limousine can parade openly in the streets of Dallas, there's a change that's come over America." Later in the five-minute piece, a firecracker explodes in an auditorium where Ford is speaking, and momentarily all are hushed in fright, but Ford recovers his composure and continues. The powerful visual allusions to the Kennedy assassination made some Ford advisers predict the loss of Texas as a consequence of broadcasting the spot, while others simply feared the unknown. Pollster Robert Teeter pretested the spot with several hundred people, but the result was indeterminate. As Bailey reported it:

They couldn't deal with it, it shook them up too much. I had no idea what the ultimate political impact would be of airing it and so the campaign decided not to run it because we concluded that we were going to win. If you're going to win you don't rock the boat. That spot was developed when we thought we were going to lose, and we wanted to shake up the audience. . . . If I had thought we were still behind, I would have been in favor of running it.

Bailey was certainly correct to deduce that his Ford spot might have wholly unforeseen consequences, and he discovered as much anew with Howard Baker's short-lived 1980 presidential campaign. During early January the Baker campaign ran Bailey ads showing Baker at the Watergate hearings, making his famous inquiry about President Nixon's involvement in the scandal: "What did he know and when did he know it?" Since the hearings had brought national attention to Baker for the first time, and the reaction among Republicans had been generally favorable even at the time (before the devastating revelations to come), the ad series seemed like a good idea. Yet, Bailey reports, "Very quickly we started getting negative calls about it. It turned out Republicans just didn't like to be reminded of Watergate."[60] The series was cancelled after only a few days.

Consultants' fears about transgressing convention and courting disaster are usually unfounded, a product of exaggerated visions of their importance to a campaign or their power to affect its outcome. More often than not, even a risk-taking "wild card" advertisement has little perceptible effect. Michael Kaye, in his "deliberate effort to be different," took a self-described gamble in Democratic U.S. Senator Dick Clark's 1978 reelection bid in Iowa. Kaye had a crippled Vietnam veteran in a wheelchair, looking directly into the camera, deliver this powerful and emotional spot:

The war in Vietnam should have taught us a lesson, but I guess it hasn't. In 1975, the CIA was involving us in another war in the jungles of Angola. But one senator, Dick Clark of Iowa, said, "No way." And he kept the President from sending military aid to Angola without the approval of Congress. Maybe if Dick Clark had been in the U.S. Senate fifteen years ago, there might not have been a Vietnam.

Though Clark was defeated, the loss was not tied even partly to this spot or the others in Kaye's creative series, which were generally believed by observers to have been an assist rather than a drag on Clark's campaign.

This suggests what most media consultants fully accept: that advertisements make some difference, but only rarely can they be assigned the major portion of credit or blame for victory or defeat. Even when a media consultant does everything "right," it may all be for naught because of an accumulation of other factors. The liberal Democratic media firm of Buckley and Rothstein produced a textbook commercial package for U.S. Senator Floyd Haskell of Colorado in his 1978 second-term bid.[61] A series of thirty-second ads in late summer on the theme "Haskell for People" handsomely displayed Haskell's pork-barrel produce for his state, positioned him as a "fighter" (opposing even a president of his own party in Colorado's interest), showed him to be close to the people in yet another "work days" gimmick, and praised him lavishly with testimonials from Coloradans aided by his Senate office. In the home stretch, his advertisements focused on his record, drawing a sharp and attractive contrast between him and his opponent, Republican U.S. Representative William Armstrong. Films of five-minute and thirty-minute duration included pleasant family scenes with his daughters (blunting the effects of an unhappy divorce) and a discussion of his notable record in World War II (making less credible his opponent's charges that he was "soft" on defense). When Haskell lost by a margin of three to two—especially disastrous for an incumbent—one of his media consultants cried, "Maybe those ads just weren't credible." More likely, Haskell's advertisements had relatively little to do with his loss. He was an aloof, shy incumbent, with no strong base of support, narrowly elected the first time in a fluke, who was running in a year when his party and his philosophy took a drubbing at the senatorial level in the western states. His advertisements may have helped to keep his margin of defeat from being even worse.

Most media consultants hope to stave off defeats of any margin by extensive contingency planning. Very frequently advertisements are prepared in anticipation of the opponent's potential strategies, and consequently many never find their way onto the television screen. New rapid production equipment is making long-range contingency production unnecessary, however. It is entirely possible, even relatively simple now, for a campaign to change advertising gears as circumstances warrant. The 1976 presidential media advisers were constantly adjusting their commerical themes to suit changing conditions and the opponent's direction.[62] Jimmy Carter, who had begun his television effort as the cinéma vérité star of documentary advertising, gradually became a "talking head" candidate of presidential stature who appeared at a desk instead of on a peanut field wearing a suit instead of jeans and discussing specific issues instead of vague generalities. Ford's campaign, ironically, moved in just the opposite direction, from being grandiose and presidential, to focusing on the warm, personal qualities of the candidate and his family.

Multiple themes and rapid changes in emphasis and image can be dangerous when a consultant is handling a live candidate, since the changes often make the candidate appear to be an unprincipled political chameleon. Referenda and initiative campaigns, however, are tailor-made for subplots galore and maneuvers worthy of an Olympic gymnast. It was partly the creative challenge of ballot measures that induced Chuck Winner to concentrate his political efforts there, rather than with candidates. His firm (Winner-Wagner and Associates) has built a national reputation for successful opposition to antinuclear initiatives, starting with Proposition 15 in California, a 1976 ballot initiative that sought to limit nuclear power construction in the nation's largest state. On its face, the measure promised to be attractive to a significant share of the state's electorate, if only because so many public opinion grinches (big industry, oil companies, and the utilities) opposed it. The initiative's backers secured almost double the number of signatures necessary to place it on the ballot while the governor, Jerry Brown, was popularizing alternative energy sources (solar, geothermal, etc.). On the other hand, the Winner-Wagner agency was guaranteed by industry to have all the money it would need to turn public opinion around, and financing is probably the most crucial element in a successful ballot measure campaign (whether for or against.)[63]

While proponents were calling Proposition 15 "the safeguards measure," Winner decided to term it "the shutdown initiative." The economic and environmental consequences were used to depict the alleged stark effects of the stifling of nuclear industry. Only two politicians were used to endorse the anticampaign, both of them selected after extensive polling: ex-Governor Edmund G. "Pat" Brown, Sr. (the current governor's father) and Robert Moretti, former speaker of the state house and a member of the California Energy Commission. Endorsements were secured mainly from apolitical "experts" (scientists, doctors, even environmentalists) since surveys demonstrated they had more credibility on this particular issue than either politicians or movie stars (the latter, perennial California favorites in political advertising). In general, Winner took the negative aspects of nuclear power and converted them into attributes. For example, "We could not try to say 'nuclear' is better than 'solar' because of public opinion, so we tried to tie nuclear power to solar power, saying we needed both of them," revealed Winner. Energy Commissioner Moretti and others related the need for nuclear power to the energy crisis and the great national goal of ending "our dependence on foreign oil" and stopping "foreign blackmail." The environmentalist claimed Proposition 15 would be bad for the environment. The physician insisted Proposition 15 would be injurious to health. The experts were always identified as "Nobel Laureates" and "eminent scientists" to whom laymen in their technical ignorance naturally defer. Interestingly, the Winner-Wagner research discovered that a large segment of the public was not even dimly aware of how electricity is made or what the alternative methods for its generation are. Considering what the public knew, and what they were being told, Winner's slogan was quite appropriate: "The more you know about Proposition 15, the less you like it."

Added to all of this was an effort to make Proposition 15 sound as extreme as possible (a "total shutdown," it was called) and to hit the voter in his pocketbook by claiming passage would cost the average family $375 per year in added energy bills. Whatever the accuracy of all these assertions—and this ballot measure occurred before Three Mile Island dramatized in a personal way the dangers of nuclear power—the research that went into their formulation and precise wording was impressive and painstaking. Thirty-five thirty- and sixty-second commercials were prepared, and each was audience-tested before airing. The "Pat Brown" spot, for instance, was originally intended for targeting to highly Democratic television audiences, but the pretest indicated that one of Brown's lines ("But look into '15' yourself") was so credible and highly rated that eventually the spot was slated for all audiences. It is a commentary on the homogenization of American state politics that Winner-Wagner produced the very same kind of commercials with similar wordings for recent equally successful battles against antinuclear initiatives in Arizona and Montana.

Yet another classic case of a corporate-sponsored defeat of a California initiative was that of Proposition 5, a 1978 measure designed to restrict smoking privileges. An alarmed tobacco industry contracted with Woodward & McDowell agency, and a brilliant campaign was produced that succeeded in transferring a threat to a special-interest group (smokers) into a threat to everyone's freedom. This was done by transferring the nonsmoking public's ire *from* the smoker's irritating habits *to* a more general enemy, the encroaching bureaucracy—always a tempting straw man. With an eye to "big brother," the anti-Proposition 5 spots made clear their theme with a number of recurring slogans: "What will the regulators try to regulate next?"; "They're at it again!"; "Let's stop them before they stop us." Often the ads did not even make clear the content of Proposition 5; but whatever Proposition 5 may be, the commercials suggested, it is associated with boogeymen and things that go bump in the night. Most of the spots feature average people in everyday situations explaining the absurdity of the smoking regulations designed by the equivalent of George Wallace's pointy-headed bureaucrats with briefcases full of peanut butter sandwiches. The sensible man's contempt for such senseless regulation, with which the audience at home is presumably identifying, is communicated by sarcastic concluding remarks ("Hey, guys—*really stupid!*"; "Have they taken leave of their senses?"; "Now really, fellas . . ."). One of the most creative ads has a black female lawyer explaining, with the instant credibility of race and profession, how Proposition 5 invidiously discriminates. Scare tactics are part and parcel of the presentation too. A policeman is pictured arresting someone for smoking in an unauthorized place. And Greg Morris makes a guest appearance in a sort of "Mission Infringement" spot, his solemn, clipped tone giving the viewer the full measure of Proposition 5's threat to the personal liberties he and his "Mission Impossible" associates have struggled so hard to protect.

In well-funded campaigns like these initiative efforts, audience pretesting of advertisements is standard, with the "focus group" device usually being utilized. A focus group is comprised of ten to fifteen individuals marshalled by a trained discussion leader. The individuals (from predetermined population subgroups) are often asked to join the session in random selections at shopping centers, providing of course they fill the prescription, and they are paid a nominal amount for their participation by the several firms that organize focus groups. Once gathered together, the group is shown the advertisements and asked a series of open-ended questions to probe their reactions to each spot. Many times the media consultants will watch the dialogue behind a two-way mirror, and the discussion is always tape-recorded for later analysis. Despite the nonrandom nature of the focus group, it can be advantageous since probes can be more thorough than in most polls, and the responses can be more unstructured than surveys permit.

There is little question that the device has been invaluable on occasion. While attending a focus group, one California consultant, Hugh Schwartz, discovered the theme that would prove to be the successful ingredient of his campaign to defeat Governor Ronald Reagan's 1971 tax reform initiative, Proposition 1. During the group session, as the text of the initiative was being circulated, Schwartz reported that "One guy took a look at it and said, 'Geez, you've gotta be a lawyer to understand this thing.' That became the theme of the campaign. Our ads all stressed the initiative was so much legalese, and that even the people who wrote it didn't understand what it would do."[64] Proposition 1 lost disastrously, its grave dug when a reporter, taking his cue from Schwartz's advertisements, asked Reagan if he understood the measure. "Hell no," the governor replied.[65]

The National Republican Congressional Committee has used focus groups extensively to improve the content and form of their national advertisements.[66] Among many other findings (which further testing has confirmed) is the revelation that candidates should not merely advocate their own points of view; their credibility is greatly increased when they present, in however biased a fashion, both sides of an argument before taking a position.[67] Focus groups frequently produce surprises and refute common wisdom. Several of William Winter's campaign aides objected to the airing of one of Robert Squier's spots for the 1979 Mississippi Democratic gubernatorial primary because it featured a relaxed black worker who continued to recline as Winter spoke to him. The fear was that blacks would see the portrayal as demeaning and suggestive of slothfulness, but when a group of black voters viewed all of Winter's commercials, they chose the one in question as their favorite. Squier said that the black observers approvingly saw the black man as declaring "I'm laying right here, whitey. In the old days I had to get on my feet for you, but I don't have to anymore."

For all their virtues, there are considerable dangers involved in reliance on focus groups. A couple of strong personalities in a group can stifle discussion or heavily influence the conclusions of other participants. And even though focus groups are not random samples, they often are treated as such. (Whenever possible, the more concrete and structured conclusions of a focus group should be tested in a poll with a representative sample.) In most candidate campaigns, though, sufficient scheduling flexibility and money are not available to permit the luxury of extensive focus-group testing. A series of six panels reviewing two to four commercials at a time costs about $2,000, and the process can add a week or more to the already tight media production schedule.

Consultant Styles

The strategies consultants choose are strongly influenced by the professional styles they have adopted and perfected over the years. There are two simultaneous and contradictory desires tugging at the consultant's creative threads. On the one hand is the tendency toward the tried and true, the proven techniques and those that are faddishly popular. Imitation, however, is not nearly as intellectually satisfying as indulging one's own creative impulses, and so usually the consultant tries to impose his own individual style—sometimes unvaryingly in very different campaigns and electoral circumstances. For those consultants lucky enough to have *established* a trend—thus earning the right to have their cake (proven techniques) and eat it too (personal style)—there is another danger, however. When a consultant's trademark becomes well known, it is easier to anticipate his approach and, by extrapolation, some of his strategy. As one national consultant boasted, "We all know each other's trademark so well. When I'm in a race against consultant X, I know pretty much what he's going to do."

What is most surprising, perhaps, is that the styles are so divergent, even opposite. Tony Schwartz has done more theorizing about the effectiveness of various media formats than any of the national media professionals. He designs only "head-on spots and symbolic spots" and opposes "cluttering" them up with jingles and slogans. Says Schwartz, "People gain comfort from visual familiarity and discomfort from auditory repetition."[68] One application of Schwartz's guideline is his practice of printing the candidate's name—on television and in all print advertisements—exactly as it will appear on the ballot, using the same typeface and complete formal name, for example. Also, toward the end of a campaign, Schwartz often produces commercials that are montages of the early ads, contending that "Usually I can evoke people's full experience of the early commercials by using bits and pieces of them, properly designed. This makes use of a principle of perception, that people most readily understand things they have seen and heard before."[69] Calling the best political commercials akin to "Rorschach patterns," Schwartz believes that "a voter wants the candidate to talk *to* him, not *at* him; to use the medium not as a large *public address* system, but rather as a *private undress* system."[70]

Schwartz's approach inevitably led him to philosophical (and then personal) conflict with Gerald Rafshoon in the one major campaign they jointly worked, the 1976 Carter presidential effort. Schwartz has been highly critical of Rafshoon's general election package for Carter, contending that it neither permitted the Democratic nominee to appear presidential nor let him speak straight into the camera and thus directly to the voter. Instead, Carter was filmed speaking to others and communicating indirectly with the at-home audience. Rafshoon, pronounces Schwartz, was using television "as a window on the world rather than a door into your home."[71] Eighteen days before the election, Carter visited Schwartz's New York studio and a series of "talking head" ads were quickly produced. Rafshoon himself understandably bristles at the suggestion that Schwartz's series reversed a bland, progressively less appealing ad campaign, yet some of President Ford's media aides believe precisely that, and most national consultants agree with David Garth's assessment of Rafshoon's media: "All I remember . . . [is] Carter running his hands through peanuts."[72] During Rafshoon's notably unsuccessful year's tenure on the White House staff as assistant to the president for communications, Carter seemed to decline in the job performance polls as steadily as he did in the 1976 campaign trial heats, and while no one could fairly assign Rafshoon much of the blame, he certainly did little of notice to arrest Carter's fall from grace. Most of the "Rafshoonery," as it came to be called, resembled the cosmetic image making typical of his ads.[73] Yet Rafshoon, deny it though he might, has apparently learned from his experiences. The critics issued far more favorable reviews of his 1980 Carter reelection spots, which Rafshoon described as "90 percent Carter and 10 percent technique." Said Rafshoon: "Our job is not to mess up the 10 percent."[74]

Next to Rafshoon, no media consultant attracted more publicity in recent years than David Garth. The New York-based media man's style can only be captured with a long string of descriptions: noisy, rough-edged, brimming with information (because Garth thinks the audience absorbs more that way) with visual statistics streaming across the screen while the announcer adds still more. Each commercial requires several viewings for all the data to be taken in and for the multiple slogans that accompany the spots to be pieced together. Garth is noted for the extensive research his staff undertakes. About five to nine "books" of material, each several inches thick, are compiled for a campaign, and a fact sheet is prepared for each commercial to document its facts and assertions. Besides this sort of exhaustive research, Garth is well known for the degree of control over the campaign he demands of each client. While most of his media peers find Garth personally obnoxious, many acknowledge that his "take-charge" manner has distinct advantages. Charles Guggenheim comments:

There's one image in politics that serves the candidate better than any other. The candidate must give the impression that he knows what he is doing. . . . David Garth helps a candidate say, "I really believe in myself, I know what I'm doing." And so by demanding that he control the campaign and by demanding that the candidate do what he wants him to do, he performs a very valuable service for the candidate.

Guggenheim's praise of the Garth approach does not imply any imitation of it. In fact, their styles could hardly be more divergent. Guggenheim came to politics from film, quite the reverse of the route taken by most other media professionals. He had been producing opinionated films on social, political, and historical subjects, and it seemed a logical step to move from advocating ideas to working for candidates who could bring them into being. Guggenheim's most famous contribution to the political filming art was his popularization of the cinéma vérité technique, which has little fixed script and no hard sell.[75] The ads are carved out of hours of film, taken by a cameraman following the candidate around as he talks to voters encountered during his scheduled rounds. The idea, of course, is to get behind the campaign's facade and reveal the candidate's real qualities. After a while, the theory goes, the camera merely becomes part of the entourage, and the candidate becomes oblivious to its presence. The candidate never fails to impress and convince the average, undecided people he sees in his travels (after proper editing), and the television viewer, watching the road show and its interpersonal victories, is supposed to identify with the filmed voters and be swayed as they have been. Yet the "stream of consciousness," rambling nature of cinema verité and its stress on personal image rather than issue substance is disturbing to some. Other consultants, such as Douglas Bailey, claim that Guggenheim's profession has always been filmmaking, not politics, and that his spots often make little political sense: "Charles Guggenheim is a good friend, but he's a filmmaker. He makes beautiful films. When he gets into political campaigns, it's almost coincidental if the film makes any political sense."

Guggenheim, a modest and unassuming man in a profession—be it film or consulting—not noted for those virtues, accurately evaluated his own work when he suggested that "Our material, just to look at as film, is probably more interesting than anybody else's. But that doesn't mean that it is necessarily the most effective politically." Neither, however, does the judgment on Guggenheim imply that cinema verité is an ineffective technique. In the hands of Robert Squier, another practitioner, the ads can be free-flowing yet sharp, forceful, and thematic. Douglas Bailey's agency, despite his criticism of Guggenheim's cinema verité work, has also used the format from time to time. Bailey himself has allowed that viewers at home enjoy being "voyeurs," watching the candidate relating to other people. The Bailey/Deardourff firm's forté, though, is the man-in-the-street interview. Ordinary individuals frequently make a better case for a candidate in their own words than scriptwriters would have been able to concoct, and the naturalness and freshness of the comments make the arguments appear far more credible than canned material. Bailey/Deardourff's ads sometimes splice together half a dozen comments using very similar phrases to suggest that a certain impression about a candidate or his opponent is widespread.

The man-in-the-street technique may appear to be contrived image making, but some consultants belittle it as dull and too cerebral. Robert Goodman, one of the liveliest and most personally appealing media consultants, declares, "Bailey and Deardourff are research people. We're more hot-blooded, more emotional. We're not afraid to say the word 'love.' "[76] Every election to Goodman is a dramatic event that needs a hero (a "soaring American eagle") and a spirit. The candidate is made heroic and the campaign is given spirit through generous provision of catchy jingles, stirring songs, noise, excitement, and clever slogans. The justification for all the hoopla is, insists Goodman, "Voting is emotional. People vote feelings rather than fact. . . . Television is a feeling medium . . . and voting decisions are based more on perceptions and style than substance." The question must inevitably arise: At what point do political advertisements become all style and no substance, pure image without a reality?

Imagery or Substance?

> Glenn Beall stands for things Marylanders have always felt but can't always express about their state. It has something to do with hearing about what our fathers have left us, respecting people, their accomplishments, their customs, their beliefs. It has something to do with fair leadership. Marylanders have always demanded that kind of leadership. That's why Maryland needs Glenn Beall in the United States Senate.
>
> —*Audio script of 1970 television spot*

A majority of Marylanders did indeed decide they needed Glenn Beall in the U.S. Senate, but this commercial could not possibly have given them any reason to do so. It was a pleasant-enough spot: magnificent film, sunset scenes on Chesapeake Bay, the candidate cheerily waving to and walking with ethnically balanced crowds, the mellifluous voice of a polished announcer perfectly matching script with scene. Pleasing, yes; informative, no. It told the viewer absolutely nothing.

This sort of vapid image making did not originate with modern media consultants; the party bosses of old were hardly known for elevating the level of political discourse.[77] That party leaders are guilty of the same vice cannot make it a virtue, however, and media consultants have transformed obfuscation into an art form with all the television world their stage. The practice is not confined to a few. As one consultant admitted before a jury of his peers, "There isn't a one of us who hasn't practiced the art of waffling, dodging, and avoiding with meaningless rhetoric."[78] Most consultants simply agree with Pat Caddell's observation that "Too many good people have been defeated because they tried to substitute substance for style."[79] And, in the end, the professionals' livelihoods depend on winning, not scoring debating points on issues. ("What do you believe in?" a fellow consultant privately asked Gerald Rafshoon in the midst of the 1976 Carter campaign. "Winning the presidency" was Rafshoon's curt answer.) Rather than avoiding issues entirely, most consultants merely are selective in articulating positions. "I tell the candidate never to lie about his real position on an issue if asked, but if it is one that's going to cost him votes, he just shouldn't publicize it," advises Joseph Napolitan.

Professionals are equally choosy in publicizing a candidate's personality traits, but there are limits to even a consultant's magic. "It is a very hard job to turn a turkey into a movie star; you try instead to make people like the turkey," says media woman Jill Buckley.[80] A live candidate is simply not as flexible a product as a bar of soap, as Bob Goodman notes:

You can't put a candidate completely in a new package. You can take his polyester off and put him in a decent-looking suit. You can have him blow dry his hair. You can teach him how to keep his eye on the camera. You can try to inspire certain attributes. But you don't have the complete freedom that you do when you're dealing with a bar of soap.

The public has preconceived notions about politics and some individual candidates that cannot be altered by the quick fix of an ad campaign. Both Edward Kennedy and John Connally discovered this in 1980. But while it is undoubtedly difficult to change the public's fixed image, it is much easier to create one where none existed (for a new candidate) or through selective emphasis on some personality characteristics and issues to cause a preexisting image to be viewed in a new context.

Not all of the image making is designed for evasion. Some of it is produced for exactly the opposite purpose: to attract attention, specifically the attention of the "free" or "unpaid" media—the press. The press at times seems even less interested in issues than do media consultants. Jill Buckley sounds a frequently heard lament: "If you gave a terrific speech on health care, you're not going to get on page 63 [of the newspaper] unless you give it in a nursing home standing on a bed with your legs wrapped in tape."[81] Television, particularly, demands "good visuals."

With the experience of dozens of campaigns, eventually consultants have also realized that all a candidate usually gains from taking a position on a controversial issue is a lot of coverage about the *controversy* generated by the candidate's stand, rather than the specifics of the position itself.[82] In the final analysis, though, candidates eschew issues and emphasize image because they believe, whether correctly or not, that most voters judge them more on feelings about personalities than on issues. Voters are presumed to want to know what kind of person the candidate is, whether he is likeable and of good character, whether he is honest and sincere, and whether he appears effective, authoritative, and knowledgeable (whatever may be the subjects.) Because of this belief, Bob Goodman "strive[s] for . . . an emotion, not a position" because "feelings decide it all. We must *like* this human being to vote for him. In most elections, the issue isn't foreign policy or inflation. The issue is really the human being."[83]

In the relatively nonparty and nonideological American political system, it is the individual *candidate* who is the center of the electoral process, and the audience responds accordingly. The electorate has a better recall of the content of "image" commercials compared with issue-oriented advertisements, for example,[84] and recall is vital considering the intense competition for the attention of the voter not just among candidates but by commercial advertisers. In 1976 Ford and Carter together were outspent on television during the general election by just two product advertisers, General Motors and Proctor & Gamble.[85] And, sadly, media consultants do not package candidates so much as they package voters' prejudices. Professionals attempt to make their candidates physically handsomer and more attractive, for instance, because (as one consultant put it) "ugly folks get less votes." Focus-group experiments have shown that respondents select the most attractive candidate of the available alternatives and impute worse motives and capabilities to less attractive ones.[86] It was with good reason, then, that political consultants interviewed for a national Republican party study unanimously agreed that "candidates should be pictured in a television spot only when they are physically attractive."[87] (What would the GOP's rather ugly Abe Lincoln have done in the television age?)

Little wonder, too, that candidates all over the country have been forcefully and painfully reshaped by consultant-ordered diets, new coiffures, refurbished wardrobes, and voice lessons. Richard Nixon, after the lesson of his 1960 presidential debates, did not have to be coaxed in 1968 to lose weight so as to reduce his facial jowls, to keep a constant suntan for color television, and to shave several times a day to alter his "shadowy" look.[88] U.S. Senator Henry Jackson of Washington, in preparation for his 1976 bid for the Democratic presidential nomination, hired speech instructors to speed his delivery and improve his pronunciation, slimmed down twenty pounds, had plastic surgery to correct sagging eyelids, let his hair grow longer, and purchased a number of "made-for-TV" suits.[89] Candidates are also "improved" by association with symbols of desired qualities or favored groups. Put a candidate on a surfer's beach or in a tackle football game or a discussion with a group of young people and he is more youthful, and the generation gap is bridged. To emphasize warmth and sincerity, the roaring fire is a perfect accompaniment, and a study with bookcases crammed full will signify wisdom and competence. To stress a candidate's power or patriotism, the emotion-laden symbols of democracy (the White House, Capitol Hill, monuments of various descriptions, the seals of office, and the ubiquitous flag) are made to order.

The brevity of most political commercials puts a premium on image making symbols, which permit a consultant to communicate far more than time would allow in words. For the same reason, sloganeering and shorthand language are also highly prized skills in the media arts. A candidate does not discuss inflation as an economist does; his purposes are better served by quipping "Prices are so high that bologna is a gourmet food."[90] Candidates who use "bumper-sticker" phrases can get their messages across more quickly in advertisements and also, when covered by the free media, cannot be edited. Tony Schwartz encourages his clients to make all their important statements in fifty seconds or less, so that they will be reported in their entirety on the evening news.[91] Media-produced taciturnity, then, has distinct political advantages, even if by nature it requires oversimplistic answers to devilishly difficult questions.

Literally every word of a spot announcement becomes important, and a good media consultant wastes no opportunity to get a point across. Several years ago spots were often concluded with the obligatory "This ad paid for by the Potzrebie for Senate Campaign Committee." Now most media professionals have adopted a new version: "This ad was brought to you by a lot of people who want to see Irving Potzrebie in the United States Senate."[92] The announcer's voice is considered vital by many consultants, who go to great lengths to secure a particular narrator for their spots. The inflection, resonance, tone, and even the speed of a candidate's voice is also of concern to many consultants. Studies have indicated that especially fast talkers are perceived as competent but not kind (and slow enunciators the reverse), so professional training is sometimes prescribed to speed up or slow down the candidate's speech rate.[93] A candidate's voice can occasionally contribute to his victory, surprisingly enough. The Ringe-Russo agency, preparing for Texas Republican William Clements's eventually successful 1978 gubernatorial effort, concluded (in the words of one of the firm's principals) that "The most important thing of all in Texas was not inflation, or taxes, or morality. It was to be a Texan . . . and we made a decision to make the keystone of our advertising program the fact that Bill Clements was more of a Texan than anybody else running."[94] In accordance with this finding, the agency used no announcer at all in the Clements advertisements, preferring to use Clements himself as the narrator. The candidate's deep Texas drawl was so appealing to the Lone Star state's voters that a telephone poll by Lance Tarrance revealed that 27 percent of Clements's primary supporters said they cast their ballots for him because of his voice![95]

The use of symbols and imagery was certainly a part of pretelevision politics, but television, itself pure image, added a sort of technological temptation to be expansive that consultants have never been able to resist. There is a film image to cure every problem, to fill every need. Lyndon Johnson's 1968 foreign and domestic disasters could be subsumed by a suitable incumbency image, advised Charles Guggenheim in a strategy memorandum never to be implemented because of Johnson's withdrawal. In words that could as easily have been written for Richard Nixon in 1972 or Jimmy Carter in 1980, Guggenheim told Johnson that his advertisements

should convince that the presidency is an awesome responsibility and the president's chair is occupied by a person with uncommon ability . . . that these are terribly critical times, that the wrong decision could lead to dangerous consequences . . . [that] the presidency [is] a lonesome job occupied by a man more misunderstood than revered, a man with uncommon talents, a man of, by, and for the land that he serves.[96]

One of President Johnson's eventual Democratic opponents, Senator Robert F. Kennedy, ended up with the same consultant, who grappled with RFK's very different problems. To soften Kennedy's "ruthless" image, for instance, Guggenheim filmed an appealing, if empty, spot with Kennedy and his children. While alternately tossing a football and hugging the little ones, Kennedy is surrounded by a breezy spring day and pleasant, sentimental string music as the narrator tenderly says, "A man with ten children can't avoid a concern about the future. It's underfoot most of the time. Each day Robert Kennedy is surrounded by a lot of reminding that we must do something about tomorrow." A man with ten cute and loving children cannot really be ruthless, implies Guggenheim, even if he never gets around to telling us what it is we must do about tomorrow. A voter should simply presume that, once in power, Kennedy would do the right thing because he cares about his children's future.

Three presidential elections later, image making had been deemed so much a part of one president's success that his national reelection chairman, opening his 1980 New Hampshire primary headquarters, was moved to insist that "The president is not a parthenogenetic, vacuous creation of television."[97] President Ford's spots in 1976 were no less image conscious than Carter's. Bailey/Deardourff agency made a not-so-subtle attempt to portray Ford in the Eisenhower "fatherly" mold, for example. Their man-in-the-street spots featured several women remarking that Ford "reminds me of my father." (One actually said, "If he were my father, I'd love him"!) The 1980 presidential campaign was no different from the one that preceded it in the continuing fascination of consultants with imagery and style. Sometimes the imagery was quiet, as in advertisements for Howard Baker (another Bailey, Deardourff project) that showed him, in an open-neck checked shirt, seated in a living room next to a wood-burning stove or commenting about his homey photographs of weddings, a firehouse, and old people.[98] And sometimes the style was noisy, as in Bob Goodman's brash spots for George Bush.[99] With music much like "Victory at Sea," with crowds roaring, "We want Bush," the candidate made his empty contribution to the presidential advertising discourse:

I've seen this country up close. I hear what Americans are saying. Yes, they want change. Yes, they want solutions. But they don't want yesterday's ideas promising everything to everybody. Americans today are ready to roll up their sleeves and rededicate this country to excellence, to principle, and to leadership from strength. And that's why I'm optimistic about our future.

As image-dominated as presidential campaigns may be, image making is much more prevalent at the state and congressional district levels, where, unlike most presidential contenders, candidates are often unknowns, with no sharply defined public images. Unknowns, if sufficiently pliant, present ripe opportunities for creative consultants. There is no better example than Bob Goodman's media work for Malcolm Wallop, Republican nominee for the U.S. Senate from Wyoming in 1976 who up-ended three-term incumbent Democrat Gale McGee in a major upset (for which Goodman's ad campaign was given a good part of the credit).[100] As the selected spots in table 3–2 suggest, few

TABLE 3-2

Selected Advertisements by Robert Goodman from the Malcolm Wallop for
U.S. Senate Campaign (Wyoming, 1976)

1. The Wallop Senate Drive (30 seconds)

ANNOUNCER:	Malcolm Wallop
WALLOP:	Time used to be on our side, but now we know better.
MUSIC:	Come join the Wallop Senate Drive, the Wallop Senate Drive/It's alert, it's alive/It's Wyoming to the spurs/The Wallop Senate Drive.
WALLOP:	[While music plays in background] The ideas that served the sixties no longer serve today. Let's put the past to rest and dedicate ourselves to a new and better tomorrow. Come on Wyoming, this is our day!
POSTER:	Malcolm Wallop for United States Senate.

2. Ride with us, Wyoming (60 seconds)

MUSIC:	["The Wallop Senate Drive," as three cowboys saddle up their horses out on the range.]
ANNOUNCER:	The Wallop Senate Drive starts here. Three riders with a proclamation.
VISUALS:	[Men are mounting horses as the music builds. Wallop is pictured in a close-up shot pulling the brim of his cowboy hat down over his eyes, á la Marlboro advertisement—except for the dark-blue business suit he is wearing. As the theme song is sung, the camera shows Wallop in slow motion, swinging a saddlebag through the air; then the three riders come over the crest of a hill. The focus now shifts to Wallop riding his horse.]
ANNOUNCER:	Go forth for Wyoming, Malcolm Wallop. Tell them in the United States Senate that the people of Wyoming are proud of their land and life, and a Wyoming senator will fight every intrusion upon it. That you, Malcolm Wallop, will serve the nation best by serving Wyoming first— the very special needs of this great state. And in so doing share its blessing with America.
VISUALS:	[Wallop is now leading a horde of cowboys on horseback, resembling a cavalry scene. They parade through town, as crowds cheer and Wallop waves.]
ANNOUNCER:	Malcolm Wallop for U.S. Senate. Ride with us, Wyoming!

3. Post Office (30 seconds)

VISUALS:	[Camera shows a letter to Mrs. John Smith with four one-cent stamps in the corner.]
ANNOUNCER:	We paid exactly four cents to mail a first-class letter in 1959. That's about the time Senator Gale McGee came to the United States Senate. Since then a lot has happened. [One-cent stamps of various sizes begin to appear across the top of the letter, down the left-hand side, then across the bottom of the letter. Camera begins to move to the right of the letter, hesitates.] Oh, yes [camera moves back to the letter], McGee is chairman of the Senate Post Office Committee. [Camera begins to move to the right of the letter again, and hesitates.] And, oh yes [as camera moves back to the letter], Mrs. Smith is still waiting for the letter.
POSTER:	Join the Wallop Senate Drive.

4. Porta-Potty (30 seconds)

VISUAL:	[Wallop, dressed as a cowboy, is saddling and mounting a horse.]
ANNOUNCER:	Everywhere you look these days, the federal government is there, telling you what they think, telling you what they think you ought to think. Telling you how to do things, setting up rules you can't follow. I think the federal government is going too far. Now they say if you don't take the portable facility along with you on a roundup, you can't go!
VISUALS:	[Wallop appears angry and disgusted, matching the announcer's sarcastic tone, as the camera pans a porta-potty strapped to a donkey tied to Wallop's horse.]
ANNOUNCER:	We need someone to tell 'em about Wyoming. Malcolm Wallop will.
POSTER:	Malcolm Wallop for U.S. Senate.

real issues existed in the campaign, and a generalized enemy (big, inefficient government) was made Wallop's target in an orgy of gimmickry. Scenery and extras reminiscent of the old West (seventy-five horses and riders, filmed by a helicopter) were combined with the accent, tone, and dramatic music of a Marlboro commercial. The stirring, patriotic presentations focus all the emotion and virtue on the candidate in the ten-gallon hat, who is transformed into a cowpoke even though he is a Yale graduate, born in New York, and a polo-playing cousin of Queen Elizabeth II. Yet any viewer of these extraordinarily moving spots would not be surprised to learn they were highly rated by voters in a national focus-group test.[101]

The boosterism and parochialism about Wyoming glorified in the Wallop ads can be seen yet again in an Alaskan setting in Goodman's package for U.S. Representative Don Young's 1978 reelection campaign. (See table 3–3.) The theme, the song, and the slogan ("Don Young, Alaskan like you") is nothing but an appeal to tribal loyalties. "What is the Don Young campaign all about?" one spot asks. "It's what the people of Alaska are all about" comes the answer, and more spectacular music and stunningly beautiful scenes of the Alaskan wilderness build the voter's pride in his state—and in that fine man who represents it. The only vague attempt at issues is the striking of a "them versus us" posture toward the ignorant, un-Alaskan federal government—a crude, incipient nationalism that says nothing of value about the problems facing either Alaska or the country.

Goodman's casting and musical productions are not standard fare at the state and district levels, but somewhat similar image techniques using other formats are common. Robert Squier is one of the best and most successful practitioners of symbolic politics in statewide races. For one of U.S. Representative John Brademas's reelection races, for instance, Squier included an appeal to blue-collar workers built around symbols suggested by the workers themselves. In doing research for the Indiana Democrat's media, Squier had talked to a local union official who disclosed that the workers were asking management for shower and locker rooms at the factory so they could enter and exit their place of employment dressed in a coat and tie. Reports Squier:

I got to thinking about it. We had been doing those blue-collar spots all wrong all these years. We'd shown the blue-collar worker dirty, coming out of the factory, and put him on the screen the way he doesn't like to be seen. He sees himself as a suburbanite. So instead we showed him the way he'd like to be seen by his family and the community.

TABLE 3–3

Selected Advertisements by Robert Goodman from U.S. Representative Don Young's Reelection Campaign (Alaska, 1978)

---

1. Alaska the Beautiful (60 seconds)

VISUALS:	[Panoramas of Alaskan scenery]
MUSIC:	Don Young, Alaskan like you/Fighting for you to stay free/Don Young, we're asking of you/Stand by our side in D.C.
ANNOUNCER:	It took some time and hard work to build the Alaska of today, and it takes hard work to keep the Alaska we want it to be. Here's the man who does that work every day. Don Young for Alaska—and what a state to work for! Welcome to the biggest congressional district in the nation and the man who fights to keep it the best. Alaska and Don Young. Let's keep a good man on the job. Don Young, Alaskan like you. [Music fades]

---

2. The Fighter (30 seconds)

VISUAL:	[Representative Young at a House committee meeting]
MUSIC:	[Same, but only one line sung:] Don Young, Alaskan like you.
ANNOUNCER:	An Alaskan with seniority and clout. When Don Young speaks, Washington listens.
YOUNG:	Let me put you on notice. Alaska is getting sick and tired of being kicked around. If you keep this up, we are going to kick back.
ANNOUNCER:	Don Young, Congressman, Alaskan like you.

---

3. Common Man Testimonial (30 seconds)

ANNOUNCER:	What is the Don Young campaign all about? It's what the people of Alaska are all about.
MAN ON THE STREET:	You know, people in the lower 48 don't realize that things are different here in Alaska. They are making laws in D.C. for the whole country, and they end up hurting Alaska most. Now, the only man I know who is fighting for the exceptions that Alaska needs is Don Young. He's not part of that Washington, D.C. crowd. He is an Alaskan. He lives in Fort Yukon. I don't know what we would do without him, to tell you the truth.
ANNOUNCER:	Don Young, Alaskan like you.

The Brademas commercials dutifully featured a blue-collar worker in his suburban setting, the proud owner of "his own home, a new car, and a new dog," surrounded by a family (and a congressman) equally proud of his success.

For all of this concern with image, by no means are all advertising campaigns consumed with trivia, obsessed with symbols, and afraid of detailed positions. In his reelection campaigns U.S. Senator William Proxmire consistently runs up to two dozen spots on specific issues. When John F. Kennedy sought the presidency in 1960, he taped a number of "talking head" commercials. Sitting in his Senate office, speaking quietly and directly to the camera, he showed how much could be communicated on a complicated subject such as health care by the candidate himself, absent any gimmicks, in just sixty seconds:

This is Senator John Kennedy, the Democratic nominee for the Presidency of the United States. One of the problems which concerns me most is our failure to meet the problem of medical care for our older citizens. Some of them are in ill health, some of them are in your family. And yet under present laws, before they can receive any assistance in the payment of their medical bills, which may be expensive, they must take a pauper's oath, they must say that they are medically indigent. I believe that the way to meet this problem is the way Franklin Roosevelt met it in the Social Security Act of 1935. I believe that people during their working years would want to contribute so that when they've retired, when they've reached the age of sixty-five for men or sixty-two for women, then they can receive assistance in paying their bills. They pay their own way, they live in dignity, they get protection. This is the way it ought to be done. This is the sound way. And I can assure you that if we're successful, we're going to pass this bill next January.

Some consultants, to their credit, insist on issue-oriented advertising. As the earlier sampling of commercials from David Garth's package for New Jersey Governor Brendan Byrne indicated, Garth's material is factual and unusually informative. The issues discussed were obviously ones thought best to stress for tactical or strategic reasons. To expect otherwise during time bought by the candidate would be folly; on the other hand, an expectation that a candidate should discuss his positions in some detail on at least a few major issues (even issues of his own choosing) is far from unreasonable. Byrne's ads concentrated on his accomplishments, unsurprisingly, but also did not avoid the more unpleasant aspects of his record, and the candidate offered much of his own defense in person. There were negative spots directed against his Republican opponent, but they were not the outlandishly ribald offerings that seem to be standard fare in some media firms.

It is significant that McClure and Patterson could conclude in their media study of the 1972 presidential election that "The problem with television's entry into national politics is that network news departments and political candidates consistently misuse the medium and underrate their audiences."[102] Political consultants should be added to the guilty list. They often ignore the finding that issue spots result in a better evaluation of the candidate by viewers[103] and that the mere appearance of an issue in a political advertisement increases the issue's importance and salience to voters.[104] They also seem to forget from time to time the role of elections in a representative democracy, which requires not merely the elevation of individuals to leadership posts but also the establishment of a raison d'être for leadership and broad mandates for governance.

As critical as one can properly be of consultants' issue-deficient advertising, it must also be admitted that television journalists do even a worse job. McClure and Patterson found that political advertising in 1972, for all its many faults, gave five times the coverage to the major issues of the day than did the evening network news programs.[105] The vast majority of the "news" was given over to campaign trivia, hoopla, polls, and "horse-race" estimates, and this sorry record was only slightly improved in 1976.[106] Malcolm MacDougall, staff director of advertising for President Ford's campaign, adroitly captured the press's video coverage of the Ford-Carter race in a personal remembrance:

I saw Carter playing softball in Plains, Georgia. I saw Carter kissing Amy, I saw Carter hugging Lillian. I saw Carter, in dungarees, walking hand in hand through the peanut farm with Rosalynn. I saw Carter going into church, preaching in church, coming out of church. I saw Carter trying to explain his ethnic purity statement. I saw Carter trying to explain his *Playboy* interview. And then I saw two full, wonderful weeks of people commenting about Carter's *Playboy* interview. I saw Ford misstate the problems of Eastern Europe— and a week of people commenting about his misstatement. I saw Ford bump his head again. I saw Ford in Ohio say how glad he was to be back in Iowa. I saw marching bands and hecklers, and I learned about the size of crowds and the significance of the size of the crowds. And I saw Carter carrying his own suitcase a lot. But in all the hours of high anxiety that I spent watching the network news, never did I hear what the candidates had to say about the campaign issues. That was not news.[107]

When political advertisements are as trivial, at least there is usually a musical accompaniment.

Gimmicks, Slogans, and Star Politics

Americans have always viewed politics as good sport, a form of entertainment, and politicians have always been willing to do just about anything to please in order to attract the voter's attention. Television offers the ingenious candidate and consultant tremendous potential for the exploitation of gimmickry, and many have risen to the challenge. The corollary of the image-making trend is a greater reliance on gimmicks, slogans, and star politics in the everlasting quest for name recognition and voter approval. There is no "visual" to compete with a good gimmick; as Clem Whitaker, one of the founding political consultants, advised his brethren many years ago, "Put on a show!"[108]

The pattern was set early in U.S. history by, among many others, Andrew Jackson, who had his supporters raise hickory poles in honor of "Old Hickory," and William Henry Harrison, an aristocrat who deceptively used the "log cabin" symbol to connote the humble birth he did not have. Modern gimmicks are more photogenic and candidate-centered.[109] The "walking" candidate is a favorite. More than a quarter century ago an obscure Nevada journalist, Thomas Mechling, trekked across his state to upset the favored candidate for a Democratic U.S. Senate nomination. Trudging across a constituency became a successful tactic again in the early 1970s. First "walkin' Lawton" Chiles plodded his way 1,003 miles down the Florida peninsula to win a Senate seat in 1970. Then Dan Walker (appropriately named) became governor of Illinois, and Dick Clark upset an incumbent U.S. senator in Iowa in 1972 using the technique. After that the dam broke, and literally hundreds of candidates have, with varying degrees of success, joined the fad and put on their walking boots.[110] A later innovation, to match the jogging craze in the United States, called for a candidate to run his way to victory—at least for a block or two for television cameras.[111] Florida Governor Bob Graham's campaign "work days" earned him national publicity in 1978, but again, he was hardly the first to use the device. Idaho Republican Steven D. Symms, found to be "missing" after his U.S. House nomination in 1972, was "discovered" several days later working in one of the state's mines. Governor Cliff Finch of Mississippi ran a "lunch pail" campaign similar to Graham's in 1975. Graham's 1978 Republican opponent also tried to use the technique during the general election, but while interstate plagiarism is tolerated by the voters, this imitation was too close to home.[112]

Sometimes candidates will go to ridiculous lengths to lure the media. Former Texas Governor John Connally, fading fast in the 1980 presidential race, campaigned nonstop for thirty-seven hours to stress his vitality (and, indirectly, Ronald Reagan's age.) An Oregon woman campaigning for governor in 1978 used a propane-powered balloon to enter and exit from her engagements,[113] and the former speaker of the Montana House, trying for a U.S. Senate nomination the same year, parachuted into one of his rallies. In Texas a Senate candidate canoed to a news conference. In Georgia Nick Belluso, a gubernatorial contender, hired a hypnotist to "mesmerize" voters in paid television spots. ("You *will* vote for Nick Belluso," the swami, turbaned and surrounded by mists, repeated.) The 1974 Peace and Freedom Party candidate for governor of California, Elizabeth Keathley, held a news conference in the nude on a beach; male reporters turned out in droves. It is somewhat reassuring to know that all of these candidates were defeated.

A candidate's slogan can be a sort of "minigimmick" in bumpersticker language, and consultants and candidates have become quite good at concocting them. Occasionally entire campaigns have been built around a slogan. John C. Danforth, in becoming the first Republican attorney general of Missouri in forty years in 1968, used the title of a well-remembered book his grandfather (the chairman of Ralston-Purina Company) had written in the 1920s to challenge the youth of his day, *I Dare You!*[114] The candidate started his speeches and headed his literature with those three words, striking a consistent and positive note that drew attention to him—no small feat in a presidential year for a contender for lesser statewide office. Most slogans center on the campaign theme (such as Graham's "Working for Governor"), on the candidate's qualifications (such as John Y. Brown's "A Businessman for Kentucky") or on general, positive, representative themes that seek to identify the candidate with his constituency ("He thinks like us"; "He hears you"; "He's on our side"; "You know where he stands.") Occasionally a theme is essentially negative, saying or implying more about the opposition than the candidate employing it (as in William Winter's "The Toughest Job in Mississippi" or the British Conservative party's "Labour Isn't Working.")[115]

Typically almost all American slogans are nonideological and decidedly not issue-oriented ("Not left, not right——forward" or "Something can be done"),[116] although New Right candidates are sometimes exceptions. U.S. Representative Steven Symms (R-Idaho), for instance, was first elected with the slogan "Let's Take a Bite Out of Government"—his buttons were in the shape of an apple with a bite out of it—or U.S. Senator Gordon Humphrey (R-N.H.)'s election slogan, "I want to be the toughest skinflint in the U.S. Senate." Incumbents are particularly prone to nonideological offerings, preferring to emphasize their accomplishments or simply their incumbency (as in Richard Nixon's 1972 "Four More Years" and "Re-Elect the President," or Senator Birch Bayh's "One Man Who Makes a Difference.") One candidate's forename lent itself perfectly to a reelection slogan. Pete Wilson, having been elected mayor of San Diego on a simple slogan of "Pete," ran for reelection as "Re-Pete."

The slogans of presidential candidates became part of the nation's political lore. Eisenhower's "Crime, Communism, and Korea" was unusually issue-oriented but is hardly representative. Lyndon Johnson's "All the Way with LBJ" and "LBJ for the USA" are more typical. Johnson's opponent, Barry Goldwater, made a serious mistake in selecting "In Your Heart You Know He's Right" as his slogan since it emphasized the extremism that was to be his undoing. (Interestingly, it was the least favorably received of five slogans pretested for Goldwater, but the candidate insisted on it anyway.)[117] George Wallace had probably the most emotion-packed presidential slogan of recent times ("Send Them a Message"), while Nixon's became the most ironic in light of Watergate ("Nixon's the One!" [1968]; "Now More than Ever" [1972]). Whatever else can be said about him, though, Nixon made good in the end on the promise of his secondary theme, "Bring Us Together." The 1976 election was a dramatic battle of slogans. Gerald Ford, emphasizing his occupancy of the White House in a desperate attempt to retain it, used "He's Our President—Let's Keep Him" in the preconvention period and two general election slogans, "He's Making Us Proud Again" and "Let's Keep to His Steady Course." Jimmy Carter's 1976 slogans ("Why Not the Best?" and "Leaders, for a Change") sound suspiciously like the themes adopted by most of Carter's opponents in 1980, a measure of the changeability of politics and the perils of incumbency.

Perhaps the worst aspect of presidential sloganeering is the myriad of repulsive forms in which the catch phrases are packaged. The 1968 Nixon organization, for instance, set an industry record for the production of campaign kitsch: 20.5 million buttons, 9 million bumper stickers, 600,000 balloons, 28,000 straw skimmers, 12,000 paper dresses, and 12,000 jewelry items.[118]

Through the years campaigns have assaulted not just the eyes but also the ears, with songs and jingles galore. But as Douglas Bailey has suggested, music must be used carefully in television political advertisements: "There is nothing better . . . than good campaign music and nothing worse than bad campaign music."[119] For certain candidates songs are simply inappropriate, and one has to agree with Bailey when he says, "It is hard for me to imagine a song ad in a Nixon campaign being effective."[120] In the main, campaign songs are best forgotten, silly variations on popular tunes that are written primarily to gain name recognition. ("Hey look him over/He's your kind of guy/His first name is Birch/And his last name is Bayh.")[121] The John Kennedy for President campaign produced one of the first television political spots built around a jingle. Resembling a movie advertisement for popcorn, the visuals were provided by animated campaign paraphernalia while the words to "Kennedy for Me" were cheerily sung:

Do you want a man for president who's seasoned through and through;
But not so doggone seasoned that he won't try something new?
A man who's old enough to know and young enough to do?
Well, it's up to you!

Of all the media professionals, Robert Goodman is the most addicted to song, and his lyrics (such as those for Senator Malcolm Wallop and Representative Don Young, cited earlier) are generally conceded to be effective and entertaining.[122] Gerald Ford's 1976 theme song, "I'm Feeling Good About America" was also thought (at least by the opposition) to have been useful and appropriate, coming as it did on the heels of the American Bicentennial.

Humor is used even more sparingly than songs in political commercials. While comedies consistently rank among the most popular television shows—and most any political campaign would make a grand situation comedy—a good portion of the electorate looks askance at candidates who take their politics too lightly, or so consultants fear. A joke also becomes old quickly, and when aired repeatedly it can be stale and irritating. Occasionally, though, humor is used with great effect. The Michigan Republican party delighted the state's voters in 1978 with the clever and witty Bailey, Deardourff spots presented in table 3–4, which compared the Democratic legislature to the "Lansing Zoo" in an attempt to increase GOP representation in the state capitol. The National Republican Congressional Committee sponsored a waggish spot aimed at the Democratic Congress in 1980 featuring an actor resembling Speaker Thomas P. O'Neill driving a car that runs out of fuel, with the punch line, "The Democrats are out of gas." One of the most telling humorous advertisements was designed by Bob Goodman for West Virginia Governor Arch Moore's successful 1972 reelection effort. Moore was in a difficult race against John D. (Jay) Rockefeller IV, who had lived in West Virginia (by design) for years but whose name was unmistakably associated with the Empire state. Using actors with bald New York accents, Goodman filmed this playful but hard-hitting spot:

INTERVIEWER: Ah, excuse me. What do you think about a West Virginian running for Governor of New York?
MAN ON MANHATTAN STREET: Like, is that a question or is that a statement? It don't make no sense neither way.

TABLE 3-4
Humorous Advertisements by Bailey, Deardouff & Associates for the Republican Party of Michigan (State Legislative Elections, 1978)

---

1. The Lansing Zoo: A Friendly Place (30 seconds)

VISUALS: [Groups of animals in captivity or in the wild, with a steady background of animal noises; same for all commercials.]

ANNOUNCER: The Lansing Zoo. Otherwise known as the Democratic State Legislature. It's a friendly place. [Monkeys applauding.] They take care of each other in fine style. [Monkeys cleaning each other.] They've fitted their nest with a $3.5 million office building just for Democrats and their staff. [Birds and rabbits in droves.] And they increased their staff an average of 166 percent per legislature, all in just the last seven years. [Hundreds of donkeys.] Maybe it's time we picked them clean for a change. [Preening animals.] After all, when we want something, like property tax reduced, they're not so friendly. [An ostrich attacks the cameraman's lens.]

---

2. The Lansing Zoo: A Shy Place (30 seconds)

ANNOUNCER: When you visit the Lansing Zoo, otherwise known as the Democratic State Legislature, do you wonder why they're so shy? [Animals run away from camera.] Where were they when they could have increased our state personal tax exemption by $100? [Flock of birds flies away.] Where were they when they could have allowed installment payments on the property tax? [Ostriches run away.] Where was the Democratic legislature when the elderly wanted property tax relief? [Herd of zebras running.] Just because they're shy, is no reason for us to be shy. [Ground hog goes into burrow.] Maybe we should help them disappear. [A hippo goes underwater.]

---

3. The Lansing Zoo: A Sleepy Place (30 seconds)

AUDIO: [Lullaby on sound track.]

ANNOUNCER: Have you noticed how the Lansing Zoo, otherwise known as the Democratic State Legislature, is such a sleepy place? [Lion yawns and rolls over.] Maybe that's why it took them thirteen months to lower the tolerance levels on PPB and four years to pass plant rehabilitation to save Michigan jobs. [Lions and tigers sleeping, some with limbs dangling from trees.] On the energy crisis the DEMOCRATIC state LEGISLATURE just couldn't quite summon the energy to do anything. Maybe they need a good long rest; looks like it. [A hippo's massive yawn.]

---

4. The Lansing Zoo: A Painful Place (30 seconds)[a]

VISUAL: [Two gargantuan rhinos, mating.]

ANNOUNCER: Do you know what is being done to us by the Democratically controlled legislature in this state? Do you have any idea how it hurts taxpayers to have the Democrats behind things in Lansing? Why would anyone want to be in this position for ten years? Isn't it about time we get the Democrats off our back?

---

[a] The fourth spot, which quite obviously would not meet television's antiobscenity standards, was not actually broadcast. Rather it was designed and used as a fund-raising device at dinners—the video equivalent of a dirty joke, which, if properly enjoyed by participants, traditionally opens checkbooks at such affairs.

NEXT NEW YORKER: I think it's preposterous. I think it's ridiculous.
NEXT NEW YORKER: Crazy, just crazy, I mean really. . . .
NEXT NEW YORKER [laughingly]:   You've got to be kidding!
NARRATOR (to man coming off bus):   A West Virginian as Governor of New York? How about it?

[Man rudely waves "interviewer" away without commenting.]

WOMAN IN THE BRONX: That makes as much sense to me as having the next Governor of West Virginia be a New Yorker.
NARRATOR: Democrats have paid for this message to reelect a good governor.

Most of the best in humorous clips end up on the cutting-room floor. Robert Squier was filming a crucial, end-of-the campaign television talk from candidate Carter to the American people in 1976 when, in the middle of an impassioned entreaty, Carter swatted a fly rather viciously.

Periodically, too, humor is used to destroy rather than to build a television image. A candidate running against an Oklahoma congressman in the 1960s was filmed walking through the state's meadows, eyes fixed on the azure sky and the bright promise of a future in Congress. His dream was shattered by a thirty-second spot produced by his opponent in which the congressman said simply, "Anyone who is looking up instead of looking down in an Oklahoma meadow doesn't know what he's walking through."[123]

Humor, jingles, slogans, and gimmicks all have a magnified role in television campaigning, but no phenomenon better illustrates the effect of media on electioneering than the development of "star politics" in the American system. Movie stars and television actors move freely from film to politics, and politicians achieve their own kind of star quality. Moreover, television fame originating in any field can conceivably be transformed into a candidacy. Perhaps the situation has become much as Californian Jerry Brown's 1978 reelection finance chairman, a former record promotion executive, described it: "There isn't much difference between plugging Donna Summers or Jerry Brown. You have a product to sell and you do it. The main difference is that in politics, there's a cutoff date when the campaign ends. A record goes on forever."

Ronald Reagan is certainly the best-known product of star politics.[124] In twenty-eight years of acting experience in films and on television, Reagan acquired invaluable political skills, from memorization and speech delivery to the negotiating talents sharpened as Screen Actors Guild president. A television performance for Barry Goldwater in 1964 gave him his christening in politics, and television rescued him again and again from difficulty during his California gubernatorial tenure and presidential races. As governor, Reagan used television to "go over the heads" of the recalcitrant Democratic legislature and take the case for his legislative proposals directly to the voters. As a 1976 presidential candidate, after he had lost the five opening primaries Reagan turned to television to reinflate his campaign and refill his treasury.[125] In 1980 Reagan used a series of "talking head" spots on the issues to soothe voters fearful of his foreign policy intentions and focus the campaign on Jimmy Carter's economic record.

Reagan's performance in the Golden State had actually been preceded by tap dancer George Murphy's election to the U.S. Senate in 1964, and has been succeeded by dozens of other star candidacies all over the country.[126] George Murphy himself was defeated for reelection by the son of the former heavyweight champion of the world, and in both 1978 and 1980 the Democratic son of actor Gregory Peck very nearly ousted a Republican congressional incumbent (aided by substantial contributions from Frank Sinatra, Warren Beatty, Johnny Carson, and others). Relatives and mates of film and television personalities frequently seem to cash in politically on associational fame. Elizabeth Taylor's seventh husband, former Navy Secretary John W. Warner, put his wife's crowd-drawing pull to good use in his successful 1978 quest for a Virginia U.S. Senate seat. Former Miss America Phyllis George performed much the same chore for John Y. Brown's 1979 campaign for the Kentucky governorship. George traveled the state, introducing her new husband and addressing his rallies herself. Said Brown's media man, Robert Squier: "The high point of the campaign was when his name recognition went above hers."[127]

Renown gained in other fields can be used to great advantage in politics. Basketball star Bill Bradley won a U.S. Senate seat from New Jersey in 1978, and his media professional, Michael Kaye, happily reminded voters of Bradley's career with the New York Knicks in one advertisement, when the player-candidate tossed a wad of paper through a miniature hoop on a dustbin as the announcer quipped, "With you on his team, he can't miss." Two former astronauts, John Glenn (D-Ohio) and Harrison Schmitt (R-N.M.), have also won Senate seats, and their media played their stellar accomplishments to the hilt. Virtually all the terminology in Bob Goodman's commercials for Schmitt was space-related, establishing the candidate as "still the hero, the astronaut who traveled to the stars" who would "accomplish missions" for the people of New Mexico.

Stars are created by politics as well, sometimes intentionally. The Butcher-Forde agency decided to make the chairman of the "Proposition 13" movement in California the very embodiment of the campaign.[128] Thus Howard Jarvis became the focus of commercials supporting the tax-cut initiative—and, interestingly, the center of attention in some of the commercials run by the opposition. (One anti-13 spot begins, "Howard Jarvis says Proposition 13 won't hurt schools—that's nonsense!") It is an old political axiom that you cannot beat somebody with nobody, and so Howard Jarvis, unopposed media star, carried the day for his ballot measure.

Officeholders are often signed by speakers' bureaus and talent firms. When Governor George Wallace of Alabama left office, for example, a Nashville entertainment agency contracted with him to handle his schedule of speeches, books, movie rights, syndicated radio shows and newspaper columns, and television appearances. The president of the agency explained his interest in Wallace: "You're looking at some basic qualities, whether it's a singer or a politician: believability, glamour, supply and demand." Gradually, over the years, the political travails of some politicians and their families become prime-time soap operas, and the politicians personally become the publicity equals of Hollywood kings and queens. Although they have had many imitators over the years, the Kennedys remain the premiere American television family. Tom Shales, television critic for *The Washington Post*, aptly described it this way:

For the American electorate . . . the Kennedy family saga has become an incredible, ongoing, heart-wrenching novel-for-television. It's "Roots," but it's happening right now. It's "The Rich Waltons," resonant with echoes of America and family values, and it's real. The story has everything—passion, tragedy, glamor, and glory. And ordeals. Lots of ordeals.[129]

The Kennedys are joined in the soap-opera circle by the Roosevelts and Rockefellers, and by many other families in individual states (the Byrds of Virginia, the Longs of Louisiana, the Browns of California, and on and on). Each of these families passes on the political torch, and offices, from brother to brother, father to son, generation to generation. Politicians without a magic name often rely on others; the cavalcade of stars and starlets and famous people from other professions who appear in political commercials every election year is lengthy. Politics, thanks to television, seems to become more star-struck each year—and more star-filled.

Media Deceptions

Star politics is not half as disturbing as the media deceptions that have accompanied the growth of televised political advertising. Deceit and systematic misrepresentation have become all too common in the consulting profession. The goal of electing the clients they have signed appears too often to justify all kinds of chicanery by consultants—in image making, choice of format, and film editing. Sometimes blatant untruths are employed, becoming televised lies writ large that can be refuted, if at all, by an opposing candidate only at great cost in time and resources. In a few cases an observer must conclude sadly that the line between a successful congressional or gubernatorial campaign and Allenwood prison has been very, very thin. Usually a consultant will hesitate to use any illegal or even questionable tactics because of the potential effect on his reputation, should his actions be discovered and well publicized. Yet the defeat of prominent clients can hurt reputations too, and impending electoral disaster can sometimes encourage a consultant, and certainly a candidate, to take chances—particularly if the political or journalistic climate is a tolerant one. Moreover, in some instances a consultant will uncritically accept the assertions and facts made by his client without checking them independently, thus becoming a party to deception because of slipshod research.

The mildest deceptions are those that modify character and image. With the right snippets of film, fiery-tempered men can be portrayed as cool and calm, and mild-mannered candidates can be transformed into aggressive go-getters. Bob Goodman has even worked wonders with his clients' physical dimensions, making a tall candidate (6'8" Senator Alan Simpson of Wyoming) appear shorter by having him lean against rails as he talked to voters, and a short candidate (5'6" Senator John Tower of Texas) appear taller by filming him in a specially reconstructed old Senate chamber where the desks were much tinier to fit the more diminutive senators of the last century. Careful editing of dozens or even hundreds of hours of film can make the delusions more serious. When California Democratic U.S. Senator Clair Engle decided to seek reelection in 1964, despite recent brain surgery that had left him with a paralyzed arm and greatly deteriorated verbal and ambulatory skills, his consultants repeatedly filmed and, with difficulty, constructed a forty-two-second commercial in which Engle, appearing perfectly healthy, announced his candidacy for a second term.

The deception went off with only one hitch: Engle died before the primary.[130] A similar misrepresentation occurred in the case of the reelection bid of a prominent southern governor in the late 1960s. The governor was an alcoholic, virtually incapacitated for portions of each day, yet his precisely edited commercials created the impression of an effective, functioning governor—a fiction of which all those involved were fully aware. (He was defeated for reelection for other reasons.)

Candidates are quick to condemn the press for quoting out of context, but they look the other way when their consultants use the same bogus tool. Maryland's Acting Governor Blair Lee, seeking to gain nomination to the office in his own right in the state's 1978 Democratic primary, permitted the airing of a commercial implying editorial support for his candidacy from the influential *Sunpapers,* which had heartily endorsed his eventually triumphant opponent, Harry R. Hughes. John Connally's consultant lifted a line from a flowery introduction of Connally delivered by Iowa Governor Robert Ray and constructed a television spot that left the impression that the popular chief executive was endorsing Connally prior to his state's crucial 1980 presidential caucuses. Ray, who was supporting Senator Howard Baker, strongly objected, and the Connally campaign withdrew the ad. One of Baker's own 1980 commercials, produced by the Bailey/Deardourff firm, was deceptively edited. Baker, who polls found had a soft image in a year when voters demanded firm leadership, was shown giving a tough, emotional, no-nonsense answer to an Iranian student's complaint as the crowd cheered wildly and gave Baker a standing ovation. In fact, the audience's approbation had come at the end of Baker's presentation, a full ten minutes after the Iranian student incident.[131]

Advertising formats can be just as beguiling as purposive editing. One format that regularly fools viewers to achieve greater credibility is the "news adjacency" design, where spots are produced to look and sound like news and are played (where not prohibited) during the station breaks of news programs. A Seattle congressional candidate in 1978 actually hired an impersonator to imitate the voice of news commentator Paul Harvey as narration for his radio spots.[132] The press in some cases assists candidates in their news deception. Congressional incumbents (and some other imaginative candidates as well) are notorious for using their office facilities to produce radio or television "actualities" with announcements or commentary by the candidates. These naturally self-serving pieces are sometimes inserted whole into news programs, without production attribution, presenting the candidate precisely as his consultants want him portrayed with the added credibility of a supposedly nonpartisan news show.

One of the most wily confidence tricks ever pulled in politics was carried off with artful use of a television format. Democrat Robert Meyner and Republican Malcolm Forbes, running for the New Jersey governorship in 1953, had purchased back-to-back hour-long slots for television broadcasts, with the first hour being Meyner's. The last few minutes of Meyner's 10:00–11:00 P.M. program was intentionally devoted to the playing of the Star Spangled Banner with a test pattern background, the traditional "sign-off" used by television stations. Almost no one was left to watch poor Malcom Forbes, who lost an audience and eventually the election.[133]

Occasionally one finds cases of absolute fraud in campaign advertising. Political treachery is hardly an invention of television, of course. Few recent campaigns, fortunately, can match the web of McCarthyite lies skillfully weaved for Republican John Butler in his defeat of Maryland Democratic Senator Millard Tydings in 1950, which included distribution of faked, composite pictures of Tydings with "Communist leader" Earl Browder and other dirty tricks.[134] Spurious news films run in movie theaters were used in the pretelevision age to defeat Democrat Upton Sinclair's bid for the California governorship in 1933.[135] Louis B. Mayer, then head of MGM and chairman of the Republican state party, put his studios to work producing newsreels that theater owners were forced to show. In the newsreels an interviewer was pictured traveling the state, asking actors posing as voters for whom they would vote in the coming gubernatorial contest. A little old lady announcing her Republican intentions explained that her "little home may not be much, but it is all I have in the world." A seedy-looking, unkempt bum unhesitatingly declared for Sinclair. "I am voting for Seen-clair. His system worked vell in Russia, so vy can't it vork here?" An army of hobos is depicted jumping off freight trains at California stops because, as one notes, "Sinclair says he'll take the property of the working people and give it to us!" Not surprisingly, Sinclair, once thought to be leading, lost decisively.

Most modern television distortions are not so heavy-handed, but they can be just as devastating. When Arizona Democratic U.S. Representative Morris Udall ran for reelection in 1978, his Republican opponent, Tom Richey, ran an advertisement designed by the Bishop and Bryant agency that claimed Udall "doesn't . . . think like us anymore." As proof, the commercial showed Udall speaking at a public hearing, declaring: "I'm for socialism because I think the owners of public lands ought to be paid something." The snippet of Udall in this spot, in which he appears to be admitting that he is a socialist—electoral suicide in the United States—is, in fact, a deliberate misrepresentation of his actual statement. Having been accused of favoring a "socialistic" course of action at a public lands hearing, Udall had replied in argument, "If paying the American public for their land is socialism, then I'm for socialism because I think the owners of public land ought to be paid something." The misrepresentation was pointed out to the candidate, but he steadfastly refused to withdraw the spot, in good part on the advice of his consultants. As one of them later commented shamelessly: "[The ad] was a successful attack if for no other reason than Udall had to respond to it and it became an issue in the campaign. . . . Whether or not he ever said he was a socialist, it pretty much cast the issue discussion in positive terms for [Richey] and in negative terms for [Udall]."[136]

The commercial produced ill-gotten gains, as Udall won only 54 percent of the vote, his lowest proportion since his first congressional race in 1961. As a Bishop and Bryant spokesman suggested, "[Udall's] response was through the print media [i.e., newspapers], and they can't match television. More people remembered the attack than remembered the response."[137] That is one of television's great dangers: the instantaneous, repetitious dissemination of false information, bought and paid for, that only an aggressive press or equally large ad expenditures by the aggrieved party can correct. If the money is not there, or the press is not alert, or if sufficient time in a campaign does not remain, the harm done—to a candidacy, certainly, but, of deeper concern, to the democratic process—can be significant.

Negative Advertising

Even when television is used to communicate political truth (at least from one candidate's perspective), the truth can be negatively packaged—attacking the opponent's character and record rather than supporting one's own. If there is a single trend obvious to most American media consultants, it is the increasing proportion of negative political advertising. Going on the offensive, "attack politics," is becoming more popular because, while vicious, it has gained a reputation for effectiveness among professionals. At least a third of all spot commercials in recent campaigns have been negative, and in a minority of campaigns half or more of the spots are negative in tone or substance.[138] Interestingly, product advertising appears to have moved in the same direction; while previously the cardinal rule of product (as political) advertising was never to mention the name of one's competitor, commercial marketers have rushed to pounce on competing brands by name.

In politics, negative advertising is believed to be more attention grabbing and exciting,[139] and to be particularly effective against incumbents. The most common circumstances under which negative ads are produced, however, are when a candidate is far behind and not gaining in the polls or when a leading candidate falls precipitously in the trial heats. Richard L. Thornburgh, Pennsylvania's winning 1978 Republican gubernatorial nominee, was lagging badly in early October when Bailey/Deardourff agency decided to air a series of hard-hitting spots, hammering away at Democrat Pete Flaherty's performance as mayor of Pittsburgh.[140] ("Can the man who drove Pittsburgh to its *knees* put Pennsylvania back on its *feet*?" asked the announcer.) While President Carter's tough anti-Reagan advertising in the general election received the most attention, the 1980 presidential campaign was replete with examples of candidates turning to negatives when times got tough. In the Republican party's prenomination contest, for instance, George Bush's advertising witnessed a startling transformation from early puffery about "a president we won't have to train" to slicing attacks on front-runner Ronald Reagan after Bush's devastating New Hampshire primary loss.[141] With each new turn in the polls, Bush's strategy changed. A harsh series of anti-Reagan ads planned for the Florida primary was cancelled, for instance, after polls showed Bush gaining a few points on the heels of his Massachusetts victory.[142]

Despite its perceived advantages, negative advertising is approached with caution and handled with care by consultants, who are well aware of its backlash-generating potential. A Republican-sponsored study of media termed the negative approach "high-risk" advertising, because "it must walk the fine line between making its point and turning off the voter."[143] Research has indicated that, in general, voters prefer positive, informational ads[144] and, above all, a spot must appear to be fair. But, as Doug Bailey notes, "The same commercial can be run by two different candidates and one would be seen as being fair and the other unfair." An underdog such as President Ford in 1976 could get away with it since the voters presumably allow for desperation and sympathize with probable losers, while Carter, the front-running candidate espousing honesty and integrity, would have appeared too political and ungracious.[145] The Ford media advisers tried to provoke the Carter camp into running negatives for this very reason, and Gerald Rafshoon's refusal to do so was called by Bailey his "wisest" decision.[146]

Some consultants, such as David Garth, "have a basic rule . . . that you don't do negative commercials until you have first established a real reason for people to go for you."[147] Garth cites Bailey and Deardourff as having violated this axiom with predictable consequences in the 1978 New York gubernatorial election, when GOP candidate Perry Duryea, who himself had no strong image, unleashed a barrage of vitriolic anti-Governor Hugh Carey spots in the closing weeks of the campaign.[148] Duryea, who had been leading in the polls, collapsed precipitously, although his negative strategy was only one of several reasons. Other consultants prefer to use only radio for negative advertising, claiming television's video dimension makes an attack seem more stark and rougher.[149]

Yet most professionals quickly lose their inhibitions whenever they believe negatives can help their candidates. Charles Guggenheim, who has proclaimed his belief in the ineffectiveness of negative spots,[150] produced a series of commercials for Michigan's Democratic gubernatorial nominee that editorials in state newspapers called a "new low" in dirty politics.[151] In the spots State Senator William B. Fitzgerald attacked Republican incumbent Governor William Milliken for causing human deformities by his alleged mishandling of the contamination of cattle feed by the chemical PPB. Not only did the advertisements themselves probably not help Fitzgerald, but Milliken's media man, John Deardourff, capsuled the editorial reaction to them in a spot that enhanced Milliken's electoral chances. (He eventually won reelection in a close race.)

Robert Goodman is another professional who has deprecated the use of negatives. Calling negative ads "normally counterproductive," Goodman sets a clear standard: "I don't think you should invade someone's living room with hostility and vulgarity."[152] But apparently he saw matters differently in Kentucky's 1979 gubernatorial race, when his spots for Republican Louis Nunn portrayed Democrat John Y. Brown, Jr., as, among other things, a gambling-aholic at the Las Vegas tables. ("Are you going to let him play with our money?" the narrator asked incredulously.)[153] "It's not negative to tell the truth about someone," insists Tony Schwartz, justifying his description of Illinois U.S.

Senator Charles Percy as "a racist."[154] Schwartz's ads for Percy's 1978 Democratic opponent, Alex Seith, had linked Percy to Earl Butz, whose derogatory comments about blacks led to his resignation as President Ford's Secretary of Agriculture. Once again, however, Percy's consultants (Bailey and Deardourff) were able to turn an attack around and stimulate sympathy for a beleaguered incumbent. Surrounded by an adoring and concerned family, Senator Percy earnestly declared in one ad of the counterattack series:

This campaign has not been easy. My opponent has called me a liar. He's called me a racist. But I have faith in your judgment. Nothing means more to me than my integrity, my family, and the chance to be your senator.

There are a surprisingly large number of other instructive examples of backlash produced by negative ad campaigns. Shortly before the 1976 California presidential primary, the Reagan organization learned that Ford's campaign planned to broadcast a package criticizing Reagan's foreign policy positions, with the tag line, "While Governor Reagan couldn't start a war, President Reagan could." DMI did a quick study for Reagan indicating that Ford supporters reacted as strongly against the attack as did Reagan's, so advertisements were placed encouraging Republicans to watch Ford's "smear" spots. As DMI's Richard Wirthlin planned it, the Ford advisers could not then have cancelled their spots even if they had wanted to do so. Wirthlin tracked a 12-point boost in Reagan's strength over a ten-day period, and he is convinced that backlash to Ford's negatives turned a close race into a landslide win for Reagan.[155] When a candidate is soundly disliked by the electorate to begin with, it is difficult to generate sympathy when he is attacked, no matter how outrageous the insult hurled. One of President Nixon's commercials in 1972 claimed that George McGovern would put fully half the U.S. population on welfare, an assertion that McClure and Patterson found even uninformed voters could not swallow whole,[156] but Nixon's secure electoral position was unshaken.

In statewide races with lesser-known contenders, it is probably easier to provoke a reaction with such practices as negative one-upsmanship. In the 1978 Pennsylvania U.S. Senate race, David Garth decided to respond to Democrat Bill Green's attacks against the campaign financing of Pennsylvania Republican John Heinz III (Garth's client) with similar charges couched in a way that proves the best defense is a good offense:

ANNOUNCER: Every day Bill Green is spending thousands of dollars of somebody's money to tell you that John Heinz is spending thousands of dollars
of his own money. It is the same tactic that John Kennedy's opponents
tried to use against him. But while John Heinz is using his own money
to show you what he's done, Bill Green is using somebody else's money
to attack John Heinz and to deliberately distort the Heinz record. Next
week you can reject the politics of negativism and desperation. You can
elect an Independent senator, John Heinz.

In multicandidate fields, this sort of mutual meanness can take its toll.
While Acting Governor Blair Lee and Baltimore County Executive
Theodore Venetoulis, the apparent front-runners in Maryland's 1978
Democratic gubernatorial primary, blasted away at one another with
negative ads, Harry R. Hughes (who barely broadcast at all) was pro-
pelled by voter disgust up through the middle to victory.

Presidential elections have produced a catalogue of the negative
options exercised by media professionals through the years. The early
years of television saw relatively few strong negative spots. The Eisenhower campaign aired one of the first, an antiwar masterpiece produced by Ted Bates and Company. Two soldiers are pictured discussing
the meaninglessness of war on a Korean battlefield, and when one is
suddenly killed, the other futilely charges the enemy while an off-
camera voice booms, "Vote Republican!" In 1960 John Kennedy's advisers had an ad designed to make light of Richard Nixon's "experience"
claims. It simply pictured President Eisenhower responding to a reporter's query about the major decisions Vice-President Nixon had influenced: "If you give me a week, I might think of one."

Negative television campaigning was far more extensive, and perhaps became institutionalized, in the election of 1964. That election
produced the most famous political ad in television's short history,
the so-called "Daisy Spot" designed by Tony Schwartz for the Johnson
campaign's Doyle Dane Bernbach advertising agency. The sights and
sounds of spring surrounded a beautiful little girl who was picking
petals from a daisy and childishly miscounting, ". . . four, five, seven,
six. . . ." As the frame freezes on her face, and closes in on her eye,
her tiny voice is replaced by a strident military one, counting down,
"ten, nine, eight. . . ." At the stroke of "zero," a nuclear explosion
is heard and the dreaded mushroom cloud appears, as President Johnson intones off camera, "These are the stakes: to make a world in
which all of God's children can live, or to go into the dark. We must
either love each other or we must die." Finally, a solemn narrator
completes the task: "Vote for President Johnson on November third.

The stakes are too high for you to stay home." The Daisy spot, still being written about four presidential elections later, was shown only once, on CBS's *Monday Night at the Movies*. It proved so controversial that it was withdrawn voluntarily, although the controversy itself was worth several million dollars in free publicity for the Democrats. It was a devastatingly effective ad not merely because it was so innately frightening and disturbing, but because Goldwater himself had set the stage for the spot's anti-Goldwater implications. The Republican nominee, while never so much as indirectly mentioned in the text, had earlier expressed his support for the use of tactical nuclear weapons. The Daisy spot, innocuous on its face, managed to evoke the negative feelings and doubts that voters already possessed about Goldwater.[157] The best political advertisements, positive and negative, follow the principle of not attempting to create, but rather capitalizing on, moods, beliefs, and prejudices already present in the electorate.

Much of the rest of the Johnson (and Goldwater) advertising package was far more negative and vicious than the Daisy spot, even though this one ad got the lion's share of press attention. Almost all the Johnson spots played on fear of what Goldwater would do as president, especially in the nuclear weapons area. In one spot a small girl was shown licking an ice-cream cone. A young woman (presumably the child's mother) substituted for the usually male narrator in a quietly alarming recitation: "Children . . . shouldn't have Strontium 90 and Cesium 137. . . . they can make you die. . . . But now there's a man who wants to be President of the United States and he doesn't like [the Nuclear Test Ban Treaty] . . . and if he's elected, they might start testing all over again." The Test Ban Treaty and Goldwater's opposition to it are the themes of several other ads. One striking spot flashes clips of many nuclear mushrooms in succession as countdowns are heard in English and Russian. Finally, President Kennedy's voice is recognized, declaring his treaty "a shaft of light through the darkness," followed by Johnson's visage and voice noting, without naming Goldwater directly, that "those who oppose [the treaty] curse the only light that can lead us out of darkness." The hot-line telephone rings in another spot, and the narrator whispers that it "only rings in a serious crisis . . . keep it in the hands of a man who's proven himself *responsible.*" Quoting Goldwater's comment that the nuclear bomb was "merely another weapon," the announcer in yet another ad repeats with disgust and incredulity, *"Merely another weapon!"*

Johnson's negative campaign was far more extensive than this brief sampling implies. A subseries was built around Goldwater's contradictory remarks about the United Nations, the Social Security System, and his political philosophy ("When somebody tells you he's for Barry Goldwater, you ask him which Barry Goldwater he's for.") Goldwater's views on Medicare are summarized by the candidate's unflattering quip, "I have personal medical insurance; my son-in-law is an intern." A Ku Klux Klan leader, with a burning cross and hooded figures filling the screen, is quoted as attacking "niggerism, Catholicism, Judaism— all the isms" and in the same breath saying, "I like Barry Goldwater; he needs our help." Goldwater's proposal to sell the Tennessee Valley Authority and stop public works projects all over the country is contrasted with his sponsorship of a federal dam for his home state of Arizona. "In Barry's book, this sort of thing is creeping socialism— except when it creeps into Arizona," a tongue-in-cheek narrator suggests. "President Johnson is president of all the people," he concludes. A large wooden map of the United States is pictured floating in water and a buzz saw rips away the eastern states as the announcer recalls Goldwater's words: "It might be a good idea to saw off the eastern seaboard and let it float out to sea." A major part of the negative effort was aimed at attracting disenchanted Republicans. Anti-Goldwater statements made by Governors Nelson Rockefeller of New York, George Romney of Michigan, and William Scranton of Pennsylvania were repeated to remind GOP voters that "even if you're a Republican with serious doubts about Barry Goldwater, you're in good company." Another long, rambling ad features a confessional monologue by an actor playing the part of a nervous and upset young Republican: "I've always been a Republican but this man *scares* me . . . so many men with strange ideas seem to be for Goldwater. . . . My party made a mistake and I'm going to have to vote against that mistake."

Goldwater gave Johnson lots of companionship on the negative front. One of his commercials linked the Johnson administration to "moral decay" as scenes of race riots, dope peddling, alcoholism, and crime appeared on the television screen. The ad, peopled mainly by blacks, was withdrawn after an outcry that it had racial undertones. Another spot, broadcast mainly in the Southwest, was also taken out of circulation voluntarily when its heavy-handed approach and very amateurish production combined to give an impression even worse than its text suggests:

NARRATOR: Let's look at the record of Lyndon Johnson. He was Bobby Baker's best friend. LBJ once said: "Bobby Baker is my strong right arm, the last man I see at night and the first one in the morning." The dark shadow of voting fraud such as the infamous Box Thirteen.* Billie Sol Estes and his connections in high places. A television monopoly forced on the people of Austin. A fourteen-million-dollar personal fortune gained on an average government salary of fourteen thousand dollars per year. Honestly, it just doesn't add up.

LITTLE BOY: Gee Dad, is all that true?

DAD: Yes, son, every bit of it.

LITTLE BOY: Will you and Mother vote for a man like that?

DAD: We won't, we can't—for your sake.

NARRATOR: Put a man of honesty, integrity, and strength in the White House. Vote for Barry Goldwater. In your heart, you know he's right.

Presidential campaigns since have seemed to try hard to equal or top the 1964 barrage of brickbats. Standing negative devices, such as the "weathervane," are repeatedly used. The weathervane ads highlight an opponent's flip-flops, and the technique has been employed by Johnson in 1964, Humphrey in 1968, and Nixon in 1972. The Ford campaign designed but did not use an ad of that variety against Carter in 1976 as well, and his staff director of advertising, Malcolm MacDougall, described the standard operating procedures in its design:

The principle behind it is simple. To make your own weathervane ad, you research your opponent's speeches over a period of about ten years. You study every newspaper article written about him during that period. You then look for the slightest indication that he may have changed his position on an issue. You make a list of all the times that your opponent's position has changed, and you are in business.[158]

The cleverest weathervane ad was produced as an anti-Nixon spot in 1968. It showed Nixon's left hand pointing eastward, his right hand westward, and his nose shifting from north to south. Nixon was so outraged when he saw the commercial that he called Hubert Humphrey personally to demand that it be withdrawn, and a rather shaken Humphrey complied. Four years later Nixon's concern (as expressed to Humphrey) that weathervane ads were demeaning to the political system was apparently forgotten, as the Committee to Re-Elect the President broadcast a remarkably similar spot that had Democratic nominee George McGovern revolving in the shifting winds of his alleged positions.

* "Box Thirteen" was allegedly the Texas vote box that was stuffed with just enough ballots to give Lyndon Johnson his first U.S. Senate victory in his 1948 Democratic primary battle with former Texas Governor Coke Stevenson.

Much like the Daisy spot, more recent negative political commercials at the presidential level have attempted to capture the essence of an already existing public sentiment about a candidate, thereby riding a building wave of emotion that is independently generated. The unpaid media stories on the 1968 election, for instance, had already established Republican vice-presidential nominee Spiro Agnew as an over-his-head, loose-talking bumbler who could not conceivably fill the office of President in an emergency. The stage was clearly set for a brilliant anti-Agnew spot that simultaneously and implicitly touted the Democrats' vice-presidential contender, Edmund Muskie. The ad offered a sign "Spiro Agnew for Vice-President" with a sound track of tittering and laughing and the closing remark, "This would be funny if it wasn't so serious." The Republicans' advertising, by contrast, hardly even mentioned Muskie, who was the recipient of reams of favorable publicity and had a popularity rating higher than any of the presidential candidates.

The 1980 presidential contest illustrated yet again the importance of understanding the public's evaluation of each candidate and structuring the advertising to fit preconceived notions. Most of President Carter's "position" spots were also, by suggestion, negative commentaries on Senator Edward Kennedy. The president's survey research discovered that voters disillusioned with his administration and put off by his failures nonetheless continued to like him personally, to believe him, and to admire the old-time family virtues with which he had associated himself. Conversely, while many of Senator Kennedy's issues were popular ones, he was mistrusted and perceived to lack the very personal qualities Carter possessed. Thus Carter's advertising took pains to invite a quiet but obvious comparison between the Kennedy and Carter families: "Husband, father, president: He's done these three jobs with distinction." And many of the spots incorporated a subliminal message about Chappaquiddick; one ad ended with these words:

You may not always agree with President Carter. But you'll never wonder whether he's telling the truth. It's hard to think of a more useful quality in a president than telling the simple truth. President Carter—for the truth.

Negative advertisements in state and congressional district contests are rarely as subtle, since the voter's knowledge about the candidate is far less complete than at the presidential level. Therefore most media consultants make their negative assertions bluntly, lest the voter miss the point. A Bailey/Deardourff spot for Ohio Governor James Rhodes in 1978 graphically made obvious the Republican incumbent's charge that Democratic opponent Richard Celeste would raise taxes.

Whenever an old-fashioned cash register rang, up popped not a number but Celeste's head. Other than sparking fears of higher taxes, most negatives in congressional elections focus on salary increases, junkets, and attendance records. One of Bob Goodman's spots for Texas Republican Senator John Tower in 1978 zeroed in on Democratic challenger Robert Krueger's low percentage of casting roll-call votes. "How'd you like to have a job where you show up just 25 percent of the time and still get paid over $50,000 a year?" an announcer asks people in the street. ' Are you kidding?" answers one. "That sounds like a con game!" another replies. Then this copy appeared on the screen: "Only one man in Texas had that job. Robert Krueger showed up 25 percent of the time but collected 100 percent of his salary."

Perhaps the ultimate negative spot was a simple, direct one produced for Republican State Senator Raymond Bateman in his unsuccessful 1977 bid to turn Democratic Governor Brendan Byrne out of office. During a thirty-second ad, one voter starkly declares, "I'm voting for Bateman because I don't like Byrne."[159] Finally, a Louisiana gubernatorial candidate in 1979 ran a negative commercial on political commercials, splicing together clips from other candidates' advertisements. His effort closed with the line, "Are you tired of all the same old political bull?" Evidently, voters were not tired enough; the candidate finished last.[160]

Political Ads and Product Ads

In the presidential election year of 1964, a producer from President Johnson's advertising agency, Doyle Dane Bernbach, approached media consultant Tony Schwartz, pulled out a photograph of LBJ, and asked, "Will you work for this product?" Candidates are far less flexible than products, of course, but there are in fact a number of similarities between product advertising and political advertising—enough, perhaps, to prove disturbing. Michael Kaye, who began his marketing career in the commercial field before switching to politics, believes that the same three ground rules apply in both areas. First, the advertiser must "know his product"; then he must "look at the competition"; and, third, he must "understand the audience." The "product's package" is then adjusted to suit all three basic conditions. Moreover, political professional Marvin Chernoff suggests that the specifics of political advertising are "defined by the commercial advertisers more than by the pollsters. Shake 'n' Bake and Coca-Cola are more important in defining our message than Pat Caddell and Peter Hart, because we compete with those [products] for the attention of the people." Chernoff sees commercial advertisers as having legitimized certain modes of advertising, which were then adapted by political media consultants for their own use.

In Chernoff's view, three eras have dominated television advertising. The product era, in the immediate post–World War II years through the 1950s, confined advertising to a discussion of the candidate/product and its virtuous qualities, and the promise implicit in those ads' descriptive superlatives led to disillusion with the product. Advertisers then began the image era in the 1960s, where the quality of a product was supposed to be judged by the desirable image created around it. Thus, Speedy defined Alka-Seltzer, the man with the eyepatch defined Hathaway shirts, and the group of three whites, a black woman, and two young people surrounding a candidate on film defined him. But with Vietnam and Watergate, image was not enough, and the electorate demanded "real people." So finally the positioning era arrived in the 1970s, and the candidate or product is now carefully and favorably located on the consumer's rational and emotional continuum in relation to all the competitors. *Implication* about rivals is the vital element in positioning. Avis is Number 2 and trying harder, while Hertz, implicitly, is fat and lazy; a Volkswagen is a bit ugly without all that chrome, yet other cars are expensive, wasteful, and obsolescent; you never have to wonder if Jimmy Carter is telling the truth, but you must do so when Edward Kennedy speaks.

The relationship between product and political advertising may not be as strong as Chernoff paints it, but there is little question that the development of both forms of advertising has been closely related. Early commercial public relations programs borrowed heavily from the established methods of political parties and campaigns, while the faster and more thorough evaluation of commercial advertising has contributed a number of major innovations to politics, from survey research methodology to audience pretesting procedures.[161] This cross-pollination has continued through the years, facilitated especially by those advertising agencies and independent media consultants that take private as well as political clients.[162] Many techniques have become standard in both fields. For example, 42 percent of all product commercials use a jingle and 33 percent use celebrity endorsements, not infrequent companions in political advertisements.[163] The identical announcers are hired by all advertisers—the same melodious, pleasing voices help the advertising go down, be the medicine political or commercial. Both types of advertising attempt to build a personality into a product, and both try to create emotional ties. How many hundreds of political commercials have imitated the exploitation of our closest relationships as Kodak film does in its "Times of Your Life" series? How many political spots have been centered around the *joie de vivre* theme of the "Pepsi Day" ads? How many politicians merely seem to repeat an unoriginal version of the McDonald's jingle, "You, you're the one . . . We do it all for you"? It is sometimes hard to distinguish between all the solid, trustworthy political candidates and Pete the Butcher of Shake 'n' Bake or Cora of Maxwell House. (Maybe while Pete and Cora are "jes' folks," the politician is necessarily presented as just like us, only *better*.) It may even be that elaborate Dr. Pepper-like production numbers are in our political future. Already county fairs, musical rallies, and "cloggers" dances have served as background for political spots, and Bob Goodman's "Ride with us, Wyoming" series for Malcolm Wallop was as close as one can come to a western drama staged for political television.

The comparison of political with product advertising can be carried too far, however, and usually is. Consumers themselves make a considerable distinction between the two ad forms. Research indicates that viewers pay significantly more attention to political advertising. While less than 20 percent of viewers can recall the average television product announcement, the average political spot is remembered by 79 percent of those who see it, and 56 percent can give a surprisingly full description of the commercial.[164] People not only consider political ads more intently, they appear to concentrate more closely on what is actually said. A study for the American Association of Product Advertisers found that only 46 percent of viewers judged a commercial spot by its content, looking instead to how the message was communicated; by contrast, McClure and Patterson discovered that 74 percent of viewers evaluated political ads on the information contained within them.[165]

This clearly suggests that advertising formats that work for products may be ineffectual politically. One superb illustration is provided by the 1976 Ford campaign, which early in the primary season disastrously employed the "slice-of-life" format so popular in product advertising.[166] "Slice-of-life" calls for paid actors in "natural" conversation during a scene from everyday life (whether at the breakfast table or in the supermarket or whatever). One of Ford's ads listened in as two "housewives" met on a sidewalk, one coming from the grocery store with shopping bags in her arms and the other standing outside a President Ford campaign office. With a squeaky-clean recitation more appropriate for a toothpaste or bathroom tissue advertisement, the women discussed the Ford record, as this excerpt suggests:

FIRST WOMAN: Ellie! Are you working for President Ford?
SECOND WOMAN: Only about twenty-six hours a day. Notice anything about these food prices lately?
FIRST WOMAN: Well, they don't seem to be going up the way they used to.
SECOND WOMAN: President Ford has cut inflation in half.
FIRST WOMAN: In half! Wow!

Designed by the president of an agency that primarily advertises products, the spots were shown only in California to universally critical reviews. Termed "heavy-handed," "amateurish," and worse by media analysts, audience testing—done after the spots were broadcast—produced laughter and ridicule among viewers who were supposed to be favorably influenced.[167]

There are other major differences in advertising a politician and a product. Pure name identification is a far more crucial element for a product than a person. Communicating a candidate's identity is only the first step to convincing a voter to cast a ballot for someone, while merely recognizing the name of a product is often sufficient inducement for a consumer to choose it over its lesser-known competitors. At least for high-visibility political offices, people consider their decisions seriously and expect to be given enough information to make a reasonably intelligent selection. Also, product advertising has a completely different scale of success, which hinges on getting a fair share of the market for a given product. That share can be quite small; 5 percent of the cola industry would represent a goldmine. Political advertising must be aimed at securing a clear majority of the market, and it must garner that majority in a short advertising season—short compared to a product cycle[168]—that culminates in a one-day clearance sale on election day.

All of these points, and other less legitimate ones, are made by political media professionals in attacking the approach to politics taken by large advertising agencies.[169] "Many agencies are so incompetent and inefficient that they can easily destroy a good candidate," exclaims Joseph Napolitan.[170] "Product advertisers are all hung up on gimmicks," says "work days" originator Robert Squier, and David Garth chimes in, "Advertising agencies . . . come up with terrific slogans that have no political reality."[171] Ad agencies are, of course, the main rivals of independent media consultants, and some of this reaction can be ascribed to self-esteem and business promotion. Yet much of the criticism is justified, because ad agencies quite naturally fail to distinguish the differing conditions and ground rules that prevail in each sphere. Political accounts are such a small portion of the average agency's profits that no great efforts are expended to alter standard operating procedures developed in the product arena. An ad agency likes to structure any account so that all major sections within the organization can take part. This means that a major share of a political campaign's billings will come from the billboard division, for example, even though most political professionals regard vast expenditures on billboards to be in good part wasted. Usually few if any individuals within an advertising agency can match a political consultant in campaign experience. By contrast, almost all media consultants have their origins in politics rather than product advertising, and for that reason alone they are probably able to give better service to campaigns, where good political judgment is still at the root of success.

Yet advertising agencies have their advantages. Besides usually employing superb artists and photographers, agency in-house time-buyers, having built up a faithful and continuing relationship with local stations over the years, have greater clout and thus usually can insure better placement of spots than political consultants.[172] On the whole, however, media consultants have looked increasingly more attractive to candidates, and today fewer ad agency executives can be found masterminding major campaigns than twenty or even ten years ago. Agencies have not been particularly upset by the loss of business; some, in fact, have welcomed it.[173] The disruption of an agency's normal schedule, coupled with the inevitable last-minute demands of a campaign, are burdensome. One agency executive explained that "The whole world is compressed in a political campaign . . . you do an ad in one day that would take seven working days on a normal account."[174] An agency's major clients can suffer in the squeeze, even though they provide the greatest profits. Procter and Gamble alone spent $460 million on advertising in 1979, dwarfing the advertising expenditure total of candidates at *all* levels in the 1976 presidential year.[175] There are also problems in collecting debts from defunct political campaigns, and they are such a small proportion of the average agency's budget that collection is hardly worth the trouble. Finally, the political taking of sides by an agency that includes hundreds of employees of all partisan and ideological stripes can prove to be divisive. In 1968 various executives of Doyle Dane Bernbach agency, which had unified behind Lyndon

Johnson in 1964, were working for Eugene McCarthy, Robert Kennedy, and Nelson Rockefeller in addition to their general election client, Hubert Humphrey.[176]

Money for Media

One advertising executive has proposed, in print, that he and his brethren should begin to "act out of principle, not the lure of money" and produce ads for candidates of their choice at cost, with no profit.[177] His sentiment is not likely to become widespread, least so among independent media professionals whose livelihoods depend on campaign accounts. The fees and commissions that media consultants earn in political campaigns are substantial, as the examples cited in chapter 1 demonstrated. Commissions bring the most profit, and usually consultants and agencies will bill their political clients an extra 17.65 percent on top of production costs, as well as pocketing the 15 percent commissions paid by television and radio stations for the advertising time purchased for airing the campaign's package.[178] A creative fee (ranging up to $25,000 a month, but usually a set fee of $60,000 or less) can also be levied.[179] Occasionally the creative fee will be increased in lieu of commissions. This is done when the certainty of a fee payment is deemed more important (generally for reasons of cash flow) than the promise of commission royalties on a less fixed schedule. Waiving commissions also occurs when a consultant is uneasy about the ability of a campaign to raise its budget and secure the money to buy enough broadcasting time to produce a rich commission lode. On the whole, however, consultants greatly prefer the more profitable commission arrangement. Major consultants, in fact, rarely take on congressional district campaigns because, while a statewide race will place the consultants' ads with dozens or even hundreds of commission-paying television and radio stations, a congressional district may include only a dozen or so stations. The commission take, then, is much less even though the same effort is devoted to producing an advertising package.

The substantial media expenditures in almost all modern campaigns insure that a percentage cut will be financially rewarding for consultants. While President Calvin Coolidge had a broadcast expenditure of just $120,000 (all for radio shows) in his 1924 campaign, Richard Nixon and Hubert Humphrey together spent about $18 million in the

1968 general election.[180] By 1972 candidates for office at all levels were putting an estimated $59.6 million into television and radio advertising.[181] The Ford and Carter organizations spent about $17 million for television time and production in the general election—well over a third of the $43.2 million in federal subsidies allotted to the major party candidates.[182] That is about the usual proportion of a campaign budget spent on media advertising, although it can range from a low of 15 percent to a high of 70 percent.[183] Candidates in weakly contested races rarely make heavy media outlays, while media costs are nearly always proportionately higher for hotly contested ones. Robert Goodman, for instance, recommends to his candidates challenging incumbents that 70 percent of their entire budget be devoted to media—a rewarding allocation for Goodman as well.[184] Certain types of campaigns also require greater or lesser media allocations. Groups supporting or opposing referenda and initiatives, for instance, usually spend the lion's share of the budget on media rather than on organization.

Geography sometimes has a decisive effect on the size of the media budget.[185] A New Jersey statewide candidate, in order to reach his electorate, must advertise (if he has the money) on New York and Philadelphia television stations—a tremendously expensive and terribly inefficient proposition, since a vast audience outside his voting district is reached and paid for. Television time bought in rural South Dakota is costly also, because the several major stations have fixed costs and a small viewing population that keeps advertising prices high.

And the production elements (choice of film or videotape, technical quality desired, the extent of filming, the actual number of spots and long commercials produced, and so forth)[186] are major determinants of cost, especially since production on average comprises 25 to 35 percent of the television budget and can easily range up to half.[187] Most political commercials appear to cost a few thousand dollars apiece.[188] This total pales by comparison with product commercials. Most 1978 television product spots cost from $20,000 to 40,000, but elaborate ones regularly run from $60,000 to 100,000, and exceptional ads have cost over $250,000.[189] On the other hand, independent media consultants charge far more for an ad package than the National Republican Congressional Committee, whose in-house media shop produces a high-quality commercial series for GOP campaigns for less than $5,000.

Media consultants and ad agencies are not the only ones who make a tidy profit on political advertising; the television and radio stations do quite well too.[190] Not only do they often get customers at off-peak times (particularly during the early presidential primary season), but political advertisers heavily favor the electronic media over newspapers, even though print media are still the preferred advertising channels for most products and businesses.[191] It is true that network news coverage of politics is costly. The 1980 presidential election coverage, for example, cost the networks an estimated $100 million.[192] But the networks have nonpolitical advertisers during news broadcasts to help finance those shows, and political candidates must pay hefty sums to reach large audiences with their spots during prime time. Thirty seconds on a top-rated network show during the 1977–1978 season cost between $60,000 and 81,500.[193] The same spot length on a special broadcast such as the Super Bowl ran an incredible $187,500. Few candidates can really afford sums of that magnitude, especially since cash payment in advance is required.[194] Fortunately for politicians, the Federal Communications Commission (FCC) ruled in April 1972 that stations cannot charge candidates more than the lowest rates they charge their best commercial clients for certain spots.[195] This "lowest unit rate" rule (or "l.u.r.") applies in the forty-five days preceding a party primary and in the sixty days before a general election. In January 1980, just before the Iowa presidential caucuses, the FCC extended l.u.r. to all political contests open to public participation.

On second glance, though, l.u.r. does not always turn out to be quite the boon it appears. How much money a candidate saves depends heavily on how much of a discount, if any at all, a station's best customers receive and on television stations' rate structure. Television stations base their assessments on how easily ads can be preempted and on the popularity of the show within which a commercial runs. The l.u.r., then, might apply to Saturday morning children's shows, which are wholly useless to candidates. Or paying the l.u.r. could mean that the spots are easily bumped out of their scheduled prime-time slots or simply not scheduled at all (and played whenever there is an available spot). This is clearly intolerable for a well-designed political media campaign, since most commercials are aimed at specific audiences or time slots. Therefore, most campaigns end up paying higher rates to avoid the web of difficulties surrounding l.u.r.[196]

With or without the cheaper l.u.r., candidates are paying far more for air time each year, at a rate of increase that has exceeded the inflation rate. Television spot-time costs increased 64 percent between 1972 and 1976, for instance, compared to a Consumer Price Index rise of a much lower 36 percent.[197] The price of one minute of network prime time doubled between the presidential elections of 1976 and 1980.[198] On individual affiliates across the country, the increases were sometimes more staggering. A thirty-second prime time spot in Portland, Oregon, cost just $55 in 1974; in 1980, the figure was $3,000.[199] Money, and a candidate's access to it, regulates the kind, quality, and quantity of televised political advertising as much as political consultants do.

Time-Buying, Targeting, and Scheduling

If money is a prerequisite for time-buying (i.e., the process of reserving particular television and radio commercial slots), so too is political skill and clout. At least as politically critical as the content of a commercial is the decision of where and when to broadcast it. While most political media consultants prefer to do their own time-buying, because of the standard 15 percent commission that they accrue for their labors, some professionals regularly subcontract with experienced national or local advertising agencies (splitting the commissions in some fashion), and for a campaign this is a far more beneficial arrangement. An agency time-buyer who is very familiar with a local market not only is an expert in audience demographics and viewing patterns, but also buys time on a continual basis for all the agency's other clients. He has the leverage and credibility to secure choice spots that a station manager might not even consider giving to an outside consultant handling a brief, one-shot customer.

Experience is essential because time-buying involves so many crucial variables.[200] A good time-buyer must know the "avails" (available slots), must be able to judge "points bought versus points delivered" (estimating audience size based on previous ratings), and must pay close attention to "psychographics" (audience makeup at any given time) and "station demographics" (the geographic regions covered by a station). The premise behind all of this is that political commercials must be carefully placed if they are to do the jobs for which they are designed; they must actually reach the intended groups of voters in order to influence them. Tony Schwartz describes the object of time-buying as "narrow-casting" rather than broadcasting political advertisements. Dissimilar kinds of people watch and listen to different sorts of programs at various times of the day. The better educated, information-oriented, undecided voters have been found to cluster around late news shows (at 10 or 11 P.M.), for example, and so a campaign seeking support from this vital swing group would try to schedule issue- and information-packed spots (perhaps in a talking head or pseudo-news format) at station breaks during late evening news programs.[201] Middle-aged housewives can be swayed with family-oriented or charismatic image spots strategically located within afternoon soap operas. Rural Americans, southerners, and blue-collar workers can be reached with down-home, musical, or even humorous advertisements during *Hee Haw*. There is also "task-oriented" time-buying, a favorite of Tony Schwartz, that allows a consultant to design spots that appeal to the mood of the voter at a particular time of day as he performs a certain activity.[202] For instance, Schwartz has produced radio spots for "car listening" when people are driving to and from work, shaping the physical characteristics of sound to be most conducive to the environment of an automobile on a highway. He also created "beach listening" spots for a gubernatorial client that were played on a Labor Day weekend.

Perhaps a good time-buyer's most useful skill is simply the sixth sense of measuring audience potential and being aware of viewer sensitivities. In a recent Indiana U.S. Senate race, for instance, the Democratic party's time-buyer only bought space for his candidate's ads during the first half of Indiana University football games, because the team was so lackluster he guessed no one would listen to the second half.[203] Mistakes in time-buying can be costly. The National Republican Congressional Committee once bought the first five minutes of NBC's *Tonight Show* for a political broadcast in the Waco, Texas, area. The reaction, discovered NRCC media director Ed Blakely, was not pleasant: "We found that you never want to preempt Johnny Carson's monologue. I think we lost votes in Waco for a long time."

Pinpoint time-buying and improved psychographics data have encouraged some consultants to design advertising packages with far more spots than ever before. While most campaigns have between a dozen and two dozen commercials,[204] Robert Squier produced seventy for William Winter's primary and general election contests in Mississippi's 1979 gubernatorial battle, most of them with a specific audience and time slot in mind. The Bailey/Deardourff agency broke all presidential records in 1976 with a total of one hour and forty minutes of thirty-second, sixty-second, and 4:20-minute spots for President Ford's campaign, but they came under criticism from some media analysts for doing it.[205] The sheer multiplicity of commercials, and their variety of formats and competing themes, were thought to have lessened the impact of an otherwise outstanding advertising package. To avoid this sort of multiple ad overkill, and also because of increasing production costs and the difficulty of buying good time in sufficient quantities, most consultants rely on far fewer spots. Frequent repetition of a few spots has its dangers, audience irritation not the least, but if a political advertisement is truly effective and useful, a viewer's perception of it, like a work of art, improves with repeated showings. If a spot is ineffective, by comparison, one airing is one too many.

A political time-buyer, unlike his product marketing counterpart, rarely has the luxury of thoughtful, smooth advance planning and un-pressured scheduling. "At its best, TV campaigning is guerrilla war-fare," observes one consultant. "You need to be highly reactive. . . . Any battle plan you lay out far ahead of time is no longer a battle—it's a ballet."[206] New production techniques (such as videotaping) allow overnight creation of spots, quite a contrast with the old eight-week lag time between planning and airing, and this development encour-ages reactive advertising and frequent revisions of media strategy.[207] Yet in any campaign there are some necessary attempts at rational planning, even if the plans and ad schedules are altered periodically.

Generally, campaigns adhere to four alternate advertising sched-ules (with all sorts of variations, of course).[208] The "flat buy" is the shopworn standard. In this method approximately the same number of spots are purchased each day for about three full weeks prior to the election. (This category includes the "blitz," when virtually every available slot is taken for the weeks leading up to election day.) The "orchestrated finish" steadily brings a campaign's advertising schedule to a peak at the campaign's close. About 10 percent of the media time budget is spent for slots four weeks away from election day; 20 percent is expended three weeks away; 30 percent a fortnight prior to the election; and a sizable 40 percent in the final seven days. Obviously this method is meant to generate momentum for a candidate, and it sometimes does, if the media budget is large enough. A third kind of advertising calendar is the "events schedule," when most of the media buys and spot time center around key "events" in the campaign, many of which are staged purely for the benefit of the advertising package. This variety of advertising is more intermittent, a kind of roller-coaster presentation, and usually does not suffice in and of itself.

The fourth and last advertising itinerary is by far the most interest-ing and novel. "Stop-start" (also called the "spurt" schedule, a term coined by Joseph Napolitan) requires early, sometimes regular saturation advertising for individual periods of a week or so months before the actual election.[209] Its goal is to create an identity where none existed at a time when there is presumably no political competition on the air, or to deal early and quickly with a major problem for an incumbent. Once the "spurt" has aired, the advertising disappears, to surface again in a different form a month or so prior to the election. Napolitan used early advertising to help Mike Gravel establish himself as a recognized challenger to U.S. Senator Ernest Gruening in Alaska's 1968 Democratic primary, which Gravel eventually won.[210] Spurt advertising can increase a candidate's "trial heat" performance in the early polls—which often measure little more than name identification—and these ratings are frequently self-fulfilling prophecies, influencing contributors and constituency organizations in their choice of candidate. DeLoss Walker, a Memphis-based political consultant, had spots broadcast for Democrat Fob James in Alabama eighteen months before a crowded 1978 gubernatorial primary. From a standing of less than 1 percent in the earliest polls, James gradually built up his recognition to become a major contender for, and the ultimate winner of, the state's governorship.[211]

A stop-start program can pay dividends for candidates in a number of other electoral situations. A nonincumbent candidate without opposition for his party's nomination has a difficult time matching the publicity gained by his eventual rival whenever the other party has a contested primary. Early advertising by the uncontested party's nominee can keep his name before the public, set the issues agenda for the general election, and put the other party on the defensive before its divisions can heal. Immediately after a primary election there is normally a lull in advertising even though the election is headline news and a topic of discussion among journalists and the general public. Tony Schwartz sees this time as another opportunity for early advertising: "Take any event that evokes discussion in the nonpaid media and frame paid media around that."[212] In addition, the Republican party has uncovered some evidence that suggests that for nonincumbent congressional hopefuls (especially Republicans) running in a presidential election year, pre-September advertising may be absolutely necessary. Voters in presidential years appear to make their House ballot choice *before* Labor Day—in a sense, getting it out of the way to concentrate on the presidential contest.[213] And finally, early advertising can help a candidate to defuse problems that can prove fatal if left unattended. When President Ford's White House chief of staff, Richard Cheney, decided to seek the U.S. House seat from his native Wyoming in 1978, he realized that he faced the charge of carpetbagger in the proud, parochial state he had left long ago. But through a superb advertising package that aired beginning in April, he reestablished his Wyoming roots with a collage of still photographs of himself as a Wyoming boy scout and a high school football hero (who married a cheerleader), while pumping voters' pride in a local boy made good, advising the President of the United States in the Oval Office and on Air Force One. Thereafter, his opponents' cries of "Carpetbagger!" fell on deaf ears, deprived of credibility by shrewd media packaging.[214]

The Problem of Time Availability

Most media consultants would heartily agree with the advice given by one of their number: "Never should the time-buyer be the determining factor in the length of spots. Each spot should be made to the length it needs to get the job done; it is a communications decision." The problem is that it has become a network and station decision as well, and there is no problem more vexing in the political media field than the limited availability of commercial broadcasting time. This is no arcane matter; fundamental questions of free speech and representative democracy are involved. Potentially, a station could lose its license for failing to give candidates for public office reasonable access to commercial time.[215] In practice, it has not happened, even though some outrageous, if isolated, examples of station arrogance exist. The core of contention is that the station or network has been permitted, for the most part, to define "reasonable access," including how many appearances a candidate is allowed, for what lengths of time, and in what kind of schedule.

One researcher reported that in five of six television stations surveyed, broadcast time devoted to political paid advertising in the last two months of both primary and general election campaigns was estimated at less than 10 percent of the total commercial time sold by the stations.[216] This small proportion during campaign peaks is not merely due to the tremendous competition for spot time—undoubtedly one major factor—but also because political time-buyers, even those with good connections, are at a serious disadvantage because of the l.u.r. There is a strict limitation on the number of prime-time network adjacencies per local station each week—an average of just sixty-six slots[217]—which intensifies the competition. Television stations, unlike newspapers, cannot "add a page" to meet advertising demand. Stations depend on advertising revenues to exist, and nonpolitical advertisers usually offer steadier and far more profitable business.[218]

The national networks are well aware of the time squeeze and its political consequences. In election years the three networks generally increase the number of adjacencies from sixty-six to seventy-five and specify that the additional slots are to be sold to political candidates, used for public service announcements, or returned. Local station sales managers also occasionally encourage local commercial advertisers to delay their advertisements until after the election period to ease the crunch. Normally, though, the problem is dealt with chiefly by limiting political advertising, even at a campaign's conclusion, by restricting the number of spots available to any single candidate. A station typically allots two to four network prime-time adjacencies per week to each presidential candidate, one or two to each U.S. Senate and House contender, and one for each of all the other candidates for public office. This may well tie up between a third and a half of a conscientious station's prime time, and yet the individual candidate still gets relatively little. The political demand for the few available slots is actually on the increase, since more campaigns at all levels are using television, and using it more extensively, than ever before.[219]

Of course, not all candidates use the spots reserved for them (and unclaimed time is usually sold to higher paying commercial advertisers). Stations insist on the reservation process, however, because of the "equal time" consideration, the requirement that a station treat fairly each major candidate by making available comparable spots to each. The equal-time requirement can result in further limitations on a candidate's airing schedule. If a candidate demands slots similar to those sold his opponent, stations sometimes cut back the opponent's allocation, awarding those spots to the petitioning candidate rather than creating additional slots or selling new ones.[220] That few stations go out of their way to make time readily accessible to candidates is not merely a commentary on the profit motive but also a product of the caution and conservatism that strict federal regulation brings. In general, the sensitivity that stations know is required in dealing with political campaigns leaves them inclined to minimize their political involvements.[221]

One Baltimore county advertising executive, who has been in his business since the dawn of television, exasperatedly told *The Washington Post*: "It isn't like it used to be. There was a time when we could buy whatever we wanted—the choicest prime-time stuff. Now most of what the stations give us is garbage."[222] Some do not even offer that. A *Post* survey of Maryland television and radio stations found a myriad of internally devised regulations that handicapped political advertisers.[223] One station refused to sell time during University of Maryland football games; another would allot only three prime-time slots per week to all the candidates; still another would accept no political ads (in clear violation of FCC guidelines). In the 1974 Massachusetts gubernatorial election, Boston's three major television stations proved just as parsimonious,[224] and it is a fair assumption, given the avalanche of complaints heard from media consultants, that there is no unique Boston-Washington axis.[225]

The lack of available time near to election day is another reason why consultants have turned to early advertising, but here too their efforts have often been stymied by stations who narrowly and unilaterally defined the start of the "campaign period" (and thus the beginning of their FCC political time obligations). When the National Republican Congressional Committee approached the networks to buy time in January of an election year, NRCC media director Ed Blakely described their unfriendly reaction and the change in attitude that came about when l.u.r. rights were waived:

"What do you mean the Republicans want to buy five minutes of time in January? There's nothing going on in January. We'll have to check with our lawyers to see if you can do that. And five minutes is a hard buy, it'll be tough." Now once they found out that we were not going to ask for the lowest unit rate and we were going to spend some money, they changed their tune: "Sure, come in, show us your checkbooks."

Networks and stations tend to make their greatest efforts for presidential candidates, and they have been especially diligent in carving out five-minute spots in presidential years.[226] Yet for state, district, and local candidates, five-minute spots are perhaps the most difficult of all to secure (partially because pre-taped programming cannot accommodate them).[227] Even presidential candidates have great problems buying thirty-minute slots during prime time. None of the three networks would agree to sell a half hour of prime time to Ronald Reagan in November 1979 for his candidacy announcement speech, and in the end his campaign was forced to buy the time on ninety-eight individual stations covering only 70 percent of the nation's households.[228]

These limitations on political broadcasting take their toll. Obviously they restrict direct communication between candidate and constituency, deny the voter information, and discourage in-depth treatment of campaign issues in longer five-minute and thirty-minute broadcasts. One study has indicated that losers in congressional races had much more trouble getting their spots on television and radio than did winners, suggesting at least an indirect relationship between success at the polls and at the station ad placement desk.[229] Incumbents are the winners in more ways than one. Normally any limitation on political advertising would work to their advantage. The media is the best way for an unknown challenger to establish himself as a credible opponent, and unpaid media alone is usually insufficient. Thus advertising time availability has an impact on competition, and the shortage of time can help to insulate an incumbent.[230] The stations' rigid cash-on-the-barrelhead policy can be devastating to candidates as well. Competition for the little available time is so fierce that choice spots should ideally be bought half a year or more ahead of time, and it is a rare statewide or district campaign that is well-heeled enough at that early stage to afford such a considerable outlay. Occasionally a presidential campaign suffers a cruel fate for the same reason. The fractured Humphrey organization in 1968 had paltry financial resources early on, and when the money finally started to flow during the final weeks of the campaign, the Humphrey staff could not buy any time at all in the crucial state of California.[231]

As bad as the situation is for candidates, it is far worse for ballot measures. "The most difficult part of any referendum campaign is buying time," Chuck Winner remarked. Those advertising slots that are reserved for politics generally go to candidates. Stations are not required to make time available for ballot measures, and referendum and initiative commercials are considered the most preemptable (i.e., the most easily bumped) political or nonpolitical spots, even though, unlike candidates' commercials, the l.u.r. rule cannot be invoked when buying time for them.[232] Consultants report that stations sometimes "blacklist" certain referenda issues on very controversial subjects and refuse to sell any time, restricting coverage to news programs and station-controlled specials. A Los Angeles radio station (KABC) went so far as to decide that no more referenda advertising would be broadcast on its airwaves because, in its opinion, corporate interests had been monopolizing the California ballot measure debates with a flood of paid time.[233]

Consultants and candidates often have not idly accepted arbitrary station and network rulings on their requests for time, and FCC and court challenges have been frequent. As early as 1952 the Democrats filed a complaint with the FCC, claiming that time was being made available to the Republicans in a partisan manner.[234] Over the years a set of FCC guidelines has been developed through piecemeal rulings that supposedly prohibit stations from flatly banning access to classes or lengths of time for political advertisers. But stations are given broad flexibility in determining what is actually made available within each class or length of time, and can in fact ban candidates from buying certain lengths and classes for "practical reasons."[235] A station can refuse to accept any thirty-second or sixty-second spot announcements, selling lengths of only five minutes or greater to political candidates.[236] Conversely, if it so chooses, a station can deny any requests for several hours of telethon broadcasting,[237] hour specials,[238] or half-hour documentaries.[239] As if that is not enough flexibility for stations, the FCC has also declared that candidates are not necessarily entitled to buy all particular placements they desire on a station's schedule (i.e., on particular shows or at a particular time of day or night),[240] and that stations can rule out advertising entirely for certain classes of candidates, usually those for lesser statewide and local offices.[241] Stated bluntly, networks and stations can really do pretty much as they please in a vast array of campaign circumstances. Just about all that is required of a station is that each candidate's request for time be treated individually and that the reasons for denial be fully articulated.[242] Because of the danger of First Amendment violations (by having a government agency decide whether the free press had judged a problem correctly), the FCC generally is limited to determining if the networks and stations have considered all the facts and offered a reasonable explanation for a decision.[243]

An important recent court ruling, supporting a surprisingly expansive FCC time access decision, may have given candidates more leverage in dealing with the stations and networks.[244] The three networks refused President Carter's reelection campaign the half-hour slots it wanted for Carter's candidacy announcement on December 4, 1979, deeming this to be within the "precampaign period." Declaring New Year's Day as the beginning of televised presidential politics, for example, CBS offered two five-minute segments instead (one during prime time, the other on daytime television.) The Carter committee appealed, the FCC ruled in its favor,[245] and the networks immediately challenged the decision in court. CBS determined the public interest as follows: "At this point in the 1980 campaign . . . the CBS Television Network has made the judgment that the public interest does not require the preemption of extensive segments of its national program service for political broadcasts of half-hour duration."[246] In fact, there was more than a little self-interest involved. Political broadcasts usually drag down prime-time ratings (not only during their airings but also by hurting the audience potential for succeeding shows), and this is particularly crucial during the autumn and winter months, advertising rates being set by reference to the audience size during that time period. The U.S. Court of Appeals quickly dispensed with the network's objections and upheld the FCC.[247] While the court decision still left the networks and stations broad discretionary powers, the FCC was, in effect, given the authority to determine the time of a campaign's beginning. The ruling will undoubtedly assist candidates and consultants to buy more air time, and earlier, in future campaigns, although it is a safe prediction that battling and bickering between the television and election camps will continue.

Besides favorable judicial developments, other possible ameliorations of the time accessibility problem are on the horizon. The growth of cable television, for instance, offers the possibility of a generous provision of free time to the candidates on some channels (although the multitude of channels probably means that such public affairs broadcasts would become "narrowcasts," viewed only by those with a pronounced interest in politics and elections). On the current national networks, there is the possibility of getting more political mileage per minute of television and radio by message compression. New technology permits the audio condensation of a spot announcement by up to 25 percent, producing a shorter, staccato ad with the same content as a longer one. Interestingly, condensed ads are not only cheaper to air but also more memorable for viewers. Speeded-up commercials actually produce heightened recall, and special equipment can improve the quality of the original sound as well.[248] Whatever the length of the spots produced, better planning and earlier time-buying can assist in securing choicer blocks of time for political candidates. The National Republican Senatorial Committee, for example, decided to spend its permitted 1980 contribution allotment in some key U.S. Senate races by buying or reserving television and radio time very early so that it would be available to GOP candidates after their nominations. (If primaries or conventions are held in late summer or early autumn, many of the best spots are gone long before the party candidates are even selected.) In a partisan split the Federal Election Commission refused to give approval to the scheme, but under the Reagan administration the vote could well be reversed.[249] Such "remedies" are, of course, nothing more than Band-Aids. Strong medicine, including a complete reappraisal of the proper contribution of media to political discourse, is in order, and chapter 6 will include recommendations for altering the substance and role of paid media advertising in American campaigns.

The Rest of the Media Package

Paid television holds such a fascination for political observers that the substantial remainder of a campaign's advertising program can be overlooked. The bumper stickers, buttons, billboards, yard signs, key chains, football score cards, calendars, pot holders, pencils, placards, and posters probably do not convert anyone to the candidate's cause, but they can establish name identification, motivate volunteers, and give the impression of momentum. They can prepare voters for the television advertising to come by familiarizing them with graphics, designs, and slogans. They can suggest the message the campaign will attempt to communicate, even by such seemingly insignificant details as color. U.S. Representative Jerry Litton's 1978 Missouri Senate campaign chose brown for his brochures because, as his spokesman confided, "All the psychological testing shows brown connotes stability and reasonableness."[250] Jimmy Carter's 1976 managers chose green to contrast with everyone else's red, white, and blue, and to symbolize freshness and rebirth.[251]

Campaign literature, with the possible exception of some particularly informational half-hour documentaries, is the most issue-oriented and factual advertising medium. Whether distributed in shopping centers, at conventions of influential groups, or through the post as direct mail, literature can be enormously persuasive and effective, although its potential is rarely realized.

Campaign literature comes in many forms: biographical sheets and booklets, handout flyers and doorknob hangers, pamphlets on the entire platform for general distribution or very specialized issues for interest groups and socioeconomic classes, and campaign biography books (which almost always fail to make anyone's best-sellers' list).[252] Much of the message contained in general appeal literature is frequently reprinted as magazine and newspaper advertising. While print advertising is not thought to have much of an impact in most modern campaigns, it can be a useful communications tool in black and ethnic newspapers and small-town weeklies, which are closely read. Magazine political advertising is making a comeback of sorts thanks to zip-code targeting. Advertisements (including fund-raising appeals) can now be placed in national magazines and printed in just the editions sent to subscribers with zip codes of a particular congressional district or state. A high proportion of magazine subscribers vote—74 percent of *Business Week* readers and 65 percent of *Time* and *Newsweek* subscribers, for instance[253]—so the money is well spent, and the cost is reasonable by comparison with other forms of advertising. Magazines also have a relatively long life expectancy, and the circulation is greater than the number of listed subscribers since they are often passed from person to person. The growth in specialized magazines also has meant that a campaign can target its message by subject matter, as well as by zip code. There is even the prospect of "talking" magazine pages in the near future.[254] Some electronic companies have already concluded contracts with leading national magazines to provide ad pages with record grooves, which yield a recorded message when a microphonograph is passed across the page. Presumably talking magazines will provide competition for the videocassette industry. Some consultants already foresee a time when video players are standard home equipment and when videocassettes of a candidate giving his pitch are mass-produced and mailed to volunteers, contributors, and the general public.

The technological marvels of the future may still be outclassed, on more than a few occasions, by a candidate's simple personal appearance. A candidate does not have to be electrifying to eclipse technology; in fact, the electronics of the unpaid media are responsible for the significance of personal appearances. Set speeches, addresses to rallies, and campaign statements are relatively unimportant electorally in and of themselves. It is the press that heightens their value by transmitting the candidate's words and gestures into almost every home in the constituency. Members of the press are coddled as a result. They are given access to the candidate and his advisers, space on the candidate's plane and rooms in his hotel (for a fee), telephones and free liquor at every stop, and the utmost consideration in scheduling campaign events, which are arranged around reporters' filing deadlines. Most campaign activities cease to be organized for their own value. They must be media events, with good visuals and dramatic action. A candidate does not hold a press conference in the campaign headquarters or give an auditorium speech to issue a statement on farm policy; he and his traveling press entourage must go to an Iowa farm with silos in the background (irresistibly including a cow-milking session during the visit). Family members are enlisted to make their own personal appearances in a number of media markets simultaneously, and the candidate is scheduled not according to the merits of the requests but by way of market rating points.

Time is eagerly sought by candidates, particularly lesser-known challengers, on interview shows and evening news programs. Paid media gives certainty of control and flexibility, but it cannot match the unpaid media for credibility or, in most cases, for size and attentiveness of audience. The three networks' evening news now reaches an average of 28 million homes.[255] The average local station, copying the national networks, is devoting more time to public affairs programs and hiring a far larger news staff.[256] All political consultants fully acknowledge that the unpaid media, more than paid media, can make or break a candidate. Edmund Muskie's early Democratic primary performances did not live up to press expectations of a front-runner's proper victory margins in the 1972 presidential contest, and he was declared to have lost a New Hampshire primary that he actually won by a comfortable margin. Jimmy Carter received just a 28.4 percent plurality win in the 1976 New Hampshire contest, 20 percentage points less than Muskie's showing four years earlier, but because he greatly exceeded the press's expectations for a dark-horse ex-Georgia governor, he became the beneficiary of a publicity bonanza. Ronald Reagan, meanwhile, garnered 48 percent of the Granite state's GOP vote against an incumbent president and was written off by the press (rather prematurely, as it turned out). In 1980 Edward Kennedy became, as one reporter wrote, "the victim of the media's mob psychology," subjected to press "overkill" with "the most intimate saturation scrutiny."[257] John Anderson, by contrast, was almost a media-sanctioned candidate, propelled along despite defeats by reporters' approval of "the Anderson difference." Merely deciding to turn their attention to races at one level or another can affect outcomes. Part of the explanation for the increasingly more frequent defeats of U.S. senators compared to House members since World War II is thought to be the unpaid media's greater interest in Senate contests and the consequent wider visibility of challengers.[258]

Free time can be crucial even to well-known presidential candidates. Jerry Brown's 1980 presidential effort depended heavily on his expected strong performance in scheduled television debates prior to the Iowa caucuses. But when Carter cancelled out, Brown's campaign effectively folded. George Bush probably wishes in retrospect that the early GOP debates in 1980 had been cancelled, since his less than dynamic, even graceless, performances appeared to belie his forceful paid advertising image. His media man, Bob Goodman, bemoaned: "The eagle performing alone on his own in television ads is terrific. That debate format is a terrible format for George. . . . It's a letdown. You see seven guys instead of the eagle and six others."[259] Candidates who are not adept at using the unpaid media suffer. Adlai Stevenson, whose statements were far too eloquent and exacting for bumper-sticker language, had a bad sense of timing that caused him to run on and to be cut off awkwardly in debate and news film.[260] On the other hand, candidates who are willing to suffer indignities and who have consultants with good contacts in television can reap great benefits. Richard Nixon's 1968 visit to Johnny Carson's "Tonight Show" and his cameo appearance on NBC's equally popular "Laugh-In" (on which he said, simply, "Sock it to me?") were viewed as media coups by his opponents. John Anderson's 1980 efforts to enlist a youthful army of campaign workers were probably given a considerable boost by his spotlight displays on NBC's "Saturday Night Live" comedy show.[261]

The value of unpaid media appearances by candidates is clearly the credibility it confers rather than its substantive content, as McClure and Patterson's media studies have pointed out. Evening newscasts, for example, tell disconcertingly little about the substance of politics, preferring the show of media events and the manufactured excitement of trial-heat polls.[262] Television reporting is understandably derided by print journalists, though television is demonstrably more influential politically than newspapers, and newspaper coverage and editorials are only rarely a significant factor in an election's outcome.[263] While television has the power of visual immediacy, however, newspaper reportage is more thorough, detailed, precise, and usually more reflective. Newspapers have always had an appeal to better educated, higher income voters,[264] but in recent years they have become an important source of campaign information for a larger proportion of the population.[265]

Radio, after experiencing a severe decline in political power after the introduction of television, is also on the rise again as a campaign tool. Almost half of presidential voters now find it an important source of campaign news,[266] and the 444 million radio sets in use in the United States (an average of 5.7 sets per household) help to explain why.[267] Even when radios were less plentiful, politicians fully recognized their value. In 1928 the Democratic and Republican presidential tickets together spent $1 million for commercial radio time.[268] Franklin Roosevelt was the first president to use radio effectively in a campaign,[269] and every president or would-be chief executive since has tried to follow his lead.[270]

Not only is there much more free "public interest" time available on radio than television, but advertising on radio can have a greater impact than on television. First of all, people are more often alone and undistracted when they are listening to it, sometimes a truly captive audience (as when driving). Radio is a time-buyer's targeting heaven as well. While television's prime-time audiences can sometimes be relatively undifferentiated, radio stations and individual programs usually have very distinctive listenerships. (Just the roll call of radio station categories reveals as much: black, ethnic, country, rock-and-roll, easy listening, all-news, etc.) Radio time is also much cheaper, so more of it can be bought with potentially greater effect with the same number of campaign advertising dollars. In large metropolitan areas such as Chicago or in suburban areas covered by large urban media markets such as New Jersey, radio is a necessary substitute for prohibitively expensive television. Moreover, radio is more flexible than television, and it is faster and cheaper to produce new radio ads in response to changing events. (Radio ads can be designed and cut in an afternoon; only videotape TV ads can be done anywhere near as quickly.)

In addition, a consultant can often deal with a controversial topic better on radio. "Radio has a way of getting things felt, without being seen. It doesn't attract attention to itself," surmises one of the medium's staunchest supporters, Tony Schwartz. For several months Schwartz ran radio spots for the New York state commerce division, featuring the voice of the commissioner of commerce, with no adverse reaction. But when a similar advertisement appeared in *The New York Times* that included the commissioner's picture, some state legislators called for an investigation, claiming state money was being used to promote the commissioner for a future bid for elective office. Schwartz also employed extensive radio advertising for Andrew Young's first congressional race in a predominantly white Georgia district, the idea being to emphasize his message and deemphasize his skin color.

While radio and television advertising are not interchangeable,[271] paid ads on either one are enhanced by a complementary commercial package on the other. This is, in fact, the definition of a successful media program: one in which no medium is completely dominant, and where all parts are coordinated to form a harmonious whole. However, because of a properly uncooperative press, the lack of available advertising time, and a host of other factors, this recipe has proven an elusive one for even the best consultant-chefs.

Media Versus Organization

Media consultants who create paid political television commercials are perfectly willing to acknowledge the value of other forms of media advertising, be it on radio, in the unpaid media, or through campaign literature and paraphernalia. What they will not accede to, for reasons of pride and financial survival, is the primary worth of campaign organization. One of the fiercest and longest running debates among candidates, consultants, and campaign budgeters concerns the relative merits of media versus organization: Where should the limited campaign dollars be spent? It is no surprise to discover that media professionals rarely recommend that less than 40 percent of the campaign war chest be spent on television and radio advertising and that the proportion occasionally ranges up to 70 percent or more. When media consultants concede any necessity for organization, it is as a second phase, a luxury that can be purchased if sufficient money is left (and there hardly ever is). Most candidates and campaign managers apparently agree with their media consultants. A Republican survey of party nominees' congressional campaigns in 1978 revealed that fully a third did not even have field organizers, an old-time campaign staple.[272] The GOP analysts were forced to conclude that "the human element of campaigning has been diminished and probably replaced by the use of more paid media." In 1976 and 1978 the proportion of voters reporting that they had been personally contacted by a candidate or a campaign worker, either in person or by telephone, was amazingly low—about 19 percent had been contacted by Republican campaigns and 14 percent by Democratic organizations.[273]

Despite their disdain for organization, media consultants such as Michael Kaye admit that "All advertising is, is a substitute for a personal call. The ideal situation would be to eliminate all advertising and have someone knock on everyone's front door. . . ." A series of studies has, in fact, suggested that organizational techniques can be quite effective, increasing a candidate's total by at least several percentage points.[274] In 1964, for example, a survey indicated that half of the political Independents personally contacted by a Goldwater volunteer voted for the Republican nominee, compared to only 29 percent of the uncontacted Independents, and 15 percent of the Democrats called on by GOP workers (as opposed to just 9 percent of uncontacted Democrats) voted for Goldwater.[275] The new sophisticated organizational technologies discussed in the next section have greatly increased the number of voters who can be reached by a limited number of volunteers, thus augmenting organization's potential electoral bonus. While some of these innovations are expensive, it is interesting to recall that in 1976, on average, presidential candidates spent about $5 in primary states, where media campaigns are the rule, for every $1 they expended in caucus states, where organization is the key to victory.[276] Jimmy Carter actually spent more on his California primary campaign (about $654,000) than he spent for all the caucus states combined. With an already noticeable drift to the caucus system apparent in some states—and with the continuation of the severe media time squeeze in the primary states—organization will almost inevitably receive a greater share of campaign resources and attention in the future.

ORGANIZATIONAL SPECIALISTS AND THEIR ACTIVITIES

Before the dawn of the new campaign technology of media, polling, and direct mail, it was the campaign organizer, not the television professional or pollster, who was the focus of press attention and the behind-the-scenes power. The great organizers such as Mark Hanna (William McKinley's campaign maestro) and James Farley (FDR's 1936 chieftain) still live in the nation's political lore. More recently, a number of campaign organizers have achieved recognition for their management abilities: Murray Chotiner (for Richard Nixon), Larry O'Brien (for JFK, LBJ, and HHH), Gary Hart (for George McGovern),[277] Jim Baker (for Gerald Ford), Hamilton Jordan (for Jimmy Carter), and John Sears (for Ronald Reagan). There is a large number of political consultants in both parties who concentrate on organization, though for the most part they are not really technologists but strategists, with an extensive set of national political contacts and lengthy (usually lifelong) lists of party and campaign attachments. The best-known organization consultants among the Democrats are Matt Reese and Mark Shields, and for the GOP, Eddie Mahe and Charles Black. All have a seemingly endless roster of involvements with national, state, and local campaigns and politicians.[278]

When a candidate hires an organization consultant, he is leasing the professional's web of associates and staking a lien on the favors owed him. The value of the consultant's contacts is not so much in the endorsements it can produce, since these are rarely considered crucial electorally.[279] Rather it is the organizer's ability to assemble a first-rate staff and, beyond, to locate and identify the candidate's likely voters—to "find 'em and vote 'em," as Abraham Lincoln once remarked—that insures his worth to any campaign. In recruiting and training campaign personnel, the organization consultant has a more taxing task than ever before, since staff size has grown considerably along with the campaign's other dimensions. The average U.S. House campaign on the GOP side now has seven full-time staffers (at least five of them paid)—about the size of most U.S. Senate campaign staffs a decade ago.[280] Presidential campaign staffs have become huge. The 1980 Carter-Mondale Committee occupied a fourteen-story building in Washington and employed 101 professionals there plus 87 more in three regional offices throughout the country.[281] Paid field workers in state offices brought the total preconvention staff to 354, with an average salary of $1,100 per month and a total monthly payroll of $400,000.[282] Volunteer workers must also be recruited, trained, and coordinated by the organization chief, and even in a congressional campaign they can number several thousand.[283]

Far more difficult a job for the organization is the identification of favorable voters and the arrangement of activities to insure that they vote, since the voting population universe in most states is numbered in the millions. The obvious solution is to target voters and geographic areas selectively, based on where the greatest number of votes can be harvested with the least effort. In selecting cities, counties, precincts, or even census tracts for targeting, organizers rely heavily on past voting patterns and turnout history, survey research information, and census and commercial marketing data.[284] Once the areas are targeted, the households and registered voters within them are personally contacted by telephone (to be discussed shortly) or by volunteer door-to-door canvassers. In 1964 the Goldwater organization reportedly contacted 3.4 million voters in 912 targeted counties of 46 states, with volunteers walking the neighborhoods.[285] In 1968 Eugene McCarthy won 42 percent of the New Hampshire presidential primary vote with the help of 3,000 student volunteers, who canvassed 60,000 homes.[286] Hamilton Jordan organized a team of 90 Georgians who personally knew Jimmy Carter to canvass fully half of the registered Democrats in New Hampshire's cities of Manchester and Nashua prior to the 1976 primary. Once the Georgians returned to their home state, they sent handwritten notes to those voters who seemed favorable to Carter. The technique was considered highly effective.[287]

In most of their massive and detailed organizational efforts, modern consultants have a superb technological partner, the computer.[288] Computers have been utilized in recent campaigns for a wide range of organizational duties: scheduling the candidate's appearances, targeting precincts for voter contact, get-out-the-vote (GOTV) activities on election day,[289] producing "walking lists" of registered voters for door-to-door canvassing and "phone lists" for telephone banks, maintaining volunteers and contributor files, and keeping financial records and accounts for eased compliance with federal and state campaign laws. It is almost impossible to find a serious campaign that does not use computers, not just for organizational purposes, but for direct-mail fund raising, compilation and analysis of polling results, and formulation of media time-buying strategies. An estimated 2,500 computer firms in the United States offer wares to candidates, and up to one-tenth of the total campaign budget is spent on computer services.[290] A modern campaign, which is a moderate-sized business and chaotic by nature, would probably not be manageable, and certainly would not be as well run, without the help of the new technology's workhorse, the computer.

REACH OUT AND TOUCH SOMEONE: INSTANT ORGANIZATION, PHONE BANKS, AND CLUSTER TARGETING

Organizational consultants have developed a number of technologies to substitute for weakened party structures (or to assist candidates not in party favor to construct an organization to rival the party). "Instant organization" (IO) is one such technology, utilizing paid callers telephoning voters from centralized banks of telephones to enlist volunteers for a candidate.[291] IO was devised and improved primarily by three individuals: Hugh Parmer, who employed IO in his successful campaign for mayor of Fort Worth, Texas; Matt Reese, while serving as director of operations for the Democratic National Committee in the early 1960s; and Hank Parkinson, who has promoted it nationally. After favorable areas are identified and targeted, and the computer has produced telephone lists by block within the targeted areas, trained callers using prepared scripts telephone the homes in each block sequentially until someone is found who will agree to be the candidate's block captain. The block captain consents to make two rounds of his neighborhood, the first to promote the candidate and the second to get-out-the-vote. Up to seven subsequent mail and telephone contacts are made to each block captain to keep his or her motivation high. The system has proven more effective in lower than higher income neighborhoods but, somewhat surprisingly, the callers apparently do not have to telephone many more than a third of the computerized telephone list for each block to find a willing volunteer.[292] IO has been a part of a diverse group of successful campaigns, from Richard Nixon's 1968 presidential effort (called "Neighbors for Nixon") to the NAACP's 1978 defeat of Philadelphia Mayor Frank Rizzo's attempt to amend the city charter so that he could seek a third term.

The "telephone banks" used in the IO system have become an organizational staple. Almost all candidates have a phone bank of some sort early in their campaigns, to identify household by household the registered voters favorable to their cause and, then, to insure their favorables turn up at the polls on election day.[293] Mainly, phone banks are staffed by volunteers (for reasons of cost), but increasingly it appears that professional paid callers are being hired to increase the efficiency and the quality of the operation. Tens of thousands of voters can be contacted, many repeatedly, with the use of a telephone bank, and the work is much quicker, less tiring for volunteers, and subject to greater control than door-to-door convassing (which nevertheless retains the advantage of personal intimacy). Richard Nixon's 1960 organization was the first to use telephones widely in a national campaign, and Nelson Rockefeller relied heavily on them in the 1964 California presidential primary. George Romney's managers in his 1966 gubernatorial reelection bid believed that the 146,000 calls to households in three key congressional districts provided the margin of victory in two of them.[294] Telephones have probably never been used as extensively as they were in the 1980 Iowa presidential caucuses, when all of the major candidates saturated the state with calls. George Bush's and Jimmy Carter's telephone banks were regarded before the caucuses as technologically superior to their rivals, and they apparently delivered not just votes for the two candidates but also a turnout far exceeding the 1976 total.[295] Carter's campaign found an ingenious use for some of his telephone bank results. Evidence indicates that some Carter workers in Maine gave lists of voters who were *unfavorable* to the president to Jerry Brown's campaign organization, in order to split the anti-Carter vote and dilute Edward Kennedy's potential support.[296]

Telephones are one of only two campaign tools (radio being the other) whose recent costs have lagged considerably behind the Consumer Price Index.[297] New innovations, such as a tele-computer phoning device (which completes far more calls per hour with a partially automated taped answering system), will probably increase the cost but also the sophistication and usefulness of the telephone.[298] There are still unavoidable problems with telephone banks, specifically the large proportion of voters who cannot be reached because they have unlisted or unanswered telephones, or no telephone at all.[299] These difficulties may well explain the results of some studies that indicate relatively few voters report being contacted prior to an election, despite the proliferation of telephone banks.[300]

Organizational techniques are being developed that go far beyond the relatively simple devices now in use, and "cluster targeting," a complex process that more accurately locates potentially favorable blocks of voters, is one of them.[301] Cluster targeting's first campaign test came in 1978 in a Missouri campaign centering on a "right-to-work" (anti-closed shop) initiative.[302] Matt Reese was hired by the United Labor Committee of Missouri just three months before an election that earlier benchmark surveys by William Hamilton had indicated labor would lose by a crushing two-to-one margin. National labor groups, however, saw the Missouri initiative as a crucial test of their ability to fend off expected right-wing challenges to labor laws in other states, and they were prepared to invest significantly to defeat the "Show Me" state ballot measure. Reese saw an opportunity to experiment with a system so costly he had been unable earlier to find a campaign well heeled and willing enough to try it. At Reese's suggestion, the Labor Council contracted for additional polling with Hamilton's firm, and also with Claritas Corporation of Virginia, a "geo-demographic" research outfit up to that point involved primarily with commercial marketing. Claritas maintains more than 1,000 bits of socio-economic census data broken into the 278,000 block groups in the United States. (A block group is of varying size but on average contains 280 households, far smaller than the average precinct.) With ten years of marketing experience for major corporations such as Time, Inc., Claritas has been able to assign each of the 278,000 units to one of forty "Clusters."[303] Each Cluster is a classification of communities that have homogeneous economic and demographic characteristics and have been proven to react in similar ways to commercial marketing techniques.[304]

There is an obvious and valuable link between macrolevel polling data, which identify the persuadable voter by group, and the Claritas clustering system, which locates geographical units to match the "persuadable" profile and thus tells precisely which areas can be canvassed, telephoned, and mailed most productively. To give valid polling results for all forty Clusters Hamilton increased his sample size to 1,350 individuals and identified eighteen of the forty Clusters as at least "fair-minded" on the right-to-work issue. A computer was employed to match registered voters' lists with the telephone directory, after which all nonpersuadables (in nonfair-minded Clusters) were purged. A total of 595,000 voters were left in 2,300 targeted block groups (out of Missouri's 6,020). Ten different contacts were made with each of these individuals, mainly by direct mail.[305] Each direct-mail letter was written somewhat differently for each Cluster, depending on the concerns about right-to-work expressed in Hamilton's survey of the Cluster members. Some 24,100 volunteer workers recruited primarily from organized labor visited 360,000 homes in targeted neighborhoods. Favorables received postcard and telephone reminders to vote. Interestingly, less than 15 percent of the total budget was spent on television time and ad production, and just 15 percent more on radio and newspaper advertisements.[306] Well over half of the hefty campaign war chest of $2.5 million was applied to organization, while the opposition, spending about the same amount, devoted a much greater share of its resources to media. The result of Reese's extraordinary organizational effort was a stunning reversal of the original polling finding. From 63 to 30 percent in favor of the initiative (with 7 percent undecided) in February, the right-to-work measure was soundly trounced by 60 to 40 percent in the November general election.

Cluster targeting is still experimental. Despite limited testing in a few candidate campaigns, it is far from certain that the technique can be applied as successfully to a personality as an issue, nor has it been conclusively proven that the "life-style" variables and measurements that comprise *commercial marketing* Clusters are the equivalent of *political* Clusters. (As was discussed earlier, the two forms of advertising are evaluated in somewhat different terms by voter/consumers.) Nevertheless, some form of "geodemographic" or "psychographic" targeting will almost inevitably become part of the standard campaign arsenal in the future.[307] The U.S. Bureau of the Census is assisting the development with the 1980 census, since for the first time reasonably priced tapes of all the collected socioeconomic data are being made available by precinct, tailormade for consultants' needs.[308] The Qube system (discussed in chapter 2) offers fascinating possibilities for organizers as well. A politician or his media associates will one day be able to make a television pitch for volunteers and receive an instantaneous computer printout of the names, addresses, and telephone numbers of all those home viewers who have been moved enough by the presentation to punch a few buttons on their television computer terminals.[309] Be it Qubes or Clusters, the new technology of election campaigns has radically affected the way campaigns are organized. The raw materials—time, money, people, and talent—are the same, but little else on the landscape would be recognizable to the party leader of yore.

Media may be overrated by comparison to organization in its contribution to campaigns, but no other technology or campaign technique is so pervasive or believed to be so important. There is some justification for the belief, since paid political advertisements actually communicate more information about issues than news programs (which says more about the news than it does about political commercials). Yet the accumulation of evidence suggests that there is every reason to be disturbed about the shape and substance of the media consultant's activities. Some charges against him are basically spurious. Candidates are not sold like soap if only because people treat candidate and product advertising differently, expecting somewhat more from a campaign sales pitch and being more attentive to it. Neither have consultants succeeded in media-manipulating the electorate consistently; when it happens, it is more a matter of luck and circumstance, because the often diametrically opposed styles of media professionals reveal how unscientific the televised electoral arts still are. And consultants' handsome fees are what the market will gladly bear, less obscene than the profits that accrue to stations and networks for advertising that should be aired in the public interest—despite lowest unit rates, which themselves are a decidedly mixed blessing.

What *is* unsettling about many of the prominent masters is their glorification of style over substance, their hero worship of imagery idols, and their trivialization of politics with an overindulgent, insatiable appetite for gimmicks, slogans, and star politics. Candidates are willing accomplices, of course, but the encouragement of media "experts" (who are royally paid because they know what a candidate *must* do to win) gives the whole sordid collection of techniques the blessing of strategic necessity. The British Conservative party commercials cited in this chapter clearly show that drama, appeal, entertainment, and effect do not have to be sacrificed once extensive discussion of issues is introduced into the paid dialogue. Moreover, the deceptions that occur in political advertising are universally deplored, and rightly so, but little is said of the trend to purely unconstructive negativism in ad campaigning. There is nothing inherently wrong in pointing out the weaknesses of the opposition—it has always been done and should be—but it must be undertaken within the framework of positive alternatives.

If the current difficulties with time availability continue, however, neither positive nor negative messages will be aired to the extent the democratic process deserves. The paucity of time inhibits communication between voters and those who seek to represent them (helping incumbents above all) and promotes brevity, blandness, and superficiality in political advertising. This latter dilemma is not the consultant's fault; it is the system's imperfection. But like the media professionals' own foibles, it must be corrected to insure that the electoral process is as fair and informative as it must be in a democracy. These matters, and related ones, will be taken up again in chapter 6.

NOTES

1. David R. Altman, chairman of Altman, Stoller, Weiss agency, writing in *The New York Times*, October 11, 1978.

2. Telephone conversation on election night, 1978, as reported in *The Washington Post*, November 9, 1978.

3. Stanley Kelley, *Professional Public Relations and Political Power* (Baltimore, Md.: Johns Hopkins, 1956), p. 141.

4. There were about 19 million sets in use by election time and 58 million viewers.

5. See Kelley, *Professional Public Relations and Political Power*, pp. 160–169, 187–201.

6. Ibid., pp. 196–197.

7. Ibid., p. 190, n. 45.

8. Marya Mannes, "Sales Campaign" (1952) from *Rhymes for Our Times* by Mannes and Robert Osborn (New York: George Braziller, 1959); as quoted by Walter Troy Spencer, "The Agency Knack of Political Packaging," in Robert Agranoff (ed.), *The New Style in Election Campaigns* (2nd ed.) (Boston: Holbrook, 1976), p. 87.

9. Dan Nimmo, *The Political Persuaders: The Techniques of Modern Election Campaigns* (Englewood Cliffs, N.J.: Prentice-Hall, 1970), p. 114.

10. See Kelley, *Professional Public Relations and Political Power*, pp. 177–184.

11. Nimmo, *The Political Persuaders*, pp. 112–113.

12. See Joe McGinniss, *The Selling of the President 1968* (New York: Trident Press, 1969). As to color's impact on political advertising, researchers have discovered that color commercials are recalled more easily than black-and-white ads, and that color increases voters' positive judgment of ads, especially for women. See Thomas R. Donahoe, "Viewers' Perceptions of Color and Black-and-White Paid Political Advertising," *Journalism Quarterly*, vol. 50 (Winter 1973): 660–665.

13. Nimmo, *The Political Persuaders*, p. 151.

14. George H. White, *A Study of Access to Television for Political Candidates* (Cambridge, Mass.: Institute of Politics, JFK School of Government, Harvard, May 1978), pp. 1–2.

15. Kelley (*Professional Public Relations and Political Power*, p. 2) notes that all

presidents at least since Eisenhower have had public relations men in the White House to help "sell" their policies. Rafshoon is the first media campaign consultant, though, to find full-time presidential employment.

16. Carter also made extensive use of the telephone.

17. Quoted in *The Washington Post*, January 5, 1980.

18. Hughes relied on unpaid media and in particular, enthusiastic front-page editorial endorsements by the *Sunpapers*.

19. See *The Washington Post*, March 31, 1979.

20. See Sidney Blumenthal, "Teddy's Media Bust," *The New Republic*, vol. 182, no. 10 (March 3, 1980): 16–18.

21. Peter Hart did not begin work for the Kennedy Campaign until December 1, 1979.

22. By 1960, 87 percent of all households had a television, so most of the growth occurred in the 1950s. In 1970 only 31 percent of all homes had two or more television sets, however.

23. Most figures are taken from a 1978 Roper poll quoted in the National Republican Congressional Committee [hereafter NRCC], "Political Advertising on Television: A Review" (Washington, D.C., October 1979): 29. Generally, women watch more television than men, old people more than young adults, children more than teenagers, but the proportions vary tremendously by time slot and program. Sunday night is the most popular television night, for example; men dominate weekend daytime television because of sports games; and women watch most weekday daytime shows. A small percentage of Americans are all but addicted to television: 16 percent watch over thirty hours per week.

24. See the Survey Research Center, University of Michigan, *American National Election Studies Data Sourcebook, 1952–1978* (Cambridge, Mass.: Harvard, 1980): Tables 5.7, 5.8, 5.9, 5.10, 5.11, 5.15, and 5.16.

25. See, for example, NRCC, "1978 Congressional Post-Election Survey" (Washington, D.C., 1979): 17. Television is apparently as influential in other countries. A 1979 study conducted by the *Sunday Times* and pollster Robert Worcester of London indicated that 75 percent of the British public rated television "very" or "fairly" useful in making their voting decision. See David Lipsey, "What Swings the Elections?" *New Society*, vol. 52, no. 916 (April 24, 1980): 165–166.

26. The 1978 Roper poll as quoted in the NRCC study, "Political Advertising on Television," p. 29.

27. McClure and Patterson, *The Unseeing Eye: The Myth of Television Power in National Politics* (New York: Putnam's, 1976).

28. Again, British television does no better. Lipsey, "What Swings the Elections?" reports that ITV ran a poll story on twenty-two of the thirty-five days of the 1979 general election campaign. After the campaign's conclusion, viewers in a separate poll ranked polls at the very bottom of what they wanted to hear about; issues were at the top.

29. As much is suggested by McClure and Patterson in *The Unseeing Eye*, p. 158, n. 3, and p. 164, n. 8.

30. See John Wanat, "Political Broadcasting Advertising and Primary Election Voting," *Journal of Broadcasting*, vol. 18 (Fall 1974): 413–422. Wanat found a positive correlation between the amount of a candidate's broadcast advertising and the proportion of the vote received in congressional election party primaries.

31. See Nimmo, *The Political Persuaders*, pp. 164–167.

32. See White, *A Study of Access to Television for Political Candidates*, pp. 5–8; and Walter DeVries and V. Lance Tarrance, *The Ticket-Splitters: A New Force in American Politics* (Grand Rapids, Mich.: William B. Eerdmans, 1972).

33. See Kenneth G. Sheinkopf, "How Political Party Workers Respond to Political Advertising," *Journalism Quarterly*, vol. 50 (Summer 1973): 334–339. See also *Campaigning Reports*, vol. 1, no. 1 (April 1, 1979); 5–6. A recent study of 375 Wisconsin party workers and 262 voters found that three-fourths of the workers felt better, worked harder, and were more confident of victory after seeing advertisements.

34. *The Washington Post*, May 13, 1979.

35. Ibid., February 16, 1980.

36. As quoted in ibid.

37. As quoted in ibid., November 27, 1979.

38. Ernest May and Janet Fraser (eds.), *Campaign '72: The Managers Speak* (Cambridge, Mass.: Harvard, 1973), p. 212.

39. *The Washington Post*, November 27, 1979.

40. Kelley, *Professional Public Relations and Political Power*, p. 162, reports that 96 percent of all Democratic paid television time in 1952 was devoted to coverage of speeches. The GOP broadcasts were much more innovative. See also Nimmo, *The Political Persuaders*, pp. 149–155.

41. See, for instance, the NRCC, "Political Advertising on Television," pp. 11, 19. Conservatives respond especially well to a "talking head" spot.

42. Ibid. "Man-in-the-street" has a proven recall of 32 percent and is the favorite format of liberal voters.

43. Personal interview with the author. See also *Congressional Quarterly Weekly*, July 22, 1978, p. 1859.

44. Some stations will sell two-minute spots as well. Networks no longer sell twenty-second spots, as they once did.

45. White, *A Study of Access to Television for Political Candidates*, p. 113, n. 7.

46. Ibid., p. 46. A Roper study confirms most of White's figures (which were provided by BBD & O). See the NRCC, "Political Advertising on Television," p. 27.

47. As quoted in *The Washington Post*, January 23, 1972.

48. *E.P.O.*, vol. 1, no. 1 (January/February 1979): 55.

49. Quoted anonymously in ibid., p. 66.

50. See Joseph Napolitan, *The Election Game and How to Win It* (New York: Doubleday, 1972), pp. 64–112, 209–227.

51. See *Campaign Insights*, vol. 7, no. 20 (October 15, 1976): 5.

52. See Keith R. Sanders, "Political Television Commercials: An Experimental Study of Type and Length," *Communication Research*, vol. 5 (January 1978): 57–70; and the NRCC, "Political Advertising on Television," p. 26. The NRCC study indicated that on the day after airing, between 50 and 80 percent of those interviewed recalled two-minute spots, while only 17 to 32 percent remembered the content of thirty-second spots.

53. As quoted in *Campaign Insights*, vol. 8, no. 8 (April 15, 1976): 3.

54. As quoted in L. Patrick Devlin, "Contrasts in Presidential Campaign Commercials of 1976," *Central States Speech Journal*, vol. 28 (Winter 1977): 243. A two-minute spot and the usual thirty- and sixty-second spots were also produced for Carter by Rafshoon.

55. Deckard, a state representative until 1974, had been out of office and out of the public arena for four years.

56. Percy was actually tricked into airing the apology ad and had only agreed to film it on condition that it would not be shown unless an audience pretesting indicated that it was the most effective approach. Douglas Bailey never conducted a test and relied on his instincts in scheduling it for broadcast.

57. Over 1100 American advertisements were viewed by the author in the course of this study, and none of these, at least, was judged to be a match for the Tory spots.

58. As governor Graham continued the "work days" gimmick, regularly securing favorable publicity in one-day stints at jobs ranging from television newsman to skid-row hosteler.

59. Devlin, "Contrasts in Presidential Campaign Commercials of 1976," p. 244.

60. As quoted in *National Journal*, March 1, 1980, p. 345.

61. See *The Washington Post*, October 10, 1978.

62. See Devlin, "Contrasts in Presidential Campaign Commercials of 1976."

63. Most voters give relatively little attention to lesser offices and ballot issues, and so the arguments with the most visibility tend to prevail. See the excellent report by the Media Access Project, "Taking the Initiative: Corporate Control of the Referendum Process Through Media Spending and What to Do About It" (Washington, D.C., 1980). This study depicts how three 1976 initiatives in Colorado went down to defeat after multimillion-dollar, corporate-financed advertising campaigns.

64. *The San Francisco Examiner*, July 24, 1979.

65. Ibid.

66. The Democratic counterpart to the NRCC does not even have a media division. It may be just a coincidence, but the GOP postelection surveys show advertisements used by Republican candidates steadily gaining relative to Democratic media. For example, in 1976 the television messages of GOP candidates had an 18 percent higher recall than did the Democrats' fare, and they were slightly more persuasive as well. Additional improvement was registered in 1978. See NRCC, "1978 Congressional Post-Election Survey," pp. 38–43.

67. In other words, instead of asserting as fact that "The Congress runs the economy," it is better to say, "Some people think that the president runs the economy, and others say that the Congress does. Well, in fact, Congress does."

68. As quoted in *The Washington Post Magazine*, February 25, 1979.

69. Tony Schwartz, *The Responsive Chord* (New York: Anchor/Doubleday, 1973), p. 100.

70. Ibid., pp. 84, 93.

71. *The Washington Post Magazine*, February 25, 1979; and personal interview with the author.

72. *The Washington Post Magazine*, July 29, 1979. See also *National Journal*, November 13, 1976, p. 1639.

73. See the Associated Press dispatch, July 30, 1979, and *The Washington Post*, November 26, 1978. Rafshoon's White House innovations included a return to the playing of "Hail to the Chief," more practice for Carter before giving speeches and press conferences (with little visible effect to most observers), and more personal courting of news media personnel by the president.

74. *The Washington Post*, March 18, 1980.

75. See *Congressional Quarterly*, July 22, 1978, p. 1859.

76. *The Wall Street Journal*, September 24, 1979.

77. See Kelley, *Professional Public Relations and Political Power*, pp. 217–219.

78. Sanford Weiner addressing the 1975 AAPC convention in Agranoff (ed.), *The New Style in Election Campaigns*, p. 76.

79. As quoted in *Campaign Insight*, vol. 8, no. 15 (August 1, 1979): 8.

80. Seminar presentation at the AAPC Annual Meeting, Washington, D.C., November 30, 1978.

81. Ibid.

82. See Malcolm MacDougall, "The Barker of Snake Oil Politics," *Politics Today*, vol. 7, no. 1 (January/February 1980): 34–37.

83. As quoted in *The Wall Street Journal*, September 24, 1979, and the *National Journal*, March 1, 1980, p. 345.

84. Sanders, "Political Television Commercials." Yet, paradoxically, issue commercials, even if not remembered well, yield a candidate higher evaluations from the audience—perhaps because they show the candidate to be knowledgeable, one of the most desired traits in an officeholder.

85. *Campaigning Reports*, vol. 1, no. 7 (September 6, 1979): 4.

86. See *Campaign Insights*, vol. 9, no. 8 (April 15, 1978): 13, and vol. 9, no. 15 (August 1, 1978): 15.

87. NRCC, "Political Advertising on Television," p. 23.

88. Nimmo, *The Political Persuaders*, p. 143.

89. *Campaign Insights*, vol. 8, no. 17 (September 1, 1979): 6, and vol. 8, no. 21 (November 1, 1977): 12.

90. This particular phrase was coined by U.S. Representative Barbara Mikulski (D-Md.). See *Campaigning Reports*, vol. 1, no. 8 (September 20, 1979): 3.

91. Schwartz, *The Responsive Chord*, p. 89.

92. This version often involves filing with the appropriate state or federal agencies the name of a rather odd-sounding campaign committee, the "A Lot of People Who Want to See Irving Potzrebie in the United States Senate Campaign Committee."

93. See *Campaign Insights*, vol. 7, no. 9 (May 1, 1976): 2.

94. William Russo speaking to the AAPC Annual Meeting, Washington, D.C., November 15, 1979.

95. Subliminally, a far larger number may have been influenced by Clements's

voice; it would seem likely that many people would not consciously cite voice as a "reason" for supporting a candidate.

96. Memorandum from Charles Guggenheim to Arthur Krim (chairman of the Democratic National Finance Committee) with a cover memorandum from Marvin Watson to President Johnson dated November 2, 1967, from the Office Files of Marvin Watson: Krim, Arthur, Box 26 (1375A), LBJ Library. Krim had recommended Guggenheim to do a preliminary thirty-minute campaign documentary on Johnson at a cost of $150,000 to $200,000, with a decision to be made at a later time on whether Guggenheim should do all the reelection campaign's film and radio production. Johnson himself appended a positive note to Watson's cover memo, indicating tentative approval. However, all negotiations ground to a halt the day Robert Kennedy announced for president, when Guggenheim personally told Johnson that because of his longstanding warm relationship with the Kennedys he would work for RFK.

The Guggenheim letter, whatever the fate of its proposals, is a fascinating exercise in grand strategy as consultants often draw it. Guggenheim saw Johnson's media schedule in three phases. First, soon after the August Democratic convention, a ten-day or two-week barrage of advertisements would be released, unexpectedly forcing the Republicans immediately to the defensive. Then, at the end of this phase, the campaign would retrench a bit with a moderate broadcast schedule until two weeks prior to the general election, whereupon completely new material, spearheaded by a thirty-minute documentary, would be aired on a saturation schedule. The documentary film especially would be "made up of moments people can retain . . . strong enough to carry into the voting booth," so as to bring the campaign to its peak at precisely the appropriate time. In a wry note, Guggenheim surmised that "the American people have accepted the presidential contest as part of their entertainment life. . . . The people expect drama, pathos, intrigue, conflict, and they expect it to hang together as a dramatic package."

97. As quoted in *The Washington Post*, June 26, 1979.

98. See *National Journal*, March 1, 1980, p. 345.

99. See *The Washington Post*, February 10, 1980.

100. See *The Wall Street Journal*, September 24, 1979.

101. NRCC, "Political Advertising on Television," p. 10.

102. McClure and Patterson, *The Unseeing Eye*, p. 144.

103. Sanders, "Political Television Commercials." See also n. 84 above.

104. NRCC, "Political Advertising on Television," p. 24.

105. McClure and Patterson, *The Unseeing Eye*, p. 144.

106. See Thomas E. Patterson, "The 1976 Horserace," *The Wilson Quarterly*, vol. 1, no. 3 (Spring 1977): 73–79.

107. MacDougall, "The Barker of Snake Oil Politics," p. 35. See also a similar discussion of television coverage of the 1972 presidental campaign in Timothy Crouse, *The Boys on the Bus* (New York: Ballantine, 1972), pp. 149–187.

108. Kelley, *Professional Public Relations and Political Power*, p. 50.

109. See *Congressional Quarterly Weekly*, October 21, 1978, p. 3060–3061.

110. While all of the candidates mentioned are Democrats, Republicans are just as athletic. For example, Republican Lamar Alexander of Tennessee walked across his state and into the governor's mansion in 1978.

111. George Bush became the first presidential campaign jogger in 1980; President Carter also jogged during the 1980 nomination campaign—but only in the Rose Garden.

112. See *Campaign Insights*, vol. 9, no. 23 (December 1, 1978): 9.

113. An unknown, she ended up finishing third and receiving 20 percent of the vote in the Democratic primary for her efforts (with a total expenditure of just $15,000.). *E.P.O.*, vol. 1, no. 2 (March/April 1979): 8.

114. Harry N. D. Fisher, "How the 'I Dare You!' Candidate Won," in Agranoff (ed.), *The New Style in Election Campaigns*, pp. 79–86.

115. The Tory theme was always accompanied by a photo of an endless unemployment queue.

116. See *Campaign Insights*, vol. 9, no. 19 (October 1, 1978): 5.

117. Nimmo, *The Political Persuaders*, p. 55.

118. *Campaign Insights*, vol. 7, no. 19 (October 1, 1976): 3.

119. Devlin, "Contrasts in Presidential Campaign Commercials of 1976," p. 246.

120. Ibid. As it happened, the Nixon "November group" media consultants produced a song spot in 1972 but decided against using it.

121. Used by Birch Bayh in his initial and successful campaign for the U.S. Senate from Indiana in 1962. *Campaign Insights*, Vol. 8, no. 5 (March 1, 1977): 10.

122. Goodman, who once wrote songs on Broadway, composes all his own campaign tunes. See *The Washington Post Magazine*, March 11, 1979.

123. *Campaign Insights*, vol. 8, no. 22 (November 15, 1977): 13. The clever congressman was Democrat Tom Steed.

124. See *Congressional Quarterly Weekly*, December 15, 1979, pp. 2823–2829.

125. The March 1976, thirty-minute broadcast raised $1 million for Reagan and helped him win the North Carolina primary against President Ford.

126. The stars are not all major ones. It is not uncommon today to see television news commentators, anchormen, or other local media personalities being elected to Congress and other offices.

127. As quoted in *The Washington Post*, October 31, 1979.

128. Nora B. Jacob, "Butcher and Forde: Wizards of the Computer Letter," *The California Journal*, vol. 10 (May 1979): 163–164.

129. *The Washington Post*, November 26, 1979.

130. Nimmo, *The Political Persuaders*, pp. 141–142.

131. Transcript of the CBS Evening News, February 8, 1980.

132. *Campaign Insights*, vol. 9, no. 21 (November 1, 1978): 16. One spot began with Harvey's traditional greeting, "Hello, Americans!" There was no statutory prohibition or FCC sanction against radio impersonations, but the ad's effectiveness was reduced because many stations insisted on adding their own disclaimers before or after the spot.

133. *Campaign Insights*, vol. 8, no. 17 (September 1, 1977): 10. Also, personal interview with former Governor Robert Meyner, Newark, N.J., July 29, 1976. Meyner was quite proud of the strategem.

134. See Kelley, *Professional Public Relations and Political Power*, pp. 107–143. Chicago public relations man Jon M. Jonkel devised Butler's regrettable strategy.

135. *The San Francisco Examiner*, July 25, 1977.

136. A Bishop and Bryant agency spokesman at the AAPC Annual Meeting, Washington, D.C., November 15, 1979.

137. Ibid.

138. This estimate was reached after viewing over 1100 commercials from many dozen campaigns. There also appeared to be a greater proportion of negatives in more recent campaigns.

139. See, for instance, Xandra Kayden, *Campaign Organization* (Lexington, Mass.: D. C. Heath, 1978), p. 119.

140. See *The Washington Post*, November 9, 1978.

141. See ibid., March 3, 1980.

142. See ibid., March 8, 1980.

143. NRCC, "Political Advertising on Television," pp. 10–11.

144. Ibid. In addition, focus-group research conducted by Lance Tarrance for Republican William Clements's 1978 Texas gubernatorial campaign indicated that undecided voters strongly prefer contrast spots—high information ads that simply contrast and highlight the positions of the candidates—to purely negative ads. Clements's final commercials, which were aimed at the undecided bloc, were thought to be instrumental in breaking a stalemate in the polls and assisting him to victory.

145. Devlin, "Contrasts in Presidential Campaign Commercials of 1976," pp. 242–243.

146. Ibid.

147. *E.P.O.*, vol. 1, no. 1 (January/February 1979): 54.

148. Ibid. See also *The Washington Post*, November 9, 1978.

149. See *National Journal*, March 1, 1980, p. 346.

150. In 1972 the McGovern campaign dropped Guggenheim as its media consultant because he refused to design negative spots. In correspondence to the author dated August 11, 1980, Guggenheim explained his position:

I was under great pressure from the campaign to go negative and to attack Nixon. This made no sense to me since the polls made it clear that the problem was not making Nixon less popular (the swing vote already disliked him) but giving them a reason to vote for McGovern. The polls showed the undecideds had no reason to vote for McGovern. He scared them—they felt him unqualified. Late in the race—with my refusal to go negative—the campaign hired Tony Schwartz. [Pollster] Lou Harris told me after the election that as the negative ads appeared, McGovern rapidly lost ground with the undecideds.

151. See *The Washington Post*, November 9, 1978.

152. As quoted in *The Washington Post Magazine*, March 11, 1979.

153. The Nunn-Brown campaign was one of the nastiest in recent times, and Goodman's negative ads were only a small part of the viciousness. See *The Washington Post*, October 31, 1979.

154. Personal interview with the author. See also *The Washington Post Magazine*, February 25, 1979.

155. See *National Journal*, December 15, 1979, p. 2092. Former President Ford, in a University of Virginia class interview on October 11, 1979, independently arrived at the same conclusion as Wirthlin.

156. McClure and Patterson, *The Unseeing Eye*, p. 131.

157. See Schwartz's own fascinating discussion of the Daisy spot in his *The Responsive Chord*, pp. 93–94. Schwartz believes the shrewdest move Goldwater could have made at the time was to agree with the sentiments expressed in the ad and to offer to help pay for broadcasting it.

158. MacDougall, "The Barker of Snake Oil Politics," p. 36.

159. As quoted in *Congressional Quarterly Weekly*, October 29, 1977, p. 2315. The ad was produced by "The Agency," a Delaware advertising group.

160. See *The Washington Post*, October 27, 1979. The candidate in the first primary was state Senator Edgar (Sonny) Mouton.

161. See Kelley, *Professional Public Relations and Political Power*, pp. 26–28. The Claritas Corporation's ten years of commercial marketing for major corporations, for example, were the genesis of the "clustering" innovation that will be described at the end of this chapter.

162. Even in agencies where political and product divisions are administratively separate, specific advertising techniques are traded if personnel are not.

163. See John Wright, "TV Commercials That Move the Merchandise," in his (ed.), *The Commercial Connection: Advertising and the American Mass Media* (New York: Dell, 1979), pp. 314–317.

164. McClure and Patterson, *The Unseeing Eye*, p. 110. These election figures are at the presidential level; recall would probably be lower for lesser offices. The National Republican Congressional Committee produced similar research findings, with political ads having twice the proven recall of product ads. These results are especially interesting in light of the fact that a thirty-second product ad usually costs far more to produce than a political ad. In addition, greater care can be taken in the technical production and filming of product ads since there is less scheduling pressure. Finally, audience pretesting is far more elaborate and frequent for product ads. Viewers are sometimes even wired to test their emotional reactions to product commercials more precisely. This practice and others like it are not used at this time in political advertising.

165. Ibid.

166. Devlin, "Contrasts in Presidential Campaign Commercials of 1976," pp. 240–241.

167. Ibid.

168. Some major corporations have advertising schedule plans drawn up for their products years in advance, including a large number of theme variations and dozens of phases. Most political ad schedules, by comparison, are truncated and simplistic.

169. See, for example, Napolitan, *The Election Game and How to Win It*, pp. 7–10.

170. Ibid.

171. As quoted in *E.P.O.*, vol. 1, no. 1 (January/February 1979): 57.

172. Some consultants, though, subcontract with the ad agencies for time-buying, giving the client the best of both worlds.

173. See Walter Troy Spencer, "The Agency Knack of Political Packaging," in Agranoff (ed.), *The New Style in Election Campaigns*, pp. 96–97.

174. Ibid.

175. See Wright, *The Commercial Connection*, pp. 335–338. Procter and Gamble, General Motors, and General Foods, the three top commercial advertisers, together spent almost $1.1 billion in advertising in 1977 alone.

176. Spencer, "The Agency Knack of Political Packaging," p. 98.

177. David Altman writing in *The New York Times*, October 11, 1978.

178. See chapter 1 for a further discussion of commission and fee structures. The 15 percent commission is a standard discount offered by all media (television, radio, newspapers, etc.) for advertising placed through agencies and consultants. Basically, the agency and political professionals simply charge their clients (political and nonpolitical alike) for the full cost of all broadcasting time bought as though the discount did not exist, and then pocket the 15 percent difference between what the clients have paid them and what they have paid the media. The 17.65 percent commission on top of production costs is yet another way of fattening the profit margin; all expenses incurred and every service provided during production (film or tape footage, lab costs, etc.) are totaled, and 17.65 percent is added on top. Alternatively, a 15 percent commission can be added separately to each expense and service (almost as a kind of "value-added tax").

179. The size of the creative fees range widely, and involve "questimating" by consultants and marketplace trading between consultants and clients.

180. Agranoff (ed.), *The New Style in Election Campaigns*, pp. 26, 32–33. Nixon outspent Humphrey in broadcast outlays by a margin of two to one ($12 million to $6 million).

181. Ibid.

182. See Devlin, "Contrasts in Presidential Campaign Commercials of 1976," p. 248, and *National Journal*, October 20, 1979, p. 1733. Carter spent only about a quarter of his preconvention budget on advertising, but it is estimated that half of the average 1980 presidential campaign budget was consumed by media ads (on television and radio, and in newspapers). See *National Journal*, February 23, 1980, p. 311, and also Herbert E. Alexander, *Financing The 1976 Election* (Washington, D.C.: Congressional Quarterly Press, 1979). The new federal election laws, to be discussed in chapter 5, have apparently checked the growth of advertising expenditures in presidential elections through the use of spending limitations and set federal subsidies. (Carter and Ford spent a million dollars less in 1976 than Nixon and Humphrey did in 1968, despite inflation.) The overall media expenditure totals, of course, remain enormous and as a proportion of the campaign budget, media expenses are apparently growing larger. While Ford and Carter spent about half of their 1976 general election public subsidies on media, Carter's 1980 media devoured about 66 percent of his general election budget and Reagan's media claimed 56 percent of the GOP nominee's general election total. See *National Journal*, January 10, 1981, pp. 50–52.

183. See, for example, White, *A Study of Access to Television for Political Candidates*, pp. 2–3, and the NRCC, "Campaign Manager's Study: 1978 Post-Election Research" (Washington, D.C.: NRCC, 1979), pp. 2, 6.

184. Of the advertising warchest itself, Goodman believes that 70 percent should be devoted to television and only 30 percent to radio and all other media. Many of his fellow consultants think radio is far more important, but in the remarkably unscientific budget allocation process, each professional has his own theory.

185. See White, *A Study of Access to Television for Political Candidates*, pp. 34–35.

186. Videotape itself is cheaper and can be produced more quickly than film, but it is less technically desirable and also far more expensive to edit. This is no minor consideration, since it can take up to 4000 ft. of film or tape to produce a thirty-second spot. Sometimes it is quite difficult to estimate in advance which technique would be more appropriate for a given campaign, but generally each consultant has a preferred medium (which fits his style, if not the campaign's pocketbook). See *Campaigning Reports*, vol. 2, no. 5 (March 6, 1980): 1–2. New production techniques to improve technical

quality (such as the use of the computer to edit and engineer commercials) are also quite expensive.

187. See White, *A Study of Access to Television for Political Candidates*, p. 38.

188. Estimate based on the author's personal interviews with political consultants.

189. Jonathan Price, *The Best Thing on TV: Commercials* (New York: Penguin, 1978), pp. 110–111.

190. See *The Washington Post*, February 10, 1980.

191. See Wright, *The Commercial Connection*, p. 333. In 1978, newspapers logged 29 percent of the $43.7 billion in advertising expenditures throughout the United States. (Local papers led the few "national" papers in revenues by a margin of ten-to-one.) Television got 20 percent of the overall total, and radio, just seven percent. (Almost all radio revenues were locally generated, while three-eighths of the television total was network profit.) Magazines, direct mail, and so forth account for the remaining percentage of U.S. advertising revenues.

192. *National Journal*, February 2, 1980, pp. 192–197.

193. Wright, *The Commercial Connection*, pp. 334–335.

194. On rare occasions, credit is extended. (See White, *A Study of Access to Television for Political Candidates*, p. 41.) But stations usually require cash on the barrelhead to avoid accusations of favoritism or, in the case of a candidate whose warchest was emptied before payment could be made for previously broadcast spots, to prevent an illegal contribution of free time. It is easy to understand why cash flow has become such a major problem for most campaigns. Contributions tend to increase as the campaign approaches election day, but all television time has to be reserved long before the money flows. Good planning, early fund raising, and many accountants have become campaign necessities.

195. See *National Journal*, March 1, 1980, p. 346; White, *A Study of Access to Television for Political Candidates*, pp. 26–30; and Seymour M. Chase, *Candidate's Checklist: The Law on Using Television and Radio* (Washington, D.C.: self-published, 1980), p. 19. The candidate must actually be in a commercial visually or verbally to qualify for the lowest unit rate (l.u.r.). The charge is supposed to be computed on the basis of what the station earned *after* paying the consultant or agency commission. This means that a candidate not using an ad agency or consultant is entitled to a discount equal to the commission earned by his *opponent's* consultant or agency (assuming that his opponent is using a consultant or agency and that the time periods advertised in are eligible for the l.u.r.). The rules surrounding l.u.r. are confusing, and the calculation of rates based on them is a complicated endeavor. While White (p. 27) notes that, because of l.u.r., "political rates are almost always less than the average rates paid by commercial advertisers and are often substantially less than those announced on the station's rate card," it is also true that most stations do not bother to compute l.u.r. precisely, preferring to charge candidates a fixed cut rate. This practice, of course, could (if challenged) be found in violation of FCC mandates. See *The Washington Post*, September 9, 1978.

196. Radio is an exception to this generalization because most radio stations base their rates purely on the number of advertisements purchased; thus, campaign savings *can* be substantial in some cases. See *National Journal*, March 1, 1980, p. 346.

197. Institute of Politics, JFK School of Government, Harvard University, "An Analysis of the Impact of the Federal Election Campaign Act, 1972–78" (Cambridge, Mass.: May 1979): 1–15. Newspaper advertising rates, with a 47 percent rise, also outstripped the CPI, but radio has proven to be a bargain, posting an increase of 28 percent (8 percent below the CPI).

198. The 1976 average was between $42,000 and $68,000; in 1980 the figure was around $100,000. See *National Journal*, February 23, 1980, p. 313.

199. See *The Washington Post*, April 1, 1980. Other examples: San Diego: 1974 price = $509; 1980 = $3000; Baltimore: 1974 price = $1100; 1980 = $3000.

200. See *Campaign Insights*, vol. 7, no. 22 (November 15, 1976): 7.

201. See also Nimmo, *The Political Persuaders*, pp. 114–118. Interestingly, these same voters do *not* generally watch six P.M. news shows, simply because their white-collar jobs keep them in the office much later than blue-collar workers.

202. Schwartz, *The Responsive Chord*, pp. 104–105.

203. Kayden, *Campaign Organization*, p. 118.

204. Campaigns for lesser statewide offices and local posts have many fewer spots produced—sometimes just one or two, but rarely more than half a dozen.

205. Devlin, "Contrasts in Presidential Campaign Commercials of 1976," p. 243.

206. Tony Schwartz as quoted in *National Journal*, March 1, 1980, p. 348.

207. See Agranoff (ed.), *The New Style in Election Campaigns*, p. 52. The eight-week process involved two weeks for writing, two weeks for taping and, finally, four weeks for production and editing prior to the broadcast date.

208. See *Campaign Insights*, vol. 7, no. 17 (September 1, 1976): 17.

209. See *Campaign Insights*, vol. 9, no. 23 (December 1, 1978): 5.

210. See Napolitan, *The Election Game*, pp. 209–237.

211. See *Campaigning Reports*, vol. 2, no. 11 (June 6, 1979): 1.

212. However, a candidate might risk alienating election-weary voters, who had looked forward to a well-deserved respite from electioneering!

213. NRCC, "1978 Congressional Post-Election Survey," pp. 14–16, 24, 48. In the 1978 off-year elections almost half the voters interviewed said they made a congressional choice in the last three weeks of the campaign, whereas in 1976 about half claimed to have made up their minds before September. It may also be that major statewide contests (for the U.S. Senate and the governorship) also cause an earlier decision to be made in House races. As the NRCC report concludes: "The presence of a race above [House contests] on the ticket impedes [House candidates'] ability to gain attention. . . ." Incumbency proves weighty under these circumstances, and that of course tends to hurt Republicans more since they hold fewer House seats.

214. Cheney partly reassembled Ford's team of first-rate consultants, including Stuart Spencer, Robert Teeter, and Richard Gardner, a former Bailey/Deardourff associate. His connections made him probably the only House candidate in the country with a seasoned team of national political professionals.

215. For a capsuled and very useful description of the legal technicalities of time availability, see Chase, *Candidate's Checklist*, pp. 9, 33–36. This is the source of many of the specific court cases referred to below. Note that a station must make available *commercial* time; simply arranging for extensive coverage on news shows, debates, and so forth is not considered a legal substitute. The FCC clearly intends that candidates have the opportunity to tell their own story in their own way during bought time.

216. White, *A Study of Access to Television for Political Candidates*, pp. 49–50.

217. Ibid., p. 51–53. An "adjacency" is an advertising time slot bordering on network programming.

218. Let no one doubt that the station advertising managers are concerned with profit, even in campaign advertising. White, ibid., p. 29, reports that prior to the establishment of l.u.r., "there was a significant incidence of price gouging by licensees attempting to exploit political clients."

219. Ibid., pp. 55–57.

220. See *The Washington Post*, September 9, 1978. The artificial demand created by nervous campaign managers who try to keep up with the opposition's every time request and to match it spot for spot probably contributes to the accessibility problem as well. See White, *A Study of Access to Television for Political Candidates*, pp. 41–42.

221. White, ibid., pp. 29–30.

222. *The Washington Post*, September 9, 1978. The adman quoted is Louis Rosenbush.

223. Ibid.

224. Kayden, *Campaign Organization*, p. 119.

225. Even presidential candidates are severely limited by local station policies. See *The Washington Post*, February 10, 1980, which examines stations covering the New Hampshire area before that state's key presidential primary.

226. McClure and Patterson, *The Unseeing Eye*, p. 107, found that 31 percent of all ads broadcast (and 75 percent of all paid air time) in the 1972 presidential contest was in the form of five-minute spots. By contrast, thirty-second spots comprised just two percent of all ads broadcast.

227. The National Republican Congressional Committee conducted a survey of

media markets in 1979 to determine the relative availability of thirty-second, sixty-second, two-minute, and five-minute spots. They discovered that thirties and sixties were available from almost all stations at all times of the day, and that eight of ten stations would sell two-minute spots in prime time. But only about a third of the stations would agree to sell five-minute slots in prime time.

228. See *Congressional Quarterly Weekly*, December 15, 1979, p. 2823.

229. NRCC, "Campaign Manager's Study," pp. 14–19. In about a third of nineteen congressional races studied, the GOP candidate encountered placement problems on radio and television. But 42 to 43 percent of the losers had problems, compared to just 14 to 20 percent of the winners.

230. Gary C. Jacobsen has concluded that restrictions on spending for television and radio advertising work to the advantage of incumbents, and it seems a logical corollary that time limitation, which also restricts access to advertising, can have a similar effect. See Jacobsen, "The Impact of Broadcast Campaigning on Electoral Outcomes," *Journal of Politics*, vol. 37 (August 1975): 769–793.

231. See Nimmo, *The Political Persuaders*, p. 63. The Goldwater campaign of 1964 was similar in some respects. Goldwater refused any form of deficit financing, so in the early campaign stages when demand on the available warchest was great, money enough could not be found to retain reservations for television slots in the last ten days of October. The Goldwater organization was fiscally flush as the election drew near, but there were no prime-time slots left to buy.

232. Stations are also not required by the FCC to sell time to individuals seeking to make independent expenditures on behalf of candidates. When financier Max Palevsky independently tried to purchase television spots for Jimmy Carter in the 1976 Democratic presidential primary in California, for instance, he was refused time. See *National Journal*, June 23, 1979, p. 1045.

233. See *The Washington Post*, April 21, 1980.

234. Kelley, *Professional Public Relations and Political Power*, p. 190.

235. See *Federal Political Candidates* case, 43 RR 2d 1029 (1978).

236. See *Anthony R. Martin-Trigona* case, 40 RR 2d 189 (1977), which reversed *WGN Continental Broadcasting Co.* case, 36 RR 2d 865 (1976).

237. See *WALB-TV, Inc.* case, 37 RR 2d 904 (1976), which involved a 1976 request by Gerald Rafshoon for five hours of Saturday evening broadcast time to stage a fund-raising telethon for Jimmy Carter. The station refused, and Rafshoon claimed the owner's denial was based on his support of Carter's Georgia rival, ex-Governor Lester Maddox. The FCC held that, since the station had offered Carter some free prime time and later additional purchasing opportunities, the refusal was not unreasonable. See also *Hon. Pete Flaherty* case, 21 RR 2d 259 (1974). Flaherty, a candidate for U.S. Senate, was denied a four-and-one-half-hour block of time.

238. See *Joel D. Joseph, Esq.* case, 40 RR 2d 274 (1977).

239. See *Mary Olive Pierson* case, 40 RR 2d 638 (1979).

240. See *Anthony R. Martin-Trigona* case, 41 RR 2d 1599 (1977).

241. See *Charles Mark Furcolo* case, 48 FCC 2d 565 (1974).

242. A broadcaster is merely required to *consider* the candidate's individual needs (as defined by the candidate) and the amount of time previously given to a candidate. In deciding to refuse a request, a broadcaster is permitted to take into account the potential disruption of local programming caused by the request, the number of candidates likely to invoke equal access rights if the time request is granted, and the timing of the candidate's request. The broadcaster must also clearly articulate the reasons for his decision, which is more likely to be upheld by the FCC if alternate paid time (of whatever length) has been offered.

243. See *The Washington Post*, March 15, 1980.

244. See ibid., also October 30, 1979 and November 29, 1979. See also *Campaign Practices Reports*, vol. 7, no. 6 (March 31, 1980): 1–4.

245. Two FCC rulings were rendered: FCC 79–750 (November 21, 1979) and FCC 79–773 (November 28, 1979).

246. Statement of a CBS executive carried in a UPI dispatch, November 7, 1979. CBS and the other networks had earlier refused to sell half hours to Ronald Reagan and John Connally.

247. *CBS, ABC, NBC v. FCC*, U.S. Court of Appeals at Washington, D.C., Nos. 79-2403, 79-2406, 79-2407 (March 14, 1980). The decision was upheld by the Supreme Court in July, 1981.

248. See *Campaigning Reports*, vol. 7, no. 5 (July 26, 1979): 2–3. There are still problems with the technology that will limit its political usefulness for the near future. See *Campaigning Reports*, vol. 2, no. 9 (May 1, 1980): 5–7.

249. See *Campaign Practices Reports*, vol. 7, no. 5 (March 17, 1980): 5–7. The President nominates all the FEC members and, while half must be Democrats, the kind of Democrats selected by Reagan (if he can get the nominations approved by Congress) might be more amenable to the GOP's plan.

250. *Campaign Insights*, vol. 7, no. 7 (April 1, 1976): 3.

251. Ibid.

252. Two relatively successful sellers were Barry Goldwater's *Conscience of a Conservative* and Jimmy Carter's *Why Not The Best?*

253. According to a survey by Simmons Media Studies of New York in 1976–1977.

254. *Campaigning Reports*, vol. 2, no. 2 (January 24, 1980): 1.

255. The Neilsen ratings show the CBS Evening News reaching 11.2 million, NBC 9.8 million, and ABC 7 million. Patterson, "The 1976 Horserace," p. 78.

256. For example, according to the Radio-Television News Directors Association, the number of television stations employing a full-time news staff of twenty or more people increased 100 percent in seven years (1972–1979).

257. *National Journal*, February 2, 1980, p. 195.

258. In 1978, 94 percent of the 382 House members seeking reelection won, while only 60 percent of U.S. senators trying for an additional term were victorious. This differential reflects a growing disparity. See *Congressional Quarterly Weekly*, April 5, 1980, pp. 905–909. The trend continued in 1980, when about 91 percent of all House incumbents were again re-elected compared to just 55 percent in the Senate.

259. As quoted in *The Washington Post*, March 22, 1980. This is a good example of a point that consultants repeatedly make: that their "image-making" advertisements dare not be too deceptive because any lies or distortions they contain can be laid bare for all to see in the unpaid media. Of course, this axiom applies most particularly to presidential candidates. Contests for many state and local offices are rarely in the limelight enough to expose distortions, especially more subtle ones.

260. Kelley, *Professional Public Relations and Political Power*, p. 172.

261. Anderson was also the star of a series in Garry Trudeau's *Doonesbury* comicstrip, which centers on college-age characters and has a large following among the same population.

262. Perhaps stung by the chorus of recent criticisms by media analysts, the networks appeared to include more purely issue segments in the 1980 news broadcasts, at least in the general election. See Michael Robinson and Margaret Sheehan, "How the Networks Learned to Love the Issues," *Washington Journalism Review* (December 1980): 15–17.

263. Nimmo, *The Political Persuaders*, p. 132–133.

264. McClure and Patterson, *The Unseeing Eye*, p. 128.

265. Survey Research Center, *American National Election Studies Data Sourcebook, 1952–1978*, Tables 5.7–5.11, 5.15–5.16.

266. Ibid.

267. See *Campaigning Reports*, vol. 1, no. 5 (July 26, 1979): 6.

268. *The Wilson Quarterly*, vol. 1, no. 3 (Spring 1977): 91.

269. See Paul F. Lazarsfeld, et al., *The People's Choice: How the Voter Makes Up His Mind in a Presidential Campaign* (New York: Columbia, 1944). Lazarsfeld concentrated on radio's impact in FDR's 1940 reelection, and he concluded that people-to-people communication had a much greater effect on individuals' voting decisions.

270. Nimmo, *The Political Persuaders*, pp. 135–137.

271. Schwartz, among others, criticizes the use of television soundtracks as radio commercials "because most of the TV soundtracks alone are lousy; they are not *made for listening* [and] a percentage of the people listening on radio didn't see it on TV anyway," so they will have nothing to recall. Recall is usually the reason given for radio airing of television audio.

272. NRCC, "Campaign Manager's Study," p. 1.

273. NRCC, "1978 Congressional Post-Election Survey," pp. 45–46.

274. See Nimmo, *The Political Persuaders*, p. 56, n. 35.

275. Ibid., p. 122.

276. See *Congressional Quarterly Weekly*, December 29, 1979, pp. 2958 to 2959. The Iowa caucuses, the first event on the new presidential schedule, are of course an exception, and many candidates in 1980 spent close to the state spending ceiling of $450,000. Interestingly, though, the top finishers on the GOP side (Bush and Reagan) had paltry media expenditures (husbanding campaign dollars for organization) while two other major candidates who finished far out of the running (Baker and Connally) together spent six and one-half times on television advertising what Bush and Reagan together had spent. See *National Journal*, March 1, 1980, p. 345.

277. Hart has since organized his own campaign efforts, and as of 1975 has been U.S. senator from Colorado.

278. Reese is profiled in Appendix C. Profiles of the others mentioned here (except Shields) can be found in Peter Lincoln, "Who's Whose: *Politics Today*'s Guide to All the Candidates' Men," *Politics Today*, vol. 7, no. 2 (March/April 1980): 32–37. Shields's career is reviewed in a lengthy sketch in *The Washington Post*, November 6, 1978.

279. Many candidates have made the fatal mistake of confusing organization with the assemblage of lists of endorsers. Endorsements usually do not matter a great deal, since the endorsers (many of whom are in public life themselves or busy with other careers) rarely work very hard or, more important, have such a hold on their followers that they can transfer loyalties. As one political operative, remembering the 1972 Democratic presidential race, recently quipped, "You want to know what endorsements really mean? Just ask President Muskie," a reference to the fact that Muskie had almost the entire party establishment behind him but lost ignominiously anyway. "Laying on of the hands" is only effective, outside of the Roman Catholic Church, in big-city machines and strong party organizations, a vanishing species. If an endorsement is worth anything, it is merely in the credibility it confers with the press and party elite, and, occasionally, for the free publicity a celebrity media event can draw. Some endorsements, though, can actually hurt a candidacy. Take, for instance, the lukewarm blessing bestowed on a victorious rival by a defeated Republican congressional candidate in the Midwest: "I find it easy to support [my former opponent]. After all, I was trained as a lawyer. I can defend almost anything."

280. *Campaigning Reports*, vol. 1, no. 8 (September 20, 1979): 1.

281. *National Journal*, January 5, 1980, pp. 11–15. Some of the principal staffers earned more than $40,000 annually, quite a contrast with the old "mom and pop" storefront political manager.

282. Ibid., February 23, 1980, p. 312. It is not just incumbent presidents who can assemble such an entourage. George Bush employed 248 workers with a total monthly payroll over $100,000 during the early primaries and caucuses of the 1980 campaign.

283. NRCC, "Campaign Manager's Study." In the congressional races surveyed, the size of the volunteer staff ranged from 100 to 3900, the average being 1157.

284. See Nimmo, *The Political Persuaders*, p. 76; also Agranoff (ed.), *The New Style in Election Campaigns*, throughout.

285. Nimmo, *The Political Persuaders*, p. 21.

286. Ibid., p. 59.

287. *Campaign Insights*, vol. 8, no. 15 (August 1, 1977): 10, and vol. 8, no. 21 (November 1, 1977): 9–10.

288. See Robert Chartrand, *Computers and Political Campaigning* (New York: Spartan, 1972); and Hank Parkinson, "Campaign '80: Battle of the Computers," a syndicated series made available through North American Newspaper Alliance Syndication, Autumn 1979.

289. See especially Rex Hardesty, "The Computer's Role in Getting Out the Vote," in Agranoff (ed.), *The New Style in Election Campaigns*, pp. 188–197.

290. Parkinson, "Campaign '80."

291. Personal interview with Hank Parkinson. Also *Campaigning Reports*, vol. 1, no. 1 (April 1, 1979): 1.

292. This is Parkinson's estimate. He also suggests from his experience that about 65 percent of the block captains actually perform their assigned chores.

293. The NRCC "Campaign Manager's Study," (pp. 20–22) reported that 87 percent

of the GOP campaigns surveyed used telephone banks—100 percent of the winners compared to 79 percent of the losers. The average number of calls made and completed was 31,000. Almost half the phone banks were staffed entirely by volunteers, about a fifth entirely by paid workers, and a third by a combination of the two groups.

294. Nimmo, *The Political Persuaders*, pp. 135–137.

295. Turnout in Iowa increased 60,000 over 1976 to a total of 225,000 in 1980, making the Iowa caucuses the equivalent of a small primary election. George Bush called first to identify his favorables and then recalled them as many as ten times before the caucuses. More than 3 million calls were made by all the Iowa candidates, at an estimated cost of about $9 million. See *Campaigning Reports*, vol. 2, no. 3 (February 7, 1980): 6. Jimmy Carter not only conducted a large-scale telephone bank system in 1980, he was also a one-man phone operation himself. He reportedly placed twenty to forty calls per night to homes in key primary and caucus states, and some blocks in New Hampshire sported a dozen residents who had met the president by phone. See *The Washington Post*, February 6, 1980.

296. See *The Washington Post*, February 7, 1980.

297. While the CPI increased 36 percent from 1972 to 1976, local telephone service went up 28 percent and long distance by 19 percent. See Institute of Politics, "An Analysis of the Impact of the Federal Election Campaign Act, 1972–78," pp. 1–16.

298. See *Campaigning Reports*, vol. 2, no. 9 (May 1, 1980): 7–9. With the telecomputer device, 130 to 200 calls can be completed by one operator in an hour, several times the current number.

299. The percentage of unlisted telephones can range over a third in major cities. See *Campaign Insights*, vol. 8, no. 5 (March 1, 1977): 6. Fully two-thirds of homes sometimes cannot be contacted because ringing telephones go unanswered. See *Campaigning Reports*, vol. 2, no. 1 (January 10, 1980): 3.

300. NRCC, "1978 Congressional Post-Election Survey," pp. 4–5. The survey showed only nine percent of Republican voters and seven percent of Democratic voters reported being contacted before the 1978 midterm elections.

301. See *The New York Times*, February 4, 1979. Much of the subsequent discussion is drawn from several public presentations by Matt Reese and the author's personal interview with him.

302. Missouri is one of the few southern or border states without a right-to-work law.

303. "Cluster" is a registered trademark of the Claritas Corporation.

304. These characteristics have been called "life-style" variables. Each Cluster's life style is denoted by level of affluence; educational level; housing pattern and degree of urbanization; ethnic, racial, and religious composition; mobility rate; and age of population. All of these measurements together produce groupings such as "Cluster 8" (upper-class mobile professionals and college students) or "Cluster 33" (urban fringe towns and rural southern areas and military bases). The idea, as Reese suggests, is that "People of similar life styles eat the same kind of food and go to the same kind of theater, read the same kind of magazines, maybe react to information the same way. Maybe vote alike." These are major assumptions, of course—especially the last one.

305. The informed and involved individual may think these multiple contacts, as with the repeated calls of telephone banks, are superfluous and redundant. But Reese offers a convincing rejoinder:

Whether the message comes from the mass media, mail, phone, or in-person, the message must be repetitive, repetitive, repetitive. Why? Because the voters are not listening; they're not terribly interested; we're not the most important thing to them. Whether Joe Smith is their governor or I am does not rank with the fact that their fifteen-year-old daughter was out till midnight last night; does not rank with the fact that their mortgage payment is due on Thursday; may not even rank with their bowling score.

306. All of the advertising was targeted and time-bought to reach the maximum number of targeted Cluster groups. Claritas provided the Cluster data broken down by media markets.

307. Psychographics is a close cousin of geodemographics. See *Campaigning Reports*, vol. 1, no. 10 (October 18, 1979): 4–5.

308. *Campaigning Reports*, vol. 1, no. 4 (July 12, 1979): 1–2.

309. *The Washington Post*, August 24, 1979. It has happened at least once already. Ralph Nader appeared on a Qube system show in Columbus, Ohio, speaking on consumer rights. As he left the studio after his talk, he was handed a computer printout with the names and telephone numbers of 700 volunteers.

Chapter 4

Direct Mail: The Poisoned Pen of Politics

With direct mail, I can speak with forked tongue. If I'm a Republican candidate I can make myself sound like a Democrat. If I'm a Democrat I can make myself sound like a Republican. I'm not saying a goddamn thing, but I get [the voters'] support. It all sounds very appealing.

The average person would never believe what we do to make this system work!

—Comments by two direct-mail consultants[1]

Most individuals greatly enjoy receiving mail. In a recent survey more people (63 percent) said they looked forward to the post than to any other of a laundry list of pleasurable activities on the daily schedule.[2] Protestations to the contrary notwithstanding, most people even delight in the so-called "junk mail" they get, at least the political variety. One study indicates that three-fourths of the individuals who are sent a piece of political direct mail actually do read it.[3]

It is this sort of statistic that has made political direct mail one of the most ballyhooed of the new campaign techniques, while remaining the least understood. Direct mail combines sophisticated political judgments and psychological, emotional appeals with the most advanced computer and mailing technologies. Used for two very distinct purposes (persuasion and fund raising), direct mail is considered a necessity by many candidates—a significant majority, in fact, now employ it in some form[4]—but few know how and why it works. This chapter aims to unravel some of direct mail's mysteries by shedding light on the methods of the process while highlighting the successes and failures of the consultants who market political mail.[5]

The Direct-Mail Artists

Direct mail differs significantly from the other new campaign technologies in that there is usually little direct contact between the candidate and the direct-mail consultant; indeed, it is not too unusual for the consultant never to meet the candidate at all. Most of the work is done with the campaign manager and finance director, and the letter package is only rarely concocted in consultation with the candidate. The basic themes of some letters are prefabricated (based on what has worked well in the past) and, as direct mailer Robert Odell remarked, "We don't have to sit down with the candidate three times a month in order to draft a letter which reflects his thinking. We can get what we need by listening to tapes of his speeches, and by sitting in on planning and strategy sessions with the staff."

The lack of contact between candidate and consultant inevitably means that in many cases the candidate is oblivious to the role that direct mail plays in his campaign, and possibly wholly ignorant of the process itself. The Nixon White House became enraged on one occasion because Hubert Humphrey had received one of Nixon's 1972 reelection direct-mail letters—an unavoidable risk in any direct-mail program involving lists of millions of names.[6] Despite the fact that Bob Odell had coordinated a remarkably successful direct-mail effort for President Ford's 1976 campaign, Ford himself could comment after the election:

I was not familiar with any direct mail that went out from the President Ford Committee, so I can't really judge whether it was helpful or harmful. It's *expensive.* . . . I don't know whether it is categorized as junk mail or not, but we get an awful lot of junk mail from the Post Office Department.[7]

One direct-mail consultant has managed to rise from out of the obscurity that seems to surround his peers: Richard Viguerie, a right-wing activist who formed a direct-mail corporation in 1965 with $400 and the membership list of the Young Americans for Freedom (YAF). Starting with his single original contract to raise funds for the YAF— which was cancelled in five weeks—he proceeded to gross $100,000 in 1965. By 1969 he was mailing over 20 million letters annually in a firm employing about forty persons. By 1977, Viguerie had collected and stored on 3,300 magnetic computer tapes more than 30 million names of conservative-leaning individuals. (Of this number, however, only about 4.5 million have ever reportedly contributed money to conservative organizations and causes.) He mailed 76 million letters, employed 300 persons, and issued annual billings in excess of $10 million.

Viguerie's success is rooted in his marketing ability, his political ideology, and his early rejection of the prevailing myth that there were only several hundred thousand people (at most) willing to give money to political causes. "I believed there were millions who, if given the opportunity, would be interested in contributing."[8] Viguerie's innate management skills enabled him to prove his point. As he rather immodestly observed on one occasion, "Look . . . I know how to take ideas and market them. The conservative movement has always been good at producing writers and debaters, but it never had anybody who knew how to market ideas to the masses. Well, that's what I've tried to do, and that's what I'm doing."[9]

The Viguerie marketing conglomerate now stretches across the entire mailing field. The Richard A. Viguerie Company (or RAVCO), of which Viguerie is president, operates out of Falls Church, Virginia, and concentrates on the creative work of direct-mail and general mail consulting in political and charitable areas. Its principal subsidiary is Diversified Mail Marketing, Inc. (DMMI), which is incorporated in Delaware while operating in Maryland. Together with its own subsidiary, Diversified Mailing Services, DMMI provides postage and mailing services of various kinds. Viguerie is a director and former president of these outfits. The American Mailing Lists Corporation, of which Viguerie is chairman, rents out the precious lists of conservative contributors, and Diversified Printing Services, Inc., produces brochures and direct-mail letters. Finally, the Viguerie Communication Corporation is the mouthpiece for the founder's conservative views and, incidentally, helps him to build his conservative mailing lists by means of the monthly *Conservative Digest*. Viguerie is the listed publisher of the 110,000-circulation magazine, a slick production that mainly reprints wire-service material and articles by conservative columnists and officeholders. The corporation also publishes *The Right Report*, a bimonthly newsletter primarily about right-wing election campaigns.[10]

There is little question that money alone does not motivate Viguerie, although his profits are hardly puny. He is a fervent, some say zealous, right-wing ideologue who is thoroughly dedicated to a conservative revolution in American life:

You know, back in Houston, when I first got burned up over the firing of MacArthur, I felt I wanted to make a contribution and save the world. . . . I haven't gotten over that, as most people past a certain age do, when they mature. I'm frustrated on any day when I haven't saved Western civilization. I get up in the morning and that's my goal until the sun sets.[11]

In direct mail the right-wing has, in fact, achieved a considerable edge over the liberals who, it is widely conceded, have not begun to match the product quality and technology of Viguerie's direct mail, or even that of other conservative firms, such as Bruce W. Eberle and Associates of Vienna, Virginia.[12] (See Appendix C, which profiles some major American direct-mail consultants.) Right-wing and anti-union groups crowd the roster of organizations using direct mail for membership recruitment and fund raising, many of them with such emotional names as Americans Against Union Control of Government and Committee to Defeat the Union Bosses' Candidates. Conservative candidates have been consistently among the most notable beneficiaries of the direct-mail surge in recent years.

Even so, liberals have not been entirely shut out of the direct-mail field. Environmental groups have been active in enlisting support with direct mail; for instance, they have pooled their resources to build a 3-million-name list of backers.[13] There is also one prominent liberal firm: Craver, Mathews, Smith, and Company (CMS) of Arlington, Virginia, which has handled left-of-center candidates and organizations such as the National Organization for Women, the National Abortion Rights Action League, and the Sierra Club Legal Defense Fund.

Like many (but not all) direct-mail firms, CMS contracts are organized around two phases, testing and full scale, and the arrangement is subject to cancellation after the testing phase (usually if the test returns are financially disappointing). The consultants design a direct-mail program for each client, sometimes stretching over several years. They create the letter copy, rent or buy the mailing lists, supervise the printing and mailing of the letters, and evaluate and analyze the program and its degree of success (sending an update to the client about twice a month).

CMS requires client and firm co-ownership of the names of contributors generated by liberal candidates' mailings so that other liberal contenders will be able to use them in future mailings. The need for such an arrangement is obvious: "Right now," according to CMS's Robert Smith, "there are literally only two or three political campaign lists for the use of liberal candidates." Most liberal candidates have to start almost from scratch in building a national reservoir of small contributors, and there simply are not many liberal direct-mail consultants and firms capable of matching or even approaching right-wing capabilities. That is why CMS sometimes takes conflicting liberal interests. In 1980 the firm signed the draft-Kennedy movement at the same time as it was under contract to the Carter-dominated Democratic National Committee. (CMS was soon fired from the DNC post.[14]) A few other individual liberal experts, such as Morris Dees, who headed internal direct-mail efforts for George McGovern in 1972, Jimmy Carter in 1976, and Edward Kennedy in 1980, are occasionally available to left-of-center candidates.

The boom in political direct mail reflects in part the development of advanced computer mailing technology that became available in the 1970s. But it is also an unexpected result of the maze of new campaign finance regulations passed in the wake of Watergate. With individual contributions limited to $1,000 per election, new sources of funds have become vital, and direct mail's ability to tap small, grass-roots contributions in great volume has seemed increasingly attractive. As Paul Weyrich, an ideological political action committee (PAC) leader and Viguerie associate, observed: "It is ironic that the election reformers who are now busy devising ways of taking Richard Viguerie out of the political process have only themselves to blame for putting him there in the first place."[15]

The Democratic congressional leaders who shepherded the new finance regulations to passage also ended up encouraging a strengthened Republican party. By drying up big contributions on which the GOP had lackadaisically depended, the revised campaign rules *forced* the party to invest heavily in a direct-mail system that has proven to be a goldmine. Thanks primarily to direct mail, the party has broadened its financial base enormously, increasing the number of national party contributors from just 34,000 in the early 1970s to 870,000 in 1980, with the average contribution of only $26.[16] (The 870,000 figure represents only the number of active contributors to the Republican National Committee. When separate contributors to two other national divisions of the Republican party [the Congressional and Senatorial Committees] are added, the number of active GOP donors is estimated at well above one million.) As a result, the national party's 1980 budget had expanded by more than two-thirds over the 1976 figure and, contrary to popular stereotypes, by 1976 the average Republican congressional candidate was raising far more of his campaign war chest in contributions under $100 than his Democratic counterpart.[17] The GOP has far outstripped the Democratic party in direct-mail fund raising, collecting about four times as much by mail in 1978 as did the Democrats. Interestingly, the Republican direct mail has also been rated superior in both persuasive ability and recall[18] to Democratic efforts. Indeed, there is some evidence that direct mail is permitting Republican challengers to compete directly with Democratic congressional incumbents' franked office mail.[19] While one national Democratic official agreed that his party was far behind the GOP in direct-mail technology, he noted that some limited headway had been made in redressing the imbalance, and there is at least awareness among Democrats of the significance of the technological gap.[20]

The Republican and right-wing predilection for direct mail—and their success in finding consultants to help them with it—suggests another distinction between direct-mail consultants and their brethren in other fields. Unlike media professionals or generalists who seek, above all, to be associated with winners, direct-mail professionals simply look for campaigns that can produce funds and spark mass contributions. In a preponderance of direct-mail funded campaigns, the themes are emotional, negative, and antiincumbent. As William Lacy of the Eberle firm commented, "In most cases in conservative direct mail, the strategy must be a negative one directed at the incumbent. We like to go with challengers. . . . With challengers you can really take out after an incumbent." Direct-mail consultants can afford to be associated with losing efforts because, for the most part, they are judged on the campaign's financial flow chart, not its electoral performance. "Nobody is going to hold us responsible for [a candidate's] general election loss when they look at how much money we raised," said Lacy.

Ironically, congressional incumbents, the targets of so much of the modern deluge of direct mail, are themselves primary beneficiaries of the new political direct-mail technology.[21] About one-third of the members of the U.S. Senate and two-thirds of the House members have used office funds to purchase direct-mail services both to assist them in their correspondence requirements and to promote their reelections (sometimes in direct violation of House or Senate rules). Letters have been drafted by staff members; direct-mail consultants hired with office funds; mailings frequently printed and posted at government expense; and often the lists of individuals to whom the letters are sent compiled, purchased, and stored with official expenditures.[22] For example, Senator Robert P. Griffin's 1972 reelection campaign in

Michigan owed much to the Senate computer. Griffin was in a close and hard-fought race in which school busing was a major issue. His direct-mail expert, Derry Daly of the J. Walter Thompson advertising firm, devised a mass-mailing program to selected nonblack blue-collar workers that was refined and electronically produced by the Senate computer. About 200,000 pieces of mail on Griffin's support of lower property taxes were sent to higher income households throughout the state, along with other mailings. On these questions, dealing solely with legislation or national issues, the only cost to the senator's campaign committee was the rental of the mailing lists of blue-collar workers, higher income households, and so forth.[23]

As impressive as the political use of direct mail has become, politicians are by no means the only or even the best commercial customers. Charities, nonprofit organizations of all kinds, and commercial marketers have long realized the value of direct mail and, much as in the areas of media, polling, and organization, the nonpolitical users developed many of the techniques later adapted and applied to campaigns and political organizations. No political candidate or group, though, will likely ever match the so-called "electronic church" in its evangelical direct-mail successes. The Reverend Jerry Falwell's "Old Time Gospel Hour" alone has 2.5 million families on its mailing list, and one of his most successful "putting out the fleece" letters in October 1979 raised $6.7 million in a month.[24] Richard Viguerie, in fact, has contributed services to the fiercely conservative Falwell's computer firm, Epsilon Data Management, Inc., of Burlington, Massachusetts, which coordinates the minister-businessman's monthly mass mailings to his postal faithful.

How Direct Mail Works

The process of direct mail is a confusing one for the layman, if only because at certain stages it often appears to be unprofitable and nonsensical. The accompanying illustration, clearly depicting the fundamentals of a presidential campaign's direct-mail system, will serve to elucidate. The "eleven steps to raise $2 million by direct mail" revolve around two different kinds of mailings, "house" and "prospecting." A "prospect" mailing is a general, mass mailing to suspected potential campaign donors—based on some characteristics or qualities thought likely to make them susceptible to a candidate's appeal for

Direct Mail: The Poisoned Pen of Politics

funds. Note that this propensity to donate is merely *suspected*, not proven. Those individuals who actually *respond* to the prospect mailing become members of the prized "house list." They are proven donors who, having contributed once, are believed good possibilities for additional donations. As such they are the targets of repeated mailings during the course of the campaign, and normally such mailings are quite profitable—in contrast to prospecting mailings, which frequently lose money or manage to pay for themselves with a wafer-thin profit.

The illustration demonstrates the potential of a well-coordinated direct-mail program, which, with an initial investment of $200,000, can produce (under ideal conditions) a gross profit of over $2 million in a year or so and, far more important, compile a house list of over 200,000 individuals. Direct mailers go back and forth between prospecting and house (or "contributor") mailings, and during the early stages of building a reliable house list, all of the profits from house mailings are reinvested in additional prospecting. Gradually, the house list grows, as does the bank balance, even though the cost of later mailings increases because more persuasive material is sent in each letter and the response rates simultaneously decline a bit since the mailings are sent repeatedly to the same house lists. Yet as the election draws near an interesting phenomenon can be seen: The response rate increases, as does the size of the average gift. The immediacy and impact of events, such as the growing excitement of a forthcoming election, significantly affect the willingness of individuals to give. This can be a bonanza for presidential candidates during the primary season, when another election is held almost every week (assuming a candidate is winning at least some of the contests).

The direct-mail strategy just described is often referred to as the "basic investment concept." An alternative "dual investment concept" is used by some direct-mail firms that do not rely so heavily on prospecting. Here only about a quarter of the profits are expected to come from the house list compiled by prospect mailings, while the other three-quarters is derived from a "master file" of past contributors to the candidate (and others like him) that is assembled from house lists of previous and current campaigns. This dual investment pattern insures that profits are made much earlier, and is thus less risky than the basic investment system, which can leave a candidate whose effort begins to flag before the final stages with little to show for all the prospecting investments.

Table 4-1 presents an analysis of two direct-mail letters, one sent

1. Raise initial investment of $200,000 to pay for the first mailing.

"House" List	Bank Balance
0	$200,000

2. Use the $200,000 to pay for 952,381 letters at 21¢ a letter.

"House" List	Bank Balance
0	0

3. The mailing produces a response rate of 2.9 percent, meaning 27,619 letter recipients give a donation (at an average of $10.82 each). The mailing returns $298,838.

"House" List	Bank Balance
27,619	$298,838

4. The whole balance is used to mail again (1,423,038 letters at 21¢ each).

"House" List	Bank Balance
27,619	0

5. This time the response rate happens to be a bit lower (2.6 percent) but since a larger list was used, more new donors are produced (36,999). The average gift is about the same as before ($10.75), producing $397,739. All the new donors are added to the "house" list total.

"House" List	Bank Balance
64,618	$397,739

6. Now the "house" list of all previous donors is mailed. The letters are bulky (with personalized enclosures) and therefore costlier (38¢ per letter), but the response rate is a high 14.8 percent and the average donation is $13.10. After deducting $24,555 in mailing costs, the profit is $100,733.

"House" List	Bank Balance
64,618	$498,472

7. Empty the bank to prospect again. At 21¢ a letter, 2,373,676 letters are sent. Less reliable lists are used, and the response rate dips again (to 2.2 percent), but the largest mailing so far still yields the most new donors yet (52,221). The average gift of $9.91 adds $517,510 to the empty bank account.

"House" List	Bank Balance
116,839	$517,510

8. Take the whole sum and go prospecting again, buying 2,464,333 letters. With a 2.0 response rate this time and an average donation of $10.68, 49,287 new donors and $526,385 are produced.

"House" List	Bank Balance
166,126	$526,385

9. Since a month and a half have passed since the last "house" list mailing, send another one. At 38¢ a letter, the costs are $63,128. The response rate, though, is 16.3 percent with an average gift of $14.20. Thus the mailing yields a hefty profit of $321,380.

"House" List	Bank Balance
166,126	$847,765

10. Take about half the money ($425,000) for a final prospect mailing of 2,023,810 letters. The 1.9 percent response rate and average gift of $10.74 produce 38,452 more donors and $412,974 (or less than the cost of the mailing).

"House" List	Bank Balance
204,578	$835,739

11. With the primaries now underway, the political excitement and attention permit regular mailings to the "house" list (about every six weeks), and produce both a higher rate of return (an average of 22 percent) and a higher average donation (about $28). The first mailing (at these average rates) brings in $1,260,196 at a cost of only $77,740.

"House" List	Bank Balance
204,578	$2,018,195

TABLE 4-1

A Direct-Mail Letter from President Ford: An Analysis

	Prospecting Mailing[a]	Contributor Mailing[a]
Period of Mailing	Dec. 1975–June 1976	October 1975
Total Names Mailed	4,883,462	210,760
Number Responding and Contributing	86,596	24,674
(Percent Response)	(1.8)	(11.7)
Average Contribution	$20.72	$25.77
Gross Income from Mailing	$1,794,658	$635,934
Cost of Each Letter Sent	$ .21	Computer: $ .27
		Robotype: $1.04
Total Cost of Mailing	$998,126	$59,549
NET INCOME FROM MAILING	$796,533	$576,385

[a] Both mailings used exactly the same letter text. There were, however, several differences in the contributor cards and mailing envelopes.

SOURCE: Letters and mailing data provided by the National Republican Congressional Committee.

in a prospect mailing and the other to a house list. Both letters, signed by President Ford to raise funds for the National Republican Congressional Committee (NRCC), used the same text and were posted during the same general time period. The prospecting letter was mailed to almost 4.3 million people, while the contributor letter was sent to little more than 200,000. Yet the response rate—the proportion of those receiving a letter who make a contribution—was so much greater for the house mailing (11.7 percent to 1.8 percent for the prospect package) that the profit from the small mailing ($576,000) approached the level of the much larger mailing ($797,000). Prospecting produced almost three times the gross income ($1.8 million versus $636,000), but mailing costs were far higher ($1 million versus $60,000). This is despite the fact that each prospect letter, a rather impersonal "Dear Friend" item, was less expensive than the computer or robotyped letter sent to the house contributors. The computer version had a computer-imprinted personalized address and salutation, and the addressee's name was invoked twice in the text (those lines being computer imprinted, with the rest offset). A facsimile of Gerald Ford's personal stationery was used. The robotyped letter, sent to contributors with the most generous donation records, was the most personalized of all—printed on a heavier bond, individually typed, and machine signed in real ink. There were five two-cent stamps on the return envelope and a large, attractive commemorative on the mailing envelope, and the return envelope was stamped "personal" in red ink, with the individual's name typed in the return address slot and the envelope addressed to Ford at the White House. (As we shall shortly observe, these items are not the insignificant details they seem.)

This sophisticated package proved to be exceptionally lucrative for the NRCC, with an unusually high rate of return on both packages, especially the house list. The presidential imprimatur was no doubt responsible, and the letter's text was kept noticeably bland (by comparison to most direct mail) in keeping with the dignified tone thought appropriate for a chief executive. A similar house list letter mailed out by the NRCC under Ronald Reagan's signature in February and March of 1976 secured a 6.4 percent response and netted $250,000— still good but far below the presidential letter's results.

Presidents and would-be presidents have often been direct-mail signatories, mainly on behalf of their own campaigns, and have consequently been parties to the evolution of direct-mail technology. In 1964 Paul Grindle, a New England businessman who had used direct mail to build a clientele for his scientific instruments firm, coordinated major persuasive mailings for Henry Cabot Lodge's New Hampshire primary write-in effort. Of Lodge's 33,000 write-in voters (enough for a victory), as many as 26,000 were estimated to have been contacted first by mail.[25] Barry Goldwater raised almost one-third of his 1964 war chest from over 300,000 direct-mail contributors, so many that gifts of $500 and above comprised just 28 percent of his total.[26] In 1972 Goldwater's Democratic presidential counterpart, George McGovern, did almost twice as well. Starting two full years prior to the presidential election, McGovern's direct-mail consultants had amassed 350,000 contributors' names (from liberal magazine lists, antiwar groups, and the 1968 Kennedy and McCarthy campaigns) by the time of his 1971 declaration of candidacy, and by the end of the campaign McGovern had a superb 600,000-member house list that had produced $12 million.[27] Another candidate who has benefited considerably from direct mail is Ronald Reagan. During the two years preceding the 1976 election, Bruce Eberle and Associates, working with the Citizens for Reagan organization, raised $6 million from a file of 200,000 contributors.[28] In 1980, after a shaky start that included poorly designed in-house direct mail, Reagan again primed the direct-mail pumps.

As the Goldwater, McGovern, and Reagan examples suggest, generally the farther right or left one goes in making a direct-mail appeal, the more successful the effort is likely to be. Yet there are many exceptions to the rule—and many ways to cheat. One of the ways in which a moderate conservative like George Bush was able to use direct mail to great advantage in 1980, even while opposing Reagan, was to write emotional direct-mail copy to the ideological right of Reagan. When there is great ideological distance between two candidates, direct mail can be made to work not just for the candidate closest to the extreme, but also for the one closer to the center. When bland moderate-conservative Republican John Dalton ran against populist liberal Democrat Henry Howell in the 1977 Virginia gubernatorial contest, Howell was perceived as such an extremist in some quarters that Dalton's direct mailer, Bob Odell, found, "We could have mailed a telephone book and raised money."

Odell also has discovered that whenever a candidate stands out in a crowded field, for whatever reason, direct-mail fund raising is enhanced. When David Treen sought the Louisiana governorship in the state's unique open primary in 1979, he was the only Republican in a large field of Democrats, and so direct mailing was productive. Drawing a strong contrast with one's opponents is clearly one key to success, but wealthy candidates whose fortunes are publicized have special problems. John Heinz's direct mail was proving to be lucrative in his bid for a Pennsylvania U.S. Senate seat in 1976, but as soon as the press focused on his substantial personal outlays in the campaign, the mailing profits "just dried right up," reported Odell. "It's easy to see why a person would doubt that $15 was going to have much impact where a guy was putting $2 million into his own race."

Referendum and initiative campaigns, oddly, have also refined direct-mail techniques. That is because tens of thousands of signatures are required to place measures on the ballot, and it is very costly and organizationally difficult to secure the requisite number in a short period of time. There are independent signature-gathering firms that will take on the task in California (for a small fee of $400,000),[29] and most direct-mail agencies will take on the task as well. The Butcher-Forde firm in California, using direct mail, qualified in just thirty days a pro-death penalty measure (Proposition 7, which eventually passed by more than two to one) and also raised $100,000 for the sponsor in campaign contributions. The firm's grisly postal packet, heralding a "Citizens' Drive to Stop Murder," included a color brochure featuring illustrations of President Kennedy's assassination and of a black man holding a gun to a judge's head with the lurid warning, YOUR LIFE IS IN DANGER.[30] Butcher-Forde agency turned a much tidier profit for Howard Jarvis ($1.8 million) in securing most of the signatures to place Proposition 13 on the California ballot in 1978,[31] and a similar amount was raised for an unsuccessful successor initiative to halve the Golden state's income tax, which appeared on the June 1980 primary ballot.[32] The latter qualifying effort was the first ever conducted entirely by mail, with more than 6 million pieces sent to registered voters' households. More than 820,000 voters signed the petitions, and about 300,000 families—5 percent of the state's households—made contributions.[33]

Mailing Lists: Finding the Committed

There is no more crucial stage in the direct-mail process than the assembling of mailing lists. Knowing to whom to send a letter is as important to the success of a fund-raising effort as the message and the candidate. There are five basic types of lists: in-house, outside contributor, compiled, commercial, and universal.[34] "In-house" lists are the most valuable, consisting of current and previous contributors to a candidate, the names of campaign volunteers, and records of individuals who have made inquiries of the candidate by mail and telephone. Past and present donors are always identified by the time of their last donation, the frequency of donations, and the amounts contributed.

A good past contributor list, if kept current, is an irreplaceable campaign resource. Congressmen have a great advantage in the access they have to the correspondence and in the constituency contact files they have built up over the years. The average House member has between 20,000 to 30,000 names on file, which are periodically updated by his staff, and most senators have even larger voter reservoirs.[35] Occasionally a campaign can gain access to "outside contributor" lists, which record donors to various causes and other candidacies. Some direct mailers believe that people who are constitutionally inclined to give to charities, religions, and educational institutions are good bets to make political contributions as well, given the right incentive. And obviously, if an individual has given to a previous liberal cause or candidacy, there is every reason to consider him a possible donor to a new liberal product.

"Compiled" lists are basically group and membership rosters. Doctors, lawyers, businessmen, labor organizations, alumni, gun owners, veterans, and scores of other professions and special-interest groups have rosters of one sort or another. Some of these lists are obtainable free from supporters, and others can be purchased. The American

Medical Association, for example, makes its membership list available at a cost of $140 per thousand names. Another compiled list that is becoming a popular source for direct mailing is the voter registration roll. Most states permit voter registration lists, including the names and sometimes telephone numbers of all qualified voters, to be bought by candidates or campaigns.[36] The National Republican Congressional Committee has found lists of registered Republican voters to be very productive in prospect mailings, and the cost of the lists when purchased from states or localities is generally far less than similar lists bought from list "brokers" or companies. On the other hand, such firms and individuals have an unbelievably wide range of "commercial" lists for sale, from magazine subscribers and all people who buy products or enter contests through the mail, to lists of all deer hunters and trout fishermen in Arizona and all burley tobacco farmers in Tennessee. Magazine lists have proven popular with liberal and conservative candidates for prospecting, since demographic information on subscribers is usually fairly comprehensive. Liberals often mail to readers of *New Yorker, New Republic,* and *Mother Jones,* while conservatives pick *Human Events, The Saturday Evening Post,* and *Grit.*[37] "Universal" lists (like telephone directories and social registries) normally are not profitable for direct mailings precisely because they are so diversified.

There are standard criteria for evaluating the worth of any mailing list to a campaign. If the individuals listed have a history of giving to campaigns (and possibly to anything), if they are politically active in some way, and if the candidate has had some previous exposure or relationship to them, the odds are good that the list will be useful for prospecting. The same holds true if the individuals are likely to agree with the candidate on some important issue or have a strong reason to dislike his opponent. Additionally, a record of contributing or purchasing by mail is a good indicator of direct mail's potential effectiveness.

List selection is becoming more sophisticated, with survey research or demographic targeting often preceding mailings to determine the precise population subgroups or geographic areas most receptive to varying candidate messages.[38] Republican U.S. Senator John Tower's campaign used "geocoded" census data to select individuals and areas most likely to respond to his 1978 reelection appeal, and about 6 million pieces of mail were sent to 600,000 households. In the end, one of every five Texas voters were from a household that had made a contribution to Tower.[39]

Direct Mail: The Poisoned Pen of Politics

Unless a campaign is being held in Texas or one of the other largest states, though, it is very difficult to make direct mail produce much of a profit. A universe of 1 million potential givers must exist before a mailing program is thought to have a reasonable chance of success, a guideline that eliminates most U.S. House and statewide contests. Occasionally, however, a direct-mail firm can make a national appeal on behalf of a state or congressional candidate, usually by show-ing—in emotional and dramatic terms, of course—how the candidate can affect national issues or how he is the focus of national attention. A conservative challenger to an incumbent liberal Democratic U.S. senator in a small state, for example, can advertise nationally on the basis that he can "rid the U.S. Senate of one of the leading ultraliberals and super-big spenders" (as one recent letter read), while the endan-gered incumbent can alert liberal forces all over the country that he "is at the top of the right-wing's national hit list."

If, as is common, a candidate or his direct-mail firm does not possess sufficient lists to begin the mailing program, then lists are either rented or bought from list brokers, who are to be found in all major cities. Rented lists can only be used for a single mailing, and a campaign is not permitted to keep a record of the names, whereas bought lists are kept permanently. Therefore if a list will be used more than once, outright purchase is generally preferred since buying charges rarely amount to more than double the rental fees.[40] Some of the national direct-mail firms have their own subsidiary list companies, such as Rich-ard Viguerie's American Mailing Lists Corporation or Bruce Eberle's Omega List Company. The quality and exclusivity of the lists main-tained by these firms determines their market value, so most direct-mail organizations jealously husband their names and use every oppor-tunity to improve them. When list firms rent out their names, they go to great lengths to insure that the lists remain inviolable, requiring a written agreement that no copies will be made and mandating that a commercial mailing house must affix the labels provided (so that the campaign does not actually see the list). Richard Viguerie goes further than most by effectively denying co-ownership of the donors produced by a candidate's direct mail. While a candidate is permitted to mail repeatedly to his contributors, he is prohibited from renting, selling, or giving the list of respondents to any other individual or group. (Viguerie is, of course, more generous with his own company, which adds all the names to his permanent central computer file for future use.) It is true that list firms occasionally exchange part of their contributor tapes to mutually expand their offerings, but generally there is little cooperation among firms or consultants (including those on the same side of the political fence). Donor lists are so highly prized that even the Republican and Democratic National Committees will not directly share their contributor lists with their own candidates.[41]

Some direct-mail consultants suspect that, as the volume of direct mail increases each election year, a point of diminishing returns will eventually be reached. "There are a limited number of people out there who will contribute to a conservative campaign or organization, but we haven't found all of them yet," reported William Lacy of the Eberle firm. "We'll reach a diminishing point; it's going to happen. I've already noticed a very slight falling off." Liberal groups have discovered much the same, to their chagrin. Morris Dees, who had been used to 5 percent rates of return for the McGovern presidential committee in 1972, found that he had to resort to all sorts of gimmicks for Edward Kennedy in 1980 (such as offering "Kennedy Club" memberships and medallions in exchange for contributions) to even approach the 1972 donor level.[42] Oversolicitation of liberal mailing lists has proven devastating to left-of-center public interest groups.[43] Where they once prospered on the returns from direct mail, most of these groups have been forced to multiply dues just to survive in the face of sharp declines in their contributions in the 1970s. It is not that individuals are necessarily giving less, says Robert Smith of Craver, Mathews, Smith, and Company, but that more organizations are soliciting money for the same causes in basically the same way: "People may, in fact, be writing twice as many checks as before, but writing twice as many checks to five times as many appeals means that each organization is getting less than half as much." Smith, like his direct-mailing rivals and associates, sees the solution to oversolicitation in further expansion of lists, greater sophistication in targeting, and more organized, systematic direct-mail programs that include clever and innovative gimmicks.

Personalization and Package Design

Gimmicks and personalization are, in fact, two of the most pronounced characteristics of the successful direct-mail package, and these qualities can be detected in each of the five pieces of a traditional package: (1) the letter; (2) the additional enclosures; (3) the contribution card;

(4) the return envelope; and (5) the carrier or mailing envelope. In each part the direct mailer attempts to attract and rivet the recipient's attention in some way, while making the approach seem as personal as possible. The overriding principle of direct mail is intimacy. As the Republican party's direct-mail expert advised GOP campaign chiefs, "It would be best to have your candidate write a letter by hand to every name on your list. And every step you get away from that weakens the letter a little."[44]

In keeping with these rules, the letter is printed on the personal or business stationery of the signatory and never on impersonal campaign letterhead,[45] and brown or ivory stationery with dark blue or brown letterhead (rather than starchy, official white) is often preferred. The body of the letter is typed on a regular-faced typewriter in black, with short, indented paragraphs of variable length that are never more than six lines long and sometimes consist of just a single sentence. The signature is printed in fine-point blue ink, closely resembling a fountain-pen–signed name. If the letter cannot be properly dated because of the production or mailing schedule, then a designation of "Monday morning" gives the effect of immediacy. Surprisingly, longer letters generally produce greater profits than shorter ones. CMS believes their letters should run a minimum of four pages (two pages front and back, single-spaced), and one of the most lucrative direct-mail letters ever sent—for George McGovern in 1972—ran seven full pages.[46] Robert Odell's rule on length is slightly different ("You should only write as much as you have to in order to get the sales job done"), yet he also determined that longer letters were a great advantage for George Bush in 1980: "It takes a couple of pages to explain to a person why George Bush should be president and how he can win. You can't do it on one page. When you try to skirt the issue and do a short letter, you end up with short results."

Direct mailers are especially careful about design and enclosures. Mass-produced brochures and literature are thought to be far too impersonal, and sending bumper stickers has been deemed a complete waste of money. Some consultants believe that enclosures are more effective for prospect mailings, when the recipients presumably appreciate additional information or it is needed to stimulate contributions. (A member of the house list is already convinced, and his letters should be kept uncluttered and direct, according to the prevailing theory.)

The enclosures contained in recent direct-mail letters indicate the range of creative gimmickry in the field. Bob Odell's letters for George

Bush included reprinted news articles with "personal notes" laser-printed in the top margins: "To Irving Potzrebie—I thought you might be interested in these recent clippings—G. B." Several consultants reported that occasionally respondents return annotated clippings with notes such as "Thanks for lending this—I'm returning it because I'm sure you'll want to keep your copy."

When Texas gubernatorial candidate William Clements sent out money requests for television advertising, his direct mailer attached a list of all the reserved spots by city, station, and program so that the individual could see precisely what he was purchasing. A 1979 National Republican Senatorial Committee mailing let respondents target their money to the Democratic senators they most wanted to see defeated. Each respondent got to judge the Democratic incumbents on a "Danger Rating Scale," and was encouraged to scratch out, as viciously as he liked, the names of his personal targets. There are all sorts of other "participation mailers," as letters including involvement devices are called. People are frequently sent "mock election" ballots to vote or "critical issues" surveys to fill out and return (along with a contribution, of course); the Republican party even charged a fee in 1979 to count a recipient's mock presidential vote. Individuals are also inundated with "status gifts." Ronald Reagan sent each of his "first supporters" a "commemorative edition" wallet-sized card emblazoned with his countenance and the supporter's computer-typed name. Multi-colored plastic membership cards are also common enticements to "join" (i.e., contribute to) various Victory Funds, Eagle Clubs, and Stars and Stripes Forever candidates. Photographs are becoming quite popular as enclosures. Snapshots of the candidate and his family or the candidate receiving an award or the acclamation of admirers are adorned by handwritten descriptive notes in blue pen ink on the back. The Republican party used three photos of President Ford to evoke sympathy and stimulate giving as he was leaving office. The highly successful piece, mailed on December 30, 1976, included poses of Ford in the Oval office, at his swearing-in, and with his family.

Occasionally large past contributors receive a worthwhile gift with a new solicitation, such as a superbly illustrated historical calendar. More frequently, respondents are made to feel as guilty as possible if they seem inclined not to contribute. The state and national Republican parties use the marvelous gimmick of a laser-printed "memorandum" from the party's finance director to the chairman, bemoaning the absence of "key supporter" Irving Potzrebie of Jonestown from the contributor's list and vowing to "keep the books open" until he opens his wallet. Many times letters will also enclose a sealed envelope with the handwritten notation, "Read this please, if you have decided not to contribute,"[47] containing a desperate, breathless final pitch for money. For doubting Thomases, unconvinced of a candidate's electoral promise, direct mailers have a cure: an official-looking "excerpt" from a fictitious "Viability Study for Candidate X," conducted by a "Washington consultant," which inevitably seems to conclude that, if the candidate can just get enough money from the person reading the note, his victory is assured and the future of Western civilization is secure. No one else, though, has matched the number and sheer diversity of enclosures in Richard Viguerie's "state-of-the-art" direct-mail packages for the Conservative Caucus's anti-SALT campaign and the National Tax Limitation Committee's drive to secure a budget balancing amendment to the U.S. Constitution. No trouble is spared, as up to a dozen different items are packed into a booklet format with perforated tear sheets. There are gifts ("Christmas Seal"-like stamps with political messages on them), participatory devices (postcards expressing strong views on the subject at hand, preaddressed to the individual's congressman), and a legion of persuasive materials—all in a package that is almost as much fun to go through as a box of Cracker Jack.

The contributor card is a crucial part of the direct-mail package, since once an individual has decided to contribute, he often determines the size of his gift while completing the card. Direct mailers have discovered that people tend to donate more when the suggested amounts listed go from greatest to smallest ($500, $250, $100, $50) rather than the reverse and when a blank is left for even larger contributions at the higher end of the scale. Some consultants actually print tax information on the card, reminding individuals of the tax credit for political gifts. The contributor is asked to sign a personalized statement as he donates: "Yes, Candidate X, I want to help you rid Washington of the superliberals. . . ." He is even asked to sign and return the card *without* making a contribution—if he can put his name to a statement only slightly milder than this: "Sorry, Candidate X. I'm afraid I cannot contribute to your crusade even though I know your defeat would condemn my children to a life of misery and enable Sodom and Gomorrah to prevail on earth." Richard Viguerie's shrewd anti-SALT package asked each respondent to signify his contribution decision by affixing one of two flags onto the reply card—either the Stars and Stripes or the "White Flag of Surrender" (printed on a blood-red background).

Even a simple envelope can be a useful tool in direct mail. The carrier (or mailing) envelope, after all, influences the recipient's decision whether or not to bother opening it. The more personalized is the address, the better is the chance that an individual will read the contents. If an envelope cannot be personally addressed (handwritten or typed), then window envelopes are generally used, allowing the typed address on the letter itself to show through. "Live" (i.e., real) stamps on the envelope are vastly preferred to either meter or bulk-mail[48] and colorful commemorative stamps are especially prized as attention grabbers. "Teaser copy" is sometimes printed on the carrier envelope as an enticement. A gun control group was very forthright. ("ENCLOSED: Your first real chance to tell the National Rifle Association to go to hell!"), while the sponsors of Proposition 13 were deceptive ("Your 1978 Property Tax Increase statement is enclosed . . . RESPONSE REQUIRED").[49] The return envelope is, if anything, even more carefully and attractively designed. Colors that contrast with the rest of the package are often used, and ideally the individual's name is personally typed in the return-address space. Sometimes a calendar appears on the envelope with a date circled, as a reminder to the recipient that the candidate needs a gift by a certain time.[50]

A bulk-mail indicia is frequently used in prospect mailings, but again, live stamps are more desirable, and for good reason. As an experiment, the National Republican Congressional Committee mailed the exact same fund-raising package to two different samples of the same list, the only difference in the mailings being that one used a bulk indicia on the return envelope, while the other had five two-cent live stamps. Incredibly, the mailing with the bulk indicia raised only $0.50 per name mailed, while the stamped mailing garnered $1.64 per name.[51] It is a fascinating commentary on human behavior that our actions can be so easily manipulated, and this illustration serves to underline the subtle but substantial impact that consultants and the new campaign technology can have in politics.

Copywriting with Emotional Ink

Direct mail is a copy medium. On television visuals supplement copy, and on radio sound effects can embellish, but direct mail has only graphics, stamps, and the printed word. Words unspoken cannot easily move, but direct-mail consultants have long known of a secret ingredient to stir the soul: emotion. "To raise money by mail you don't have an hour of explaining things across the table to someone," insists CMS's Robert Smith. "You have to do it in a couple of pages of print. The message has to be extreme, has to be overblown; it really has to be kind of rough." Smith's axiom for the political left applies as well on the right. One antiabortion group, for example, sent out a "Stop the Baby Killers" letter in 1979 to 50,000 Catholics, Baptists, and members of other religious faiths, calling for the defeat of five pro-abortion "baby killer" incumbents in the U.S. Congress. The words "baby killers" and "murder" appeared forty-one times in the text of the letter.[52] When someone in the antiabortion movement complained to Jim Martin, a former Viguerie employee, about the extreme emotionalism of the letter, he replied as a businessman who knew the role of emotion in direct mail: ". . . the bottom line in my business is to raise money."[53]

The letter tone for in-house mailings, particularly to high donors, is usually softer, since these givers already have some sort of commitment to the candidate. But in prospect mailings, the tacit rule among direct mailers is that there are no rules—anything goes in the pursuit of profit. Tom Mathews of CMS sees little justification for appealing to reason or "freight[ing] a direct-mail letter with a great deal of doctrinaire political language" because the letter's purpose is "not to convince him of anything [but to] motivate the person to send some money."[54] The mailing list, if chosen carefully, is supposed to have guaranteed a predisposition to believe in the candidate. Direct mail, consultants insist, must make the quantum leap between belief and action—painful action (the parting with money). And only emotion can do that, they argue.

A candidate near the extreme ends of the spectrum can be himself in direct mail, but for more centrist candidates, emotion must be manufactured, either by selective and exaggerated emphasis on a couple of issues or by sharp, personal contrasts with the opponent. Involvement devices can also be useful for centrists. Robert Smith advises campaigns contemplating a direct-mail program to "Find your candidate a nasty enemy. Tell people they're threatened in some way. . . . It's a cheap trick, but the simplest."[55] Events that generate their own emotion can also be harnessed with great effectiveness by direct mail. One of CMS's most profitable letters for the pro-choice National Abortion Rights Committee was mailed shortly after Congress cut off Medicaid abortion payments in response to a 1973 Supreme Court ruling liberalizing abortion laws. And one of the firm's best fund-raising letters for the American Civil Liberties Union came on the heels of the furor created by Nazi demands for marching privileges in Skokie, Illinois.

Almost every line of copy is related either to emotionalism or personalization.[56] The letter is always in conversational (if ungrammatical) English, it is written from one person to another (not from one to thousands), and it is spiced with dozens of "you" 's and "I" 's. The salutation is as personal as possible (individually typed to the addressee if possible, but "Dear Friend" if not).[57] The opening paragraph, the most crucial part of the entire letter, is usually succinct and breathless. It is designed to rivet the reader's attention and pique his interest immediately, explaining in an intimate or momentous way why the letter is written, what the common ground with the reader is, or how the candidate's election will be vital to the recipient's own welfare. Urgency is the mood most often created in the first few words, as these examples of opening lines indicate:

If you're like me, you've received literally thousands of pieces of mail this summer. But I urge you to pay special attention to *this* letter, the MOST IMPORTANT LETTER you'll receive this year.

I believe you've been waiting 25 years to receive this letter. . . . But unless you step forward . . . there may never be another like it.

I need your advice. And I need it right away.

This is the most urgent letter I have ever written in my life.

These same lines recur frequently in national direct mailings, since they have been found effective. As one consultant wryly reported, "We usually write about ten 'most important letter ever written' letters a year—but not to the same group, obviously. It's always good for one shot." There are other approaches besides urgency. Involvement phrasing is sometimes used: "You and I can save America" or "Will you go to the White House with me on October 1st?" Guilt is always handy ("The Republican party can't afford to lose people like YOU!"), and the personal touch can charm ("I need your advice immediately" or "Would you do a very special favor for me?"). Frightening the recipients can certainly work with appropriate lists. Former military personnel responded generously to a letter that began "If you and I don't do something immediately, our country's vital security interests will be sold down the river." California suburbanites were gripped into giving by a direct-mail piece that opened like this: "If a bloodthirsty criminal like Charles Manson had you or your family brutally murdered, that criminal would not face the death penalty under current California law. We can change the law."[58]

The body of the letter is devoted to selling the candidate and his chances and closing the sale with a contribution. Boosting the candidate and his electoral prospects usually comes first. A Republican party direct-mail manual advises campaigns to "think in terms of how your candidate's election will provide something for the reader that your opponent cannot provide. In selling terms—think of benefits to the reader."[59] Testimonials and endorsements in the body of the letter can also bolster a candidate's credibility and pave the way for the quarter of the letter spent in actually asking for the contribution.

In general, the reader is asked to make a *specific* contribution; the amount is computer- or laser-printed in the body of the letter and is based either on the recipient's contribution pattern or his projected potential given the list from which his name was taken. Previous donors are never asked to give precisely the same amount as they gave before. Rather, the last previous gift is noted and gratefully acknowledged, and a percentage increment (10 to 25 percent) is added to comprise the new donation request. The pitch for funds is normally based on the campaign budget, which is identified as the minimum necessary to win, according to "the experts." The candidate explains an immediate need for a certain amount ($25,000 or less) to be used for a specified purpose (radio and television time being the favorite justifications).[60] The recipient can even be asked to buy "four prime-time radio spots for $312.18"; the more precise the request, the better it is likely to be considered. Finally, adding to the sense of urgency, the reader is given a make-or-break deadline by which time the money must be in the candidate's hand.

All the while the letter continues to make personal connections of various sorts. These are raw, scratchy "blue pen" underlinings, dashes, and checkmarks "personally" added by the candidate to emphasize parts of the typescript. If the letter was individually addressed, then the heading of all pages after the first reads, "Page two (three, etc.) of letter to Irving Potzrebie," and the addressee's name is parenthetically interspersed throughout the text in computer- or laser-printed lines ("And now, Mr. Potzrebie, let me turn to another matter of interest"). The phrasing is kept direct and simple with lots of conversational connecting phrases ("It would mean a lot to me personally," "NOW—here is the most important part," "But that's not all," etc.). William Lacy of the Eberle firm says that the level of writing complexity for direct mail is kept to "about the sixth- to eighth-grade level," not because all or even most of the respondents are that illiterate, but so that the message can be quickly and securely grasped. Lacy and others apply the "Magic Word Test" to their letters: "You add up the number of words under five letters in your copy, and if you've anywhere under 65 to 70 percent, you have problems."

The final paragraph usually restates the candidate's greatest attractions and attempts to end on a dramatic and very personal note. Sample closing lines give the flavor of the climax:

Success in the 1980's will be measured by *your* support today.

When we meet in person, I'll be honored to shake your hand. And you—with good cause—will be proud of your actions today.

I need help from my friends. Can I count on you again, Irving?

The survival of America is on the line. Let me hear from you *today!*

The signature follows, usually that of the candidate, but occasionally of someone who is well-known to the people on the mailing list (the president of the American Medical Association for doctors, for example) or who has special credibility on the issue stressed in the text (a retired general for a letter on national defense, for instance). Believability is important. The Republican party almost sent out a letter that would have been jointly signed by President Ford and Ronald Reagan at the time they were hotly contesting the 1976 GOP presidential nomination. But the party's fund raisers concluded after testing that average people simply could not conceive of the two sitting down together for any cooperative purpose at the time, so they scrapped the original plan and enclosed two separate letters, in the same package, one from each man.[61]

Postscripts are standard devices on direct-mail letters, because people have been found to pay close attention to them. (A "P.P.S.," in the signer's handwriting, often follows the typewritten postscript for added emphasis.) The requested donation and specified deadline are almost always repeated, along with still more phrases evoking guilt, urgency, patriotism, and hatred of the enemy:

If I fail to win your support . . . I'll begin to despair of success in 1980. I've figured and refigured our chances of raising dollars every way I can. There's just no way to make it without you.

I will be given a list of contributions soon and I certainly hope your name is on this list.

George Meany and the Democrats hope you'll ignore my letter.

We are waiting for your verdict. As far as we're concerned, you'll be passing judgment on America's future.

But the emotionalism of direct mail is not always so hard and virulent. Richard Viguerie's ingenious "wife letter" is a good example of the soft sell, which pulls the heartstrings instead of pumping adrenalin. Written in longhand by the candidate's wife on personal, pastel stationery, the letter is an expensive,[62] photo-offset production that is mailed in a ladylike envelope with full postage (no bulk reduction, and using live stamps). It is even shipped back to the candidate's hometown for a local postmark! In the four-page letter the wife gives a chatty rendition of her family history, children, and marriage, lightly connecting it all to her husband-candidate's concerns about inflation, taxes, energy, and other problems. The text is opened and closed with references to housewifely and childbearing duties ("The baby's crying so I must close for now," ended one), and a photo of the happy family, pets included, is enclosed with a "hand-scrawled" inscription. A similar package was used extensively both in the primary and general election for Illinois Republican Dan Crane in his successful 1978 congressional bid, and his campaign was funded in good part with the proceeds.[63] The personal connection was clearly made, and voters repeatedly thanked Crane for the family snapshot, which reporters found displayed in homes throughout the district.

The "wife letter" has been widely mimicked, but that is the fate of most effective direct-mail packages. Richard Viguerie himself discovered a 1980 Reagan fund-raising letter that was almost precisely copied after one he had mailed for another GOP presidential contender fifteen months earlier.[64] The same format, the same issues, and many of the same words were used; ten of the first eleven paragraphs were virtually identical. Direct-mail letters are not copyrighted, and the techniques are certainly standard. If direct-mail consultants were as emotional as their letters, charges of plagiarism would often fill the air.

Production and Mailing Schedules

Artful, inventive wording can greatly increase the profit margin of a letter, as can the quality of the letter's production, and it is in this area that technological precision has made its most significant impact.

"I started out typing envelopes, 500 a day, each of them individually stuffed [with letters]" recalled Bob Odell. "Now I'm at the point where I'm not sure I can keep up with the new technology." The added degree of personalization, which multiplies a letter's effectiveness, is a direct result of changes in technology. The first direct-mail letters were unvarying, mimeographed copies in an envelope carrying a computer-printed label. Then window envelopes came into widespread use (with the label affixed to the inside letter). The computer-typed letter, at first in all uppercase type and then in more natural lower and upper, was a major advance, since each letter was individually typed even if identical in message. Next came the computer "fill-in" letter, where the addressee's name was interspersed in the initial attempt at personalization. Simultaneously, advanced photocopying and printing equipment was being developed, allowing continuous production and unheard-of quantities of letters to be mailed each day.

The latest generation of word processing machines, such as the IBM System 6, is nothing short of phenomenal.[65] Five or more items in a reasonably priced direct-mail package can now be personalized in some way, and the machines' operation is far more flexible than previously. The System 6 can be equipped with a separate memory unit to store names and addresses for frequent use, or the information can be electronically stored on an unlimited number of plastic discs, each disc storing about 3,000 names and all the personal background and organizational information available about each name. There is even a third alternative, the leasing of computer memory space in a "remote" location (in another city, perhaps), with a simple telephone tie-line connecting the System 6 with its distant partner. Another new marvel, a 3800 laser printer, uses a "burning" process to print 10,000 lines per minute (compared to the computer's 1,200 lines), and can print sideways and upside down. New package preparation machines easily convert the long printed forms into manageable, mailable packets, with all enclosures neatly cut and properly folded. Some of these new machines enabled George Bush's campaign to mail out a million fund-raising letters in the few days following his 1980 Iowa caucus victory—an instantaneous response that permitted the Bush organization to capitalize on the fleeting fame of a single presidential preliminary.

The exact schedule for posting a direct-mail package necessarily varies considerably from campaign to campaign. Generally prospect mailings are done as soon as a list is available, so that house donors can be identified and added to the files as quickly as possible. Mailings to house donors, though, must be more carefully planned, and there are usually specific times during an election when awareness will be heightened or the sense of urgency and immediacy will naturally seem greater. Just before or just after a candidacy announcement, at the time of a major media broadcast or blitz, and shortly before the primary or general election are all dramatic entry points for direct mail. After Ronald Reagan broke his primary losing streak with a North Carolina victory in 1976, for example, the Eberle firm sent just 85,000 pieces to previous donors and received $778,000. And whereas Reagan's pre-announcement mailing had netted only about $300,000, a package mailed to coincide with the announcement of his candidacy showed a profit of double that. Edward Kennedy, interestingly, used a 1980 defeat as the springboard for one of his direct-mail appeals. Right after he lost the Iowa caucuses in a landslide, he sent out 5,000 mailgrams to all of his $100-and-over contributors, noting that "Most difficult period of campaign behind . . . President Carter slipping on Iranian issue that helped him win Iowa . . . Cutting expenses to the bone. Must have New Hampshire and Maine television money in two weeks. . . . Can I count on you?"

Direct mailers try to avoid the summer period, when many people are away, and December/January, when many are financially drained from the holidays, but there are few other clear scheduling "rules." Many of these rules are made to be broken; two consultants reported their most successful mailings are regularly sent in early January and around the Fourth of July, presumably because of the lack of competition from other mailers who have read the "rules" too carefully. Standard guidelines are also quoted, and often disregarded, about the frequency of mailings. Normally, the house list is mailed every thirty to forty-five days, but within a month or so of the election another letter is sent each fortnight. For instance, Bob Odell mailed every forty-five days for John Dalton's Virginia gubernatorial campaign in 1977, netting $40,000 to $60,000 from each letter to the 50,000-member house file. Generally, 5 to 10 percent of those on the house list will give with each mailing (averaging perhaps $25 a head).

Patrons can certainly be oversolicited, and complaints are sometimes heard. Wyatt Stewart, then head of the Republican party's direct-mail operation, vividly remembers the chairman of the board of Pepsi Cola, one of the most influential GOP contributors, demanding a meeting with the senior party and congressional leadership to explain to him "this crappy way of raising money" after he had received more than two dozen letters in a few months' time.[66] As it turned out, the magnate got his meeting, heard the explanation and received a full briefing on the program, and reportedly left calling direct mail the "lifeblood" of the GOP's treasury.

As long as the complaints are not too loud, though, and as long as the mailings are at least breaking even (i.e., covering the full costs of the mailing, at a minimum), additional packages are thought to be advisable. The limit may actually be one of creativity, since mailings can continue to be made as long as it can be argued that a financial need legitimately exists and a candidate's appeal can be stretched and amplified without repetition and boredom. The most important job of each new contributor letter is to upgrade previous gifts, of course. The Republican party has had a lengthy program of trial-and-error testing to determine the percentage increase that is best to request for each category of donor. In general, there is just a small percentage upgrading for gifts of under $100, but for gifts of $500 and more, a major increment is added. It is helpful to thank the individual for the original contribution first, citing the amount and specifically what it bought for the campaign; for larger donors, some sort of certificate and memento might be sent along as a symbol of gratitude. Occasionally reminders are used to prod negligent givers. For robotyped letters to large contributors, carbon copies are kept and sent along with a new cover letter if a recipient has not responded to the original within a few weeks.

Because the art of direct mail is still inexact, and conditions and circumstances vary so greatly from candidate to candidate and election to election, there are few guaranteed techniques. Direct-mail consultants (not unlike their media cousins) frequently contradict each other; what one thinks is a crackerjack idea, another discounts as wholly worthless. The direct-mail industry, and the professionals who run it, like to operate on the principle "If it ain't broke, don't fix it," but most are insecure (and wise) enough to realize that last week's magic may not work for this week's candidate. Therefore, a testing phase is sometimes added to insure that a mistake is not too costly. Testing requires taking a 1,000 to 2,000-person random sample from the mailing list and posting the prepared copy to this small group first. This adds four to eight weeks to the schedule, of course, but the adjustments and improvements that can be made before the entire list is mailed can increase the profit margin substantially. Richard Viguerie prefers to test the list as much as the letter, and he will sometimes start with several lists thought to be good for a certain candidate and solicit a sample of each. If the rate of return is significantly higher for one than the others, that list is used; if none of the lists produces, either the letter is altered or new lists are used.[67]

Indeed, given the primitive nature of the direct-mail "science" and the considerable financial risk involved in each mailing, it is surprising that testing is not almost universal. Some firms clearly recognize the need for more research. Craver, Mathews, Smith, and Company, for example, spends an average of several thousand dollars a month collecting and recording precise data on their packages for future planning purposes. Many direct mailers foresee a time when they will commission extensive psychological testing of word patterns, colors, and approaches, and use focus groups and much more sophisticated list selection techniques. For the moment, though, direct mail is a decidedly trial-and-error technology, where professionals rely on instinct and whim as much as test results. One consultant cited an instance where he had disposed of $10,000 worth of already printed letters because he had last-minute doubts about the mailing's success. Better to do that than mail at great expense a package that does poorly—which is exactly what very often happens.

The frequent omission of the testing phase is often the fault of the candidate and not of the direct mailer. Many campaigns simply come too late to a direct-mail firm for testing, and many times for doing anything at all. Direct mail needs the longest lead time of all the new campaign technologies, about eighteen months (if testing is to be included). Prospecting is a lengthy and arduous process that must be completed at least six full months before election day. By that time a campaign badly needs money to reserve media time and prepare itself organizationally. Prospecting produces little or no profit, and half a year's worth of mailing to a substantial house list is necessary to get a full return on the investment made to acquire the donors. In rare cases it is possible to shorten the schedule somewhat, but generally this can only be done with a high-visibility or very emotionally charged campaign, or when a valuable and bulky house list already exists. George Wallace, for instance, had a superb roster of contributors from his 1968 and 1972 presidential bids when he began a third effort for 1976. As early as May of 1975, Wallace already had raised $3.5 million by mail with only a $1.4 million investment.[68] Getting an early start clearly matters in direct mail, and while a substantial investment that does not show immediate results and must be spent eighteen months before the election is difficult for many candidates to understand or to raise, those who manage to do both can earn a campaign advantage. A Republican party survey showed that 38 percent of their

1978 congressional winners began their direct-mail appeals by the first quarter of the year, while only 8 percent of the party's losing candidates had started that early.[69]

Costs and Response Rates

Direct mail has long been criticized, in many cases deservedly, for its lack of cost effectiveness. Even after prospecting is over, candidates sometimes receive only a few cents of every dollar raised by direct mail.[70] This is partly due to high overhead and fixed costs. From 1976 to 1980 a 16 percent increase in postage rates and a 15 percent increase in paper costs were not always matched by a similar cost-of-living increase in the size of the average contribution.[71] Some of the new printing machines require a capital investment of $175,000 apiece (or $4,000 per month on a rental basis). In fact, when the balance sheets are examined closely, it appears that direct mail is exceptionally profitable for just a few of the clients who use it, and only modestly successful for the bulk of the rest.

Results should not be measured only by the net dollar figure raised, of course, since direct mail is a convincing form of advertising and probably a volunteer motivator as well. But most candidates hire a direct-mail consultant with campaign financing in mind, and there are those who are sorely disappointed with the results. Congressman Philip Crane, who contracted early with Richard Viguerie for his 1980 presidential bid, was certainly one of the disaffected.[72] When figures in the summer of 1979 showed that Viguerie had taken 64 cents of every dollar he had raised for Crane in fees and expenses,[73] Crane ordered Viguerie to stop operations. Ending their formerly close relationship—many of Crane's strategy meetings had been held in Viguerie's home—Crane rented his own computer and attempted to continue direct-mail fund raising from his central campaign office (using the 83,000-member house list that had been compiled by Viguerie). Viguerie retaliated by switching to John Connally and filing a legal suit against Crane, claiming several hundred thousand dollars in unpaid fees. The final figures, showing a half-million-dollar profit to the campaign out of $2.8 million raised by mail, were not disastrous by the usual yardstick of prospecting. Crane and his campaign managers did not clearly appreciate or understand the finer points of the direct-mail process, which requires reinvestment of most early profits for the promise of greater returns later from a mushrooming house list. However, the direct-mail process fails to allow for the cash-flow problems inherent in campaign financing; money, lots of it, is always needed yesterday for a host of important campaign items, and to expect campaigns to defer all other major expenditures is unrealistic, especially given the overpromise that accompanies consultants' direct-mail promotion.

Prospecting is also popular with direct mailers because of the size of the profits involved. Clients usually pay a fixed fee per thousand letters sent, from which a consultant takes his share and covers his expenses.[74] Prospect mailings are sent to many more individuals than contributor mailings, since in prospecting one casts the net over a wide area of favorable sea in hopes of a catch. In-house mailing is more akin to fishing in an aquarium, and far fewer fishing lines are needed—which means less profit to the consultant on a fixed-letter-fee basis. A few consultants do not charge by the quantity of mail sent, preferring to set a consulting fee and taking a certain percentage of the gross profit. Bob Odell, for example, has a monthly fee of between $1,000 (for regular customers like state party organizations) up to a maximum of $5,000, with a guaranteed 10 percent of the gross profit. All mailing expenses, of course, are paid from the campaign's share. Odell will also agree to permit the campaign to conduct any portion of the mailing operation within its own organization to save costs.

More typical of the fee practices of direct mailers is the Craver, Mathews, Smith arrangement. The first phase, testing, is the most expensive because even though few letters are sent, there are fixed costs that must be paid. A large, national organization may have a 50,000-individual test mailing, which would cost about $20,000, a maximum of $6,000 of which is CMS's fixed fee. Assuming the testing results are positive and the campaign or organization proceeds to a full-scale program, the CMS consulting fee is set at $2,000 per month, with a production fee (also pure profit) of $15 per thousand pieces of mail. Normally the consulting and production fees accruing to CMS account for about one-tenth of the total campaign cost. This is by no means the industry standard; Viguerie is thought to clear double the CMS percentage. Actually it is production and design costs and not consultant profits that devour the greatest portion of the contribution take from a direct mailing. For each package the copywriting and conceptual design cost several thousand dollars in staff time. Artist fees and typography expenses also mount, and the production costs can run several hundred dollars per thousand letters.[75] When many campaigns begin a direct-mail program, they may lack the considerable initial investment required to make the first prospect mailings. In some cases, direct-mail firms have been known to extend "front-end credit," that is, to delay billing for the costs of postage, production, and fees until the money from the mailing begins to flow in.[76]

As for the direct-mail letters themselves, the ultimate test of each one is simply how many donations it stimulates and in what amounts. House mailings, as opposed to prospects, almost always make money—as one consultant put it, "A house mailing that loses money usually results in an account executive getting shot"—but *how much* money it raises is key. The mailing costs of the average letter sent to a house list are about double that of a prospect letter (50 to 60 cents versus 25 to 30 cents)[77] because more personalization and better quality materials are employed. But the investment is more than rewarded. While the average rate of return for prospecting is somewhere between 1.5 and 2.0 percent,[78] and about $15 is spent to get each $18 in donations, the rate of return for a house mailing should normally run between 8 and 12 percent (and, therefore, for every $1 spent, $10 is gained). But since a direct-mail program includes far more prospecting than house mailing, a campaign or organization is lucky to end up with $2 for every $1 invested when the books are fully balanced.

Rarely, a response rate for a house mailing will soar to the 30 percent range. Bruce Eberle and Associates recorded a phenomenally high 32 percent response to a letter sent for the American Council for Free Asia just after President Carter broke full diplomatic relations with Taiwan and established them with the People's Republic of China in 1978. (The letter's virulent emotionalism probably had something to do with it. "For brutal political purposes Mr. Carter plans to send 17 million men, women, and children into Communist slavery," the letter read in part.)[79] Interestingly, most consultants seem able to predict the dollar average of contributions to their packages but cannot fathom the eventual response rate. This is because the more scientific parts of direct mail (package design, degree of personalization, and choice of lists) give a good indication of how much each respondent is likely to donate, while the artful side of direct mail (how well the package appeals to the eyes, mind, and emotions) is indeterminate and cannot be measured without testing.

In presidential politics at least, it is easier to assume that one's campaign profit will be larger than in other elections. The "matching funds" provision of the new campaign finance laws, permitting dollar-for-dollar matching of donations under $250 for qualified candidates, is a bonanza for campaigns using direct mail. The vast majority of direct-mail gifts are well under $250, which means that almost all mail contributions can be fully matched—and the response rate is effectively doubled.[80] This windfall also cheers candidates in most states that provide public financing for campaigns, and as public finance systems become more widespread, direct mail will be a major beneficiary.

But even with the matching funds provision, campaigns are not very well suited to direct mail—although political consultants can hardly be expected to admit it. Permanent organizations are in much better positions to benefit from a sustained direct-mail program than are temporary campaigns. Proper prospecting should be continuous, and concentrated for a longer period than a campaign usually allows. Once a contributor base has been identified, moreover, it should be massaged over a period of many years to yield a generous profit. A campaign is over before the most lucrative phase of direct mail can really begin. By contrast, an organization in the second or third year of solicitation can normally secure membership renewal from 50 to 75 percent of current members, at a tidy profit for each renewal. Two or more supplementary solicitations each year for extra money usually generate about a 10 percent response rate and an average gift approaching $20. It is not uncommon for an organization to realize up to a 300 percent return on its original investment in a full, three-year direct-mail development program. Perhaps it is only a matter of time before incumbent officeholders mimic the experience of organizations and contract with direct-mail consultants continuously. Already defeated presidential contenders intending to run again (such as George Wallace) have followed precisely this course, and at least one incumbent U.S. senator, Republican Jesse Helms of North Carolina, has used direct mail extensively throughout his term to fund his own and others' ideologically palatable activities.

Expanding to "Direct Response"

The shrewd candidate does not rely exclusively on direct mail for campaign fund raising. Traditional fund-raising dinners, testimonial gatherings, coffees, and cocktail parties retain their appeal, and with good reason. They often provide needed financial resources in the early stages of a campaign at a time when direct mail, still in the prospect stage, cannot. Direct-mail consultants are reasonably aware of their medium's limitations, and have recently sought to expand the borders of their operations. Some have even begun to call themselves "direct-response" professionals, because they are applying what they have learned to new media: television and the telephone. It is in these areas that direct mailers see the greatest potential for future growth.

At the simplest level, a direct-mail letter can be used to emphasize or presage a campaign message in another medium. Thus, a letter can tell its recipient to be on the lookout for certain television or magazine advertisements about the campaign (and those advertisements, when seen or read, can then serve as propaganda reinforcement and as a prod to answer the direct-mail solicitation). Other media can also be an advance cue to a voter that he will be receiving a direct-mail letter, arousing some slight degree of anticipation and possibly increasing the chances that the piece will be opened and read. The use of multiple media is especially effective when it is simultaneous. The electronic church has shown the way. On the Reverend Jerry Falwell's national "Old-Time Gospel Hour," for instance, a message is frequently emblazoned across the television screen: "Become a FAITH PARTNER. Call 1–800–453–2400. This is a FREE CALL." Now politics has taken up the toll-free banner. In September 1978, the Federal Elections Commission (FEC) issued an advisory opinion giving permission to Illinois Democratic U.S. Senate candidate Alex Seith to add a toll-free number to his media ads and to take pledges on VISA, Bank Americard, and Master Charge credit cards.[81] (The FEC opinion applied only to national offices, but most states have since added their approval for state offices.)

With television and home telephones almost universal in the United States, and an estimated 120 million people owning bank credit cards, the convenience alone probably increases the volume of gifts. Not only was the old method cumbersome—televising the address and hoping the viewer would record it, write a check, prepare an envelope, and stamp and mail it—but it allowed the emotion of the advertisement's message to subside because of the time lag between seeing it and sending off a donation.[82] Contributing is in some ways akin to impulse buying, and in this respect the televised-telephoned immediacy of "direct response" is far superior to the more deliberative, if equally emotional, direct-mail letter. The greatest advantage for the candidate, however, is the instantaneous availability of the contributed money. Even before the donors are billed, he can collect all the credit card pledges from the bank, while the donor gets a month's reprieve before facing the bill.[83] There is icing on the cake: The system efficiently produces all of the information required by the FEC to identify contributors (normally a campaign headache), and the lists that are generated have notable secondary uses (for volunteer recruitment, get-out-the-vote contacts, and follow-up direct mail).[84]

Sometimes through a merger of mailing and telephone banks just the telephone has been used in combination with direct mail. The Eberle firm has been a leader in this new area, beginning a program for a client with traditional prospecting to compile a donor list. As the election nears, however, the house list is converted into telephone sheets with each respondent's contribution record fully noted.[85] Trained callers then telephone each individual, read a prepared script that is shorter than, but equally as emotional as, a good direct mail letter, and follow up each pledge immediately with a "mailgram" thank you and contribution card. The response rate, even after the reneging pledges are accounted for, on average has been double the best return for a direct-mail letter. After initial testing for the Texas Republican party and Jeffrey Bell's 1978 U.S. Senate race in New Jersey, a full-scale program was developed for the Council for Inter-American Security (CIS), an organization opposed to the ratification of the Panama Canal Treaties.[86] With a house file of 60,000 built after thirty mailings to 6 million prospective donors, Eberle's telephone vendor began calling the list a month before the final U.S. Senate vote on the treaties, asking donors to help pay for radio spot advertisements. More than half of all those reached pledged a gift—an astounding percentage—and fully 70 percent honored their pledges in full. The next step will involve prospecting by telephone, but this will only be profitable when the selection of lists becomes more sophisticated and precise, or if mailing price increases and fixed costs exceed telephone costs.[87]

The Republican party has also experimented with telephone bank fund raising and has found that with a good list, it is not unusual for between a quarter and a third of the donors reached to make a specific pledge, with an average gift between $30 and $50.[88] Over half of the pledges are normally honored with a single mailed reminder, and half of the neglectful remainder pay up with a second notice. Interestingly, 60 percent of those who are pushed to pledge a specific amount on the telephone will send it after the first mailing, but just 30 percent of those who pledged to contribute without indicating an amount will do so, and operators are therefore encouraged to press respondents for concrete pledges. Just as with polling, finding people at home and getting them to answer the telephone is not easy; between 50 to 60 percent of all calls are not completed on the first try, and the average caller can only place fifteen to twenty calls per hour.

Also like polling, the tedious nature and precise scripting of telephoning generally requires paid callers to insure quality control. To improve telephoners' performances, some consultants have actually installed mirrors in front of the telephone tables to encourage a smiling, friendly disposition. (One experiment indicated that mirrors increased contribution rates by 10 percent![89]) The Carter campaign in 1980 hired actors in some places, on the assumption that they can take on a relaxed posture more easily and thus sell the wares better.

Other than the fact that the telephone message must be much shorter than a letter—the CIS script was only ninety-eight words—telephone solicitation closely follows the direct-mail pattern, seeking to upgrade previous donations, asking for gifts for specific purposes, and communicating urgency, immediacy, and emotion (with the added element of friendliness). After expressing the candidate's "personal" appreciation for specific past contributions and giving a brief, chatty, newsy "insider's" update on the candidate's progress, the dramatic punchlines are presented:

Mike [the candidate] is trying to raise $12,400 in the next four days, which he desperately needs to counter his opponent's last-minute television blitz. Could you help Mike to win and send another gift of $_____? [Respondent's answer.] Great! I'll tell Mike right away—he'll be very grateful—and I'll mail a pledge card to you today.

As if anyone could resist such a charming plea, direct-response technicians are hard at work perfecting a grand new telephonic scheme in which the candidate will actively (reactively?) participate. A breathless operator will announce to a startled Mrs. Jones as she picks up her home telephone: "Mrs. Jones, I have [the candidate] on the line—do you have a moment?" At which point a high-quality computer tape that pauses at the sound of a human voice will lull the listener with the candidate's words (and request for money). That is not all. Mrs. Jones is asked for her questions or opinions, and once she is through, the candidate responds on the topics she has raised, fished out by the operator and the computer from among hundreds of prerecorded sermonettes. Already a primitive version of the system has been used by U.S. Senator Jesse Helms, and the electronic church has major plans for it.[90] Much like the new organizational techniques, but in a costlier fashion, telephone fund raising permits candidates to reach out and "touch" someone.

Direct mail is a field far less in the limelight than media advertising or polling. Success is judged by a every different standard, too: A good financial balance sheet counts for more than winning. The mail consultants rarely work closely with the candidates, who are often ignorant of direct mail's impact on their campaigns, and the mailers accordingly wield little postelection influence. (Richard Viguerie is an exception to most generalizations about his brethren.) The consultants tend to gather around candidates who can produce the greatest profits, primarily candidates near the ends of the political spectrum, or they try to portray centrist candidates as being closer to the ends than they are. The right-wing has been far more diligent than the left in the direct-mail field, but other groups have developed a solid mailing capacity (including the Republican party, congressional incumbents, and referendum activists).

The direct-mail process revolves around the accumulation of good house contributor lists, mainly through prospecting, a casting of the net over wide waters to find the politically committed who have the giver's impulse. Prospect lists (in-house, outside contributor, compiled, commercial, and universal) are available from list brokers who sell and rent them, and from large list companies, some of them subsidiary firms of the direct mailers' empires. Good lists are pure gold, and they are hoarded by many consultants, who sometimes have more generous access to a client's contributors than the client himself. In order to be worth the effort, a direct-mail program for a candidate must be national in scope, be based in one of the heavily populated states, or have some national significance (even if manufactured). A profitable program usually takes eighteen months, and in many ways direct mail is better suited to permanent organizations than campaigns. A lack of cost effectiveness, a bad fit with the money cycle of a campaign, and oversolicitation of lists are some of the problems that plague political direct mail, not infrequently leading to disputes between consultants and their clients.

The recurrent themes of direct mail are emotionalism, personalization, and gimmickry. The copy tends to be negative, sometimes vehemently so, particularly when a well-known incumbent is the target. The difficulty in triggering contributions using simple print media alone encourages exaggerated drama, intimacy, and urgency, even in "soft sell" items such as the "wife letter." Every part of a direct-mail package is crucial—from the letter and enclosures to the contribution card and envelopes—and tricks of the trade are contained in every line of copy, from the date and salutation to the signature and postscript. A direct-mail letter to a donor is not a discrete unit but rather is part of a series, and the cumulative goal is to upgrade the gift. Testing has helped some direct-mail operatives to refine their upgrading techniques, but it is surprising that testing has been at such a primitive level. In fact, direct mail is no different from the other new campaign technologies in one major respect: It is still more an art than a science, relying heavily as much on trial-and-error and the political instincts of its practitioners as on the machine marvels that have made it possible. But, also like the other technologies, its future trend is firmly set in the direction of scientific precision.

NOTES

1. The first remark is by Herb Sosnick of Direct Mail Marketing of San Francisco, as quoted in *Today* newspaper, vol. 2, no. 13 (November 30, 1979): 1. The second remark was made by Wyatt Stewart, at the time the direct-mail and financial chief for the National Republican Congressional Committee, in a personal interview with the author.

2. From *Public Opinion,* vol. 2, no. 4 (June/July 1979): 40. Collecting the mail outscored watching television, participating in hobbies, sleeping, bathing, getting home from work, and eating lunch and dinner, among fourteen other activities. (Sex was not included on the list.)

3. See *Campaign Insights,* vol. 8, no. 5 (March 1, 1976): 5. The percentage reading any direct-mail letter varies with the degree of the letter's personalization, as will be discussed shortly.

4. In a GOP study of the party's 1978 congressional campaigns, 84 percent had used some form of direct mail, but most was persuasive rather than fund raising, and much of it was done without any real expertise. Winners used more direct mail and started sending it earlier than losers. See National Republican Congressional Committee [hereafter NRCC], "Campaign Manager's Study: 1978 Post-Election Research" (Washington, D.C., 1979): 2, 8–10.

5. More than 300 political direct mail letters were reviewed and analyzed in prepa-

ration for this chapter. About three-quarters were designed for candidate campaigns, the other quarter for ballot measures and fund raising/membership recruitment by political action groups of various kinds. Almost all were written for campaigns or organizations operating between 1974 and 1981. All of the letters were designed primarily with fund raising in mind (although there were necessarily persuasive elements in them). This chapter concentrates on the fund-raising aspect of direct mail, which is by far the more important and widely sought role.

6. Humphrey happened to be on a list used for a general "prospecting" mailing, a term that will be explained shortly.

7. Class interview, University of Virginia, October 11, 1979.

8. As quoted in *Campaigning Reports*, vol. 1, no. 2 (June 6, 1979): 6. Much of the discussion in this section is also taken from a personal interview with Viguerie.

9. As quoted in *The National Observer*, February 21, 1979.

10. Viguerie is also a director and stockholder in Rhatican and Associates, Inc., a public relations consulting firm headed by his close associate, William Rhatican, a former vice-president of RAVCO.

11. As quoted in *New York Magazine*, June 9, 1975.

12. The Eberle firm is much smaller than Viguerie's, and mailing and printing are subcontracted to other organizations. Only the creative package and graphics are actually done in-house.

13. See *The Washington Post*, June 2, 1979.

14. See *The Washington Post*, July 6, 1979, and July 24, 1979. The DNC claimed that CMS had broken an understanding that the DNC was to be the firm's exclusive national political client, which CMS, of course, denied making. CMS later coordinated direct mail for John Anderson's Independent 1980 bid for the presidency.

15. Paul Weyrich, "The New Right: PACs and Coalition Politics," in Michael J. Malbin, *Parties, Interest Groups, and Campaign Finance Laws* (Washington: American Enterprise Institute, 1980), pp. 72–73.

16. There were still about 400 contributors of $10,000 to the national party in 1979, but their total gifts comprised less than a tenth of the overall budget. More than eight in ten of the GOP's contributors give less than $25 and all but a few percent give less than $100.

17. See Institute of Politics, JFK School of Government, Harvard University, "An Analysis of the Impact of the Federal Election Campaign Act, 1972–78" (Cambridge, Mass.: May 1979): 1–19.

18. See NRCC, "1978 Congressional Post-Election Survey" (Washington, D.C., 1979): 44–45.

19. See NRCC, "A Survey of Selected 1976 House Races" (Washington, D.C., 1977): 16. The frank is the free mailing privilege enjoyed by members of Congress. It is the reproduction of a member's signature in place of a stamp, the cost of postage being covered by a separate congressional appropriation.

20. Personal interview with William R. Sweeney, executive director of the Democratic Congressional Campaign Committee. Already the percentage of small donor support of the Democratic national party has been increased to 30 percent in 1979, from a virtually nonexistent proportion two years earlier.

21. See *National Journal*, July 21, 1979, pp. 1445–1452.

22. Ibid. About 90 congressmen have advanced IBM "System 6" self-contained computer mailing units, while 210 others lease computer time-sharing capacity from private firms.

23. Ibid.

24. See *The National Journal*, December 22, 1979, pp. 2142–2145; and *The Richmond Times-Dispatch*, January 1, 1980.

25. Dan Nimmo, *The Political Persuaders: The Techniques of Modern Election Campaigns* (Englewood Cliffs, N.J.: Prentice-Hall, 1970), pp. 126–127.

26. Ibid., p. 64.

27. Robert Agranoff (ed.), *The New Style in Election Campaigns* (2nd ed.) (Boston: Holbrook, 1976), p. 147.

28. See *Campaign Insights*, vol. 9, no. 20 (October 15, 1978): 1.

29. See David Magleby, "The Initiative and Referendum in the American States,"

University of Virginia Newsletter, vol. 56, no. 6 (February 1980): 3. In 1978 the usual charge was 50 cents per signature obtained, with half the amount going to the ballot measure's sponsors and the other half to the firm for profits and expenses. Magleby notes that deceptive practices of some signature-gathering firms—such as using misleading descriptions of ballot measures to induce voters to sign petitions—have led to restrictions on paid signature collection in Colorado, Idaho, Massachusetts, Ohio, South Dakota, and Washington. See "Public Hearings on the Initiative Process," Assembly Committee on Elections and Reapportionment, California State Legislature (hearing held in Los Angeles, October 10, 1972), p. 39.

30. See *Today*, vol. 2, no. 13 (November 30, 1979): 1.

31. Nora B. Jacob, "Butcher and Forde, Wizards of the Computer Letter," *The California Journal*, vol. 10 (May 1979): 162–164.

32. See *Campaigning Reports*, vol. 2, no. 3 (February 7, 1980): 4.

33. The average gift was about $9.40.

34. See NRCC, *Financing Republican Congressional Campaigns* (Washington, D.C., 1979), pp. 99–100.

35. See *National Journal*, July 21, 1979, pp. 1445–1452.

36. Ibid. Unfortunately for challengers, some states allow only elected officials to buy the registration lists—yet another incumbency advantage.

37. *Campaign Insights*, vol. 8, no. 12 (June 15, 1977): 1.

38. The "Cluster targeting" system discussed in the last chapter is one such example. See also *Campaign Insights*, vol. 7, no. 2 (January 15, 1976): 1.

39. Data presented during seminar presentation at the AAPC Annual Meeting, Washington, D.C., November 15, 1979. In a Tarrance survey for Tower, 63 percent of Tower's supporters indicated that the mail was one of their primary sources of campaign information; almost none of Democratic Senate nominee Robert Kreuger's supporters mentioned mail.

40. Actual purchase of lists also permits "merging and purging," that is, both eliminating names that are duplicated in other lists already possessed by the campaign and identifying the individuals who have previously donated to more than one group or candidate (and thus are likelier future donors). Purging is an especially important function, since some previous donors simply stop giving, and up to 25 percent or more of any list must be annually purged to account for deaths, mobility, and so forth. Rental fees range from about $35 per 1,000 names up to $80 for very active files; buying charges are about double, usually hovering around $100–$125 per 1,000 names. A list broker normally receives a 20 percent commission from the owners of the list whenever he rents it out.

41. Institute of Politics, JFK School of Government, Harvard University, "An Analysis of the Impact of the Federal Election Campaign Act, 1972–78," pp. 1–19. The Republican National Committee, however, does share its lists with state Republican party organizations and also helps them to maintain their own lists with a cooperative computer program.

42. See *Campaigning Reports*, vol. 2, no. 3 (February 7, 1980): 1–2. Of course, differences in the two candidacies and the issues of the day could account for the profit discrepancy. Dees, though, believes that oversolicitation of the same liberal lists is primarily responsible for the drop-off.

43. See *The Washington Post Magazine*, November 26, 1978, pp. 12–31.

44. NRCC, *Financing Republican Congressional Campaigns*, p. 97. See also pp. 105–108.

45. If the signatory is an elected official and his office stationery is being used, the direct mailer must be careful to use and reproduce it at campaign expense. A disclaimer similar to the following is sometimes added in minute print: "No taxpayers' funds were used in the preparation or mailing of this correspondence." This normally accompanies the required disclaimers of the campaign committee's name and the Federal Election Commission's address.

46. The CMS philosophy is expressed in *Campaigning Reports*, vol. 1, no. 4 (July 11, 1979): 3–4.

47. Another popular version reads: "Do not open this note *unless* you've decided *not* to contribute."

48. Meter is preferred to indicia, if that is the only choice available. Live stamps are even available (precancelled) for third-class mail, which is the rate normally used in direct mail.

49. One of the Proposition 13 letter's enclosures gave an estimate of what the individual's 1978 property tax would likely be without passage of Proposition 13. The estimates were wildly inaccurate, as it turned out, because of computer error.

50. Bold direct mailers occasionally enclose two envelopes to try to double the contribution total with a single mailing expense. Each envelope has a calendar printed on it in with a due date circled in red. The double-gift goal is also emphasized in the letter text.

51. Another direct-mail consultant claimed that crookedly applied stamps work best. He reportedly called his mailing house to complain that live stamps were being applied to his mailing envelopes too *neatly*, distracting from the all-important personalized image (since the human hand almost always affixes a stamp in a slightly cockeyed fashion). Whether or not there is any merit to this claim, there is a persistent myth among political consultants, which started as an inside joke among direct mailers, that there exists a machine specifically designed to apply stamps in a crooked fashion. In fact, the natural imperfections in the mechanical process automatically result is less-than-precise stamping.

52. See *The Washington Post*, August 22, 1979.

53. Ibid.

54. From a talk given at an AAPC fund-raising seminar, Baltimore/Washington Airport, June 8 , 1979.

55. From a talk given at the AAPC Annual Meeting, Washington, D.C., November 30, 1978.

56. See the NRCC, *Financing Republican Congressional Campaigns*, pp. 161–170.

57. "Dear Friend" is considered to be a perfectly acceptable "personalized impersonal" salutation, while other traditional openings ("greetings," "to whom it may concern," etc.) have been found to be too stiff.

58. This line was used in a Butcher-Forde letter for Proposition 7, a pro-death penalty California initiative that passed overwhelmingly.

59. NRCC, *Financing Republican Congressional Campaigns*, pp. 161–170.

60. Ibid. emphatically warns campaigns *not* to "ask your supporters to pay salaries, offices, telephones, or supplies—yes, they know you use them. But don't mention them in a fund-raising letter." Presumably this is because these items lack sex appeal, and the ego gratification from buying television time is probably not the equivalent of purchasing paper and pens.

61. The Reagan letter began, "I am joining today with President Ford . . ." and the Ford letter had a similar opening.

62. Because of the costly reproduction process for a handwritten letter, and the use of full postage, the "wife letter" is more than twice as expensive as the average direct-mail piece. See *The Washington Post*, January 7, 1978, and October 28, 1978, for a review of the "wife letter's" impact on the congressional campaign of Illinois Republican Dan Crane, who in 1978 won a U.S. House seat (joining his congressman—brother Phil Crane).

63. The "wife letter" was sent to 50,000 homes prior to the Republican primary, and to 100,000 selected households—about half the families in the district—one and a half weeks before the November election. The general election letter was specifically targeted to appeal to Democrats and Independents.

64. See *The Washington Post*, December 15, 1979. The earlier letter had been for U.S. Representative Phil Crane.

65. Some other examples of advanced word processing equipment are the IBM Mag Card II, the IBM 66/40 High Speed Document Printer (Jet Ink), the Wang System 20, the Vydec 1400, and Xerox 850. See also *National Journal*, July 21, 1979, pp. 1445–1452.

66. Part of the problem, in this case, was the chairman's multiple residences.

67. *Campaign Insights*, vol. 7, no. 5 (March 1, 1976): 5.

68. Wallace's core list numbered about 200,000 individuals.

69. NRCC, "Campaign Manager's Study," pp. 8–10.

70. See *Congressional Quarterly Weekly*, December 24, 1977, p. 2651. See also *Campaign Insights*, vol. 18, no. 14 (July 15, 1978): 13.

71. See *National Journal*, February 23, 1980, p. 313.

72. See *The Washington Star*, July 24, 1979 and August 8, 1979; and *The Washington Post*, May 12, 1979.

73. Later estimates, provided by Viguerie himself, were even less sanguine for Crane. Out of a total of $2.8 million raised by Viguerie, $2.3 million was spent to raise it.

74. In some cases the set fee is paid per letter sent, ranging from 15 to 40 cents per letter. When the fee is per thousand letters, it can range anywhere from $180 to $400, and the consultants' profit portion of the fee is usually between $15 and $30.

75. CMS gives a general estimate of $220 in production costs per thousand letters in a prospectus to possible clients, and breaks down the figure like this:

Postage (1,000 pieces at bulk rate):	$ 84.00
Mailing lists (1,000 names at $40 per thousand):	$ 40.00
Envelopes (outside and business reply— 1,000 each):	$ 19.00
Mailing house charges (per 1,000 pieces):	$ 16.00
Printing (1,000 copies of standard package):	$ 61.00
TOTAL:	$220.00

As the prospectus notes, however, this can only be a general estimate because "there is no way of pinning down these costs until final decisions are made on the package to be tested, the lists to be used, the volume to be mailed and the best prices to be obtained at the time."

76. See *The Washington Star*, June 23, 1975. This extension of credit is not unlike that of the Rafshoon Agency's leniency with the 1976 Carter campaign for which Gerald Rafshoon was criticized.

77. These are general estimates. The larger the mailing, the smaller will be the per-letter cost because of fixed fees and expenses.

78. CMS estimates that a cheaply produced prospect package can break even on a rate of return as low as .75 to 1.25 percent, but this is probably rare. For example, if it costs $220 per thousand letters to produce a direct-mail package, it will take a two percent response with an average gift of $11 to break even—*before* the consultant's management fee, production fee, expenses, *and* the other design costs are billed.

79. The letter was also highly personalized, had a strong lead ("This is the most important letter I've written to you"), communicated urgency throughout ("Remember, this is a crisis situation"), offered a specific solution (a lawsuit to block Carter's abrogation of the U.S.-Taiwan treaty), had a vivid, handwritten teaser on the carrier envelope ("EMERGENCY"), and had superb enclosures, live multiple stamps, and tightly written copy.

80. This is only one of many ways the new campaign finance laws have worked to the benefit of consultants and the new campaign technology (and to the detriment of political parties). This is one of the subjects to be taken up in chapter 5.

81. There was at least a partial precedent for the FEC action. The Democratic telethons of the 1970s had taken pledged credit card contributions via televised telephone numbers.

82. In the few states that continue to prohibit credit card political contributions, a mailgram (deliverable within forty-eight hours) is usually sent to anyone who calls the toll-free number. This method is far more expensive, however: about $3 per contributor, versus $1.80 for a credit card donation.

83. A credit card "pledge" is no ordinary nonenforceable pledge. Usually telephone-bank fund raising is plagued by people who renege, but a credit card transaction is legally binding. An individual who makes a political pledge, then, is subject to the same late-payment interest rate charged for all other items and can lose charging privileges or face a bill collector if he has a change of mind after the fact!

84. The Qube system, discussed in chapter 2, is a made-to-order "direct response" system along similar lines, although its widespread use is some years away. See *The Washington Post*, August 24, 1979.

85. House list donors who do not have home telephones can still present a problem of varying proportions, however. The Eberle firm identified telephone numbers for only one-half of its best donor lists.

86. See *Campaigning Reports*, vol. 1, no. 4 (July 11, 1979): 7–9.

87. Eberle Co. estimated the cost of its telephone program for CIS at as high as $8,000 per thousand pledges, so unless the circumstances look particularly auspicious, telephoning can be a financial gamble.

88. NRCC, *Financing Republican Congressional Campaigns*, pp. 5, 190–200.

89. See *Campaigning Reports*, vol. 2, no. 5 (March 6, 1980): 1.

90. See *The Richmond Times-Dispatch*, January 1, 1980.

II

Democracy and the New Campaign Technology

Chapter 5

Parties, PACs, and Political Consultants

Back in New Jersey, I pushed Bill Bradley to attack the party. The party people wrote him off. So we did an anti-machine commercial in Bradley's primary campaign which had the party leaders up in arms. Someone was using a mold to make something. Finally in the end you see somebody holding a little statue of a guy in a business suit and the idea was that Bill Bradley is not tied to old ideas and old solutions. He isn't the typical politician. He comes from a different background. The little figure is laid down and next to it are about twelve more identical figures. The very last line said, "Vote for Bill Bradley unless you want another politician out of the same mold."

—MICHAEL KAYE
Media Consultant

We are entrepreneurs for a good cause, for one human being, not a party label.

—ROBERT GOODMAN
Media Consultant

Consultants have become possible because of the decline of the political parties . . . and the consultant has made the parties even more irrelevant. If what I've said is the truth, it's a goddamn shame. I think the parties are necessary.

—MATT REESE
Generalist Consultant

The rise of political consultants and the decline of political parties are related. Consultants have helped to grease the slippery pole down which the parties have slid, and most of them make no pretensions of strong party loyalty. They are, as Bob Goodman suggests, "entrepreneurs for a good cause," and that cause is the candidate, not the party. The atrophy of the political party system in the United States can hardly be blamed on consultants; often the consultants have more been beneficiaries of the web of forces that have brought the parties so low. On the other hand, the independent professionals' activities, and their success, are undeniably contributing to keeping the parties down.

In this chapter we shall examine the relationships between the parties and the consultants, and we shall assess the effect of the new campaign technology on the parties—what it has been and what, with resolve, it might be. First, however, we must consider two vital political developments that have drastically altered the way in which the electoral system functions. Both the mushrooming of so-called political action committees (PACs) and the passage of new campaign finance laws (principally FECA) have had major consequences for both political consultants and political parties. But while the PACs and FECA have brought joy to consultants and their bank accounts, they have laid more misery at the doorsteps of the long-suffering parties.

The Growth of Political Action Committees

A modern political action committee is defined either as a "separate segregated fund" of a corporation, labor union, or trade association, or as a self-sustaining organization, both of which are formed for the purpose of supporting candidates. The "separate funds" are always connected to a parent organization (the union, corporation, or association) and can be supported administratively by the parent. Self-sustaining PACs must pay all of their own administrative costs. Before the campaign finance reforms of the 1970s, the use of *corporate* (but not union) funds to establish and administer PACs was prohibited, which effectively barred the PAC as a vehicle for most corporations to influence politics.[1] The Federal Election Campaign Act of 1971 (FECA) and the major amendments of 1974 and 1976[2] lifted the ban on the use of corporate funds in stages and legitimized a significant new role for corporate groups in federal elections.[3] The PAC, which had long been organized labor's essential tool, became the property of business as well—and, in the eyes of most observers, has vastly strengthened the position of business in the political system.

It is one of the greatest ironies of recent American politics that organized labor, *not* business, brought about these changes in statutory law. The 1971 FECA had removed the general ban on corporate money for establishing PACs but then had reimposed it on most companies by forbidding the use of funds by any company that was a government contractor. Because of union-held manpower training contracts, unions feared that they would run afoul of the law and so got friendly congressional sponsors to lift the government contractor ban in 1974. The unions were betting that corporations would not take advantage of the new provision, and they clearly lost their bet. Not long after the 1974 amendments passed, the U.S. Chamber of Commerce, the National Association of Manufacturers, and the Republican National Committee all began to run seminars on PAC formation and to push corporate executives in that direction. As labor had assumed, most corporations were hesitant at first and wanted to see if the new Federal Election Commission (FEC) would really approve full-fledged corporate PACs. The crucial test ruling was announced by the FEC in November 1975 on request from the Sun Oil Company. That company's political action committee, SunPAC, was permitted to use company funds to solicit political contributions from salaried employees. The 1976 FECA amendments limited corporate PAC solicitations to twice-a-year mailings to executive employees and stockholders (and union PACs to annual communications to union members), but the rush to form business PACs was on.

Just from 1976 to 1978 the number of PACs rose from 1,242 to 1,938, and their total spending increased from $30.1 million to $77.8 million. New business PACs comprised by far the largest share of the growth; whereas only 695 business PACs existed by 1976, two years later 1,239 could be counted. In 1978 all PACs accounted for $35.1 million of the $199 million in contributions received by congressional candidates, and one researcher estimated that business and business-related groups outspent labor by better than two to one.[4] Between 1976 and 1978, corporate PAC gifts to candidates more than doubled, while labor's PAC donations showed only a 25 percent gain.* The

---

* Labor's figures do not, however, include separate spending for registration, get-out-the-vote, and other activities, which may amount to as much as $20 million in an election year.

vast majority of all PAC funds fatten the coffers of incumbents. The average congressman running for reelection in 1978 got 27 percent of his treasury from PACs, the average challenger less than 13 percent.[5] PACs, after all, are created in part to secure influence, and incumbent reelections are always probable and thus better financial investments, with a surer rate of return. Ideological PACs are, of course, an exception, regularly preferring challengers to distasteful officeholders.

Political action committees operate at the state and local as well as the national level. In the state of California alone there are over 500 PACs at work, and in 1978 contributions to the state's candidates topped $21 million (with business PACs comprising slightly over half the total).[6] Everyone from the American Horse Council to Howard Jarvis's American Tax Reduction Movement has established a PAC somewhere. Besides labor unions, businesses, and trade associations, religious organizations and, rather oddly, politicians have been among the busiest in the PAC field. The Reverend Jerry Falwell's Moral Majority, Inc., and the California-based Christian Voice each have their own PAC, and liberal Democrats have been targeted for defeat by them.[7] Congressman Jack Kemp (R-N.Y.) has his own PAC, The Committee to Rebuild American Incentive, that has helped candidates supporting the Kemp-Roth 30 percent tax cut bill (and, coincidentally, furthered Kemp's budding career).[8] Ronald Reagan, John Connally, George Bush, and Robert Dole, 1980 GOP presidential contenders, all had their own PACs at some time during the prenomination period.[9] Reagan's "Citizens for the Republic" (CFR) is the largest candidate-based PAC ever formed, begun with $1.5 million in leftover 1976 campaign funds and fueled with direct mail using Reagan's contributor list. CFR made $615,000 in donations to over 400 Republican candidates across the country in the 1978 midterm elections and paid all of Reagan's traveling expenses and its own staff costs.[10] The "Connally Citizen's Forum," Bush's "Fund for a Limited Government," and Dole's "Campaign America" also gave to midterm candidates, though like CFR the greatest proportion of their budget was devoted to their own organization and presidential contender.[11] The advantages of candidate PACs, other than self-promotion and the gratitude and goodwill they engender among the party faithful, are yet another consequence of the Federal Election Campaign Act. They avoid FECA's contribution limits—individuals can give only $1,000 to a candidate but $5,000 to a multicandidate PAC—and enable a presidential candidate to raise and spend money without it counting against the maximum spending limits imposed by FECA.[12]

Yet another increasingly prominent form of political action committee is the ideological PAC. The National Committee for an Effective Congress (NCEC) on the left and the Committee for the Survival of a Free Congress (CSFC) on the right are typical. Both provide organizational assistance to ideologically compatible candidates, irrespective of party. The NCEC is much the elder of the two and was founded in 1948. It describes itself as a "bipartisan progressive" group dedicated to civil rights, civil liberties, and internationalism. Rather than giving money, the NCEC provides specific services, such as the hiring and paying of the campaign manager, polling, targeting, and organizing. In a normal election year the NCEC will assist in some way up to sixty House candidates and a dozen Senate contenders. Russell Hemenway, executive director of the NCEC, sees his organization as a substitute for the Democratic National Committee, which "provides almost no services to candidates," and for political consultants who "are looking for campaigns that can pay hefty bills."

Many of the same goals are shared by the CSFC, which has sought to imitate somewhat the NCEC and the AFL–CIO's Committee on Political Education (COPE).[13] "I make no secret of the fact that I admire their [COPE's] operations and have to some extent modeled our committee on the labor groups . . ." says CSFC director Paul Weyrich.[14] Founded in 1974 with financial support from Joseph Coors, the conservative Colorado brewer, the CSFC plays a central role in the so-called "New Right," along with Richard Viguerie's direct-mail outfit and another political committee, the National Conservative PAC.[15] Like the NCEC, the CSFC helps candidates assemble a skilled campaign team, usually contributing about $500 a month to pay the salary of a field organizer. The CSFC acts almost like a political party, recruiting candidates, refining candidates' political abilities, performing electoral organizational chores, devising strategy, and constructing campaign staffs. An extensive five-day "candidate school" is held by the CSFC four to six times every two years, and is attended by prospective congressional contenders and campaign managers from the conservative wings of both parties, who pay a registration fee of $500 per person. The schools enlist incumbent congressmen and consultants as instructors, and are organized around problem-solving groups that enable the CSFC directors to evaluate each political candidate's performance. At the end of the course, a simulated election is held, which sometimes serves as an informal primary of sorts since more than one candidate from the same district attends. In 1978 three Republican House contenders from the same Wisconsin constituency attended the CSFC school, and the PAC decided that one of them, Toby Roth, was clearly superior (and the most conservative). After the school's adjournment Roth received the group's blessing, and he went on to win his party's nomination and to defeat an incumbent Democratic congressman in November.

In explaining the explosive growth of PACs, most (but not all) roads lead to FECA. The 1974 lifting of the ban on corporate funding of PACs was crucial, certainly, and the tighter public disclosure requirements, by revealing the previously obscured extent of each corporation's involvement in politics, has produced a "Keep up with the Joneses" mentality among business and trade association circles. FECA's $1,000 limitation on individual contributions and its more permissive $5,000 PAC limit encourage candidates to rely on PACs as a more generous source of funds.[16] Also having an effect on the extent and pace of PAC expansion is a growing group of political consultants, such as national generalists Hank Parkinson and Roy Pfautch, who specialize in assisting PAC formation and activity. The professionals are finding PAC consulting to be more stable, continuous, and profitable than candidate work, and almost all consultants have advised at least one or a few PACs from time to time.

The Influence of PACs: Rivaling the Parties

"The fact is that PACs work," editorialized *The New York Times*. "They give companies a very large bang for their bucks."[17] Thus a Common Cause study of the 1978 congressional defeat of a consumer-oriented hospital cost-containment measure showed, for example, that the American Medical Association's PAC had contributed $101,259 over a three-year period to the members of the House committee that defeated the bill. And a report compiled by Ralph Nader's Public Citizen's Congress Watch indicated that four of five House members who voted to reduce a "windfall profits" tax on the oil industry in June 1979 had received oil PAC money in 1977–1978.[18] (Of the fifty-eight congressmen who received more than $2,500 from oil interests, fifty-five voted to dilute the tax.)

Cumulatively PAC money comprises a large share of most congressional treasuries. The number of House candidates receiving over $50,000 from PACs more than tripled in just two years, from 57 in

1976 to 176 (including 106 incumbents) in 1978.[19] As the latter statistic suggests, PAC money is very carefully targeted primarily to incumbents (and other likely winners).[20] The desire to pick winners also leads many PACs to delay their contributions until victory is thought likely for one or the other candidate, and occasionally PACs hedge their bets by contributing to *both* major party candidates although public disclosure of campaign contributions has tended to discourage this practice.

The PAC bias toward incumbents means that even corporate committees normally dispense a great deal of money to Democrats. Business groups provided about 60 percent of the contributions received by the Democratic National Committee in 1978, for instance, and Democratic congressional incumbents in the same year got twice as much money from business as from labor.[21] A Republican National Chairman, William Brock, was actually driven at one point to harshly criticize corporate PACs for their contribution patterns, although gradually a PAC turn toward challengers (mainly Republicans) has been detected[22]—if only because challengers are usually financed at lower levels than incumbents and are considered more likely to notice and remember a PAC gift if elected.

Because of FECA restrictions, no candidate can receive so much from a single PAC that his vote can be called controlled by a single committee. But related PACs from an industry or set of interests potentially can have that corrupting effect.[23] And PACs have certainly been known to exert considerable influence in legislative matters, sometimes none too subtly. U.S. Senator Charles Mathias of Maryland charged in 1979 that one PAC had threatened to withhold contributions from his reelection campaign if he voted against a bill its industry favored.[24] This sort of PAC hardball is sometimes played electorally as well. Single-issue and ideological PACs target candidates for defeat far more frequently than they choose candidates to elect.

More worrying than PACs' influence on lawmaking and elections, though, is their effect on the political parties. Both parties seem to be resigned to the age of PACs. Like Willie Sutton who robbed banks "because that's where they keep the money," the parties have begun to direct their attentions to the overflowing PAC treasuries and have hired consultants to insure they get their fair share of PAC money.[25] The GOP assists its candidates in soliciting PACs, helping its nominees to secure appointments with PAC officials and directing them toward committees that are likely to donate to them.[26] Behind the facade of cooperation, however, lies the inescapable incompatibility and competitiveness between parties and PACs. Many political action committees are slowly but surely developing into rival institutions that raise money, develop memberships, recruit candidates, organize campaigns, and influence officeholders just as the parties do (or are supposed to do). PACs already outfinance the parties, partly because they drain away potential gifts to them, permitting supporters to tell the Democratic or Republican committee that they have already given at the office.[27] PACs also outspend the parties by a large margin. While the two parties were contributing $10.8 million to their congressional nominees in 1978, PACs mustered a $35.1 million expenditure.

As the pattern of incumbent contributions suggests, PACs are not organized along party lines and are not likely to be ever. In the words of one PAC official, "We believe you have to be pretty cold-blooded concerning your giving policy. You simply have to support candidates who support you . . . regardless of party or philosophy."[28] The ideological PACs, of course, make no pretense about their aims. Most of them view the parties with undisguised hostility, attacking them for a lack of ideological clarity and working to defeat the more moderate choices of party leaders in primaries. Paul Weyrich of CSFC proudly cites the case of Republican right-wing political novice Gordon Humphrey of New Hampshire, a former airline pilot who upset incumbent Democratic U.S. Senator Thomas McIntyre in 1978. The GOP senatorial campaign committee gave assistance to Humphrey's more moderate primary opponent, but CSFC helped to engineer a primary victory for him. Now, reports Weyrich, "Gordon is less than enthusiastic about the party," which suits CSFC just fine. It is easy to agree with Weyrich's observation that "both political parties would have an all-night celebration if we were to go out of business." The problem for the parties can be succinctly stated: Groups like CSFC are in no danger of going out of business. In fact, they are flourishing.

Effects of the New Campaign Finance Laws

"The three most important things in politics are money, money, and money," drawled the late U.S. Senator Everett Dirksen on one occasion, and he was surely right. The way in which the financial superstructure of a political system is arranged will determine who has access to political office and how they get there. The health of the party system and the fortunes of political consultants, among many other considerations, lie in the balance. The new campaign finance laws, which have drawn only patchy mention so far, are actually crucial elements in the rise of political consultants and the diminution of the parties, and their widespread effects deserve a more thorough treatment.

Watergate and the public's perception of the role of "big money" in the Nixon administration's corruption helped to pave the way for FECA.[29] In 1972, 153 individuals and couples donated $50,000 or more to Richard Nixon's reelection campaign, and 20 of them gave $200,000 or more. (One contributor, Clement Stone, weighed in with $2.1 million.) By contrast, George McGovern's effort was supported by only twenty-seven gifts of $50,000 or over, of whom just five gave more than $200,000.[30] One of the objectives of FECA was to reduce the influence of large donors by limiting each individual to a maximum contribution of $1,000 per candidate per election, up to an overall ceiling of $25,000 to all candidates annually. (Primary and general elections are counted separately.) A political action committee has a more generous limitation: $5,000 per candidate per election, and there is no overall annual spending ceiling. A PAC can also give up to $15,000 to a national party committee each year and up to $5,000 a year to other political committees. An individual can donate up to $20,000 to a national political party and up to $5,000 to PACs and other political committees, *but* those gifts are subtracted from the $25,000 ceiling. Apart from these contribution limitations, the law also requires disclosure of the names of all over-$100 donors and also of the way in which campaign money had been spent.

Public financing of presidential (but not congressional) campaigns was also provided for. To qualify for federal subsidies, a candidate is required to demonstrate broad appeal by raising $5,000 in each of twenty states from individual contributions of $250 or less. Once qualified, a candidate can secure "matching funds" (federal subsidies) for up to $250 of a donation. If a contribution exceeds $250, only the first $250 is "matchable," which makes four gifts of $250 each worth far more than one gift of $1,000. In addition, only individual gifts are eligible for matching funds; PAC money is on its own. Finally, the spending of candidates who qualify for and accept public financing is strictly regulated. There is a state-by-state spending ceiling and an overall spending ceiling for the presidential preconvention preliminaries, and in the general election the two major party candidates are limited to spending a lump-sum public subsidy ($29.4 million in 1980, up $7 million from 1976). To interpret and enforce the law, Congress created the Federal Election Commission (FEC), which has regulatory authority over campaigns for federal office.

Broadly speaking, the new campaign laws had five objectives:[31] (1) to reduce the impact of "big money" and the influence of large contributors; (2) to eliminate, as far as practicable, fraud and deception in campaign finance; (3) to strengthen the position of the political parties; (4) to encourage candidates to cast their financial net widely, increasing participation in campaigns by broad-based appeals rather than simply relying on the gifts of a few; and (5) to enable people from all economic levels to seek public office, minimizing the importance of personal wealth. From the perspective of several election cycles, it is obvious that FECA and the three means chosen to accomplish these aims (disclosure of donors, limitations on campaign spending, and public financing of candidates) have not lived up to expectations.

Indeed, each of FECA's goals is at least partly unmet, and in one major respect—the strengthening of political parties—FECA has had precisely the opposite effect. Granted, a number of FECA provisions reasonably take into account the parties' interests. Each national party committee is permitted to make a special general election expenditure on behalf of its presidential nominee (2 cents for each person of voting age, plus a cost of living increase, amounting to $4.6 million in 1980). The Democratic and Republican senatorial campaign committees are also given the right to donate up to $17,500 to each of their Senate nominees. FECA is also broadly supportive of the two-party system in its restriction of access to public funds by third parties. A new third party or Independent presidential nominee can only receive public funds retroactively, once the election is concluded, and just if the party or candidate received more than 5 percent of the national popular vote. Any monies so received will only be in proportion to the third party's percentage of the vote.

But other than these and a few other provisions, FECA has proved to be *harmful* to the major parties. It simply does not create a party-centered system of campaign finance. The stringent reporting requirements and the intricate specifications for the splitting of costs when an expenditure benefiting all of a party's candidates is made have discouraged party umbrella spending, for example, and have encouraged candidates to stay clear of the party and its other nominees. The finance law also restricts the contributions of a political party to each of its own candidates to just $5,000—putting the political parties on exactly the same footing as nonparty PACs. There is little question that this restriction has damaged the parties. One study reported that in 1972 about 17 percent of the budgets of congressional candidates had been donated by the parties, but by 1978 the proportion had declined to a paltry 4.5 percent.[32]

The campaign laws also cause the national party committees to compete with their own candidates for limited fund-raising dollars to a greater degree than ever before, through a combination of contribution limits and a single, small income tax credit covering both candidate and party gifts.[33] It is little wonder that the national party committees guard so jealously their direct-mail lists and generally refuse to share them with party candidates. Moreover, FECA dealt a severe blow to local party organizational and volunteer activity because the limited campaign dollars that were permitted to be spent had to be carefully managed, controlled and disclosed, resulting in a centralization of most campaign tasks and an elimination of grass-roots programs. "Before the election laws," grumbled a local party official in Illinois before his state's 1980 presidential primary, "we could buy TV time, arrange radio commercials, and raise money locally to pay for them. We had some control over the format and the content. Now it's all run from Washington."[34] As consultant Stuart Spencer explained FECA's impact:

Volunteer work is really hurt because of the new campaign finance laws. The little old lady has got no place to go, and the real spark for the parties is the grass-roots activities. If you had gotten excited about Dwight Eisenhower, you'd have gone out and gotten a storefront for a headquarters. If you did that today it would be charged against our budget. And I'd say, "Close the son-of-a-bitch up; I don't want to spend the money on that!"

The intimidation of the new rules, the threat of prosecution, and the bulky expenditure reporting requirements also have taken their toll. One Republican county chairman in 1976 was actually photographed on a ladder, painting out the name of Gerald Ford from a campaign sign since the local party committee had discovered it had exceeded the tiny $1,000 maximum it was permitted to spend on behalf of the national ticket. In reflecting on the 1976 presidential campaign, David Broder remembered that "In many big-city neighborhoods and in most small towns, there was nothing to suggest that America was choosing a president—no local headquarters, no bumper stickers, no buttons, and almost no volunteer activity."[35]

FECA's $1,000 contribution limit on individual gifts has also been a godsend for the parties' vibrant rivals, political action committees. PACs, with a $5,000 contribution limit, can offer a greater reward for a more efficient expenditure of a candidate's time and efforts, since individual donations are usually solicited in high-overhead dinners and parties, while PACs are organized and centralized. As a consequence, the proportion of money raised by congressional candidates from PACs doubled from 1972 to 1978, to fully a quarter of congressional campaign expenditures. Because of the role of public funding in presidential campaigns (and the matching funds available for individual but not PAC gifts), political action committees have so far played a lesser role in presidential politics, but PAC contributions are growing at a fast clip at that level as well.[36]

Not only have the new campaign finance laws weakened parties by strengthening PACs, they have also boosted the role and influence of another group of party competitors, political consultants. Many consultants viewed FECA with concern at first, primarily because the 1974 amendments mandated overall spending limits on congressional campaigns that the professionals feared would drastically reduce the amount of money expended on their services. But after the Supreme Court struck down the spending ceiling sections of FECA in the 1976 case *Buckley v. Valeo*,[37] consultants saw FECA in a new light, and for good reasons. As Xandra Kayden has surmised, "Those who spend large portions of the campaign budget will have a greater role in decision making,"[38] and since the disclosure requirements naturally tend to direct campaign money to easily disclosable activities such as media advertising and polling, media and polling consultants' roles in a centralized campaign structure are probably increased. Certainly the power and profits of direct mailers and other campaign fund raisers have been enhanced by FECA. The contribution limitations and matching funds for $250-and-under individual gifts fit direct mail like a glove, and contemporary candidates rely on direct mailers and professional money raisers the way their predecessors did on "fat cats" and "financial angels." "Blessed are the gatherers," President Ford's finance chairman in 1976, Robert Mosbacher, was quoted as saying. "No $1,000 contributor is of tremendous value. It's the guy who'll go out and raise $100,000."[39] Consultants also gain from FECA's stimulus to centralized planning. Because of limits, campaigns are forced to plan better and map out their budgets earlier and more precisely—exactly the skills that generalist consultants are touted to possess. There is little doubt that FECA makes the management of cash flow and an early start in fund raising at least as critical to a candidate's success as any issue proposal he might make in the course of his campaign. Almost 60 percent of the GOP House winners in 1978, for instance, began their fund-raising efforts in the first quarter of 1978, while losers started much later and sought over half their money in the last months of the campaign.[40]

While FECA's favors to political consultants and PACs and its deleterious effects on the political party system are of central concern here, its unforeseen and unintended consequences have hardly been so restricted. It was thought before passage, for example, that FECA would tend to benefit better-known presidential candidates, since unknowns would be unable to seek out the dispersed base of supporters necessary to meet public funding matching requirements. In fact, the 1976 success of Jimmy Carter and the public funding qualification of fringe candidates such as the U.S. Labor party's 1980 candidate, Lyndon Larouche, proves just the opposite: that little-known outsiders can gain access to matching funds and even compete effectively *because* of the public financing system.

FECA was also designed to neutralize the advantage of personal wealth, but the Supreme Court, again in *Buckley v. Valeo,* struck down all limitations on a candidate's expenditure of his own personal resources, claiming any prohibition to be an infringement of the First Amendment right of free speech. Since then a dramatic rise in the use of candidates' personal fortunes has been noted, with candidate and family money comprising on average about 9 percent of the campaign budget.[41] Republican congressional contenders, for example, spent about $20,000 of their own funds in 1978, whether they won or lost.[42]

The merchandising of access to officeholders has not slowed, either; the marketing techniques now are wholesale instead of retail. Whereas before FECA an incumbent candidate would have assiduously courted a few financial angels, now there are "President's Councils" and "Senators Clubs" offering frequent meetings with the governing elite in exchange for a large contribution. The "National Finance Council," a creation of the Democratic National Committee, charges $5,000 for admission and arranges meetings for its membership with the powerful on a regular basis. Membership in the National Republican Senatorial Committee's "The Senate Trust" costs $10,000, with half a dozen private dinners per year with GOP U.S. senators as the reward.[43]

Moreover, FECA has made any individual who can draw a paying crowd potentially powerful and has thus given a lift to "star politics." Hollywood's finest can contribute their talent gratis without going over the $1,000 limit—holding a benefit concert for a candidate, for example, that draws large numbers of small donations, all matchable with public funds.[44] Jimmy Carter was the first presidential candidate to tap the fund-raising power of popular bands. In 1976 the Allman Brothers and The Marshall Tucker Band helped deliver $350,000 to the Carter war chest. (This figure includes matching funds.) Carter's Democratic rivals quickly caught on, and Jerry Brown raised $160,000 in one day at a 1976 concert featuring singers Helen Reddy and his girl friend, Linda Ronstadt, and repeated the performance in 1980 with a Ronstadt-Eagles-Chicago starfest. Edward Kennedy's 1980 campaign kitty benefited from art rather than music. Andy Warhol donated one of his creations, and the Kennedy staff had 500 lithographs printed, for sale at $1,000 apiece.

Two other unintended FECA effects are worth noting: The finance law acts to slim the field of presidential candidates while fattening campaign staffing. The trimming is accomplished through a cutoff of federal funding. If a presidential candidate finishes with less than 10 percent of the vote in two successive primaries, the flow of all federal matching funds ceases in thirty days.[45] Several 1980 contenders, including Jerry Brown and Robert Dole, felt the FECA ax before they had withdrawn from the competition. The staff inflation is accomplished by the burden of paperwork imposed on a campaign and by the legal and financial complexity of complying with FECA. Detailed reporting requirements have discouraged local party committees from joining the fray, but campaigns themselves hardly have a choice. So an estimated 5 to 7 percent of a presidential preconvention budget is now consumed by lawyers and accountants.[46]

Enough of FECA's shortcomings had become evident by 1979 to prod Congress into making some minor and a few moderately significant reforms in the law. The Congress passed HR5010 in December 1979 after bipartisan agreement was reached within the House and Senate Administration Committees.[47] While it avoided the more controversial and serious reforms needed in the areas of PACs and public funding, and only went a little way toward redressing the unhealthy tilt of the present system against political parties, HR5010 did achieve some useful objectives. The paperwork requirements were reduced in several respects, with fewer reports and less detail being asked from most candidates. More important, the law permitted state and local party groups to revive grass-roots participation and make unlimited purchases of campaign materials for volunteer activities (buttons, bumper stickers, yard signs, brochures, and the like). Certain kinds of voter registration and get-out-the-vote drives on behalf of presidential tickets were also permitted without financial limit at the state and local levels, and financial reports to the FEC were waived if annual expenditures for volunteer programs did not exceed $5,000 or nonvolunteer projects more than $1,000. (Previously, if total spending went above $1,000—a ridiculously low threshold—a party committee was forced to fulfill all the FEC's reporting stipulations.) Volunteer political activity itself was encouraged by an increase to $1,000 from $500 the amount of money an individual could spend in providing his home, food, or personal travel to a candidate without having to file a contributor's report. And, in yet another small step in the right direction, a volunteer was permitted to spend up to $2,000 on behalf of a party before the amount was treated as a contribution. It is one of the few provisions on record that favors the beleaguered political parties more than individual candidates.

The Independent Expenditure Loophole

One particular anomaly of the federal election rules gives PACs a tremendous potential advantage over parties and could play havoc with attempts to limit the influence of large donors. That anomaly, the provision for independent expenditures on behalf of a candidate, was not a part of FECA but a Supreme Court mandate (from *Buckley v. Valeo*). The Court held that Congress could not impose spending limitations on PACs and individuals who desire to advocate a candidate's election without consultation with his campaign. The Federal Election Commission, acting after the Court's decision, defined an independent expenditure as one made by a person or committee "expressly advocating the election or defeat" of a candidate that is "*not* made with the cooperation, or with the prior consent of, or in consultation with, or at the request or suggestion of, a candidate or any agent or authorized committee" of the candidate.[48] The expenditure, in other words, must truly be independent of the candidate and his campaign; otherwise it would come under the regular contribution limitations. While there is no ceiling on the amount, or stipulation regarding frequency of, independent expenditures, they must be reported to the FEC once they exceed $250. Further, a group of individuals collectively making independent expenditures that amount to more than $1,000 in a calendar year is considered a political committee, subject to registration and periodic reporting obligations.

Only limited use of the independent expenditures loophole has been made since 1976 but, like corporations' rush to form PACs, this form of election spending could well become commonplace once the initial caution and unfamiliarity is overcome. Already its popularity is on the upswing. While less than 0.2 percent of all campaign money spent in 1976 was independent in nature, the 1978 figures indicate that the two top independent spenders alone exceeded the entire total of independent expenditures for 1976 House and Senate candidates, and new records were set again in 1980 at both the presidential and congressional levels.[49] To this point, independent expenditures have almost always involved advertising in some form, where an individual or committee purchases time and space to endorse or attack a candidate, or support or oppose a group of candidates based on an issue or set of issues. Henry C. Grover, a former Texas legislator and Ronald Reagan supporter, independently spent more money than any other individual in 1976 ($63,000) for pro-Reagan newspaper advertisements prior to the Texas and Michigan GOP primaries. And in 1980 Reagan was assisted by an independent backer in the South Carolina primary. Having already spent two-thirds of the nationwide spending limit, Reagan's campaign was unwilling to invest a significant amount of money in the Magnolia State, so U.S. Senator Jesse Helms used funds from his own PAC to launch a television promotion on behalf of the eventual Republican nominee. Liberal financier Stewart Mott spent well over $100,000 just a few weeks later to air advertisements for John Anderson's presidential effort while he was still competing in the GOP primaries.[50]

Political action committees have been slower to investigate the independent route, but when they do, the result is often a major investment. PACs are better situated than most individuals to organize an effective independent program, since they have the administrative structure and the experienced staff that individuals lack. PACs also have direct access to the expertise of political consultants, many of whom are on retainer to them. The American Medical Association's AMPAC has been a path breaker in exploring independent action. In 1978 the committee spent over $42,000 on advertisements supporting favored congressional candidates in six popular magazines distributed throughout sixteen congressional districts and the state of Georgia.[51] The National Conservative Political Action Committee (NCPAC) has also concentrated on independent expenditures, but of the negative variety. The group spent about $700,000 in 1979 alone, primarily for television advertising to attack liberal U.S. senators up for reelection the following year.[52] All told in 1980, NCPAC's independent spending in the congressional contests and presidential race (where they backed Ronald Reagan) exceeded $2.3 million.

There are notable obstacles in the path of any group or individual attempting to undertake an independent course of action. Beyond the reporting burdens imposed by the FEC, which are particularly onerous for individuals, there is the frustrating and difficult prohibition against contact with the candidate or his agents. The AMPAC executive director, for example, felt obliged to require each member of the committee's staff and board of directors to identify any congressional candidate with whom they had had direct or indirect contact for over a full year, so as to eliminate possible violations of the FEC's standards.[53] Additional FEC regulations restrict the flexibility of independent campaigns. Individuals are forbidden from pooling their money for an independent effort, thus preventing liberal or conservative persons from combining their resources in order to afford national television time, for instance.[54] Even if the time could be afforded, there is no guarantee ads would be run. As the discussion in chapter 3 on media time availability indicated, many stations refuse to consider the sale of spots or programs for independent campaigns, and the Federal Communications Commission does not require them to do so. The Internal Revenue Service added another inhibiting factor in 1980 by preliminarily ruling that contributions to "negative campaigns" are not eligible for the income tax credit on political donations.[55] Last, there is the fear and the danger that an independent campaign would distort or interfere with a candidate's strategy, by perhaps raising an unpleasant issue on a controversial subject or erroneous charges. Candidates, therefore, often try to discourage independent efforts on their behalf.[56] In Idaho, for example, the Anybody But Church Committee, a PAC affiliated with NCPAC, ran independent television commercials against Democratic U.S. Senator Frank Church in 1980. One spot showed empty Titan missile sites in the state and accused Church of opposing a strong national defense. But the ad backfired when Church pointed out that the Titans had been replaced by a new generation of more effective missiles under a program he backed. After this incident, Republican U.S. Senate candidates in two other states denounced similar NCPAC media campaigns against their liberal incumbent opponents, openly fearing a sympathy backlash.

Despite all of the real and potential problems involved with independent expenditures, political observers are virtually unanimous in predicting expansion in the field. There is talk among PAC officials of independent polling for a favored candidate to better design an independent media package, of independent telephone banks to identify a candidate's voters and get them to the polls on election day, and of independent persuasive direct-mail programs. One executive of AMPAC was willing to predict that within a decade, half of all the money in the growing treasuries of political action committees would be spent for independent activities—a challenge to the limitation goals of FECA, certainly, but no less a challenge to the influence of political parties.

Political Consultants and Party Decline

The decline of the American political party system has been the subject of exhaustive investigation and debate over the last decades, and the phenomenon cannot be simply explained or easily reversed. The parties are certainly not lifeless, and the requiem masses sometimes said for them are a bit hasty. Then, too, much of the nostalgia for strong, vibrant parties is a product of poor memory or creative imagination, since historically American parties in most regions only fitfully performed the Herculean roles often attributed to them retrospectively.[57] Yet some fairly objective measures do indicate a lessening of popular and participatory fervor in and about the parties. For example, the proportion of voters who identify with one of the two major parties has slipped significantly, from about 74 percent in 1952 to 60 percent in 1978.[58] The practice of ticket-splitting (simultaneously casting a ballot for at least one Democratic candidate and one Republican candidate) is also no longer rare, with at least three-quarters (and probably more) of the population having split a ticket at least once.[59] Organizationally, the machines have almost all been dismantled, state and local party committees in many areas have atrophied, and volunteer participation in party activities is considered by most observers to have waned greatly.

There are dozens of major and minor causes for the shift away from party loyalty and straight ticket voting and for the rusting of party machinery. That these changes could come about at all is a measure of the relatively nonideological nature of American politics and the lack of class-based party identification on the European model, depriving American parties of the social and economic reinforcements that induce deeper loyalty to a compatible political organization. In earlier times the American parties could compensate somewhat as the supplier of essential services and favors, at least in urban areas. But the dawn of the social welfare state, when services became a matter of right and not privilege, combined with progressive civil service reforms (which eliminated much of the parties' reward system), removed much of the personal connection between party and voter. The slowing of the flow of immigrants starved party organizations in the cities, and the general decline of the central urban areas and growth of less organizable suburbs, with better educated and more affluent residents, had an effect as well. Suburban voters formed the heart of a new breed of knowledgeable, informed, issue-oriented Independents, convinced that the parties were nearly indistinguishable—useless shells that never fulfilled their platform promises.

One by one parties lost their most important jobs: dispenser of patronage, provider of services, supervisors of elections and suppliers of ballots, prime centers for entertainment and social activities. Public financing replaced much of the party fund-raising role for candidates, and television became the provider of news and information on public affairs to the average voter, emphasizing candidate personality rather than party identity. The parties were increasingly deprived even of their raison d'être, the selection of candidates. The democratic impulse is never far from the surface in the American electorate, and the steady growth in the primary system of nomination is one indication of it. Nominees for most major state and local offices in almost every region are chosen in party primaries, some open to all members of the electorate without regard to party registration (if there is party registration at all). The number of presidential primaries has mushroomed from fifteen in 1960 to thirty-seven in 1980, and almost three-quarters of all national convention delegates are selected by the primary method (or are bound to reflect the primary results).[60] Contrary to the situation in the convention or mass caucus nominating systems, the influence of party leaders and activists is normally diluted or nonexistent in primaries, and a party is not infrequently shackled with candidates who are completely unknown to it, which must nonetheless lend them its label. Indeed, many candidates win party nominations by running as outsiders against the "party bosses"—popular and enduring straw men in American campaign history.

The weakness of the parties exaggerates the worst aspects of a candidate-centered system, allowing extremes to develop such as the Committee to Re-elect the President.[61] CREEP functioned virtually as a surrogate party. It had its own internal advertising agency; a direct-mail operation with four mailing offices; 7 computer centers; 10 regional headquarters and separate branches in the states and many localities; 250 telephone bank outlets; many group divisions (youth, labor, ethnic, etc.); and a rather unique security outfit that all Americans became well acquainted with. CREEP even appointed its own precinct work-ers, leaving all the "party" candidates to fend for themselves, and brooked no interference in its affairs, undertaking no action (for the general good of the Republican party or anything else) that might interfere with its supreme goal of electing one candidate.

The "personality cult" campaign and the general deterioration of the party system are perfectly acceptable to most political consul-tants. In fact, they themselves, along with their electoral wares, have played a moderate part in personalizing and glamorizing American politics and in the continuing decline of party organization. While certainly not initiating the party's decline, they have nonetheless aided and abetted the slide, sometimes with malice aforethought. The gen-eral weakness of the party gave consultants their original opening in California, and the opportunity has been seized since by professionals in other states under similar conditions.[62] Candidates saw skills and technologies possessed by consultants that were unavailable from the parties and, as journalist David Broder suggests, "The availability of professionals for hire to individual campaigns has been one of the things which has enabled candidates to operate independently of the parties." The services provided by consultants, their new campaign technolo-gies, have undoubtedly supplanted party activities and influence. "The new technologies make parties, if not obsolete, certainly obsolescent," asserts generalist consultant Joseph Napolitan. Part of it is a matter of mystique. Party leaders used to be the ones thought to have the keys to success, THE secrets to winning elections. Now political consul-tants have the magic and the technique; independent professionals are the new experts, and their advice and support are considered to be more valuable publicly and privately than almost any party leader's.

Pollster Patrick Caddell clearly identified the alternate nonparty route that consultants have provided to willing politicians:

Parties traditionally provided the avenue by which candidates reached voters. What we've done with media, what we've done with polling, and what we've done with direct organizational techniques is that we have provided candidates who have the resources (and that's the important thing, the resources), the ability to reach the voters and have a direct contact with the electorate without regard to party or party organization.

[margin note: candidates can appeal 1 to 1]

Caddell's polling, for example, now reports the voter's attitudes and opinions more directly, more intricately, and more accurately to the candidate than the old party leaders ever could have done, no matter how closely they had their "ears to the ground." Like polling, television and radio have replaced the party as the middleman between the candidate and the voter. The uncontrolled media (and consultants as well), not the party leaders, determine the battlegrounds, arbitrate among candidates, and interpret election results. Paid media advertising represents the candidate more fully and more attractively than the party was ever able to do. Even most of the old party organizations could not hope to match the sophistication of "Cluster targeting" or other organizational techniques. And direct mail can, in certain circumstances, raise funds far more efficiently and lucratively than any political party, using other means, has ever has done.

Consultants have busied themselves not just by enabling candidates to make electoral declarations of independence from the parties, but also by equipping party-rivaling political action committees and single-issue groups with the tools of the campaign management profession. The modern manifestation of single-issue movements has stimulated an extraordinary degree of public hand wringing, although it is really nothing new. Antiabortionists or antigun controllers are merely latter-day reincarnations of prohibitionists or greenbackers.[63] The difference, of course, is that single-issue movements today have consultants and new campaign technology. Direct mail, for instance, is made to order for single-issue organizations, feeding on precisely the same emotional virulence that gave birth to them.

[margin note: is this bad?]

Consultants, then, are managing to circumvent the parties in two ways—with candidates and with issue movements and PACs. By no means are all consultants equally guilty of the charge. Many of them have had strong ties to the parties in the past and retain their early loyalties (if only for business purposes). Stuart Spencer is typical of the professionals who were politically nursed by the parties. Viewing each contest as "an opportunity for the GOP," he has consistently and steadfastly worked for Republicans across the ideological spectrum, from California U.S. Representative John Rousselot (a former member of The John Birch Society) and Ronald Reagan to Nelson Rockefeller and U.S. Senator Don Reigle (when he was a liberal Republican congressman, before he switched parties and won a Michigan Senate seat as a Democrat). Robert Goodman frankly ties his prosperity to his party ("Our business has grown because the Republican party has made us a part of their family"), and his and Spencer's sentiments are

[margin note: ? of what?]

[margin note at bottom: So what, more people are independents today anyhow. Also, is this "homogenizing" politics as subculture cags?]

matched on the Democratic side by those of consultants such as Matt Reese and Robert Squier.

A few consultants work closely with party committees as well as party candidates, helping to strengthen the organization. A third to a half of all Market Opinion Research's political work is done for the Republican National Committee or state and local GOP groups, and MOR's president, Robert Teeter, wishes the proportion were even higher: "If I have a preference between working for the party or for individual candidates, it would be for the party because it's more stable—an ongoing, operating entity where our work continues after each campaign." Robert Odell is fully in agreement with his fellow Republican, and perhaps even more dedicated to and enthusiastic about the party. His direct-mailing firm has contracts with thirteen state party organizations, one-third of his business, and he has taken great pride in building up their fund-raising capacities.

But attitudes such as these are exceptional. Most political consultants are at least passively hostile to the parties, the more ideological among them, contemptuous. At times consultants can sound like the evangelical populists they often portray their candidates to be, railing against the evils of boss rule. "Really the only major function of the political party structure these days is to nominate the candidates for president, and my personal feeling is that we'd all be better off if this responsibility also were placed in the hands of the people," Joe Napolitan has written.[64] Bob Goodman, in tones echoed time and again by his fellow independent professionals, lauds consultants for unshackling candidates, putting them beyond the reach of the petty party barons:

We have enabled people to come into a party or call themselves independent Democrats or Republicans and run for office without having to pay the dues of being a party member in a feudal way. Meaning kiss the ass of certain people and maybe down the line they'll give you a shot at public office.

Parties are usually viewed as one more obstacle in the way of the client's election. "In most places the party operation does not do a great deal to help a candidate get elected the first time, and [it] is more of a hassle than it's worth," concludes Douglas Bailey. Many party-consultant relationships are marked by sharp conflict, explained by Napolitan as the result of party workers' jealousy of consultants, who "have replaced organization regulars in making important campaign decisions" and who are possible usurpers of "what they [party workers] consider their rights to patronage."[65]

A natural consequence of the consultant's antagonism toward the party is his willingness to run his candidates apart from, or even against, their party label. It was difficult to know whether GOP nominee John Heinz was a Democrat or Republican in his 1976 Pennsylvania Senate race, since David Garth fashioned his media campaign around an anti-party theme: "If you think Pennsylvania needs an *Independent* senator, elect John Heinz." One of Garth's spots actually featured a glowing "endorsement" of Heinz's character by Jimmy Carter (delivered in March of 1975) to further confuse the voter. Scrambling labels may seem unfortunate to those concerned about the role of party in elections, but at least the party is not under direct attack, a common tactic in party primaries. Milton Shapp won the Democratic nomination for the Pennsylvania governorship in 1966 in a major upset thanks to Joe Napolitan's "Man Against the Machine" theme.[66] Michael Kaye's commercial advertisement for Bill Bradley cited in the beginning of this chapter suggests the convenient whipping boy that gained a New Jersey U.S. Senate nomination for a New York Knick in 1978.

When they are not running against it, most consultants simply ignore the party, in campaigns and in the way they run their business. The now-defunct Baus and Raus agency of California managed to work for Richard Nixon, Barry Goldwater, and Edmund G. "Pat" Brown, Sr., within the span of a few years. Elliot Curson Advertising, which did a good deal of Ronald Reagan's preconvention media in 1980, had most recently handled Peter Flaherty, the liberal Democratic nominee for governor of Pennsylvania in 1978. As noted in chapter 2, the DMI polling firm once worked simultaneously for the Democratic and Republican U.S. House candidates in the same district. Two partners of Dresner, Morris, and Tortorello, a formerly Democratic polling outfit, were convinced by the third principal that "labels aren't that important anymore," and the firm is now regularly taking two-thirds Democratic clients and one-third Republican—ranging from one end of the two-party spectrum to the other.[67]

Sanford L. Weiner, a former president of the American Association of Political Consultants, who began by representing conservative Republicans and whose clientele is now increasingly Democratic and liberal, dismissed his party contradictions by noting that "no one in California cares that any firm represents both Democrats and Republicans. . . . Strict partisanship just isn't that important anymore."[68] Another pace-setting California firm, the Butcher-Forde direct-mail agency, is positively proud of the agency's and directors' utter lack of personal professional adherence to any party or political philosophy.

One of the firm's senior associates described himself and his fellows as "pure advocates," declaring, "We're businessmen first, and politics is our business. . . . It's whoever gets to us first."[69] Their list of recent clients is a grab bag of politicians on right and left, from liberal Democratic U.S. Senator Alan Cranston to Howard Jarvis and State Senator John Schmitz (former presidential candidate of George Wallace's American Independent Party). In addition to toying with the idea of an independent candidacy of his own and aiding George Wallace's direct-mail efforts, Richard Viguerie has at times been quoted as favoring the dissolution of the Republican party, and enjoys working against either party's moderate or liberal candidates.[70] Viguerie's hostility to the organized party and his designs against it are only slightly more grandiose than those of many consultants and leaders of ideological PACs. As Viguerie's right-wing associate, Paul Weyrich of the Committee for the Survival of a Free Congress, put it, "The parties—they water down, water down, water down until they get something that everybody agrees on, which means nothing to anybody. The political parties have helped to destroy the political parties." With a little help from political consultants, he might have added.

A Party's Rejoinder: GOP Renewal

One of the two major parties has decided to fight back and has begun to acquire the techniques of the political consultant to further its own candidates—and, in the process, nurse itself back to health. The Republican party at the national level has organized exemplary direct-mail and media operations centered around two subsidiaries of the Republican National Committee (RNC), the National Republican Senatorial Committee (NRSC) and the National Republican Congressional Committee (NRCC). The NRSC assists GOP U.S. Senate candidates while the NRCC aids Republican contenders for the U.S. House of Representatives. It is difficult not to be impressed by the GOP's assemblage of organizational and technological tools. The NRCC, for example, carefully selects 100 to 120 target House districts each election year where Republicans are believed to have a chance to oust incumbent Democrats or fill open seats, and the committee's five full-time field representatives then go to work to recruit outstanding candidates, normally identifying willing participants in forty to fifty of the districts.[71] If the party feels it has located a particularly strong candidate in a "likely-to-win" district, and other key Republicans in the district and state agree, the NRCC will even back the candidate in a party primary.

The assistance, in both a primary and general election, can be considerable. Both the NRCC and the NRSC have collected voluminous records on House and Senate members' votes and activities. There is also a growing storehouse of postelection research, including studies of voters, nonvoters, campaign managers, and candidates conducted by national polling firms (D.M.I., MOR, and V. Lance Tarrance and Associates among them). The Congressional Committee sends a weekly publication called "News from the Other Side" to 2,500 newspaper editors in congressional districts with Democratic incumbents, contradicting the Democrats' views and offering a Republican alternative. The Republican organizations also help their candidates to solicit PACs and political consultants. An extensive and somewhat evaluative list of consultants is kept current, as is a roster of PACs that have donated to GOP candidates in the past. The party assists candidates in securing appointments with PAC decision makers as well.

Campaign management colleges are yet another regular project of the Republican National Committee. In operation since 1974, the college consists of a week's strenuous training in campaign techniques for twelve-hour-per-day sessions. About twenty "students" are selected to participate in each college, most of them slated to manage GOP House or Senate campaigns. All costs are paid by the Republican party, and the sessions can be held for new groups as often as once a month in an election year. In addition, the special projects division of the RNC sponsors a separate school for campaign press secretaries and more than a dozen three-day "basic instructional" workshops for all interested campaign staffers at sites scattered throughout the country. (On average, a workshop will draw about eighty participants.) The candidates themselves are not ignored, and the RNC, in cooperation with incumbent Republican congressmen, frequently brings candidates and prospective candidates to Washington long before the advent of the campaign to polish their skills and learn new ones.

The media division of the NRCC is particularly noteworthy, and its evolution is powerful evidence of campaign technology's potential usefulness to a party and its nominees. In 1971 the old broadcast services division of the RNC employed just three people and offered a very limited list of services. The new media division is so active and involved that it is difficult to summarize all of its programs. Audio and videotape "actualities" (i.e., tapes featuring the candidate) are transmitted to every radio and television station in a House member's district and are then used (normally unedited) by the unpaid media on news programs. The taping and transmission can be accomplished within a single working day, so that a congressman's activity in the morning can be highlighted on the six o'clock news. In some respects the NRCC media division has become a part-time Washington correspondent for many stations across the country.

Campaign needs, though, are the major focus of the media division. As was discussed in chapter 3, commercials for both radio and television are produced for a phenomenally low price (at least compared to what political consultants charge). An entire advertising package, counting salaries, overhead, and all production costs, can be delivered for less than the $5,000 contribution the national party is permitted to make to each of its candidates.[72] The media division is flexible enough to do as much or as little as a campaign needs, sometimes doing the entire ad package from start to finish, other times simply working with a candidate's political consultant or local agency to plan Capitol Hill filming. As of 1980, even the time-buying for many GOP candidates was done by the NRCC, saving campaigns as much as 90 percent of the normal 15 percent agency commission fee. Postproduction and editing facilities were also added in 1980, a measure that resulted in even lower media charges for GOP candidates. A major expansion of the division's scope occurred as well. While only 8 media campaigns were taken by the NRCC in 1978, almost 50 were handled in 1980, and 300 individual commercials were produced.

The most interesting part of the media division's program is the attempt to improve the image of the Republican party with television advertisements. FECA has indirectly encouraged the party to expend funds in this way by limiting its contributions to candidates, and the GOP has made a virtue of necessity, marketing its party label in a way that it hopes will have beneficial side effects for its nominees. After Watergate's devastation, in-house media research indicated that the GOP could not talk about issues effectively until its general image and credibility improved. Out of that finding came the "America Today" series, a group of well-targeted five-minute spots that centered around a "human interest" topic (such as the needs of the disabled or the cardiopulmonary-resuscitation method) and showed what individual members of the Republican congressional delegation were doing about it. "We picked as narrators congressmen who could project what we wanted to say institutionally about the party: that Republicans care about people," reported NRCC media director Ed Blakely. A service element was built into each spot, and viewers were urged to "write REPUBLICANS, Box 1400, Washington, D.C., and we will send you a free brochure telling how you can get involved and what you can do." Each ad closed with pictures of all the GOP House members flashed for a third of a second each as an announcer reminded listeners that "'America Today' was brought to you as a public service by the Republicans in Congress, 146 men and women working to improve the government and the quality of life of the people of this nation." Each stage of the development and production was accompanied by careful testing with focus groups, and a cyclical schedule of broadcasting (three weeks on the air, then two weeks off, then two weeks on again, and so forth), with different spots shown each cycle, was designed, similar to an advertising schedule for a commercial product. An extensive study by Robert Teeter's MOR firm demonstrated that the ads "succeeded in producing changes in the evaluation of the GOP."[73] Viewers thought that Republicans were more caring individuals than they had previously believed and, interestingly, the ads concurrently reduced viewers' favorable impressions of Democrats by 3 to 13 percent on rating scales for nine desirable attributes. The image polishing did not necessarily translate into more votes, but Independent voters, in particular, appeared more receptive to Republicanism afterward.

The same study found that another GOP series of commercials was much more directly useful in corralling voters. The "Issues of the '80s" spots, aired once "America Today"'s image making had run its course, gave standard Republican dogma on a host of topics, such as government spending and rising food prices. After seeing the ads (in the absence of countervailing advertisements, of course) a gain of 19 percent was registered for the GOP side.[74] This package led to an even more strongly partisan ad campaign first aired early in 1980, a $9.5 million series (briefly discussed in chapter 3) that attacked the Democratic Congress using themes from a Teeter poll conducted for the RNC. With the tag line "Vote Republican—for a Change," the thirty-second, sixty-second, and five-minute ads attacked the Democratic Congress and lampooned its leaders. One spot had an actor resembling House Speaker Tip O'Neill driving a car until it ran out of gas. Another featured an unemployed factory worker asking pointedly, "If the Democrats are so good for working people, then how come so many people aren't working?" The inspiration for the series, incidentally, was provided by the advertising package run by the British Conservative party in 1979, which helped to make Margaret Thatcher prime minister.

Many of the RNC and associated divisions' activities are paid for with profits from a remarkably successful direct-mail operation. Direct mail has brought the Republican party from near-bankruptcy (in 1975 the party raised just $300,000 of its $2.3 million budget) to a financial position unrivaled in its history. The direct-mail packages for all of the national GOP groups collected about $20 million in 1979, at a cost of only about 35 cents per dollar raised. The Republican party now has reliable lists containing the names of over one million donors, which are maintained by a 25 percent annual replacement (because of donor mobility, death, etc.). All the GOP's direct-mail programs are coordinated by the Stephen Winchell and Associates firm. (Winchell, a former employee of Richard Viguerie, was selected after his old boss refused to take the account, demurring because he wanted "to destroy the Republican party by drying up all the contributions to it"—or so charged NRCC finance director Wyatt Stewart.) The GOP has been taking full advantage of a provision passed by Congress in 1978 that gave "qualified political parties" the right to mail letters under the nonprofit rate of 2.7 cents a letter,[75] rather than the usual third-class rate of 8.4 cents.[76] The RNC has even experimented with direct response, combining television ads and toll-free numbers with credit card contribution pledging. After some strained negotiation in 1978, for example, the NRCC convinced former President Ford and Ronald Reagan to appear together in a sixty-second spot attacking the Democratic Congress and urging credit card contributions to the GOP by means of a toll-free number.

The NRCC plans to stay at its present level of direct-mail solicitation so as to reserve contribution potential for state party committees. In fact, much of the effort in the direct-mail division and in the other RNC subsidiaries is to transfer technology to the state level and strengthen state parties in the process. Twenty state organizations are already tied into the RNC's "mother computer" via long-distance telephone lines. Access to the computer is made available for a very small fee (about $7 an hour, plus a one-time $300 start-up fee), and each of the subscribers gains entry to a sophisticated data processing network called "REPNET" that contains five major programs for financial accounting and reporting, political targeting and survey processing, mailing list maintenance, donor preservation and information, and correspondence and word processing.[77] In another attempt to help the state parties (and to improve the GOP's congressional redistricting fortunes in the wake of the 1980 census), the RNC formed a political action committee called "GOPAC," headed by Delaware Governor Pierre DuPont, which contributed well over $1 million to state legislative candidates in 1979 and 1980 contests.[78]

There is no Democratic equivalent of GOPAC, of the advanced Republican direct-mail program, or of the peripatetic NRCC media division. In almost every respect the Democratic operations are pitifully inadequate by comparison with the GOP's; even where there is some visible activity, the effort is a pale shadow of its rival's work. The Democratic National Committee (DNC) and the Democratic Congressional Campaign Committee (DCCC) do schedule several dozen campaign training programs around the country, but the three-day seminars and weekend workshops cannot compare with the more extensive and informative Republican gatherings.[79] The Democratic congressional committee does not have the staff to be more expansive, with just nine full-time staff members in 1979 compared to the NRCC's fifty-five. The DNC's direct mail, even with occasional help from Craver, Mathews, Smith, and Co., is relatively primitive—sometimes using offset, with no address, poor enclosures, and little personalization. Thanks mainly to the difference in direct-mail sophistication, the Democratic party was able to give only one-fifth as much as its Republican counterpart to its 1978 U.S. House candidates and only one-seventh as much to its Senate nominees.[80] During 1979 and 1980 the national Republican party and its allied Senate and House campaign committees raised $111 million and gave $9.9 million (besides campaign services) to congressional candidates. The comparable figures for the Democratic party and committees were a paltry $18.9 million raised and $2.3 million donated to candidates for Congress.[81]

The technological and organizational gap between the two parties is certainly wider now than it has ever been, but there are indications that Republicans have been more willing and able than Democrats to experiment with new techniques during the entire age of political consultantship. Certainly this has been so since the 1952 presidential campaign, when the Democratic public relations agents were limited to purely technical functions while Eisenhower's agency managers had far more latitude and influence.[82] In the very same year the Republican Congressional Campaign Committee (the NRCC's predecessor) made $1.7 million in expenditures, and the Democratic committee spent next to nothing.[83] Robert Squier, who has worked closely with some officials of the Democratic National Committee, suggested that the

Democrats have not matched the GOP in campaign technology "because of a lack of money, a lack of leadership, and a lack of understanding how and why a party has to be involved in modern campaigning."

There are other factors at work as well. The pre-1980 Republican party, as the perennially disappointed underdog, had to try harder and had to be willing to experiment with new ideas since the old ways were obviously not enough for victory. The Democratic party had been more electorally secure and consequently had less incentive to build the party or change its ways. "The Democratic party as the majority party is simply not frustrated enough," surmised William Sweeney, executive director of the Democratic Congressional Campaign Committee, before his party's 1980 disasters. Many more of the Democratic elite had been in office as well, with the personal staff perquisites that accompany incumbency, making the strengthening of party staff somewhat less important than for office-hungry Republicans. Labor's COPE operations also proved to be a ready substitute for the party's weaknesses, and, until the growth of PACs, COPE's efforts could only be directly challenged with GOP resources. Moreover, it may be that the business and middle-class base of the modern Republican party naturally produced a greater managerial emphasis among its directors, many of whom are drawn from the same sector of society. Whatever the roots of its technological edge, it has proved to be a significant advantage to the GOP in electing its candidates, in strengthening itself, and in competing effectively with rival PACs and political consultants.

The Democrats' jarring defeats in 1980 may well shake the party out of its lethargy and spur it on to modernization.[84] There is little question that the Democratic party's potential is great if it chooses to exploit its base—RNCC's Wyatt Stewart boasted that he could apply GOP direct-mail techniques to the much broader based Democratic party and "do twice what the Republican party is doing today." Direct mailer Robert Smith, a Democrat, is harshly critical of his party's leadership because of the very point that Stewart makes, and he sees what the Democratic party's future *could* be with proper application of a technology similar to direct mail:

The Democrats have dragged their feet and dragged their feet because of a lack of leadership, and lack of commitment to building a huge "small donor" base, and a lack of understanding of the basic investment strategy involved in direct mail and what it can deliver. The Republicans by contrast have made a fortune. The Republicans represent 20 percent or so of the population and they have a huge donor base, hundreds of thousands of names raising millions of dollars. Democrats represent 40 percent or so of the public, and they have a very small donor base raising very little money. The Democratic party should raise almost $100 million a year. That's their potential.

While the GOP has made the best of the circumstances, both political parties have been buffeted by a number of forces unleashed by new campaign finance laws and the technologies of political consultants. The mushrooming corporate PAC movement, ironically spurred by labor's legislative maneuverings, has matched COPE and benefited mainly incumbents. With a contribution limit five times greater than that of individuals and equal to the parties, a political action committee rivals the party for the affections of candidates, and if the PAC is ideological and organization oriented, it can become a sort of surrogate party. A further expansion of PAC activity and influence, through provision of new services and the exercise of the independent expenditure provision, is almost guaranteed.

While FECA was strengthening PACs it was weakening the parties, despite its objectives to the contrary. Competition between the parties and its nominees over scarce funds, reduction of volunteer participation, and a boost to star politics were all unintended but demonstrable effects of FECA. Political consultants were among the biggest gainers, becoming more necessary than ever for long-range planning and efficient management of larger staffs, and direct-mail fund raising from small donors became one of the most sought-after technologies. Not just FECA but also the weakened parties themselves gave political consultants their modern opening, and they used the opportunity to hawk techniques that replaced the party as the middleman between candidate and voter. A few independent consulting professionals are strongly supportive of the party system, but most are indifferent or even hostile to it, frequently running their client-candidates against or around the party label and also assisting the development of PACs' competitive facilities. Whereas most consultants are nominally loyal to one or the other party for business reasons, a growing number are proud switch-hitters, mercenaries available for hire to the first or top bidder. Others, for ideological reasons, are openly contemptuous of the parties, opposing a flexible party system in toto. However, one of the parties has begun to fight back; the Republicans are showing the way, and their shrewd and sophisticated moves suggest one solution to the democratic and ethical dilemmas posed by the rise of political consultants and the new campaign technology. It is to these vital considerations that chapter 6 turns.

NOTES

1. This anticorporate PAC provision was one of the only parts of the Federal Corrupt Practices Act of 1925 (43 Stat 1070) that is considered to have accomplished its purpose. See *National Journal*, October 23, 1976, p. 1515, and April 10, 1976, p. 470; also *Congressional Quarterly Weekly*, January 10, 1976, pp. 46–49.

2. 86 Stat 3(1971); 88 Stat 1263 (1974); 90 Stat 475 (1976).

3. See Edwin M. Epstein, "An Irony of Electoral Reform: The Business PAC Phenomenon," *Regulation* (May/June 1979): 35–41.

4. Ibid. PACs had given only about $22 million in the 1976 congressional elections.

5. See *The Washington Post*, May 18, 1979.

6. See *The San Francisco Examiner*, July 23, 1979. Eleven different categories of PACs are recorded and registered by the California Fair Political Practices Commission. The most generous PACs in 1978 were those of realtors, teachers, growers, and doctors.

7. See *National Journal*, December 22, 1979, pp. 2142–2145; and *The Los Angeles Times*, August 5, 1979. These religious PACs have not been nearly as active as their leaders once projected they would be. See *Congressional Quarterly Weekly*, September 6, 1980, pp. 2627–2634.

8. *The Washington Post*, May 20, 1980.

9. *The Washington Post*, February 3, 1979.

10. CFR had between eighteen and thirty full-time personnel, plus occasional contracts with political consultants. Reagan was CFR's chairman until he formally announced his presidential candidacy in 1979.

11. Only 6 percent of Dole's PAC money and 11 percent of Bush's went directly to candidates. Out of CFR's $2.5 million budget, about $1.9 million was spent for its own operation.

12. The spending limits only apply to candidates who accept federal matching funds, but almost all presidential contenders have necessarily done so.

13. See Paul M. Weyrich, "The New Right: PACs and Coalition Politics," in Michael J. Malbin (ed.), *Parties, Interest Groups, and Campaign Finance Laws* (Washington: American Enterprise Institute, 1980), pp. 68–81.

14. *National Journal*, October 23, 1976, p. 1514, and January 5, 1980, p. 20. See also *Congressional Quarterly Weekly*, December 24, 1977, p. 2652.

15. *National Journal*, January 21, 1978, pp. 88–92.

16. See Institute of Politics, JFK School of Government, Harvard University, "An Analysis of the Impact of the Federal Election Campaign Act, 1972–78" (Cambridge, Mass.: May 1979).

17. June 7, 1979, edition.

18. *The Washington Post*, July 24, 1979. The energy PACs registered a sevenfold increase in number from 1976 to 1979, and gave an estimated $6 million to congressional candidates between 1977 and 1980. See Alan Berlow and Laura B. Weiss, "Energy PACs: Potential Power in Elections," *Congressional Quarterly Weekly*, November 3, 1979, pp. 2455–2461.

19. *The Washington Post*, July 23, 1979.

20. See *National Journal*, April 10, 1976, p. 475.

21. William T. Mayton, "Nixon's PACs Americana," *The Washington Monthly* (January 1980), pp. 54–57.

22. See *The Washington Post*, February 2, 1979. For example, the 1979 House freshmen had received $3.3 million in PAC money during their 1978 bid for office, an average of about $43,000 each. The chairman of House committees had only gotten an average of $45,000 apiece, indicating more targeting of PAC money to likely newcomers. See also *Congressional Quarterly Weekly*, November 22, 1980, pp. 3405–3409. Moreover, with the GOP takeover of the U.S. Senate and the addition of nearly three dozen Republicans in House seats in 1980, Republicans will begin to benefit more substantially from lingering PAC bias toward incumbents.

23. See the example of energy PACs in Berlow and Weiss, "Energy PACs," pp. 2455–2461.

24. As reported in *The Washington Post*, May 21, 1979. Mathias would not name

the PAC, but it was identified by other sources as that of the Bristol-Myers Company, a pharmaceutical firm.

25. The GOP has been more diligent in this, as in most campaign matters. See *The Washington Post*, October 1, 1978.

26. National Republican Congressional Committee, [hereafter NRCC], *Financing Republican Congressional Campaigns* (Washington, D.C., 1979), pp. 205–209. See also *Campaigning Reports*, vol. 2, no. 3 (February 7, 1980): 9–10.

27. Institute of Politics, Harvard University, "An Analysis of the Impact of the Federal Election Campaign Act," pp. 4–8.

28. As quoted in *Campaigning Reports*, vol. 1, no. 6 (August 9, 1979): 10.

29. See *National Journal*, February 9, 1980, pp. 229–231.

30. This partisan financial pattern had been reversed in 1964, when the Johnson/Humphrey Democratic ticket collected 69 percent of their $9 million total in sums over $500. The Goldwater/Miller team, fueled by a superb direct-mail program, spent over $16 million, only 28 percent of which was given in amounts over $500. See Herbert E. Alexander, *Financing the 1964 Election* (Princeton, N.J.: Citizens' Research Foundation, 1966), pp. 84–85.

31. Xandra Kayden, *Campaign Organization* (Lexington, Mass: D.C. Heath, 1978), p. 163.

32. Institute of Politics, Harvard University, "An Analysis of the Impact of the Federal Election Campaign Act," pp. 1–3.

33. Ibid., pp. 1–19.

34. *National Journal*, March 15, 1980, p. 439.

35. *The Washington Post*, September 30, 1979.

36. See *Congressional Quarterly Weekly*, February 23, 1980, pp. 569–571.

37. 96 S.Ct. 612 (1976) or 424 U.S. 1 (1976).

38. Kayden, *Campaign Organization*, pp. 171–172.

39. *National Journal*, February 9, 1980, pp. 229–231.

40. NRCC, "Campaign Manager's Study: 1978 Post-Election Research" (Washington, D.C., 1979), pp. 2, 5.

41. Institute of Politics, Harvard University, "An Analysis of the Impact of the Federal Election Campaign Act," pp. 1–3.

42. NRCC, "Campaign Manager's Study," pp. 2, 4.

43. There are a number of similar groups in both parties. See *The Washington Post*, March 12, 1979, and April 22, 1979; also *National Journal*, May 23, 1981, pp. 920–925.

44. See *The Washington Post*, February 25, 1979. For a concert admission payment to be matchable, the FEC requires that the ticket be purchased in advance with the buyer's name and address recorded. On occasion, this has somewhat reduced the matchable proportion of concert funds, but naturally campaigns take pains to fulfill all requirements for as many participants as possible.

45. There are loopholes for a candidate. He can notify the FEC in writing twenty-five business days prior to a primary that he does not want a certain contest to count against his eligibility. Or if a candidate secures 20 percent or more of the vote in a primary after his funding cutoff, the flow would be resumed. Primaries occurring on the same day, incidentally, are counted as one, and the results added together.

46. See *National Journal*, February 23, 1980, p. 313; and *Time*, December 24, 1979.

47. See *Congressional Quarterly Weekly*, January 5, 1980, pp. 33–34. After President Carter signed it into law (with some reluctance since it potentially barred contributions to his campaign by all federal workers), HR5010 became officially recorded as Public Law 96–187.

48. Federal Election Commission, U.S., "Campaign Guide for Presidential Candidates and Their Committees" (Washington, D.C.: FEC, October 1979), pp. 9, 36–37.

49. See *National Journal*, June 23, 1979, pp. 1044–1046, and May 23, 1981, pp. 920–925. For the 1980 elections alone, 112 PACs and individuals spent $16.2 million in independent expenditures.

50. See *The Washington Post*, April 9, 1980.

51. See Nathan J. Muller, "Political Advertising in National Magazines," *Practical Politics*, vol. 2, no. 1 (November/December 1978): 16–20, 28.

52. See *The Washington Post*, August 17, 1979; *Campaigning Practices Reports*, vol. 7, no. 5 (March 17, 1980): 2–4; and *Congressional Quarterly Weekly*, November 22, 1980, pp. 3405–3409.

53. Internal memorandum from AMPAC Executive Director William L. Watson dated June 28, 1978. Also the author's personal correspondence with Donald P. Wilcox, general counsel of the Texas Medical Association, dated December 18, 1979, and with Peter B. Lauer, assistant director of AMPAC, dated December 27, 1979. The staff and members of the board were required to submit a signed certification of noncontact and a promise to refrain from making any contact with any campaign unless specifically authorized by AMPAC.

54. A major court suit was filed in 1979 by liberal and conservative activists challenging this ruling and others: *Mott, et al. v. FEC*, U.S. District Court for the District of Columbia, 79–3375, December 17, 1979. See *National Journal*, December 22, 1979, p. 2165. However, the suit was unsuccessful and dismissed in July 1980.

55. *The Washington Post*, April 4, 1980, The ruling was requested by the Democratic party with NCPAC's campaigns in mind.

56. See the *Congressional Quarterly Weekly* Special Report, "The 1980 Elections," Supplement to vol. 38, no. 8 (February 23, 1980): 457, 462, 466.

57. See, for example, David Adamany's commentary on campaign finance in Malbin (ed.), *Parties, Interest Groups, and Campaign Finance Laws*, pp. 319–320.

58. Data from the University of Michigan's Center for Political Studies. In 1952, 47 percent of the population identified with the Democratic party, 27 percent with the Republican party, while 22 percent were Independent and 4 percent were classified as apolitical. By 1978 Democrats were down to 39 percent, Republicans to 21 percent, with Independents nearing a plurality (at 38 percent) and apoliticals at 2 percent.

59. Walter DeVries and Lance Tarrance, *The Ticket-Splitters: A New Force in American Politics* (Grand Rapids, Mich.: William B. Eerdsman, 1972). The numbers and proportion of ticket-splitters in the population have almost certainly risen since the DeVries and Tarrance study.

60. See *Congressional Quarterly Weekly*, December 29, 1979, pp. 2957–2965. In 1980, 76 percent of the GOP national convention delegates and 71 percent of the Democratic delegates were either elected in primaries or bound to reflect the results.

61. Robert Agranoff, ed., *The New Style in Election Campaigns* (2nd ed.) (Boston: Holbrook, 1976), p. 15.

62. Stanley Kelley, Jr., *Professional Public Relations and Political Power* (Baltimore: Johns Hopkins, 1956), p. 62.

63. See Arthur Schlesinger in *The Wall Street Journal*, May 10, 1979.

64. Joseph Napolitan, *The Election Game and How to Win It* (New York: Doubleday, 1972), pp. 17–18.

65. Ibid.

66. See ibid., pp. 162–208. Shapp lost the general election that year but came back to win the statehouse in 1970.

67. Telephone interview with Nicholas Tortorello, January 21, 1980.

68. Sanford L. Weiner, "The Role of the Political Consultant," in Agranoff (ed.), *The New Style in Election Campaigns*, p. 59.

69. Telephone interview with Harvey Englander, senior associate of Butcher-Forde, January 21, 1980. See also Nora B. Jacob, "Butcher and Forde: Wizards of the Computer Letter," *The California Journal*, vol. 10 (May 1979): p. 163.

70. See *National Journal*, January 21, 1978, p. 91; and *Congressional Quarterly Weekly*, October 23, 1976, p. 3028, and December 24, 1977, p. 2650.

71. *National Journal*, January 5, 1980, pp. 21–24.

72. If the total cost exceeds $5000, or if the NRCC has already made a monetary contribution to a campaign, then the candidate merely reimburses the NRCC for any amount above the $5000 maximum. A precise, computerized accounting of all work performed by media division personnel is updated daily, and, to avoid illegal extension of credit to candidates, accounts are payable in advance or on delivery of the advertisements.

73. The MOR study consisted of 1200 original interviews and 506 follow-ups, and was conducted from December 1977 to January 1978. "America Today" 's audience recall

was unusually high for a show of its nature (40 percent), and 73 percent of those who watched termed it "worthwhile." NRCC, "Political Advertising on Television: A Review" (Washington, D.C. October 1979), pp. 8–9; and NRCC, "1978 Congressional Post-Election Survey" (Washington, D.C., 1979), pp. 38–39.

74. NRCC, "Political Advertising on Television," pp. 19, 25.

75. The nonprofit rate was later raised first to 3.1 cents and then (as of July 1980) to 3.5 cents.

76. See *The Washington Post*, April 22, 1979. The 5.7 cents difference is, in effect, a government subsidy to the parties. There has also been controversy as to what constitutes a "qualified party," with all manner of political groups trying to cash in on the provision.

77. The five components of REPNET mentioned here are: CPA (Computerized Political Accounting System); ADONIS (Automated Donor Information System); UNICORN (Universal Correspondence and Word Processing); MAIL CALL (Mailing List Maintenance System); TARGET 20 (Political Targeting and Survey Processing System).

78. See *Campaigning Reports*, vol. 1, no. 5 (July 26, 1979): 1; and also vol. 2, no. 1 (January 10, 1980): 1.

79. *National Journal*, January 5, 1980, pp. 21–24.

80. See *National Journal*, May, 23, 1981, pp. 920–925.

81. See *Campaign Practices Reports*, vol. 7, no. 5 (March 17, 1980): 6. See also *National Journal*, September 27, 1980, pp. 1617–1621.

82. Stanley Kelley, Jr., *Professional Public Relations and Political Power*, pp. 144–160.

83. Ibid., p. 216.

84. The drubbing administered Democrats at the polls in 1980 did seem to produce at least one salutary effect for the Democratic party: a consensus among its leaders and officeholders that the party needed to acquire some of the new campaign technologies, especially a direct mail fund-raising program. Democrats took their first major steps toward organizational and financial modernization in 1981, although the task will not be quickly or easily accomplished. See *National Journal*, May 23, 1981, pp. 920–925.

Chapter 6

Conclusion: Political Ethics and Representative Democracy

Political consultants may be little different from people in all walks of life who, knowing that honesty is the best policy, often settle for second best. There is, however, a crucial qualitative distinction between the tax fiddlings of a restaurateur and the finaglings of an individual who affects the democratic process in a vital and intimate way. Frequently over the course of this book, new and disturbing questions have arisen about the ethics and democratic consequences of political consultants. Why are the ethical standards of the consulting profession so "flexible"—and what, if any, are those standards? What is it that permits all other aspects of campaigns and elections—indeed, all other American institutions—to be carefully scrutinized in the press while consultants emerge from press commentaries unscathed or even anointed? How have consultants affected the electoral system and the kind and quality of representation in American government? These queries, and others like them, will be addressed by examining them first in the context of the consulting profession generally, then within the confines of each of the technological specialties that have been the special focus of this book (polling, paid media, and direct mail). Finally, the implications of these findings for the American party system will be discussed and some remedies for the ills that abound will be proposed.

Conclusion

The Consulting Profession's Ethical Code and Democratic Effects

At least since the days of Cicero, who called campaigning "a most wretched custom," electioneering has had a double-edged reputation. On the one hand it has been viewed as a necessary and even somewhat useful part of democratic ritual. On the other hand it has been seen as a seedy and self-advertising public spectacle that frequently attracts to its banner ignoble and untrustworthy denizens of society's darkest corners. Consultants often appear as innocent and as devious as the electioneering skills they market. There is nothing inherently evil about their new techniques; any technology of itself is morally neutral and can be used for good or ill. But that truism suggests precisely the question that must be asked: How are consultants *using* their tools and their prestige, and what standards guide them?

As one might expect, the consultants answer the question quite differently than their critics. On two separate occasions, generalist consultant Joseph Napolitan defended his peers and stated the ethical case for his profession:

If we were to work on just one campaign for just one candidate and felt very strongly about it, we might be more tempted to pull out all the stops and win at any cost. But when you know that you've got to come back the next year, and the years after that, you know that you must survive on your reputation, and if the reputation stinks you're not likely to get clients, or at least the kind of clients you want.[1]

If word gets around that you're not ethical, you can get wiped out of this business very quickly. Sure, there are some whores in our business—I could name one or two, but no more, and probably many fewer than in any other semiprofessional service industry.[2]

Certainly, a blot of campaign scandal on the record can be extremely costly to a political consultant. Generalist Roy Pfautch, for example, was an unindicted co-conspirator in one of the Watergate spin-offs, the so-called "Townhouse operation" that funneled laundered money to certain Nixon-supported candidates. As a result, Pfautch paid six-figure legal fees, faced grand juries in several states, and was a focus of devastatingly bad national publicity. He was dropped by many, though not all, of his political clients.[3] "When the going gets tough, the politician gets going—the other way," Pfautch notes ruefully, although one can hardly blame any candidate for avoiding a tie-in to

Watergate. The lesson for other political consultants came across loud and clear. Moreover, because most consultants are well-known across state boundaries, they can expect adverse national publicity if they violate the law or engage in any unethical conduct even in a single local election. Scandal can put a dent, at the least, in a consultant's business, if not eliminate it altogether.

Others dispute the contention that consultants adhere closely to a set of ethical guidelines merely out of fear of ruin. Political professionals are, after all, businessmen and electoral junkies who keenly desire profit and victory, and as human beings, they are as susceptible as anyone to the belief that they will not be caught, that "It won't happen to me." The price of defeat to the professional is not to be underestimated either. Lost future accounts and a damaged reputation are just two of the costs that accompany losing. As a consequence, "anything goes" is the standard that many professionals actually accept. William Butcher of Butcher-Forde believes that it is fair to use any material or take any approach that is not "in bad taste," leaving the definition to be determined on a case-by-case basis.[4] Another consultant opposes a formal and specific code of ethics for the profession, suggesting that the Ten Commandments should suffice.[5] This sort of flippancy, and the avoidance of ethical challenge with a win-at-all-costs philosophy, will be encouraged all the more if a nascent trend in California becomes a new industry standard. Some contracts in the state that spawned and nurtured political consulting have featured a clause offering a bonus to a firm if the client wins the election.[6]

Given the underlying sentiments for success and profit that all consultants share to some degree, it is not surprising that few of them are willing to criticize one another publicly or declare any electoral practice off-limits, or even undesirable. While airing their jealousies freely in private, professionals are far more circumspect in public, rarely criticizing another consultant, whatever the offense. Consultants are blood-brother members of the same fraternity, and while they may carp and make snide remarks about one another in the bosom of the family, the norms of professionalism will cause them to close ranks whenever under attack or when their livelihood is threatened.

This principle is institutionally demonstrated by the halfhearted attempt of the consultants' trade association, the American Association of Political Consultants (AAPC), to devise a code of ethics. In 1971, two years after the AAPC was founded, the members began to debate the need for some sort of statement on professional ethics.[7] For several additional years the AAPC dragged its feet, the principals unable to agree on even a loose set of guidelines. Finally in September 1975 a compromise code was adopted, and a revised version is reproduced in table 6–1. As a brief glance will indicate, the standards are general and flexible, which is not unusual for an ethics' code. Some of the clauses are taken directly or are paraphrased from the Code of Fair Campaign Practices (drawn up by the Fair Campaign Practices Commission) and the "Code of Ethics for Political Campaign Advertising" of the American Association of Advertising Agencies (first adopted in February 1968). Most of the clauses have no practical impact whatsoever. Violations of the campaign laws (clause 1) or failure to pay one's bills (clause 14) are, of course, illegal and prosecutable offenses with or without the AAPC code, and the pledge to work for equal voting rights (clause 2) and the Carteresque promise to appeal to the good and decent virtues in the American people (clause 3) are pleasant window dressings. Other sections, such as the fifth clause (catering to the press) and the twelfth clause (catering to each other), are clearly in the consultants' own interests. Some of the toughest provisions have escape hatches. The professionals must only *urge*, not require, their clients to sign a Fair Campaign Practice Code (clause 6), and consultants boldly promise never to lie *intentionally* about their clients or the opposition (clause 10). Primarily, however, the standards are blatantly violated. Only *overt* appeals to prejudice (clause 4) are avoided in practice, mainly because they do not work, but subtle shadings of bias (slogans such as "You Know Where He Stands") are welcome weapons in the campaign arsenal. If clause 7 on the confidentiality of client information were not widely violated, this book, for one, could never have been written. Anyone who follows politics sadly recognizes how frequently "personal and scurrilous attacks" (clause 8) are the basis of one or both sides' campaigns, and some of these efforts have borne the unmistakable fingerprints of political consultants. Clause 9 on the documentation of campaign charges is flagrantly disregarded by all but a handful of professionals, most of whom rely almost entirely and unquestioningly on their clients' staffs for information. One almost blushes upon reading clause 13; there surely must be few professions that can match political consulting in kind and quantity of conflicts of interest, from working both sides of the party fence simultaneously to accepting favors from elected exclients to contracting with lobby groups to influence the same men and women one has helped to elect.

TABLE 6–1

*Code of Ethics of the American Association of Political Consultants
(adopted September 1975)*

1. We pledge to observe the letter and the spirit of the laws and regulations on campaign financing and spending.
2. We pledge to work for equal voting rights and privileges for all citizens.
3. We pledge to appeal to the good and commendable ideals in the American voters and not to indulge in irrational appeals.
4. We pledge to condemn any appeal to voters based on race, religion, or national origin.
5. We pledge to be honest in our relationships with the press and to respond candidly to questions we can answer with appropriate authorization.
6. We pledge to urge our candidates to sign Fair Campaign Practice Codes and to abide by their provisions.
7. We pledge to respect the trust and confidence of our clients, and not to reveal confidential or private information either during or following our period of professional relationship.
8. We pledge to refrain from personal or scurrilous attacks on a candidate or members of his family, and to do everything within our power to prevent others in the campaign from making such attacks.
9. We pledge to document and report factually any criticisms we make against our opponent or his record.
10. We pledge not to disseminate false or misleading information intentionally, and to exercise special care to make certain all information disseminated by our campaign organizations is accurate and factual.
11. We pledge not to indulge in any activity which corrupts or degrades the practice of political campaigning and counseling.
12. We pledge to treat our colleagues with respect and never intentionally to injure their professional or personal reputation.
13. We pledge not to represent competing or conflicting interests without the express consent of those concerned.
14. We pledge to pay promptly, and in full, suppliers, producers, consultants, and staff members retained and hired by us, and to do whatever possible to assure that our clients make full and prompt payments to those who provide campaign services or materials.
15. We pledge to repudiate the support of any individual, group, or organization which resorts to practices forbidden by this Code.
16. We pledge that if any of us has evidence indicating that any member of the AAPC has willfully ignored or circumvented these pledges, we will fulfill our obligation to report such infractions to the President and the Board of Directors of the AAPC, who shall be empowered, after thorough investigation, to expel any member found guilty of violating this Code.

Source: Brochure published by the American Association of Political Consultants.

Most of the AAPC code is clearly too generalized and vague to be enforceable, but some of the clauses potentially could be—if the will to do so were there. Although the code provides for an investigating mechanism (clause 16), it has not once been invoked, nor is it likely to be. Notwithstanding the many unethical examples presented earlier, and many more not mentioned herein, it is an excellent bet that there will never be more than a token internal investigation of a code violation, if that much. One of the members of the AAPC board of directors, when presented with a number of hypothetical transgressions of the code, would only go so far as to say that "the AAPC would *probably* investigate in some fashion if a complaint was brought." Matt Reese, a former AAPC president, was frank when asked to explain the lax enforcement of the ethics code: "We're not concerned enough, I guess."

The AAPC's lackadaisical attitude about ethical matters is especially regrettable because policing its profession would be a valuable function for an otherwise desultory and lifeless trade association that presently is of little consequence to anyone. Moreover, as Charles Guggenheim correctly observes:

The AAPC is giving the impression that we are just perfecting the techniques of winning, and it doesn't matter who runs as long as they ask us to work for them. . . . They get together and discuss how to win, how to manipulate, when they should be getting together to discuss whether the process is ethical and right, and how to improve it.

A concerted effort to enforce its code would not be pointless posturing on the part of the AAPC, since any action the association might take against a consultant would give the offender a feared dose of adverse publicity. An invigorated AAPC might even be able to perpetuate Watergate's effect on campaign ethics. In the first presidential election after the Nixon scandals, candidates and consultants were on their best behavior, conscious that the eyes of the press and electorate were trained upon them, searching for any ethical missteps. For the first time since the Fair Campaign Practices Commission was formed in 1954, in 1976 no complaints were filed alleging unethical campaigning at the presidential level, and complaints in gubernatorial and congressional races were 40 percent below average.[8]

In the absence of an institutional watchdog such as an invigorated AAPC, political candidates themselves simply must be on their guard to a much greater degree than most are at present. Unfortunately, candidates and campaign managers are relatively unfamiliar with the new technologies and the consultants, knowing both mainly by their glowing reputations, a condition that produces extreme deference. Even without an advanced level of sophistication, though, clients themselves could prevent some consultant abuses by shopping around, contacting several professionals, and carefully weighing the alternatives and comparing the costs, just as they normally would for any competitive vendor. This is a more difficult practice to follow with national consultants, of course, because the demand for them is so great, but with second-level, lesser-known professionals, the suggestion is realistic. As in all other market transactions, *caveat emptor.*

A client should be on constant guard against several common unethical practices. Overselling is a trademark of many consultants. A range of services much wider than the professional's expertise is frequently offered, and clients would do far better in many cases to contract only for the service or activity that earned the consultant his presumably good reputation. Some consultants also take on far too many campaigns, vastly overextending themselves and promising far more than they can deliver effectively. One result is that a candidate who thought he would be getting a "name" consultant's attention and advice is shunted to subcontracted agents or less experienced associates (sometimes very junior, election-year hired hands). As related in chapter 1, George Bush devised one remedy for this; when he signed on media man Bob Goodman, he contractually specified that Goodman could take only a very limited number of other campaigns in 1980.

Occasionally, however, a candidate is a willing participant in a consultant sham of "overselling," agreeing to buy merely the professional's name for fund raising and promotional purposes. This practice is the industry's own form of prostitution and is baldly unethical. Candidates should also be alert for "recycled material." It happens all too often that a consultant will, with only minor additions and deletions, pass off earlier research or survey work as new material, conducted specifically for the current client (who consequently pays a full fee for second-hand data). Finally, one of Watergate's many lessons for candidates was a warning to remain fully apprised of one's employee's activities and to make it clear what sorts of practices are unacceptable. One consultant (with a perfect electoral record for a decade and a half) attributed part of his success to his phenomenal "guessing" ability. He was able to guess so well because, in addition to his intuition, he had used eavesdropping devices, informants on the opponent's staff, and visitations to the opponent's printer to barter advance examination of forthcoming tracts.[9]

Many unethical practices are clustered in the financial area. Many consultants are deliberately vague about their commission fee policies because the practices are so outrageous. Some firms mark up every single vendor's invoice by a generous percentage, occasionally including personal expenses (travel, etc.) in the markup. This mercenary padding of the profit margin at every opportunity is yet another way (on top of other fulsome fees and payments) that consultants increase the costs of campaigning. Markups are less offensive as long as the candidate is actually receiving the materials and services promised, of course. On rare occasions, a consultant's fee is nothing more than the loot of an unarmed robbery. Joe Napolitan cites the admittedly unrepresentative case of a Senate candidate who spent $700,000 and had virtually nothing to show for it.[10] Maryland gubernatorial candidate Francis B. Burch, the state's attorney general, was forced to go to court in 1978 to reclaim fees paid organizational consultant James G. Goff for promised work never produced.[11] U.S. Senator John Heinz of Pennsylvania actually won a $55,000 court-ordered refund from his agency, George Young and Associates, Inc., in 1979. Heinz's campaign had filed a suit the day after his 1976 election alleging that the firm leased "campaign headquarters" storefronts that were never opened, rented billboard space without using it, and wasted the campaign's money in several other ways.[12] All of the financial abuses are not designed to cheat clients; a few of them benefit candidates as well as the consulting firms. For example, the Nixon-publicized methods of "laundering" money still have their adherents. One media professional, Marvin Chernoff, claims to know of major Democratic consultants who have occasionally laundered large corporate "gifts" for candidates. In order to accomplish this, the corporation usually awards a lucrative and remarkably untaxing public relations contract to a consultant, who then offers his firm's services to the favored candidate at a low, cut-rate price. "Any media shop can launder money very easily—but we don't do that because we could go to jail very easily," notes Chernoff.

Consultants take care of themselves in other decidedly unethical ways. It is common practice for consultants to arrange, and expect, state or local government contracts once they help a governor or mayor win an election. "You win the race for a client in order to get service contracts," explained one proud political consultant. Some elected executives, sadly, are more than willing to reward their consultants with contracts and the like, but should they be shy about it, they can expect their agencies to ask. One major advertising agency in Salt Lake City, Harris and Love, offered outright to "eat" (i.e., scratch) a major billing cost for Governor Scott Matheson's 1980 campaign in exchange for a contract with the Utah state travel agency.[13] (Their ploy failed.) Other consultants use their association with the powerful to secure contracts with special interest groups, political action committees (PACs), and lobbies that plan to use the professional's contacts to meet their legislative goals. In other words, consultants sell pieces of the influence they have accumulated and the access they have to officeholders. Robert

Goodman, for example, secured the account of the West Virginia Coal Association after his agency handled the successful gubernatorial campaign of Republican Arch Moore in 1972. Most professionals, such as Chuck Winner, refuse to acknowledge the real and potential conflicts involved in such arrangements: "We've done a lot of work for congressmen over the years and have a good relationship with a lot of them, and now we're doing lobbying work in Washington. You'd say that's a conflict; I don't."

Those who disagree with Winner, however, think such sweetheart deals and influence peddling should be banned. Political consultant firms simply should not handle the accounts of groups that are lobbying officials the consultants have helped elect. Also worrisome is the practice of some politicians (including former President Carter) of keeping their campaign consultants on permanent staff retainer once in public office, while permitting them to take dozens of other political and private clients at the same time. The idea of image consultants controlling public policy as well as elections is distasteful enough, but the added problems of conflict of interest posed by such arrangements should be sufficient to prohibit them.[14]

Inevitably, one wonders why the reasonably vigilant and dedicated corps of national political reporters has not been more diligent in ferreting out instances of ethical abuse among consultants and in focusing more critically upon their activities. It is somewhat disheartening to those who have a romanticized view of the press to learn that, alas, journalists too are susceptible to sweetheart deals. A symbiotic relationship has developed between the press and political consultants, which has helped both groups enormously. As columnist Jack Germond explains, consultants are a major reason why reporters are able to cover campaigns more thoroughly and accurately than ten or twenty years ago:

The good consultants understand they have a continuing relationship with political reporters. . . . I've known John Deardourff for twenty years and I'm going to know him another twenty years and a lot of campaigns. John knows very well (and so do I) that I would not sell him out on something that he told me off the record, for example. Neither is he going to tell me a flat-out lie. Two years from now we are both going to want to trust each other again. It is a two-way street, and it has made a hell of a difference to both of us.

In return for the contacts and information, the press treat their valued sources with kid gloves. Beyond letting consultants off with little scrutiny, they help to fill their coffers by building their reputations and

sick, Sabato

press

writing and airing "gee whiz" stories about the wondrous wizards of political consulting. Even when the professionals lose, the press (if not the candidates) give consultants the benefit of the doubt, quoting their cumulative win-loss record, which allows for a few bad years.

There is a desperate need for the press to stop treating consultants as the gods of the political wars and to end their sweetheart arrangement. Only the press is in a position to reduce consultants to human size and to examine the damaging effects they and their new campaign technologies are having on the American political system. Only the press can publicize the shockingly unethical practices that are so pervasive. Political consultants, particularly the nationally recognized ones, are intelligent, capable, and highly skilled in the political arts, much more so than the regular staffers of most campaigns or—one fears to add—the average group of candidates and officeholders. Yet respect for their abilities and gratitude for their favors should not result in permission for them to go about their business absolutely unchecked. A democratic society cannot rely on the self-professed virtues of any group of men and women who work for private gain in the name of the public trust. Neither can it rely on elected representatives to regulate the behavior of a group to which they are especially indebted. Barring a major public scandal involving consultants that would have editorial writers and the electorate clamoring for statutory regulation of the profession, there is little chance of legislative remedy (even if a workable one could be devised).[15] Consultants have too much influence and too many ties with elected public officials who pass the laws, and it is doubtful that officeholders would be inclined to damage people whose skills they think they need to win elections. It is up to the press, then, to demand the contractual details of consultant-candidate arrangements, to equip themselves more fully to analyze and critique the consultant's work and technologies, to spotlight the relationships between consultants and public officials, and consultants and lobby groups, and to hold consultants more accountable for their actions when they ill serve clients or the public at large. Political consultants are public figures by their own admission and solicitation, and since they undeniably have a degree of power and influence, they deserve to be watched as closely as each of the other American power centers.

Wholly apart from the ethical questions that consultants' activities raise, the profession has wrought substantial effects on the democratic process over the years. One effect is the assist consultants have given to the homogenization of American state politics. Pollsters have long noted the trend toward less diversity and more uniformity in the politi-

false!

311

cal cultures of the American regions. As pollster Patrick Caddell commented, "I can see from the beginning of the decade when I started to the end of the decade that the regional differences—which are still there to some extent—have narrowed. The country has become much more homogeneous." By carrying new techniques and technologies from one place to the next in a kind of political cross-pollination, consultants have contributed to the homogenization, although it is hardly due to them alone. Television generally, other forms of communication and marketing, and industrialization have all had a major impact, for example. It is not that state political cultures have become entirely indistinct. Journalist David Broder rightly cautions, "You can go overboard on this. Campaigns in Wyoming still look very different from campaigns in Maryland." And, as media consultant Bob Squier notes, to fail to take account of varying state traditions and attitudes in an attempt to mass-produce campaigns is to court electoral disaster: "The style and the look, the feel and the message, all of it is different from place to place. People that are successful in the field are open to the differences from place to place, and people who lose are people who tend to approach every situation in the same way." Rather it is the medium of the message that is now standardized, that helps to shape the way politicians and people outside politics conceive of a campaign and what they expect from it. "Mom and pop" operations are dubbed likely failures, for example, while a candidate who advertises on television and sends direct-mail letters and bandies polls about is considered a real contender.

In addition to homogenizing state politics, consultants may also have made politics more competitive in some areas. Where one party had been weak and the other dominant, an infusion of new campaign technology from the outside has occasionally made a candidate of the weaker party into a winner both by substituting for the failures of his party and by emphasizing his personality over his party label. At the same time, consultants have helped to reinforce the political status quo by preferring incumbents to challengers in most cases—the win-loss record must be preserved—and by discouraging potential candidates who are early-on labeled "long shots" or "probable losers." (The labels, of course, are reinforced once no major consultant will take their campaigns.)

Whatever campaigns they do choose, political professionals have surely added to the spiral of campaign costs, not merely by charging exorbitant fees and commissions (the equivalent of which they all claim they save for their clients by wise decisions), but also by making enormously expensive technologies standard items in modern campaigns. Consultants have also lengthened campaigns. The Carter and Bush presidential examples are more than matched on the state level, where four-year campaigns for U.S. Senate and governor are not unheard of. When Donald Stewart, who had been campaigning full-time for an Alabama U.S. Senate seat since the summer of 1977, won a two-year term in November 1978, he opened his 1980 reelection headquarters one day after his election. (It did not help him, incidentally. He lost renomination in 1980.) Longer campaigns like Stewart's are encouraged by consultants because the new technologies, such as polling and direct mail, have long lead times; planning and organization can obviously be more thorough; and, most important, this solves the professionals' need for stable, continuous campaign work.

While the campaigns may be getting longer, their focus is becoming narrower. Consultants tend to like to run tunnel-vision campaigns, elminating all "dry," "extraneous" issues (the stuff of government) to zero in on one or a few glamour topics or, as consultant William Butcher calls them, the opponent's "fatal flaws": "If we find the opponent has a fatal flaw, we'll point it out relentlessly. We'll hammer at it over and over and over and over and over again. I know we've driven some people up the wall, even in our own campaigns. Because there is no overrepeating a fatal flaw."[16] Fortunately, the press can broaden the discussion and force campaigns to react, but this does not obviate a concern political scientist Stanley Kelley expressed even before the new technological wonders came on the scene. What does it mean, he asked "for our system of government to have political discussion increasingly monopolized by members of a restricted skill group"?[17]

The practices that concern us in our own country become an outrage when exported abroad. American political consultants' involvement in foreign elections is nothing short of interference in the sovereign affairs of other nations (and it is irrelevant whether they are invited to participate or not). The potential for trouble and misinterpretation is too great to permit this sort of activity to continue. After decades of CIA skulduggery and the congressionally sponsored U.S. confessions of foreign intrigue in the 1970s, the specter of the ugly American seems all too real around the globe. Beyond the unfortunate image of the cigar-chomping, behind-the-scenes Yankee manipulator an American consultant abroad inevitably calls forth, it is expecting a bit much for the citizens of another country, upon learning of a certain consultant's management of one of their politicians' campaigns, to divorce the consultant from his American clients, which might well include the president and influential senators. A connection will naturally be assumed, and the intimations have the potential of being quite damaging to American interests. After all, when an American citizen votes in another country's elections, he risks losing his citizenship. It seems only proper that an American's attempts to influence millions of votes in a foreign election and to directly interfere with another democratic country's most sacred tradition, its electoral process, should be similarly frowned upon and disciplined.

Polling Pitfalls in a Representative Democracy

There are a number of unethical and dishonest practices in the political polling industry, some widespread and others relatively rare but of concern nonetheless. Little-known polling firms have, on occasion, been suspected of wholly or partly manufacturing survey results (the infamous "instant poll"). Major polling consultants have not infrequently been thought to hedge or publicly misrepresent unfavorable survey results for the benefit of their candidates, and sometimes to refuse to give a full and frank analysis to a candidate when a poll contains bad news.[18] Commonly, also, pollsters fail to make a clear distinction between survey findings and their own opinions, relishing too greatly their position as vox populi. While efforts to use campaign volunteers as interviewers to reduce the costs of polling are welcome, some firms have been notoriously slipshod in the quality of volunteer training and supervision they offer and require. Less than vigorous volunteer training by Patrick Caddell's Cambridge Survey Research in New Hampshire in 1978, for example, has been held partly responsible by some observers for the misleading poll results that lulled U.S. Senator Thomas McIntyre into overconfidence and defeat. Similarly, Cambridge Survey Research and other organizations have been criticized for being "poll mills," producing prefabricated, "cut-and-paste" surveys that are not adequately tailored to local circumstances and varying campaigns.

Charles W. Roll, Jr. and Albert H. Cantril, both polling analysts themselves, cited some disturbing if exceptional illustrations of unethical conduct by political pollsters.[19] One firm, trying to outbid another for a Senate candidate's business, offered to produce two surveys for the price of one: an accurate poll for internal use and another more optimistic model for press and fund-raising consumption. Another firm made a habit of manufacturing low favorability ratings for incumbent governors, then threatening to release them unless its organization was hired by the state or campaign—a unique kind of blackmail by poll. In 1978, after a newspaper poll showed New York's incumbent U.S. Senator Charles Goodell running a poor third in his bid for election to a full term, a Goodell staffer reported being contacted by a pollster to inquire whether the senator would be interested in buying a survey showing him ahead. A businessman in a southwestern state considering a race for the governorship commissioned a "confidential" poll only to discover that the pollster had leaked the findings to a national party figure (who happened to be from the businessman's state) in order, apparently, to secure a contract with the national party.

While many categories of abuses have been ignored by national political pollsters, they have taken an interest in addressing the problems of confidentiality and partial leaking of surveys. The major political surveyors have all endorsed poll reporting standards devised separately by the American Association for Public Opinion Research (AAPOR) and the National Council on Public Polls, prodded perhaps by the threat of congressional legislation on the subject raised on Capitol Hill from time to time.[20] The AAPOR code insists that professionals must include in any press release the essentials about how a survey was conducted and inform their clients in detail about these elements at the same time. At a minimum AAPOR believes the following data should be disclosed by the pollster and reported by the journalist in full:

1. The identity of *who sponsored* the survey.
2. The *exact wording* of questions asked.
3. A *definition of the population* actually sampled.
4. The *size of sample.* For mail surveys, this should include the number of questionnaires mailed out *and* the number returned.
5. An indication of what allowance should be made for *sampling error.*
6. *Which results are based on parts of the sample,* rather than the total sample. (For example: likely voters only, those aware of an event, or those who answered other questions in a certain way.)
7. *Whether interviewing was done personally,* or by telephone, mail, or on street corners.
8. The *timing* of the interviewing in relation to relevant events.

Each of these pieces of information is crucial if a fair evaluation is to be made of a survey's accuracy and objectivity. Knowing, for instance, whether a poll's questions were asked of all eligible voters, or just likely voters, or perhaps the entire population (registered and unregistered) is essential for judging the results. Even a matter as seemingly unimportant as the exact period of time during which the interviewing occurred can make all the difference. For example, a survey of voters a week before and a week after the taking of the American Embassy hostages in Iran in November 1979 produced considerably different results for the Carter-Kennedy Democratic presidential race, with Carter moving from decided underdog to potential winner almost overnight. This is not an isolated incident; events have the power to change public opinion rapidly and drastically, and this has been proven repeatedly.

The Canadian Daily Newspaper Publisher's Association has suggested a couple of sensible additions to AAPOR's list.[21] The nature of the group doing the interviewing should be identified, since there is a professional world of difference between trained interviewers and a candidate's hastily and haphazardly assembled volunteers. Further, the method by which the persons interviewed were chosen should also be specified. Completely random samples are, of course, prohibitively expensive, so some brief description of how restricted the "randomness" was would be helpful. Another disclosure guideline is added by the Opinion Research Corporation of Princeton, which believes that an explanation of any special analytical or statistical procedure employed in a poll (such as multidimensional scaling) should be appended to a news release.[22] A final standard might be in order as well—one to insure the confidentiality of all respondents in any public disclosure of polling data. Most pollsters consider implicit the guarantee that a respondent's individual answers will never be personally attributed, but considering the tendency of some campaigns to mix general canvassing with nonrandom polling,[23] a formal commitment to preserving respondents' anonymity would be useful.

It is unfortunate that some pollsters, particularly lesser-known regional and state surveyors, are less than conscientious in complying with these standards, which are frequently violated in whole or in part. Not just pollsters currying favor with the press but also campaign workers who are trying to generate momentum are "partial leakers," the prime offenders of ethical disclosure. Clearly, AAPOR's guidelines and the others suggested here should be adhered to in the polling industry without exception, and should be strictly enforced by the press if not by the pollsters.

It is to the role of the press that any discussion about polling in a democratic society inevitably leads. Just as with consultants generally, the press must, in the end, be a significant check on the activities of private pollsters. And yet most reporting of surveys lacks the wisdom and sophistication necessary to distinguish image from reality for the general public. Observers in the polling field have identified a number of major errors in press reporting of surveys, most of which the press copies from mistakes of the pollsters themselves.[24] First, Americans are wrongly assumed to hold a firm opinion on every issue, when in fact many poll questions create public opinion where none existed before. The press also frequently fails to note whether a poll is surveying the opinions of the general population or of registered and likely voters, a crucial distinction in election surveys. Then, too, journalists seem to accept hypotheses as fact: "If the election were held today," for example, should be a tacit signal of unreality. Press coverage is too bare-boned as well. The exact wording of the questions, an absolutely essential item if readers or listeners are to exercise independent judgment about potential wording bias, is often deleted. (Even when the wording is given, the picture remains incomplete, since the order and substance of *previous* questions could well have biased responses to a later one.) Not just AAPOR-recommended elements are deleted; the potential for change in the figures, or strategies that could accomplish those shifts, are rarely discussed, and the relative intensity with which each side holds its view is usually ignored. The press seems to accept polling statements without question or probe. (What, for instance, does "we want a reduction in taxes" really mean, and with what acceptable consequences?) So too do journalists assume polling accuracy, when there is potential for error at every stage. Whatever the accuracy of the poll, there is an unfortunate reporting tendency to oversimplify and to overstate the significance of any single survey, a practice difficult to avoid, perhaps, in a business like news that lives from day to day. Polls are certainly ephemeral, and occasionally chimerical. To ballyhoo each new poll with a great flourish is to overinflate the importance of a single snapshot of an object moving in time; it is an institutionalization of today at the expense of tomorrow.

Part of the reason why the press is so keen to report polls is that many news organizations have made substantial payments to polling firms to get them, and newspapers and networks want to get their money's worth. There are disturbing sidelights to this arrangement, though. The news media are creating their own conflict of interest; they *make*, not just report, news by commissioning polls, and they have a vested interest in promoting their pollster and purchased surveys to the exclusion of other polls that may contradict their findings and interpretations. Neither is the arrangement free of ethical difficulties for the pollster. The media demands speed and lives under the pressure of absolute deadlines, and imposing these constraints on the polling process is dangerous. In order to fill the reserved spot on the nightly news, for example, the pollster may have to sacrifice quality to produce the data in time, then oversimplify the results to avoid running over the two-minute allotment on the program itself. There are also obvious dangers and conflicts of interest for both pollsters and journalists when pollsters work simultaneously for candidates and the media.

The proliferation of television network–pollster contracts for weekly or even daily tracking of the candidates' standings is especially worrisome. The constant drumbeat of horse-race statistics has damaging effects on the electoral process. Today's polling prophecies can become tomorrow's self-fulfilled headlines because they provide "objective" evidence, for instance, that a candidate is dead in the water—insuring that he stays there by drying up his contributions, if nothing else. Candidates usually dismiss unfavorable polls with the comment "The only poll that counts is on election day," but because of the usual relationship between fund raising and the perception of a candidate's chances, the comment is wishful thinking. Network polls also feed the "numbers game," helping to set up expectations for a candidate's victory margin that can convert an honest victory into a measured defeat. After examining the catalogue of ills that press polling is at least partly responsible for, an observer cannot help but wish that horse-race and scoreboard journalism could be abolished. The electorate, after all, is not betting on a daily double, but attempting to elect a president or governor or senator.

Polls, a wag might say, have a lot of depth on the surface but deep down they are shallow, and the sooner journalists accept the fact the better will polling coverage be. A new kind of journalist, well grounded in survey methodology, is needed if polls are to be kept in proper perspective and the pollsters themselves are to be checked. One auspicious development is the decision by major newspapers (including The Washington Post and The New York Times, as well as some regional journals) to develop in-house polling expertise. At least one journalist on each major newspaper should be able to conduct and analyze polls, and advise on the proper way to present and frame other pollsters' surveys. It also might be a useful idea to extend rudimentary instruction about polling to the citizenry in general, perhaps through senior-level high school civics classes and certainly within appropriate courses in a college curriculum. Any modern, discerning voter simply must be able to understand, interpret, and not infrequently ignore polls.

The American mania about polls in itself is somewhat worrying, suggesting some sort of societal insecurity that encourages almost daily temperature and blood pressure readings via surveys. The most disturbing aspect, though, is the tendency of public opinion polling generally, and campaign polling in particular, to reinforce a potential or incumbent officeholder's role as constituency delegate while weakening his role as governmental trustee. It is true that polls *can* have decidedly positive effects in a democracy. Roll and Cantril suggest, for example, that polling "can help uncover the common ground amid the din of conflicting claims, and help leaders find the bases of consensus" and "can provide a check on the claims of special interests which represent themselves as advocating the public interest." All the while, as they see it, polls are "enhanc[ing] the strength of the democratic process by improving communication between the leader and the led," uncovering items of public policy misunderstood or ignored by the public that leaders can then seek to address.[25] But these beneficial consequences presuppose strong leaders have won office, and campaign polling may do far more to assist weaker candidates who reposition themselves on any and every issue to pander to popular opinion. The predominance of polls in modern election campaigns has undoubtedly helped to insure that, more than ever before, candidates blow with the prevailing winds.

If the candidate becomes a slave to public opinion, then the former candidate once in office is likely to be subservient as well. After all, officeholders, in the natural course of political events, become candidates again as their terms near an end—if in fact they ever stop campaigning. Polls are the deceptively attractive means to retain popular support while attaining "pure democracy," the populist's dream. Some political pollsters welcome government by poll; one suggested that polling is a "very democratic" development "because the poll is much like an old town meeting where everybody gets a chance to say what they think." This novel adaptation of Huey Long's "every man a king" principle may be appealing, but it is wrong and unhealthy. Polls are not even good examples of pure democracy; they lack both the cues of leadership and the influence of rational discussion that are components of town meetings. A fundamental problem with polls is that the opinions of those who are misinformed, uninformed, or apathetic are given equal weight with those who are knowledgeable, concerned, and involved. The concept of a *representative* democracy incorporates an essential acceptance of *trusteeship* as a legitimate and necessary element of rational government in a diverse, multifaceted society. Polls test, and possibly deny, the legitimacy of the trusteeship doctrine. They are fundamentally populist, purporting as they do to represent "the will of the people" and implicitly defying those in power to contradict the people's collective judgment and wisdom.

In the prepolling era, when public opinion was more obscure, profiles in courage were less risky and more plentiful, but few candidates and public officials are bold enough today to defy the vox populi in such a clearly expressed and well-publicized form as a public opinion poll. As a sad consequence, the trustee officeholder may be nearing extinction, while the pure delegate—little more than a humanoid Qube system—multiplies and flourishes. What is true of the officeholder is even more prevalent among candidates for whom the election (also vox populi) looms above like the sword of Damocles. The nonincumbent, running without the responsibility of office, is especially tempted to rely on polls. The survey-manufactured positioning of candidates obscures differences between the contenders and their parties, and reduces the distinctions between the democratic alternatives, possibly frustrating the voters in the process and increasing nonvoting by suggesting "there's not a dime's worth of difference. . . ."

No one can reasonably assert that public opinion should not be a vital element in campaigning and governing in a democracy. But it should only be *one* element. The specifics of public policy must be designed within the broad framework of public opinion, certainly, and experience and investigation has clearly demonstrated that polls can reveal that generalized outline. But to suggest that the *details* of public policy should be shaped by an often ill-informed electorate, and to claim further that the details are accurately discerned through polling, is pure folly. Assuming that citizens understand and agree with the basic rationale of representative government—and it *has* been the American form of government for two centuries—it is doubtful whether the electorate would really expect to be consulted on more than the fundamentals of public policy anyway. Leadership, one suspects, is still the quality most admired, however begrudgingly, in elected public officials. Walter Lippmann's wise words on the proper role of public opinion powerfully convey the dangers of polling excess:

The notion that public opinion can and will decide all issues is in appearance very democratic. In practice it undermines and destroys democratic government. For when everybody is supposed to have a judgment about everything, nobody in fact is going to know much about anything. . . . Effective government cannot be conducted by legislators and officials who, when a question is presented, ask themselves first and last not what is the truth and which is the right and necessary course, but "What does the Gallup poll say?"[26]

An abandonment of political polling is wholly unrealistic and, even if possible, would sacrifice the beneficial uses that polls have. What is warranted is a lowering of the pollsters' voices, singly and generically, and a deflation of the publicity afforded polls to a point more in keeping with their real significance and usefulness, and in a form more cognizant of their numerous shortcomings. The pollsters can hardly be expected to limit their own livelihoods, or willingly acquiesce in the lessening of their influence. The responsibility and the challenge belong to the press, which has done so much to increase the prominence of polls and compound their nasty side effects, and to candidates and officeholders, many of whom need to rediscover the values and virtues of trusteeship government in a representative democracy.

Media Sales, Deceptions, Negativism, and Access

If I sell a car, I am not a bad guy. The minute you add one ingredient, the politician, all of a sudden it becomes distasteful or wrong. I am still waiting for someone to say why it is wrong. Why is it wrong to sell politicians?

By no means is media consultant Michael Kaye alone among media professionals in voicing this complaint. The respectable consultant is proud of his salesmanship skills and sees his trade as eminently honorable. Yet the ad man's selling instinct among political consultants is the most degrading and repulsive aspect of their profession. Adlai Stevenson was surely correct to claim, "The idea that you can merchandise candidates for high office like breakfast cereal is the ultimate indignity to the democratic process."[27] Electoral politics must not be reduced to barter or a grand-scale bazaar or a campaigner's New York Stock Exchange where tickertapes record votes. There are other qualities necessary to the functioning of representative democracy—rarified, dignified, even sentimental elements of which hard-sell makes a mockery.

Consultants certainly do not bear the entire blame for campaigning that emphasizes personality, gimmickry, and negativism. The unpaid media are just as wedded to the carnival aspects of politics, and politicians willingly embrace them. The voters deserve a share of guilt as well. Their collective lack of close attention to public affairs often forces the consultant both to package a candidate attractively just to catch the electorate's eye and to make the candidate's advertising package entertaining to keep the eye trained on the message long enough for effect. It is just this sort of knowledge that led Patrick Caddell to advise President-elect Carter in December 1976 that "The old cliché about mistaking style for substance usually works in reverse in politics. Too many good people have been defeated because they tried to substitute substance for style; they forgot to give the public the kind of visible signals it needs to understand what is happening."[28]

With advice like this, it is no wonder that campaigning seems to have degenerated into personality cults and the incessant search for star quality, name recognition, malleability, and media "sensibility." The obvious result is the replacement of workhorses with showhorses—politicians who enjoy running to the exclusion of governing. There is no better current senatorial illustration than Larry Pressler, Republican U.S. senator from South Dakota, who jumped from the House of Representatives after two undistinguished terms to the U.S. Senate at the age of thirty-seven and began an abortive presidential campaign literally only months after taking his seat in the upper chamber. He is considered to be one of the most media-conscious and adept officeholders on Capitol Hill, staying in constant, personal touch with newspaper publishers and radio and television directors all over his state, writing many of his own press releases, and always alert for any available "media event" opportunities—all the while producing little legislatively.[29] One well-researched *Wall Street Journal* feature article on Pressler concluded, "As a campaigner, he is superb. . . . But as a legislator, Mr. Pressler isn't much."[30] Pressler himself was content to comment, "I just want to be a good person," an answer that has apparently satisfied South Dakotans, who gave him a two-to-one victory in his maiden Senate run.

Consultants have been contributing to the darker side of politics in ways other than star promotion. Their marks have been detected on some of the more shameful modern acts of political deception. Campaigns were deceptive long before television, of course, and the deceptiveness of many television advertisements is in the eye of the beholder. The factual inaccuracies or exaggerations and the personal slanders that attend so many advertisements are not subject to flexible interpretation, however. Consultants have a clear, ethical obligation to check thoroughly the facts and claims of the candidate and his staff before producing radio and television commercials based on them. Mistrust of politicians and distaste for politics among people generally probably stems, in good part, from vile and misleading campaigns. If restoring voters' respect for the political system is not incentive enough, then consultants should remember the words of V. O. Key, Jr.: "Voters are not fools." Most human beings can sense honesty, and they respond well to frankness and truthfulness. Not many hard-bitten political professionals seem to accept this basic axiom. Matt Reese, addressing an AAPC convention of consultants generally well known to him, once remarked, not entirely tongue-in-cheek, "Voters are most likely to be persuaded when we tell them the truth. That's shocking to this crew, isn't it?"[31]

While deceptiveness cannot be regulated out of existence, a couple of specific practices can be banned. "Pseudonews" spots, made to sound like part of a news program and scheduled in the vicinity of news shows, are undoubtedly confusing and deceiving to some viewers and listeners, and should be expressly prohibited by the Federal Communications Commission or by individual stations. In addition, the current FCC warning against use of so-called "subliminal advertising," which employs consciously inaudible sounds or unseen images to subconsciously affect people's inclinations, should be strengthened and effectively enforced. Subliminal messages are already being used in other fields.[32] Some department stores in the U.S. and Canada have installed a device called a "black box" that emits an antitheft warning ("I am honest; I will not steal") rapidly and at a very low volume, mixed among the usual music offerings. Even though barely audible, the sound seems to register in the recesses of the mind, and, moreover, the subliminal suggestion may influence behavior under some conditions. One store chain installing the black box reported a 37 percent reduction in shoplifting and employee theft. Subliminals briefly became a subject of controversy in the 1950s, when the theater practice of flashing "Hungry? Eat popcorn" signs between frames of feature films was exposed. (The tactic was generally believed to have been dropped.) A subliminal message has also been used in at least one television commercial, a children's toy advertisement—the words "Get It" were momentarily flashed across the screen—but afterward the FCC issued a warning against further subliminals.

FCC warning or not, consultant Douglas Bailey "wouldn't doubt for a moment that subliminal advertising has been used" in campaigns.

In fact, the inventor of the black box, Dr. Hal C. Becker, reports being approached by local, state, and national campaign operatives and politicians, all with inquiries about the obvious political applications of his device—a projection of name or slogan could be done, for a start—and some with generous offers of money.[33] While a general receptivity to the subliminal message, as in hypnosis, appears to be a necessary precondition to actually influencing behavior, and thus a staunchly Democratic voter could not be instantly persuaded to vote Republican, subliminals could well prove to be effective with floating voters and those with very weak partisan links. Currently only the fact that the technology is not widespread probably prevents abuse, a circumstance that could easily change. Elaborate equipment can detect subliminal frames and audio tracks, and it is far from outlandish to suggest that the FCC should have it at the ready. For the moment, the FCC would do well to reemphasize and toughen its original pronouncement on subliminals and to prevent the airing of pseudosubliminals like this television advertisement for an unsuccessful Democratic primary gubernatorial candidate that actually was broadcast in Georgia in 1978:

CANDIDATE: This Is Nick Belluso. In the next ten seconds, you will be hit with a tremendous hypnotic force. You may wish to turn away. Without further ado, let me introduce to you the hypnogenecist of mass hypnosis, the Reverend James G. Masters. Take us away, James.

HYPNOTIST: (In strange garb, surrounded by mists) Do not be afraid. I am placing the name Nick Belluso in your subconscious mind. You will remember this. You will vote on Election Day. You will vote Nick Belluso for governor. You will remember this. You will vote on Election Day. You will vote Nick Belluso for governor. . . .

Just as deceptive campaigning makes voters more distrustful of politics, so too must negative advertising intensify the everpresent dislike of politicians. A voter always has five principal ways to express himself in a two-party election: voting for or against either of the party nominees, or not voting at all. The trend toward negative advertising has surely increased the proportion of the electorate that votes *against* rather than *for* candidates, and, even more disturbingly, negative ad campaigns have been consciously devoted to reducing voter turnout—a shocking and thoroughly reprehensible development in a political democracy. Voting participation in the U.S. has been declining steadily. While 63.1 percent of the voting-age population cast a ballot in the 1960 presidential election, only 53.9 percent did so in 1980. Off-year congressional elections have fallen from 46.3 percent participation in 1962 to approximately 34 percent turnout in 1978. And the 39 percent of eligible voters who trooped to the polls in presidential primaries between 1948 and 1968 had dwindled to just 24 percent by 1980.[34] As with the decline of political parties, the phenomenon of declining turnout has many causes, from the low participation registered by eighteen- to twenty-year-olds since they were enfranchised in 1971 to the lower spending limits imposed by the Federal Election Campaign Act (FECA). In some cases, negative advertising campaigns can certainly be added to the list. Television is, after all, a spectator's medium, not a participant's, and politics may often seem like just another game show, where the players compete and accumulate points to the passive delight or disappointment of those at home on the sofa. If negative ads produce revulsion about politics, a viewer can simply decide to tune out on election day.

Once upon a time, campaigns encouraged stay-at-homes to vote as a regular practice. As noted in chapter 1, the first paid television spot ever, in 1948 for President Harry Truman, was a get-out-to-vote message. In 1960 an often-broadcast Democratic advertisement featured John Kennedy reminding voters to participate, noting that "Millions throughout the world are denied that right." Almost all of Lyndon Johnson's 1964 spots ended with the tag line, "The stakes are too high for you to stay home," and one ad was blunter: "If it should rain on November third, please get wet." But many modern campaigns are far more on the model of the 1974 Ohio gubernatorial contest that pitted former two-term Republican governor James Rhodes against one-term incumbent John J. Gilligan. As one of Rhodes's consultants, Douglas Bailey, remembers the election setting:

That campaign was one where both candidates were perceived essentially negatively. There wasn't really any strong support for Rhodes and there wasn't any great support for Gilligan. So Gilligan made the mistake of trying to change people's minds about him. Rhodes didn't make that mistake. He just ran an anti-Gilligan campaign from the beginning.

And run a negative campaign Rhodes and the Bailey-Deardourff agency certainly did. Their shrewdest ploy was to concentrate Rhodes's negative commercials in the heavily Democratic Cuyahoga County (Cleveland area) media market. Democrats were puzzled by the tactic, since conventional wisdom suggested that one never wastes advertising dollars communicating with the other candidate's strong adherents. Once the results were in, however, the wisdom of the strategy became apparent. In the year of Watergate, when other Democrats were sweeping to victory in Ohio and across the country, Gilligan was narrowly defeated for reelection, to almost everyone's surprise. Cuyahoga County's returns were the key to Rhodes's upset. In 1970 when Gilligan had first won election as governor, he had received 67.2 percent of the Cuyahoga vote (and 54.2 percent statewide). In 1974, after the Rhodes commercial onslaught, Gilligan's percentage in Cuyahoga dropped almost 9 percentage points (to 58.4 percent) compared to a drop in the rest of the state of only about 5 percent.[35] Gilligan would still have won, though, if the voting turnout in Cuyahoga had kept pace with the statewide participation rate. While the statewide rate slipped only three-tenths of 1 percent, the turnout decline in Cuyahoga was a stunning 18.6 percent, a fall-off of about 105,000 voters from four years earlier.[36] The Bailey-Deardourff negative advertising package had succeeded in moving many Democratic voters to the ranks of the nonvoting by introducing doubts and damaging information about the Democratic party candidate. Strong Democrats were not going to vote *for* a Republican or even *against* a Democrat, so they exercised one of their other options and abstained in sufficient numbers to elect Rhodes by a wafer-thin 11,500-vote plurality in a turnout of more than 2.6 million.

It is not possible to eliminate negative advertising completely, nor is there anything wrong with a fair comparison of one candidate's background and ideas with another's. But negative spots should be as factual and informational as possible, and should be "contrast ads," that is, commercials that do not merely attack the opponent but also show specifically how the candidate paying for the ad is better. Whether the spots are positive or negative in theme, the time has come for greater reliance on the "talking head" format, however "dull" or "uncreative" it seems to media consultants. A new and reasonable requirement in political advertising would be the stipulation that a candidate must appear and speak in each of his commercials for at least half its length. And whenever time permits, the spots should be at least five minutes long. It is not that nothing of importance is ever said in thirty or sixty seconds. Rather, there is simply a greater chance of more information being communicated in greater depth with longer blocks of time. Talking-head spots have been shown to produce considerable audience recall, and five-minute commercials have low tune-out factors, so consultants cannot credibly argue that either of these reforms would affect their communicative effectiveness.

Until the time availability crisis is resolved, however, consultants cannot be criticized for producing brief spots. If the discussion about the problem in chapter 3 suggested one broad conclusion, it was that television and radio stations have far too much flexibility and freedom to decide the placement and, in essence, the length of political commercials. Stations vary considerably in their policies at present, some selling only short spots and others just long spots, some giving political ads good placement and others relegating them to virtually worthless slots. Such a haphazard, crazy-quilt pattern is unacceptable for the media aspects of the most important ritual of democracy. The public, not the stations and networks, owns the airwaves, and it should be able to reclaim legally a significant share of commercial time for its political education during campaign periods. Concrete, uniform, and generous standards are clearly needed, and only the FCC and Congress can provide them.

Ideally the American system would be modeled after Great Britain's. In the U.K.'s 1979 general election, for example, each major party was given five ten-minute television broadcasts sprinkled throughout the campaign, and lesser parties were allotted fewer slots based on the national percentage of the vote they received in the prior election. Moreover, each segment was broadcast simultaneously on all channels. While viewers could still turn their sets off (or, in the U.S., switch to cable TV), audience tune-out was held to a minimum. Furthermore, in apportioning time to parties instead of candidates, voters were reminded that they were making a choice between parties, not merely between personalities.

Regrettably, this sort of mandatory allocation system is no panacea. While it would be feasible at the presidential level in the U.S., it is much too simplistic to be applied at state, district, and local electoral levels. The constraints on stations include a fixed supply of air time, varying local conditions and market situations, and a multitude of candidates and offices being elected. For instance, many media markets reach dozens of congressional districts, while others incorporate only one or a few, so some stations would be deluged with demands for time and others hardly affected by a uniform guideline.

Other solutions, therefore, are required to provide more general relief. A study group at Harvard's Institute of Politics has made some useful recommendations to ease the media access crunch, and the FCC and Congress would do well to adopt them.[37] The group proposed replacing the advertising revenue lost when lowest unit rate political spots substitute for more lucrative commercial ads with tax deductions for the stations. Networks and stations should be permitted to deduct from gross income all lost advertising revenue during prime time and two-thirds of their loss during other times. The networks should also be required legally to release to their member stations each week of a campaign a reasonable number of sixty-second to five-minute segments (perhaps totaling ten to fifteen minutes in all), which would be for sale only to candidates. Such an allocation would more than double the current average and loosen the present tight quotas and rules established by stations to limit access. Finally, candidates need relief from television and radio's cash-on-the-barrelhead advance payment standards. Political spots should be scheduled prior to payment and paid for in installments as the campaign progresses and funds begin to flow in. These reforms are necessary not so much for the good of the candidates as for the edification of the voters. The free flow of information is an absolutely essential component of democratic elections, and the problem of time availability cannot be permitted to slow the flow to an unenlightening trickle.

Hate Mail and the Political Postal Barons

The ethical and democratic issues seem more clear-cut in the field of direct mail than in any other technology. Perhaps this is true because the technique is so extreme, almost a parody of modern politics and the embodiment of its worst excesses. Subtlety is most definitely not a part of the direct-mail process. When direct-mail copywriters decide to imitate an idea, they do not borrow; they steal, plagiarizing whole letters and specialty devices. There is nothing illegal about the widespread practice, since letters are not copyrighted, but at the least it encourages the crass and sordid side of the profession. Fraud is yet another rather blatant activity among some in the field. Money has occasionally been raised by mail for groups that do not exist and that serve as fronts for snake-oil artists. Individuals have also conned direct-mail firms by setting up fictitious groups and pocketing the profits raised for them. At a minimum a direct mailer has the responsibility to investigate thoroughly a client's legitimacy before signing him on. Even when a mailing is legitimate, few contributors are cognizant of how little of the gift actually winds up in the candidate or cause's coffers, due to costs and the mailer's fees and profits. A statement on each contribution form, estimating the proportion of each donation devoured by "administration," is clearly warranted.

Some list brokers are frequently dishonest too. Claiming to have a productive list, they give a small "random sample" for pretesting purposes that, just as predicted, yields a high rate of return. Upon purchasing and mailing the entire list, however, an organization discovers the return rate drops off sharply, and for a good reason: The most generous donors on the list comprised a very nonrandom random sample. The legitimate direct-mail firms have their own ethical problems with lists. It is outrageous that some mailers allocate to themselves greater rights of ownership to donor names than to their own clients. The amassing of endless lists of contributors of a particular political persuasion is frightening, and not simply because it concentrates such awesome power in one or a few individuals. There are legitimate questions of privacy at issue. People and their political predilections are bought and sold at whim by list brokers. The secret ballot may become a pleasant fiction when the entire population ends up pegged and computerized in a direct-mail contributors' bank (and a telephone canvasser's computer tally sheet). Some of the direct-mail groups so opposed to "Big Government" are beginning to have an unsettling "Big Brother" potential themselves.

Direct mail is often nothing more than mass-produced and lovingly refined hate mail. It is the standard industry practice to exaggerate broadly, just on or over the edge of lying. One direct mailer drew the fine lines of his profession's ethics: "I wouldn't quote somebody *completely* out of context; I wouldn't write something that was *blatantly* untrue." Direct mail is thus the conveyor of misinformation and the purveyor of oversimplification and superheated emotionalism, all of which are notoriously destructive to rational political decision making and a civilized political process. It is disturbing to realize how easily many of us are manipulated. Personalization, gimmickry, or a false "RESPONSE REQUIRED" stamp on an envelope can actually induce some people to make contributions, for instance.

The trivialization of politics (à la "wife letter") and the promotion of impulse and emotion over rationality and considered thought are but two of the upsetting side effects of the political direct-mail industry. A separate and stringent code of ethics for direct mailers alone, shunning emotionalism, personal attacks, and other unsavory practices, would be a welcome law-and-order brake on the Wild West free-for-all that presently prevails. Some remedy is a necessity, for as a blue-ribbon citizens' commission in Orange County, California concluded in 1977:

Some of these consultants regard a campaign as the equivalent of warfare, in which anything goes, short of overt violations of the law. . . . Deceptions and misrepresentations, especially unleashed at the last minute through computerized mailings, seem to have become, for some, a standard campaign technique.[38]

Consultants, Campaign Technology, and the Future of the Party System

Supporters of a strong modern political party system should be wary of embracing a romantic myth that has developed in the wake of the decline of party organization: that the old system of "boss control" (where it actually existed) was somehow far superior to the reformed politics of today. To be sure, the method of primary nomination and, perhaps, a rigid and complex quota representation of women and minorities may have helped produce some less than stellar presidential candidates, but, on the other hand, the party bosses gave the nation many a statesman like Warren G. Harding and corruption so vile that democracy was mocked. In fact, it is precisely because the parties are now reformed, more open and representative, that they are deserving of support and can potentially stave off their own degeneration, prevent the final triumph of personality politics, and serve as the basis for institutional stability and accountability in the American democratic system. One shudders to consider the nonparty alternative, as one historian has depicted it:

Political adventurers will roam the countryside like Chinese warlords or Iranian ayatollahs, recruiting personal armies, conducting hostilities against some rival warlords and forming alliances with others, and, as they win elections, striving to govern through ad hoc coalitions in legislatures.[39]

The parties need help to counter the ravages of political action committees (PACs), political consultants, and campaign finance laws. The worst way to go about providing assistance would be to limit further the amount of money flowing into political campaigns. Contrary to popular impression, there is not *enough* money available. Milton Shapp, pursuing the Pennsylvania governorship, once remarked, "I'm not trying to buy the election; I'm trying to sell myself!" There is a distinction, because (like it or not) political candidates are competing with thousands of products and hundreds of other concerns that crowd the average person's day. Granted, campaign costs have risen dramatically; the $540 million spent in all political races in 1976 was over 300 percent higher than in 1952, while the Consumer Price Index rose 115 percent and the electorate's size only doubled.[40] Yet television costs and the other expensive components of the new campaign technology easily account for much of the disparity, having risen dramatically in price and far outstripped both the CPI and most candidates' available resources.[41] When the half-billion-dollar 1976 campaign expenditure total is compared with the $33.6 billion spent on product advertising in the same year, the relatively low level of political spending becomes more apparent.

FECA, too, reduced significantly political spending at the presidential level. The 1972 McGovern and Nixon general election campaigns spent warchests of approximately $30 million and $60 million, respectively. Despite a 33 percent inflation factor between 1972 and 1976, FECA allocated the Ford and Carter general election campaigns just $21.8 million apiece. The democratic consequences were obvious, and at the local level fewer people than observers could ever remember were involved in the electoral process. Furthermore, FECA's limitations on donations have been a bonanza for incumbents, who can raise money in limited amounts far more easily than challengers and who are rarely beaten because of it.[42] FECA was intended to help open up the system, but instead it has significantly contributed to "tenuring in" incumbents and narrowing access to public office.

If the current system is to be changed effectively and usefully, then the severe restraint on personal contributions will have to be loosened. The current limitation of $1,000 on an individual's gift should be raised to $5,000 so that individual contributions are at parity with the PAC limit. No remotely honest candidate can be purchased or even compromised for that amount, and inflation alone has effectively reduced the worth of the current amount by almost half. Additionally, the national and state party committees should be permitted to give any party candidate at least several times the amount of money a single PAC can contribute, and tax credits for gifts to the party should be expanded. A Harvard Institute of Politics study suggested that the current 50 cents-on-the-dollar credit should be expanded to a dollar-for-dollar credit for the first $50 in gifts to political candidates *and* the first $50 given to a political party by each taxpayer, and that tax credits for gifts to nonparty committees (such as PACs) should be eliminated.[43]

Unfortunately, Congress (composed of 535 incumbents) has been trying to correct the obvious imbalances in the campaign finance system by taking precisely the opposite tack. The Obey-Railsback bill, which the House of Representatives approved in 1979 with the strong support of Common Cause, would have reduced the maximum PAC contribution to a House candidate from $5,000 to $3,000 per election, with a $70,000 ceiling on PAC gifts from all sources in a single year. (Even though Obey-Railsback did not apply to Senate candidates, the Senate feared eventual pressure to expand coverage to their own house and so killed the bill.) The impulse to reduce the influence of PACs is an understandable one, especially given the unsavory practices and occasional coercion of employees that has marked the mushrooming growth of political committees.[44] But corporate money and all other special-interest money has always found its way into the political system, and severe limitations on it will almost inevitably be frustrated. New clamps on PAC gifts would, one can safely predict, merely result in an accelerated rush toward independent expenditures and cause a proliferation of separate but closely associated PACs, each eligible to give the maximum amount. Because of the Supreme Court's decision in *Buckley v. Valeo* and subsequent court rulings, no legislative recourse to contradict these tendencies is possible. And there is simply *not* enough money in political campaigns as it is, and the raising of the individual contribution limit not only reduces the relative influence of PAC money but also increases the pool of resources available to candidates. This Madisonian solution is somewhat akin to the argument in *Federalist No. 10.* By encouraging competing interests to flourish, the resources of any single special interest become less significant.[45]

Probably it would also be useful to abolish the spending ceilings for publicly funded campaigns. Political scientist Herbert Alexander, among others, has long advocated the establishment of funding "floors" rather than the imposition of "ceilings," using public funds to guarantee that every party nominee has a minimum amount to spend in automatic federal allocations but permitting each nominee to raise as much as possible from private sources, with PAC and individual contribution limits prevailing.[46] The system is similar to those existing in Western European democracies and in Israel, and it has a number of desirable effects. It provides candidates with a guaranteed degree of access to the electorate, permitting them to reserve television spots in advance and to plan better with a stabilized flow of funds, and reduces their dependence on the aggregation of special-interest money. At the same time political involvement in the form of contributions is fully encouraged, and the system is more open and responsive because fewer limitations on giving will probably increase campaign spending and reduce the security of incumbents.

If public funding is eventually extended to congressional campaigns, the funds should be distributed through the political parties, which should be granted considerable discretion in the allocation of the money to their candidates. A portion of the federal subsidy should be retained by each state party for administrative costs and organizational activities that benefit all the party's nominees (including registration drives, canvassing, get-out-the-vote efforts, etc.). The parties should also be ceded the responsibility of certifying and determining the eligibility of candidates, and of handling much of the present paperwork of the less than efficient Federal Election Commission. Decentralization generally is an attractive solution to the problems of the overburdened FEC, and the state party organizations would be substantially enlivened and strengthened in the process. Most important, candidates would be tied more closely to the parties, particularly if the parties were given, as they should be, a certain amount of flexibility in distributing the public warchest—able to choose, perhaps, to reward a loyal party candidate with a bonus portion while disciplining a maverick or an "antiparty" primary nominee by reducing his share. Some of the states have already shown the way in strengthening party organizations through public financing. Of the seventeen states with public funds provisions, eight (Idaho, Iowa, Kentucky, Maine, North Carolina, Oregon, Rhode Island, and Utah) channel candidate subsidies by way of the parties, and a preliminary assessment of the consequences does indeed indicate that party organizations have been major beneficiaries.[47]

As far as the health of the parties is concerned, political consultants have, to this point, been part of the problem, but their skills and technologies may be exactly what the doctor ordered to restore parties to a salubrious and predominant position. The fact that most consultants are not strongly ideological and are already polarized (for business reasons) within the two-party system is helpful, and it suggests that regardless of their personal views about the efficacy of political parties, they will adjust to reality and accommodate to a party-centered system if ever it can be developed. Close inspection of the new campaign technologies strongly suggests that it *can* be developed by centering the most advanced technology within the state and national party organizations. Not only can the new techniques be marshalled on behalf of the parties, but the excesses of political consultancy can be trimmed, and more equal access to the treasures of technology can be guaranteed for all candidates of both parties once they are no longer reliant on the whim of professionals and the haphazard political consulting market.

In the 1950s the parties began on the right track, and were actually using public relations firms at a greater rate than individual candidates, sometimes contracting with an agency on behalf of the entire party ticket.[48] But instead of making full use of the expertise or establishing permanent ties, the parties began encouraging their candidates to retain their own consultants outside of the party establishment.[49] The parties thus helped to sow the seeds of their own decline, missing a golden opportunity to develop internally the techniques that would become so pervasive in less than a decade. After independent consultants demonstrated technology's political power, the parties finally began to realize what they had lost and what potentially they could have. Ironically, FECA, which had weakened the position of the party in so many ways, and consultants, often contemptuous of parties, combined to offer a backhanded opportunity that the down-and-out Republican party seized. Because spending limitations and ceilings impose planning requirements and reward centralized efficiency, the long-dominant power flow from state and local parties to the national committee was reversed. FECA assisted the nationalization of the federal party structure by introducing economies of large-scale production. Concurrently, FECA also specifically allowed for parties to hire consultants on behalf of a candidate or to provide similar, in-kind services of their own design.[50] Consultants, meanwhile, were so deluged with statewide and presidential work that they refused to take on most of the less lucrative U.S. House campaigns, leaving a major consulting need unfilled. The Republican party accepted the challenge of centralization and gradually began to bridge the gap in congressional campaigns.

The GOP itself has only started down the road of technological reform, and, of course, the Democrats have not really begun. Ideally, each party will develop a full range of campaign services and permanently employ a staff complement of experts who can meet the electoral requirements of party candidates and tie them more closely to the party as they help elect them. The services, shorn of generous fees and commissions, can also be provided far more cheaply to campaigns than by independent consultants, as the National Republican

Conclusion

Congressional Committee's media division has proven, and the rise in campaign costs might consequently be retarded. Just as important, some of the enormously talented consultants could be drawn closer to the bosom of the parties through party sponsored multicandidate contracts, which could provide the consultant's guidance to several or more candidates economically while using the internal services of the party to reduce costs (by, say, filming and processing all of a media consultant's advertising scripts). Parties would still be competing with private consultants, of course, but at least the consultants would *have* competition. And with contribution and spending limitations in effect, it is a rare candidate who will turn down high-quality, cut-rate party services—which the GOP has already demonstrated are possible—for a more expensive private contract.

Once the basic campaign services are established in-house, the party's horizons are broadened considerably, and it can begin to put its machinery to work for its own organization. A strengthened financial and membership base, thanks to direct mail and direct response, will give a party the resources to organize extensive registration drives, canvassing efforts, and get-out-the-vote projects. Party-based general media campaigns (such as the recent Republican series) can start to substitute for purely personalized candidate advertising, and party polling could be continuous and standardized. State and national parties have only begun to take advantage of the so-called "61-day rule," for instance. The FEC permits a party to make available party-purchased polls and other research to its candidates sixty-one days after the results are received for just 5 percent of the poll's original value.[51] Also, a party can conduct one poll for several candidates or an entire slate in a state, divide the cost among them, and give all of them immediate access to the findings. Just as with U.S. House races, where consultants' interest has sagged, the parties can extend both the party's influence and its technologies to ignored local and state legislative races where expensive advanced techniques are almost unknown at present. Finally, the new campaign techniques can help to professionalize the state and local parties, and a national party will inevitably want to transfer its technology to subordinate party committees, building a massive network of electoral machinery as it does so. A few state parties have already been pacesetters. The Indiana GOP, for example, has an extensive direct-mail fund-raising program, produces television advertising for its party ticket, recruits candidates and volunteers on a systematic basis, and has built a solid local party apparatus as well.

While the national and state parties are repairing themselves and constructing grand new operations, the press can do the parties a good turn by exposing the inherent conflicts of interest among consultants who work for candidates of both parties simultaneously. Even some consultants recognize the unethical and democratically damaging nature of the practice. "It is very hard working both sides of the fence," says Patrick Caddell. "Some of my colleagues have done it, and I think that it is wrong and there should be more attention paid to it." Political consultants who are too greedy, cynical, arrogant, egotistical, or irresponsible to accept the party-based groundrules of the American electoral system should be frozen out of the political process, and the parties should actively discourage candidates from fattening their bank accounts. Too many consultants are no better than renegades within the system, and their skills are being used for self-serving and destructive purposes.

There has been no greater change in American politics in recent years than the manner in which candidates run for public office. The very character of electioneering has been altered irrevocably by the revolution in electoral techniques: the advent of targeted direct-mail appeals, sophisticated television and radio advertising, continuous polling, and the establishment of campaign management firms and multistate consultancies. The new campaign technology and the political consultants to whom the technology is tied have wrought significant changes in the electoral process in a short time.

The ethical and democratic concerns presented in this chapter cannot be avoided, if only because the consulting industry is growing at such a fast clip and expanding in all directions, at home and internationally, and is becoming (or has become) universally accepted as a campaign necessity within the United States. The problem with consultants is not so much that they (and everyone else) exaggerate what their technologies can in fact do, although it is comforting and relieving to discover that no foolproof magic can transform a sow's ear into a silk purse; rather, what is truly disturbing is the way most independent consultants view their work and the officeholders this view has produced.

The political consultant rarely sees his responsibilities as extending beyond those he has to his client. And yet the political professional, as a vital and powerful actor in democracy's greatest dramas, undeniably has broader responsibilities—to the public at large, to the political process, and to the electoral system. Closer association with the political parties, whether voluntary or forced, may help to harness consultants'

Conclusion

considerable talents for a higher and more constructive purpose than the election of individual candidates.

Until the vision of party-dominated consulting comes to pass, however, the manner in which independent consultants select and elect candidates will be of central importance and of increasing concern. A candidate's adaptability to the new techniques of campaigning, not his competence, has become the standard by which he is judged by political professionals, and this has obvious and depressing consequences. One very prominent consultant was unusually frank and reflective in comments he made on his profession:

As political consultants, we have inadvertently done great damage to the political process, while doing excellent work. We pick people who we, subconsciously or consciously, think are good at using the technologies that we have to offer. In other words, we simply look for good candidates. Whether they become good officeholders is no longer a factor. In fact, we can compensate pretty well for their not being good.

Political consultants and the new campaign technology may well be producing a whole generation of officeholders far more skilled in the art of running for office than in the art of governing. Who can forget Robert Redford as a newly elected, media-produced U.S. senator at the end of the film *The Candidate* pathetically asking his campaign manager, "Now what do I do?" The difficulty today lies not so much with the new techniques, which can be used to reinvigorate the party system, as with consultant-created candidates who think that the packaged campaign answers are the real answers, that the blue smoke and mirrors of politics are the sum and substance of policy making.

NOTES

1. Joseph Napolitan, *The Election Game and How to Win It* (New York: Doubleday, 1972), pp. 3–4.

2. As quoted in *National Journal*, November 4, 1978, p. 1777.

3. Interestingly, he was retained by most of his political action committee and corporate clients, and to this day he returns the loyalty by concentrating on PAC business and avoiding candidate campaigns.

4. As quoted in the *San Francisco Examiner*, July 25, 1979.

5. Napolitan, *The Election Game and How to Win It*, p. 5. Napolitan quotes another consultant's statement to this effect.

6. *San Francisco Examiner*, July 23, 1979.

7. See *National Journal*, November 4, 1978, pp. 1776–1777.

8. See *Campaign Insights,* vol. 8, no. 1 (January 1, 1979): 3.

9. As cited by Dan Nimmo, *The Political Persuaders: The Techniques of Modern Election Campaigns* (Englewood Cliffs, N.J.: Prentice-Hall, 1970), p. 73.

10. Napolitan, *The Election Game and How to Win It,* p. 12.

11. See *The Washington Star,* September 8, 1978.

12. Telephone interview with Stewart Dalzell, the Heinz campaign's treasurer and general counsel, January 21, 1980. See Civil action 76–3440, U.S. District Court for the Eastern District of Pennsylvania, and see also *National Journal,* November 4, 1978, p. 1777.

13. It was Governor Matheson's response that was exceptional. Not only did he not yield to the suggestion, he sent out a memorandum insisting that this contract be awarded strictly on merit and without the slightest hint of favoritism. As it happened, the agency got the contract eventually, but only because the other bidder dropped out of the competition.

14. Carter's arrangements with Gerald Rafshoon and Patrick Caddell illustrate the conflict-of-interest potential. See *Playboy* magazine's interview with Caddell (February 1980, p. 64), and *The Washington Post's* coverage of White House staffer Rafshoon's extension of credit to candidate Carter in 1976 (June 22, 1979).

15. This is particularly true in an age of antiregulation, though one is sorely tempted to suggest that political consultants should be forced to register with the Federal Election Committee and to disclose at least a minimum of information about their activities (including a list of clients and fees). Such a register would be a reasonable starting point for press inquires and investigation.

16. As quoted in the *San Francisco Examiner,* July 24, 1979.

17. Stanley Kelley, Jr., *Professional Public Relations and Political Power* (Baltimore: Johns Hopkins, 1956), p. 38.

18. Nimmo, *The Political Persuaders,* p. 88.

19. Charles W. Roll, Jr., and Albert H. Cantril, *Polls: Their Use and Misuse in Politics* (New York: Basic Books, 1972), pp. 12–13.

20. Ibid., pp. 158–159. AAPOR first adopted a code for the public disclosure of polls in 1968, and the National Council on Public Polls added its own version in 1979. No legislation has passed Congress, in part because of the First Amendment problems inherent in restricting the press's access to polling data.

21. See *The Washington Post,* May 4, 1979.

22. *National Journal,* December 15, 1979, p. 2093.

23. See Roll and Cantril, *Polls,* pp. 162–163.

24. Michael Wheeler, "Reining in Horserace Journalism," and Burns W. Roper, "The Media and the Polls: A Boxscore," *Public Opinion,* vol. 3, no. 1A (February/March 1980): 41–49.

25. Roll and Cantril, *Polls,* pp. 52–55.

26. Quoted without specific source attribution by Haynes Johnson in his column, "Polls," *The Washington Post,* March 2, 1980, p. A-3.

27. As quoted in Vance Packard, *The Hidden Persuaders* (New York: Pocket Books, 1957), p. 172.

28. The quotation is from Caddell's "Initial Working Paper on Political Strategy," a sixty-page memorandum written for Carter at his request.

29. See *Campaigning Reports,* vol. 1, no. 8 (September 6, 1979): 1.

30. See Albert R. Hunt, "I Just Want to Be a Good Person," *The Wall Street Journal,* May 20, 1979, p. 1. See also a *Washington Post* feature article on Pressler, "Larry Pressler's Complete Book of Running," July 30, 1979, p. C-1.

31. Annual meeting of the AAPC, Washington, D.C., November 16, 1979.

32. See *Time* magazine, September 10, 1979.

33. Telephone interview with Dr. Hal C. Becker of Metairie, Louisiana, September 13, 1979.

34. See Martin Plissner and Warren Mitofsky, "What If They Held an Election and Nobody Came," *Public Opinion,* vol. 4, no. 1 (February/March 1981):50–51; *Congressional Quarterly Weekly,* February 2, 1980, pp. 286–287; and *Congressional Quarterly Weekly,* July 5, 1980, pp. 1874–1875.

35. From official election returns provided by the Office of the Secretary of State, Columbus, Ohio.

Conclusion

36. Gilligan's percentage of the vote dropped in Cuyahoga not because more Democrats were necessarily convinced to vote against him, but because so many Democrats failed to vote and Republicans presumably turned out in the normal numbers (thus inflating their percentage of the vote).

37. Campaign Study Group, Institute of Politics, Harvard University, "Increasing Access to Television for Political Candidates" (Cambridge, Mass.: Institute of Politics, July 20, 1978). See also George H. White, *A Study of Access to Television for Political Candidates* (Cambridge, Mass.: Institute of Politics, Harvard, May 1978).

38. As quoted in Nora B. Jacob, "Butcher and Forde: Wizards of the Computer Letter," *The California Journal*, vol. 10 (May 1979): 162. The commission's harsh words were directed primarily, it was believed, at the Butcher-Forde agency, which is headquartered in Orange County. Butcher-Forde, often cited as a particularly aggressive offender of ethical sensibilities, is not really unrepresentative of the industry's standards, but the agency has been more brazen than most. In 1978 the California commission fined Butcher-Forde for recruiting a third candidate in a particular race (and even paying his filing fee) in order to increase a client-candidate's chances of winning an election.

39. Arthur Schlesinger, Jr., writing in *The Wall Street Journal*, May 14, 1979.

40. *National Journal*, October 20, 1979, p. 1734. However, estimates of pre-Watergate campaign spending are probably low because detailed records of campaign expenditures simply did not exist for most campaigns. See Nimmo, *The Political Persuaders*, pp. 64–65.

41. See Institute of Politics, JFK School of Government, Harvard University, "An Analysis of the Impact of the Federal Election Campaign Act, 1972–78" (Cambridge, Mass. May 1979): 1–8.

42. See Gary C. Jacobson, *Money in Congressional Elections* (New Haven: Yale, 1980). Jacobson found that the most important factor in defeating an incumbent congressman is raising money. Poorly funded challengers almost never win.

43. Institute of Politics, "An Analysis of the Impact of FECA," pp. 1–18. The separate tax credit for parties would help to reduce the present competition between parties and their candidates for the same available dollars.

44. See William T. Mayton, "Nixon's PACs Americana," *The Washington Monthly* (January 1980): 65–67; and Walter K. Moore, "The Case of an Independent PAC," in Michael Malbin, *Parties, Interest Groups, and Campaign Finance Laws* (Washington, D.C.: American Enterprise Institute, 1980), pp. 64–65. See also a suit brought by the International Association of Machinists union against the FEC, alleging that the solicitation by corporate PACs is inherently coercive and therefore illegal under FECA (specifically, 2 U.S.C. § 441b). Although the union's arguments were rejected by both the FEC and a U.S. district court, the specifics of the charges are quite instructive about PAC activities. *Machinists v. FEC*, U.S. District Court for the District of Columbia No. 80–354. Also, *Campaign Practices Reports*, vol. 7, no. 4 (March 3, 1980): 5–6.

45. This point is made by Michael Malbin writing in *Today*, vol. 2, no. 19 (February 8, 1980): 10.

46. Herbert E. Alexander, "Statement on Senate Bill 623," June 7, 1979.

47. See Ruth S. Jones, "State Public Financing and the State Parties," in Malbin (ed.), *Parties, Interest Groups, and Campaign Finance Laws*, pp. 283–303. See also "State Financing of Political Parties and Candidates," *Comparative State Politics Newsletter*, vol. 1, no. 1 (October 1979): and "Survey on State Campaign Financing," in *Comparative State Politics Newsletter*, vol. 1, no. 2 (January 1980): 16–23.

48. Alexander Heard, *The Costs of Democracy* (Chapel Hill: University of North Carolina, 1960), p. 415. In 1956–1957, eighteen GOP state committees and fifteen Democratic ones employed public relations firms.

49. Kelley, *Professional Public Relations and Political Power*, p. 35.

50. A party-purchased consultant's fees are either counted as an in-kind contribution to the candidate (thus subject to the regular gift limits) or as a special party expenditure made on behalf of the presidential candidate in the general election.

51. After 180 days there is no cost to the candidates at all; between 16 and 60 days, there is a 50 percent charge.

Appendix A

Major American Political Consultants[a]

Name of Individual	Location[b]	Party Affiliation[c]	Ideological Leaning[d] (if any)	Scope[e]	Classification[f]	Specialty[g]
Roger Ailes & Associates, Inc.	New York City	R	—	N	S	Media
Johnny Allen & Assoc.	Washington, D.C.	D	—	N	S	Campaign organization/staff management
Bailey, Deardourff & Associates, Inc.	McLean, Va.	R	M-L	N	G	Media
Bishop & Bryant	Washington, D.C.	R	—	N	S	Media/management
Black, Manafort & Stone, Inc.	Alexandria, Va.	R	C	N	G	
The Bradley Group	San Francisco, Calif.	D	—	R	G	
Buckley/Rothstein	Washington, D.C.	D	M-L	R	S	Media
Butcher-Forde Consulting	Newport Beach, Calif.	N	C	R	S	Direct mail/media
Patrick Caddell (See "Cambridge Survey Research")						
Cambridge Opinion Studies, Inc.	New York City	D	—	N	S	Polling
Cambridge Survey Research	Boston, Massachusetts	D	M-L	N	S	Polling
Cerrell Associates, Inc.*	Los Angeles, California	D	—	N	G	Polling
Chernoff/Silver & Associates	Columbia, South Carolina	D	M-L	R	S	Media
Civic Service, Inc.	St. Louis, Missouri	R	—	N	G	
Cook, Reuf, Associates		D	—	R	S	Media
The Communications Co.	Columbia, South Carolina	D	M	N	S	Media
Craver, Mathews, Smith and Company	Washington, D.C.	D	M-L	N	S	Direct mail
Decision Making Information	Arlington, Virginia	R	—	N	S	Polling
DeVries and Associates	Santa Ana, California	D	M	N	G	Polling
Dresner, Morris, and Tortorello	Wrightsville Beach, N.C.	N	—	N	S	Polling
Bruce W. Eberle and Associates, Inc.	Vienna, Virginia	R	C	N	S	Direct mail

Firm	Location					Services
Arthur J. Finkelstein and Associates	Mt. Kisco, New York	R		N	S	Polling
Garth Associates, Inc.	New York City	D	L	N	G	Media/management
The Robert Goodman Agency, Inc.	Brooklandville, Md.	R	—	N	S	Media
Arnold Grossman	Denver, Colorado	D	—	R	S	Media
Guggenheim Productions, Inc.*	Washington, D.C.	D	M-L	N	S	Media
William R. Hamilton & Staff, Inc.	Chevy Chase, Md.	D		N	S	Polling
Peter D. Hart Research Associates, Inc.	Washington, D.C.	D	M-L	N	S	Polling
Image Dynamics, Inc.	Baltimore, Md.	N	—	N	S	Graphics/bond issues
Ruth Jones Ltd.	New York City	R	L	N	S	Media time-buying
The Kamber Group	Washington, D.C.	D	M-L	N	S	Direct Mail
Michael Kaye	Los Angeles, California	D		N	S	Media
Eddie Mahe, Jr.*	Washington, D.C.	R	—	N	G	Campaign management/organization
The Management Group	Washington, D.C.	R	M-L	N	S	Fund raising
Market Opinion Research, Inc.	Detroit, Michigan	R	L	N	S	Polling
Martilla & Associates	Boston, Massachusetts	D	—	N	G	Media/strategy
Joseph Napolitan Associates, Inc.*	New York City	D		N	S	
National Direct Mail Services, Inc.	Bethesda, Maryland	R	M	N	S	Direct mail
National Order Systems, Inc.	New York City	N		N	G	Toll-free telephone fund raising
Richard Parker and Associates	San Francisco, Calif.	D	L	N	S	Direct Mail
Parkinson Associates	Washington, D.C.	N	L	N	S	
Penn and Schoen Associates	New York, N.Y.	D		N	S	Polling
Political Financial Services	Washington, D.C.	R	—	N	S	FEC accounting/reporting
Public Response Associates	San Francisco, Calif.	D		R	S	Polling
The Public Sector	San Francisco, Calif.	R		R	S	Polling
Gerald Rafshoon Agency	Washington, D.C.	D		N	G	Media
Matt Reese Associates*	Arlington, Va.	D	—	N	G	Campaign organization
Ringe/Russo	Boston, Massachusetts	R	L	N	S	Media
David Sawyer	New York City	D	M-L	N	S	Media
Tony Schwartz*	New York City	D		N	S	Media
Mark Shields & Associates	Washington, D.C.	D		N	G	
Shosteck Associates	Silver Spring, Maryland	N		N	S	Polling
Spencer-Roberts & Associates*	Irvine, Calif.	R		N	G	
Robert Squier (See "The Communications Co.")						

Name of Individual	Location[b]	Party Affiliation[c]	Ideological Leaning[d] (if any)	Scope[e]	Classification[f]	Specialty[g]
V. Lance Tarrance & Associates, Inc.	Houston, Texas	R	—	N	S	Polling
Triad, Ltd.	Washington, D.C.	N	C	N	S	Magazine advertisements
Richard A. Viguerie Co.	Falls Church, Virginia	R	—	N	S	Direct mail
Delos Walker and Associates, Inc.	Memphis, Tennessee	D		R	G	
Sanford Weiner & Associates	San Francisco, California	D	—	R	S	Media, public relations
Whitaker-Baxter Campaigns	San Francisco, California	N	—	R	S	Referenda/initiatives
F. Clifton White and Associates*	Greenwich, Connecticut	R	—	N	G	
Stephen Winchell & Associates	Washington, D.C.	R	—	N	S	Direct mail
Richard Wirthlin (See "Decision Making Information")						
Winner-Wagner & Associates	Los Angeles, Calif.	D	—	N	S	Referenda/initiatives
Woodward & McDowell, Inc.	San Francisco, California	R	—	N	S	Media/management
George Young & Associates	Los Angeles, California	R	—	N	G	

* Asterisk designates prominent "first-generation" consultants still in the business. Italics indicate those consultants and firms considered to be most prominent in the field.

ᵃ This list (alphabetized by first key word or surname) is not intended to be exhaustive, but it contains the names of most major American political consulting firms that have had staying power and that are among the best in the field. For easy references, several well-known consultants are listed twice (by firm name and individual name).

ᵇ Only the location of the firm's main office is listed here. Several firms have one or more branch offices.

ᶜ R designates "Republican," D designates "Democratic," N designates "no consistent party affiliation." The party affiliation designation refers to the firm's *clientele*, although in most cases the same party affiliation is shared by the principal members of the firm. A party label listed here means that at least 90 percent of the firm's work is for the party indicated.

ᵈ Most consultants work for candidates across the ideological spectrum of one political party, but a few firms have demonstrated a fairly consistent (though rarely monolithic) ideology in their choice of clients. Those firms' ideology is designated liberal (L), moderate (M), conservative (C), moderate-liberal (M–L), or moderate-conservative (M–C).

ᵉ Most of the individuals and firms listed here are national in scope, but a few outstanding regional consultants are included. N designates "national." R designates "regional."

ᶠ A generalist (G) consultant is one who advises on most or all phases of his campaign and who coordinates most or all aspects of the technology employed by the campaign. A specialist (S) concentrates on one or two aspects of the campaign and peddles expertise in one or two technological specialties (such as direct mail, polling, media, organization and management, get-out-the-vote, etc.).

ᵍ Consulting firms usually offer a wide range of services, but many of the offerings tend to be "add-ons." Usually a firm or a consultant has built a reputation around provision of one service (or perhaps two). This "reputational service" is listed here. In most cases no specialties are listed for consultants designated as generalists.

SOURCES: Personal and telephone interviews, periodic consultant directories issued by the Democratic and Republican National Congressional Committees, political conference rosters, and press notices.

Appendix B

Research Sources

Interviews[a]

Recorded personal interviews were conducted between June 1979 and January 1980 with several dozen political consultants and others familiar with the consulting field. The following text indicates the name of each person interviewed, the location of the interview, and the date(s) on which the interview(s) took place. The tapes and transcripts of each of these interviews has been preserved.

GENERALIST CONSULTANTS

Joseph Cerrell, Cerrell Associates, Inc., Los Angeles, California, August 6, 1979.

Walter DeVries, DeVries and Associates, Inc., Wrightsville Beach, North Carolina, June 28, 1979.

Joseph Napolitan, Joseph Napolitan Associates, Inc., New York, New York, July 24, 1979.

Hank Parkinson, Parkinson Associates, Washington, D.C., July 23, 1979.

Roy Pfautch, Civic Service, Inc., St. Louis, Missouri, July 27, 1979.

Stuart Spencer, Spencer-Roberts & Associates, Newport Beach, California, August 2, 1979.

MEDIA CONSULTANTS

Douglas Bailey, Bailey, Deardourff and Associates, Inc., Washington, D.C., September 18, 1979.

Marvin Chernoff, Chernoff/Silver and Associates, Columbia, South Carolina, November 8, 1979.

David Garth, Garth Associates, Inc., New York, New York, September 7 and October 3, 1979.

Robert Goodman, The Robert Goodman Agency, Inc., Brooklandville, Maryland, December 18, 1979.

Charles Guggenheim, Guggenheim Productions, Inc., Washington, D.C., October 26, 1979.

Michael Kaye, Los Angeles, California, August 6, 1979.

Tony Schwartz, New York, New York, September 7, 1979.

Robert Squier, The Communications Company, Washington, D.C., June 20, 1979.

Richard Woodward, Woodward and McDowell, Inc., Los Angeles, California, August 24, 1979.

POLLING CONSULTANTS

Vincent Breglio, Decision Making Information, Washington, D.C., September 19, 1979.

Patrick Caddell, Cambridge Survey Research, Washington, D.C., January 15, 1980.

William Hamilton, William R. Hamilton & Staff, Inc., Washington, D.C., July 23, 1979.

Peter Hart, Peter D. Hart Research Associates, Inc., Washington, D.C., August 21, 1979.

Herschel Shosteck, Shosteck Associates, Silver Spring, Maryland, June 20, 1979.

Lance Tarrance, V. Lance Tarrance & Associates, Inc., Houston, Texas, November 28, 1979.

Robert Teeter, Market Opinion Research, Detroit, Michigan, January 15, 1980.

DIRECT MAIL CONSULTANTS

William Lacy, Bruce W. Eberle and Associates, Inc., Vienna, Virginia, and Charlottesville, Virginia, July 6 and October 30, 1979.

Robert Odell, National Direct Mail Services, Inc., Bethesda, Maryland, September 19, 1979.

Robert Smith, Craver, Mathews, Smith, and Company, Arlington, Virginia, August 24, 1979.

Richard Viguerie, Richard A. Viguerie Company, Falls Church, Virginia, October 26, 1979.

ORGANIZATIONAL/VOTER CONTACT CONSULTANTS

Eddie Mahe, Jr., Campaign Manager, Connally for President, Washington, D.C., October 26, 1979.

Matt Reese, Matt Reese Associates, Washington, D.C., November 30, 1979.

Larry Schwartz, National Order Systems, Inc., New York, New York, July 30, 1979.

OTHER CONSULTANTS

Joy Hamann, Joyce and Martin Advertising, Las Vegas, Nevada, August 3, 1979.

Chuck Winner, Winner-Wagner and Associates, Los Angeles, California, August 7, 1979.

POLITICAL PARTIES

Ed Blakely, Media Director, Republican National Congressional Committee, Washington, D.C., November 2, 1979, and November 19, 1980.

Research Sources

James Killough, Republicans Abroad, Republican National Committee, Washington, D.C., September 27, 1979.

Nancy Sinnott, Campaign Director, Republican National Congressional Committee, Washington, D.C., October 12, 1979.

Wyatt Stewart, Finance Director, Republican National Congressional Committee, Washington, D.C., November 2, 1979.

Steven Stockmeyer, Executive Director, Republican National Congressional Committee, Washington, D.C., October 12, 1979.

William Sweeney, Executive Director, Democratic Congressional Campaign Committee, Washington, D.C., October 12, 1979.

PACS AND INTEREST GROUPS

Al Barkan, Director, COPE (AFL-CIO), Washington, D.C., November 30, 1979.

Russell Hemenway, Executive Director, National Committee for an Effective Congress, New York, New York, July 30, 1979.

Paul Weyrich, Director, Committee for the Survival of a Free Congress, Washington, D.C., June 19, 1979.

ACADEMICS, JOURNALISTS, OTHERS

Herbert Alexander, Director, Citizens' Research Foundation, University of Southern California, Los Angeles, California, August 7, 1979.

Larry Berg, Director, Institute of Politics and Government, University of Southern California, Los Angeles, California, August 6, 1979.

David Broder, Political Reporter, the *Washington Post*, Washington, D.C., September 14, 1979.

Gerald Ford, former President, class interview, Charlottesville, Virginia, October 11, 1979.

Jack Germond, Political Reporter, the *Washington Star*, Washington, D.C., September 19, 1979.

Julian Kanter, Archivist of Political Television Commericals, Highland Park, Illinois, July 28, 1979.

Austin Ranney, Resident Scholar, American Enterprise Institute for Public Policy Research, Washington, D.C., September 27, 1979.

Research

Research was conducted primarily at the University of Virginia, Charlottesville, Virginia, but also at a number of other locations in addition to consultants' offices, including:

The Brookings Institution, Washington, D.C.
Democratic National Committee, Washington, D.C.
Republican National Committee, Washington, D.C.
Lyndon Baines Johnson Library, Austin, Texas
New College and Rhodes House Library, Oxford, England.

Conferences

Research material was gathered at a number of trade and academic conferences including the following:

American Association of Political Consultants, Annual Meeting, Washington, D.C., November 30–December 2, 1978.

American Association of Political Consultants, Fund Raising Seminar, Baltimore-Washington International Airport, June 8, 1979.

American Association of Political Consultants, Annual Meeting, Washington, D.C., November 15–16, 1979.

American Enterprise Institute for Public Policy Research, "Parties, Interest Groups and Campaign Finance Laws," Washington, D.C., September 4–5, 1979.

Campaign Practices Reports, (Plus Publications), "Campaigning—Reform Style," Washington, D.C., November 8–9, 1979.

Campaigning Reports (Plus Publications), "Technique '80," Washington, D.C., December 6–7, 1979.

ª Only personal interviews are listed here. Numerous telephone interviews were also conducted, and discussions with consultants at conferences as well as conference presentations by consultants served as source material for this study. Personal correspondence with several dozen other consultants was of considerable assistance, too.

Appendix C

Sketches of Some Major American Consultants[a]

Individual (Firm, Location)	Personal Party/ Ideology[b]	Personal Background	Firm Background	Sampling of Clients (Current and Former)[c]
Generalist Consultants				
Joseph Cerrell (Cerrell Associates, Inc., Los Angeles, Calif.)	Democratic; moderate	Student political activist at U.S.C.; worked for Pat Brown's gubernatorial campaign in 1958, then became executive director of California Democratic party.	Formed firm in 1966; national clientele but concentration in West Coast area; active Board of Directors member of American Association of Political Consultants.	Kennedy presidential (1960); Johnson presidential (1964); Humphrey presidential (1968 and 1972); Jerry Brown gubernatorial (1974); new speciality in California judicial campaigns.
Walter DeVries (DeVries and Associates, Wrightsville Beach, N.C.)	Democratic (formerly Republican); moderate	Academic-consultant; M. A. and Ph.D from Michigan State in political science and social psychology; executive assistant to Gov. George Romney (R-Mich.) from 1962–67; former senior consultant to Market Opinion Research; coauthor of *The Ticket-Splitters* and *The Transformation of Southern Politics*.	Firm formed in 1970; just self and an assistant, with all particulars subcontracted; teaches at Duke; former Vice-President of American Association of Political Consultants.	Romney presidential (1967); Pat McCullough gubernatorial primary (D-Mich., 1978); heads N.C. Opinion Research; conducts polls for Raleigh *News and Observer*.
Joseph Napolitan (Joseph Napolitan Associates, Inc., New York City)	Democratic; moderate	College English literature major, became sportswriter, then political reporter for Springfield, Mass., newspaper; got start in politics by managing winning campaign of long-shot candidate for Springfield mayor.	One of most prominent early generation consultants; opened office in 1956, branched into overseas campaigns; founder of American Association of Political Consultants; co-founder of International Association of Political Consultants.	Humphrey presidential (1968); Milton Shapp gubernatorial (D-Penn.); U.S. Sen. Mike Gravel; Gov. George Ariyoshi (D-Ha.); Venezuelan presidential campaigns.

Individual (Firm, Location)	Personal Party/ Ideology[b]	Personal Background	Firm Background	Sampling of Clients (Current and Former)[c]
Hank Parkinson (Parkinson and Associates, Washington, D.C.)	Independent (formerly Republican); moderate	Reporter-consultant; long history of involvement in local and state campaigns; debater and public speaker at Univ. of New Mexico (B.A.) with graduate work at U.S.C.; author of several books on practical politics.	Founded Campaign Associates in Wichita, Kan, in 1962; in 1979 formed new company, Parkinson and Associates, and became Senior Political Editor of Plus Publications (now defunct); formerly published *Campaign Insights* and edited *Campaigning Reports* (see bibliographical essay).	Especially active with lobbying and political action committees such as Alabama State Farm Bureau.
Roy Pfautch (Civic Service, Inc., St. Louis, Mo.)	Republican; moderate-conservative	Ordained Presbyterian minister; politically active in undergraduate college (Washington University, St. Louis, Mo.); worked on series of successful Missouri campaigns.	Established small firm in 1963; took mainly congressional races; became "Watergate casualty" through involvement in Townhouse Fund; left candidate campaigns and turned to issues and political committees.	Sen. Robert Dole (R-Kan., 1968); Thomas Curtis senatorial (1968, R-Mo); U.S. Sen. Glenn Beall, Jr. (R-Md., 1970); now works primarily for political action committees such as the American Medical Association's AMPAC.
Matt Reese (Matt Reese Associates, Arlington, Va.)	Democratic; moderate-liberal	Gregarious West Virginian who coordinated JFK's 1960 victory in that state's crucial primary; joined Democratic National Committee in 1961 as Deputy Chairman and Director of Operations, organizing major 1964 voter registration drive; B.A. in political science from Marshall University, Huntington, W.Va.	Formed firm in 1966, only half dozen full-time staffers, rest of work contracted out to 25–30 "regulars"; specializes in organizational techniques; 73% winning record in more than 187 races since 1960; past president of American Association of Political Consultants.	Robert Kennedy presidential (1968); Sen. Birch Bayh; Sen. Claiborne Pell; Sen. Thomas Eagleton; 1978 Missouri right-to-work referendum for Labor Council; Gov. Jay Rockefeller; Gov. Joseph Teasdale; foreign campaigns for president in Philippines and Costa Rica.

Name/Firm	Party; Ideology	Background	Notes	Clients
Stuart Spencer (Spencer-Roberts and Associates, Irvine Calif.)	Republican; moderate	Politics began as an avocation: volunteer work and Young Republicans activity; first political job with Los Angeles County Republican Central Committee.	Formed association with Bill Roberts in 1960 with $500 each and 3 clients; became one of the "name" GOP national firms; Roberts left in 1974 because of health, but name kept; Spencer was one of President Ford's closest advisers throughout 1976 campaign, and he took up the trusted senior counselor's role again in Ronald Reagan's 1980 general election entourage.	Ronald Reagan presidential (1980); President Ford presidential (1976); Nelson Rockefeller presidential (1964); Reagan gubernatorial (R-Calif., 1966); U.S. Rep. Donald Riegle (R-Mich.: now a Democratic U.S. Senator); U.S. Rep. John Rousselot (R-Calif.).

Polling Consultants

Name/Firm	Party; Ideology	Background	Notes	Clients
Patrick Caddell (Cambridge Survey Research, Boston, Mass. & Washington, D.C.)	Democratic; moderate-liberal	Began polling as high school student, Jacksonville, Fla. (1967); B.A. from Harvard in political science.	President of firm, formed after Caddell's service as George McGovern's presidential campaign pollster (1972) at the age of 22; had small office near White House during Carter administration, leaving most of firm's work to partners in Boston; formerly all-political firm becoming increasingly nonpolitical.	President Carter (1976, 1980 campaigns); Democratic National Committee; U.S. Sen. Joseph Biden (D-Del., 1978); Gov. Robert Graham (D-Fla, 1978); polled in almost all states.
William R. Hamilton (William R. Hamilton & Staff, Inc., Chevy Chase, Md.)	Democratic; moderate-liberal	Former media analyst for United States Information Agency (USIA); former instructor in social statistics; M.A. in political science from University of Florida.	Firm is national but has most business in southern and border states; vast proportion of business is political—for candidates or public issue groups.	Gov. Jimmy Carter (D-Ga, 1970); Humphrey presidential (1968); Muskie presidential (1972); Sen. Adlai Stevenson III (D-Ill.); Gov. Reubin Askew (D-Fla.); Sen. Herman Talmadge (D-Ga.); Henry Howell (D-Va.).
Peter D. Hart (Peter D. Hart Research Associates, Inc., Washington, D.C.)	Democratic; liberal	From political family; started in polling with Louis Harris; became research director of Democratic National Committee; also polled for Oliver Quayle.	Organized firm in 1971-72, which is now about 60 percent political; has done work for a number of liberal Republicans.	Sen. Edward Kennedy presidential (1980); U.S. Rep. Morris Udall (D-Ariz.) presidential (1976); Gov. Ella Grasso (D-Conn., 1974); Sen. John Heinz (R-Penn., 1976).

Individual (Firm, Location)	Personal Party/Ideology[b]	Personal Background	Firm Background	Sampling of Clients (Current and Former)[c]
V. Lance Tarrance (V. Lance Tarrance and Associates, Houston, Texas)	Republican; moderate-conservative	Native Texan with long involvement in state's politics; former director of research for Republican National Committee; Census Bureau official during Nixon administration; co-author of *The Ticket-Splitters*; former teaching fellow at Harvard's Institute of Politics; adjunct professor of political science at Rice University and uses their computer operations.	Left vice-presidency at D.M.I. to set up own national firm headquartered in Houston (1977).	John Connally presidential (1980); Sen. John Tower (R-Tex., 1978); Gov. William Clements (R-Tex., 1978); Sen. Pete Domenici (R-N.M., 1978); at D.M.I. helped in 1976 Reagan presidential campaign.
Robert Teeter (Market Opinion Research, Inc., Detroit, Michigan)	Republican; moderate	Former instructor in small Mich. college; worked for Gov. George Romney (R-Mich.); helped organize Environmental Protection Agency; M.A. from Michigan State.	Firm founded in 1941; Teeter became head of political division, then company president; only one-third of firm's work political; president of National Association of Political Pollsters.	Nixon presidential (1972); Ford presidential (1976); Bush presidential (1980); Gov. William Milliken (R-Mich.); Gov. James Rhodes (R-Ohio); Sen. David Durenberger (R-Minn.).
Richard B. Wirthlin (Decision Making Information, Santa Ana, California)	Republican; conservative	Devout Mormon; has devoted years to developing polling, targeting, and computer-simulated modeling for campaigns.	Former partner with Breglio (1963–67); formed D.M.I. in 1969 and serves as president; runs Santa Ana office; particularly conducting polls for the administration.	Reagan presidential campaign (1976, 1980); Sen. S. I. Hayakawa (R-Calif.); Sen. Barry Goldwater (R-Ariz.); Sen. Peter Dominick (R-Colo.); Sen. Bob Dole (R-Kan.); Gov. Dan Evans (R-Wash.); Gov. Albert Quie (R-Minn.); several hundred House campaigns.
Vincent Breglio (Decision Making Information, Santa Ana, California)	Republican; moderate	Ph.D. in social psychology from Brigham Young University; former instructor at Long Beach State University.	Vice-president of D.M.I.; heads Washington office; on leave of absence from firm as of 1981 to serve as executive director of the National Republican Senatorial Committee.	

Media Consultants

Douglas Bailey (Bailey/Deardourff and Associates, Inc., McLean, Virginia)	Republican; moderate	Doctorate in international relations; joined Harvard faculty as Henry Kissinger's assistant in 1960; became official of 1964 Rockefeller presidential campaign and met John Deardourff there.	Bailey and Deardourff formed Campaign Consulting in 1967 with a Boston lawyer, who left after the firm's move to Washington in 1968; advertising capacity added in 1969; considered most prominent Republican media firm.	George Romney presidential (1968); Gerald Ford presidential (1976); Howard Baker presidential (1980); Gov. James Rhodes (R-Ohio); Gov. William G. Milliken (R-Mich.); Sen. Charles Percy (R-Ill.); Sen. Richard Schweiker (R-Penn.); Sen. Charles Mathias (R-Md.).
John Deardourff (Bailey/Deardourff and Associates, Inc., McLean, Virginia)	Republican; moderate	From small town in Ohio; graduate of Wabash College and Fletcher School of Law and Diplomacy; head of domestic policy research in 1964 Rockefeller presidential campaign; worked for John Lindsay in 1965 New York City mayoralty election.		
Marvin Chernoff (Chernoff/Silver Associates, Columbia, S.C.)	Democratic; liberal	Former owner of an office equipment store in Cleveland; began political work as a volunteer in Carl Stokes's successful Cleveland mayoral campaign in 1967.	Formed firm in 1974 after working on Charles Revenel's gubernatorial campaign in South Carolina; primarily regional firm, but going national.	Gov. Bill Clinton (D-Ark.), U.S. Sen. Donald Stewart (D-Ala.); Sen. Frank Church (D-Idaho) in 1980; U.S. Rep. John Jenrette (D-S.C.); League of Women Voters (ERA).
David Garth (Garth Associates, Inc., New York City)	Independent; liberal	From a very liberal background with active political parents; volunteer in politics, particularly in New York State, throughout life; salty and blustery; model for consultant in movie *The Candidate*; first surfaced as co-chairman of Draft Adlai Stevenson presidential committee, 1960; first major media campaign was for John Lindsay mayoralty, 1965.	Firm concentrates on media, but is management oriented; Garth Assoc. media style is rough-cut and unusually fact filled; one of the most widely publicized firms.	Gov. Hugh Carey (D-N.Y.); Gov. Brendan Byrne (D-N.J.); Gov. John Gilligan (D-Ohio); Sen. John Heinz (R-Penn); Mayor Ed Koch (D-N.Y.); Mayor Tom Bradley (D-L.A.); Joffrey Ballet; New York Jets; three presidential campaigns: Eugene McCarthy (1968); John Lindsay (1972); John Anderson (1980).

Individual (Firm, Location)	Personal Party/ Ideology[b]	Personal Background	Firm Background	Sampling of Clients (Current and Former)[c]
Robert Goodman (Robert Goodman Agency, Brooklandville, Maryland)	Republican; liberal	Degree in philosophy from Haverford College; apprenticed in Baltimore advertising agency in 1950s; emotional, creative, enthusiastic.	Agency started in 1959 with two other partners; hardly political at first, now half political; opening provided in management of Spiro Agnew's Md. gubernatorial campaign, 1966; afterward, consultants to Republican National Committee for four years.	George Bush presidential (1980); Sen. Malcolm Wallop (R-Wyo.); Sen. Alan Simpson (R-Wyo.); Sen. Rudy Boschwitz (R-Minn); Sen. John Tower (R-Tex); Gov. Arch Moore (R-W.Va.).
Charles Guggenheim (Guggenheim Productions, Inc., Washington, D.C.)	Democratic; liberal	Primarily a documentary film producer; background in film and cinema more than politics; creative and issue oriented; long personal history and involvement in St. Louis area; winner of Peabody television and Cannes film awards.	Began political filming for St. Louis bond issue in 1955; Adlai Stevenson's presidential campaign in 1956 was first candidate effort; political proportion gradually increased to peak dominance in 1970, declined afterward by Guggenheim's choice.	Robert Kennedy presidential (1968); George McGovern presidential (1972); Edward Kennedy presidential (1980); Gov. Patrick Lucey (D-Wisc.); Sen. Phil Hart (D-Mich.); Sen. Ernest Hollings (D-S.C.); Gov. Carlos Romero Barcelo (Puerto Rico).
Gerald Rafshoon (Rafshoon Communications, Washington, D.C.)	Democratic; moderate	An Atlanta advertising agency executive, Rafshoon's activities centered primarily on Georgia and marketing until his relationship with Jimmy Carter began in 1966.	Rafshoon sold Rafshoon Advertising of Atlanta in 1979, retaining the Washington-based public relations firm of Rafshoon Communications; joined White House staff in July 1978 for a year.	Jimmy Carter's Georgia gubernatorial races (1966, 1970); Carter presidential (1976, 1980); Mario Cuomo mayoralty (New York City, 1977); Henry Howell gubernatorial (D-Va., 1977).
Tony Schwartz (New York City)	Democratic; liberal	Radio buff as child; young graphic artist in Manhattan in 1940s; built one of the first portable tape recorders; became sound expert; taught at Fordham; author of *The Responsive Chord*; refuses to travel, clients must come to New York; has won two Academy awards.	Independent television and radio ad producer; has worked closely with Joseph Napolitan; been associated with over 300 campaigns; 1948–54, founder and art director of a N.Y.C. advertising agency; first achieved national fame after 1964 LBJ "Daisy" commercial.	LBJ presidential (1964); Humphrey presidential (1968); McGovern presidential (1972); Carter presidential (1976); Gov. Jay Rockefeller (D-W.Va.); Sen. Pat Moynihan (D-N.Y.); Sen. Abraham Ribicoff (D-Conn.); Sen. Claiborne Pell (D-R.I.); Coca-Cola; Holiday Inns; American Airlines.

Robert Squier (The Communications Company, Washington, D.C.)	Democratic; moderate	Did television package for Gov. Orville Freeman (D-Minn.) while still a student at the Univ. of Minn. in 1956; at 29 directed television division of Democratic National Committee; desired public broadcasting career originally, was documentary filmmaker for National Educational Television, won two Emmy awards.	A veteran of over 100 campaigns, Squier has a small outfit concentrating on media spots and occasionally telethons (like Humphrey's 1968 election eve); handled press for Carter during Camp David Mideast talks; coordinated Carter's election eve broadcast; devised Bob Graham's "work days" gubernatorial campaign (D-Fla., 1978).	Humphrey presidential (1968); Carter presidential (1976); Gov. John Y. Brown (D-Ky.); Gov. William Winter (D-Miss.); Sen. Howell Heflin (D-Ala.); Muskie presidential (1972); Elizabeth Holtzman senatorial (D-N.Y., 1980).
Chuck Winner (Winner-Wagner Associates, Los Angeles, California)	Democratic; liberal	Youthful Eisenhower Republican; became active in Young Democrats; volunteer in Pat Brown's gubernatorial campaign (D-Calif., 1958); JFK youth coordinator, western states, 1960; later Democratic State Director of Finance; finance manager for LBJ California campaign, 1964.	Formed firm with Joseph Cerrell, 1966–69; left politics to form small marketing company; reentered politics in partnership with wife, became Muskie campaign manager in western states, 1972; Winner-Wagner firm began in 1975; last candidate taken in 1976, afterward only private clients and referenda.	Mainly initiatives and referenda work; pro-nuclear referenda in several states; anti-Proposition 13 in California; many private clients such as Rockwell International.
Richard Woodward (Woodward-McDowell, Inc., San Francisco, Calif.)	Republican; conservative	Began as corporate executive; then, dissatisfied, worked on San Diego city politics under Mayor Pete Wilson, who put him in touch with Spencer-Roberts agency; 1964 worker in Nelson Rockefeller's California primary campaign.	Became director of San Francisco office of Spencer-Roberts agency in 1968; in 1971 formed company with Jack McDowell, a Pulitzer Prize winning journalist.	U.S. Sen. S. I. Hayakawa (R-Calif.); Sen. Gordon Humphrey (R-N.H.); opposed California's Proposition 5 (anti-smoking initiative).

Individual (Firm, Location)	Personal Party/ Ideology[b]	Personal Background	Firm Background	Sampling of Clients (Current and Former)[c]
Direct Mail Consultants				
William Butcher *Arnold Forde* (Butcher-Forde Consulting, Newport Beach, Calif.)	None	A Chicago native, Forde is a former Calif. realtor who had intentions to run for office; worked first for local Democratic Committee, then Democratic National Committee; now enjoys manager's role. Butcher started working on campaigns at 14; had a direct-mail firm for candidates from 1967–70; dissolved it to form current firm.	Butcher and Forde have a total payroll of 49; direct mail is the specialty, but media and management are done too; firm has worked for Democrats and Republicans, with no ideological pattern.	Howard Jarvis's Proposition 13 "tax revolt" initiative; Jarvis's National Tax Reform Movement.
Bruce W. Eberle (Bruce W. Eberle and Associates, Inc., Vienna, Va.)	Republican; conservative	Professionally an engineer, Eberle was long active in the right-wing Young Americans for Freedom and other conservative groups.	Founded in 1974 in the basement of Eberle's home with a $2,000 investment; now has a large and young staff of conservatives oriented to candidates challenging incumbents.	Citizen's for Reagan presidential committee (1976); Jeffrey Bell senatorial (1978, R-N.J.); many conservative groups opposing SALT II, U.S.-China policies, etc.
Robert Odell (National Direct Mail Services, Inc., Bethesda, Md.)	Republican; moderate–conservative	Odell's career has been closely tied to the Republican party; summer internship with GOP Congressional Campaign Committee led to full-time position; later exec. director of Republican National Finance Committee (1971–74).	Firm started in 1974; kept relatively small (20 employees) and about 20 campaigns over 6 years; Odell took 1975–76 leave of absence to direct President Ford's re-election finance committee.	George Bush presidential (1980); Gov. William Clements (R-Tex.); Perry Duryea gubernatorial (R-N.Y., 1978; Gov. John Dalton (R-Va.); Sen. Bill Armstrong (R-Colo.); Sen. Arlen Specter (R-Penn., 1980).

Robert Smith (Craver, Mathews, Smith, and Co., Arlington, Va.)	Democratic; liberal	Like other principals in his firm, Smith worked in Common Cause organization; also former community organizer for city of N.Y. and private youth groups; B.A. in political science and sociology from Berkeley.	Company is mainly in the business of building organizational memberships; only 25% of work is political; fired as consultant for Democratic National Committee when they aided Draft Kennedy committee in 1980; rehired by DNC in 1981.	John Anderson presidential (1980); Morris Udall presidential (1976); Sen. George McGovern; Sen. John Culver; Sen. Birch Bayh; A.C.L.U.; women's and abortion rights' groups.
Richard Viguerie (Richard A. Viguerie Company, Falls Church, Va.)	Independent (tending more Republican); conservative	New Orleans native with B.A. in political science from Univ. of Houston, Viguerie was a local campaign manager for John Tower's Senate race against LBJ in 1960; then Washington political consultant and national president of the Young Americans for Freedom; committed conservative ideologue.	Began firm to raise money for the YAF in 1965 with $400 investment; firm now worth $10 million and has 4.5 million conservative donors listed in its computers; used firm as base for national conservative organizing.	George Wallace presidential (1972); Phil Crane and John Connally presidential (1980); Sen. Jesse Helms (R-N.C.); National Conservative Political Action Committee and hundreds of conservative causes.

ᵃ See appendix A for additional information and notes.

ᵇ The party affiliation listed is that of the individual *and* most of the firm's clientele. The ideological leaning is the individual's; most firms do not select clients on the basis of ideology within the chosen party.

ᶜ Many clients have signed on the same consultants repeatedly. Because of space limitations, the specific years of campaign involvement are not listed for each client in this column.

SOURCE: The reader is referred to the bibliographical essay, since dozens of sources (and the personal interviews) contributed to these vignettes.

Bibliographical Essay

Political consultants have not drawn a fair share of the attention of political scientists. Only a few major books on consultants have been written in the last quarter century, headed by Stanley Kelley's *Professional Public Relations and Political Power* (Baltimore: Johns Hopkins, 1956) and Dan Nimmo's *The Political Persuaders* (Englewood Cliffs, N.J.: Prentice-Hall, 1970). Robert Agranoff's edited volume, *The New Style in Election Campaigns* (Boston: Holbrook, 1976, 2nd ed.), has also proven to be a very useful addition to the basic literature.

Journalists have done a far better job than scholars in keeping up with the electoral activities (though not necessarily the questionable practices) of political consultants. Current and thorough inquiries are often to be found in the pages of the *National Journal* and *Congressional Quarterly Weekly*, and quite a number of them were cited in this study. Political newsletters and trade journals (such as Alan Baron's *Baron Report*, Rowland Evans and Robert Novak's *Evans-Novak Political Report*, and *Campaigns and Elections* magazine) provide an endless stream of advice, gossip and tidbit, some of which is actually revealing. Four now-defunct publications (*E.P.O.*, *Practical Politics*, and Hank Parkinson's *Campaign Insights* and *Campaigning Reports*) also fit into this category.

Occasionally consultants have taken pen in hand and produced memoirs and campaign tips. The best of the lot is a pair of books by two New York-based consultants: Joseph Napolitan's *The Election Game and How to Win It* (New York: Doubleday, 1972) and Tony Schwartz's *The Responsive Chord* (New York: Anchor/Doubleday, 1973). More than a dozen consultants contributed articles to *The Political Image Merchants* (Washington: Acropolis, 1971), ed. Ray Hiebert, Robert Jones, John Lorenz, and Ernest Lolito. Two dated but still useful works by consultants are *Politics Battle Plan* (New York: Macmillan, 1968), by Herbert M. Baus and William B. Ross and *The Image Candidates* (New York: Macmillan, 1968), by Gene Wyckoff. A refreshingly humorous view of the consultant's role is found in Harry Miles Muheim's novel, *Vote for Quimby—and Quick!* (New York: Macmillan, 1978).

There are literally hundreds of "how to win your election" books and manuals in circulation, and in the main their recitation of "do's" and "don't's" is uninspired and tedious, not to mention repetitious: plagiarism seems rampant. A prospective candidate or campaign manager would be better advised to approach his national party committee. Both the Republican and the Democratic National Committees have a wide range of publications on virtually every phase of campaigning. The Republican offerings tend to be more detailed and elaborate, reflecting their technological edge, but even the Democratic fare is up to date and useful. Several major PACs and organizations such as Labor's COPE have information on election activities. The two parties, by the way, also keep current lists of political consultants serving their candidates.

Bibliographical Essay

A few major books and references are listed below for each major category of campaign technology. For the most part, only more recently published works are cited. A lengthier bibliography that includes complete citations and many more entries for each category was compiled during this study, and is available at cost from the author. The reader should also consult the superb bibliography assembled by Lynda Lee Kaid, Keith R. Sanders, and Robert O. Hirsch (*Political Campaign Communication: A Bibliography and Guide to the Literature:* Scarecrow Press, 1974), which contains 1,539 entries published prior to its copyright date.

Media: Unquestionably the most important book is Thomas E. Patterson and Robert D. McClure's *The Unseeing Eye: The Myth of Television Power in National Politics* (New York: Putnam's, 1976). The authors' trail-blazing investigation of the effects of paid and unpaid television on voters in the 1972 presidential election exploded many of the beliefs long-held by political media consultants. Joe McGinniss's *The Selling of the President 1968* (New York: Trident, 1969) brought to the attention of the public some of the advertising methods employed in the 1968 presidential election. No better book on the unpaid media exists than Timothy Crouse's *The Boys on the Bus* (New York: Ballantine, 1972), a look at the 1972 presidential contest from the perspective of the print and television journalists who covered it.

Polls: Nothing has taken the place of classics like Walter Lippmann's *Public Opinion* (New York: Harcourt, 1922) or V. O. Key, Jr.'s, *Public Opinion and American Democracy* (New York: Alfred Knopf, 1961), but for explanations of the technology and the puzzling contradictions of modern political survey research, one must look elsewhere. Two more recent books by noted pollsters nicely fill the need: See Charles W. Roll, Jr., and Albert H. Cantril, *Polls: Their Use and Misuse in Politics* (New York: Basic Books, 1980, 2nd ed.); and George Gallup, *The Sophisticated Poll-Watcher's Guide* (Princeton: Opinion Press, 1972).

Direct Mail: Disappointingly little has been published in this vital political field. The most insightful analyses of the direct-mail process are found in the numerous *Congressional Quarterly Weekly* and *National Journal* articles cited herein. The National Republican Congressional Committee has put together a first-rate "how-to" monograph on direct mail and other financing methods (*Financing Republican Congressional Campaigns,* Washington: NRCC, 1979), which includes several dozen excellent samples of direct-mail pieces. See also Richard S. Hodgson, *Direct Mail in the Political Process* (New York: Direct Mail/Marketing Association, 1976); and Bob Stone, *Successful Direct Mail Marketing Methods* (Chicago: Crain, 1979, 2nd ed.)

Organization: Xandra Kayden's work, *Campaign Organization* (Lexington: D.C. Heath, 1978), is a thorough if limited review of the organizations of one senatorial and two gubernatorial campaigns. Several political activists have contributed books on the subject, including Sam Brown (*Storefront Organizing,* New York: Pyramid, 1972) and Jerry Bruno and Jeff Greenfield (*The Advance Man,* New York: Morrow, 1971). Unfortunately, other than in scattered newspaper, magazine, and electioneering manual articles, the new organizational technology has received scant coverage.

Parties/PACs: The modern decline of the political party and the growth

357

of independent-minded voting has been documented and described in such books as David Broder's *The Party's Over* (New York: Harper and Row, 1972), Walter DeVries and Lance Tarrance's *The Ticket-Splitter* (Grand Rapids: Eerdemans, 1972), and Jeff Fishel's *Parties and Elections in an Anti-Party Age* (Bloomington: Indiana, 1979). The growth of PACs has not been ignored, but neither has it been held to light in much of the current literature. Michael J. Malbin's edited volume from an American Enterprise Institute Conference, *Parties, Interest Groups, and Campaign Finance Laws* (Washington: American Enterprise Institute, 1980), is a much-needed addition. And again, the reader is referred to a number of investigative articles in the *National Journal* and the *Congressional Quarterly Weekly* cited herein.

Campaign Finance: All of Herbert E. Alexander's works are required reading for the student of campaign finance in American and foreign elections. *Financing the 1976 Election* (Washington: Congressional Quarterly, 1979) is perhaps his most comprehensive and illuminating work to date. Gary C. Jacobson's *Money in Congressional Elections* (New Haven: Yale, 1980) and his various articles on campaign finance are also basic sources. Several reports and monographs published by the Campaign Study Group of Harvard University's Institute of Politics have proven invaluable in my own study, especially when combined with the Federal Election Commission's periodic publications, such as *Campaign Guides* (for presidential and congressional candidates), *Campaign Finance Law* (an annual update that includes state statutes), the *FEC Record* (monthly), and the FEC's *Annual Report*.

Ethics: There are references to the ethical problems of political consulting in virtually all of the general works on consultants and new campaign technology, but the most sustained treatment can be found in Nimmo, *The Political Persuaders;* Kelley, *Professional Public Relations and Political Power;* and Agranoff (ed.), *The New Style in Election Campaigns*. See also Stanley Kelley, Jr., *Political Campaigning: Problems in Creating an Informed Electorate* (Washington: Brookings, 1960).

Name Index

Subject Index

Subject Index

Philadelphia (Penn.), 40, 201
Philippines, 58, 348
photographs, in direct mail, 238
Pittsburgh (Pa.), 166
Plains (Ga.), 152
Playboy, 153, 338*m*4
"points bought vs. points delivered," 182
political action committee (PAC), 13, 24, 25, 27, 50, 224, 248*m*, 258*n*5, 268–84, 298*m*, *n*6, *n*7, *m*10, *m*11, *n*22, *n*24, 299*n*49, 300*n*53, 309, 330–37, 339*n*44; effect of FECA on, 268–84; growth of, 268–72; and independent expenditures, 281–84, 332; and political consultants, 25, 56, 72–73, 272, 278–79, 287–90, 337*n*31; as rival of political party, 272–74, 330–37; at state and local levels, 270
political consultant. *See* consultant, political
Political Consultants, American Association of. *See* American Association of Political Consultants
Political Consultants, International Association of. *See* International Association of Political Consultants
polling, 7, 14, 15, 30, 60, 65*n*27, 68–110, 117, 122, 139, 153, 185, 200, 203, 206*n*28, 226, 256, 271, 284, 286, 293, 312, 339, 349–50; analysis and interpretation as elements of, 96–100; costs of, 49–53, 73, 77, 79–81, 106*n*34–35; democratic effects of, 68, 73–74, 81–92, 314, 321; development of, 69–75; ephemeral nature of, 81–82, 92, 102; errors in, 69, 78, 82, 83–86, 92–102; ethical problems with, 60, 314–21; firms, 69–75, 110*m*100, 349–50; and focus groups, 77–81, 90, 106*n*28; in individual states, 70, 71; influence of, 38, 41, 81–92; interviewing in, 75–81, 86–89, 92–102, 106*n*41, 110*m*02, 314, 316; kinds of, 75–81; margin of error in, 75–81, 86, 97–99, 106*n*34, 109*n*91; and the "numbers game," 85–86, 194, 318; presidents and, 68–70, 73–75, 105*n*7, 173, 316; political vs. commercial, 80; question wording in, 78–79, 83, 85–87, 93–96, 109*n*93; 317; role of interviewers and respondents in, 78, 100–102; sampling for, 69, 71, 75–81, 90, 91, 96, 105*m*4, *m*17, 106*n*32, 109*n*86, 316; screening interviewees in, 78, 85–87, 98–99, 107*n*55, 110–95; straw, 69, 71, 105*m*4, 110*n*95; subgroup analysis in, 87–88, 89–90, 98–99; undecideds in, 99; uses and misuses of, 83–86, 90–91, 92–102. *See also* consultant, political; pollsters
poll mills, 314
pollsters, 48, 66*n*63, *n*81, 68–110, 349–50; democratic effects of, 81–92, 83–85, 314–

21; ethics of, 60, 314–21; fees charged by, 49–53, 73, 77, 79–81, 106*n*34–35; influence of, 38, 41, 81–92. *See also* consultant, political; individual listings of pollsters; polling
Portugal, 61
positioning, 175
postelection poll, 107*n*43
postelection relationships, of consultants and candidates, 10, 40–43, 309–10, 338*n* 13–14
postscripts, in direct mail, 244–45
PPB, 158, 167
P.R. *See* public relations
president, 31; campaigns for, 4, 9, 20, 21, 22, 27, 28, 30, 35, 37, 39, 40, 46, 48, 59, 65*n*25, *n*45, 66*n*43, 68, 69, 70, 74, 83, 84, 85, 89, 108*n*67, 92, 110*m*05, 112, 115, 116, 119, 121, 126, 133, 135, 140, 141, 144, 145, 152, 156, 159, 166, 167, 169, 172, 173, 181, 188, 197, 270, 277, 285, 316, 331, 347–55
press: and campaign coverage, 117, 118, 119, 144, 152–53, 163, 173, 193–94, 206*m*18, *n*25, *n*28, 216*n*256, *n*259, *n*262, 287, 313; the "numbers game" and the, 84–86, 194, 318; polling and the, 68, 315–19, 321, 338*n*20; relationship of consultants with the, 4, 6, 10, 15, 19, 20, 22, 23, 26, 39, 74, 84–86, 165, 307, 310–11, 338*m*5
pretesting, 138, 177, 211*m*64
primary, system of nomination, 198, 218*n*295, 285, 330
Princeton (N.J.), 70
probability survey, 96–97
Proctor and Gamble, 145, 178
"propensity to vote" scale, 99, 110*n*95
Proposition 1 (tax reform), 138
Proposition 2 (parks bond issue), 53
Proposition 5 (anti-smoking), 52, 137–38, 353
Proposition 7 (pro-death penalty), 232, 261*n*58
Proposition 13 (anti-property tax), 24, 57, 161, 232, 240, 260*n*49, 353, 354
Proposition 15 (anti-nuclear), 56, 135–37
prospecting, in direct mail, 226–34, 237, 246, 249, 250–55, 259*n*6
pseudo-news spot, 126, 163, 183, 323
psychographics, 182, 203
Public Citizen's Congress Watch, 272
public financing. *See* finance, campaign
Public Interest Opinion Research, 94
public relations, profession of, 10, 57, 339*n*48
Puerto Rico, 57
pure democracy, 319
purposive sample, 109*n*89